M000297647

MEMOIRS OF A BYSTANDER

A Life in Diplomacy

Mr. BOOKS
10-D Super Market
Islamabad
Tel: 2278843/45 Fax: 2278825

MEMOIRS OF A BYSTANDER
A Life in Diplomacy

IQBAL AKHUND

Karachi
Oxford University Press
Oxford   New York   Delhi

Rs 350.00

Oxford University Press, Great Clarendon Street, Oxford OX2 6DP
Oxford New York
Athens Auckland Bangkok Bagotá Buenos Aires Calcutta
Cape Town Chennai Dar es Salaam Delhi Florence Hong Kong Istanbul
Karachi Kuala Lumpur Madrid Melbourne Mexico City Mumbai
Nairobi Paris S~ao Paulo Singapore Taipei Tokyo Toronto Warsaw
and associated companies in Berlin Ibadan

Oxford is a registered trade mark of Oxford University Press

© Oxford University Press 1997

The moral rights of the author have been asserted

All rights reserved. No part of this publication may be reproduced, translated,
stored in a retrieval system, or transmitted, in any form or by any means,
without the prior permission in writing of Oxford University Press.
Enquiries concerning reproduction should be sent to the
Rights Department, Oxford University Press, at the address above.

This book is sold subject to the condition that it shall not, by way
of trade or otherwise, be lent, re-sold, hired out or otherwise circulated
without the publisher's prior consent in any form of binding or cover
other than that in which it is published and without a similar condition
including this condition being imposed on the subsequent purchaser.

First published by Oxford University Press, 1997
This edition in Oxford Pakistan Paperbacks, 1998

ISBN 0 19 577997 5

Second Impression 2000

Printed in Pakistan at
Mas Printers, Karachi.
Published by
Ameena Saiyid, Oxford University Press
5-Bangalore Town, Sharae Faisal
PO Box 13033, Karachi-75350, Pakistan.

The author in his United Nations office, March 1987.

CONTENTS

LIST OF ILLUSTRATIONS

frontispiece
The author in his United Nations office, March 1987.

DEDICATION

*To my wife Lala
and to our grandchildren
Teymour, Tatiana, Zorina, Dunya.*

ACKNOWLEDGEMENTS

I wish to thank my children who besides encouraging me to write, provided the instruments for doing it, a laptop computer and printer and taught me to use it; to Brown University in Providence, Rhode Island, and the Pakistan Institute of International Affairs, Karachi for the use of their libraries; to Farzana Shakur of the PIIA for taking time out during a very busy period to trace some important references; to Micki and Stavy Vershuren for resolving a computer emergency; to Erik Safdar and Roshanara for help in reviewing and revising the manuscript and to Tyaba Habib, for the mind and heart she put into editing and giving shape to the book.

PREFACE

In the more literate countries of the world, memoirs of public men is a well-established literary genre. Retired generals and diplomats, in particular, are prone to sharing their memories and experiences with their fellow men. It gives one the opportunity to drop names, to take credit for things done, or merely witnessed; to magnify one's own role; to vindicate, justify, propagate; or merely to re-live what has been and rue what might have been.

In Pakistan the practice has not yet quite taken hold. We treat the past as another country to which one visit was enough. A well-read instructor at the Quetta Staff College once said to me, 'In our country accumulated experience is not passed on; each generation has to start afresh.' There exist indeed lacunae in the nation's collective memory. Most of Pakistan's founding fathers died taking their memories with them. The Quaid himself, Liaquat Ali Khan, Shaheed Suhrawardy, and many lesser lights left relatively few papers, notes or diaries that would throw light on the historic and tumultuous events in which they played a part. The circumstances behind some of the most crucial events in the country's history remain shrouded in secrecy—the assassination of Pakistan's first Prime Minister, Liaquat Ali Khan; military action and defeat in East Pakistan; and, notwithstanding the public attention focused on the event, the trial and execution of Zulfikar Ali Bhutto. There were obvious reasons for these matters being hushed up, but even on subjects of more general public interest, silence prevails. After nearly half a century of Independence, no Foreign Office papers have been published. Many matters remain the subject of speculation and conjecture including the 1948 tribal incursion into Kashmir; how it came about that having accepted Moscow's invitation, Liaquat Ali went instead to Washington; how and why Pakistan joined the Baghdad Pact and SEATO.

This book covers a relatively narrow canvas. It is a footnote to
the early years of Pakistan's diplomatic history. There are no
disclosures made and no secrets unveiled. Much of what is written
here is known or surmised. Nor is this a memoir in the sense of
being an account of my own career, but rather of what I saw and
heard and sometimes took part in. I hope it will be of interest as
an inside account of the diplomatic trade by someone who
practiced it for forty-odd years.

These memoirs span a period of nearly sixty years, from the
thirties to the nineties—decades of tumult and transformation
that saw wars and cataclysms, the fall of empires and the decline
of ideologies; and now at the threshold of the twenty-first century,
the world seems to be moving away from the nation state to the
global village. Loyalties shrink as the world becomes one world.
These were years that saw the end of the British Empire in India
and the emergence of Pakistan. The turbulence that followed
has not ended yet, either between the two countries, or within
them. Each is still trying to come to terms with itself even as it
shies away from coming to terms with the other, though the two
processes are closely and fatefully interlinked.

The title perhaps smacks of false modesty but is true in three
ways. Firstly, a diplomat today, despite his title of 'Ambassador
Extraordinary and Plenipotentiary', is essentially an observer who
remains tethered to the government he represents by the cord of
modern telecommunications. A Pakistani diplomat is a bystander
in the further sense that the options of action and initiative
available to a country of Pakistan's size and situation are limited.
Pakistan is not among those few countries that have the power or
influence to shape world events and who are, relatively speaking,
free agents on the world scene. Like the great majority of the
world's states, Pakistan must take things as it finds them and
adjust to them as well as it can.

Lastly, to some extent, by temperament too I am a bystander.
Throughout my life I always had the feeling of standing a little
outside of whatever was going on, watching things happen even
when I participated in the unfolding of events. This sense of
detachment has stayed with me through a long career during
which I was involved in, or witness to, events that were important
in the history of our nation and on the world stage. I don't know
whether such an attitude is necessarily useful in a diplomat, but

in a writer it may cause his work to appear as lacking in a point of view. I trust that the reader will not find that to be the case with this book.

In the popular mind a diplomat is a smooth talker who should not be taken at his word. The profession has been tarred from the inside, alas! by the treacherous pun of King James' ambassador to Rome, Sir Henry Wooton, 'An ambassador is an honest man sent to lie abroad for the good of his country.' Nothing can be further from the truth, for a diplomat's word is his currency, and if he debases it by telling lies, no one will accept it any more. A diplomat must always tell the truth, and nothing but the truth, though he need not at all times tell the whole truth.

Pakistan's short but troubled history has been marked by many sudden shifts and contradictions, and Pakistani diplomats had to spend a good bit of their working life explaining these vicissitudes. This was not as difficult as may be supposed, for behind the many changes of government and regime, national policy remained broadly unchanged. But a certain detachment helped one to maintain a sense of proportion and to put in perspective, at least in one's own mind, the virtues of the 'present government' and the villainies of the previous one. A young woman from Lahore, very put-together and of her times, recently asked me whether I still had faith in the country's future. I replied, 'Yes, I do.' To this she said, 'That is the difference between your generation and mine; we no longer believe in the future!'

But I don't think that is true of young people in general, or was true of the young woman herself. The remark came from a sense of anger at the way things have gone in Pakistan but also of a frustrated hope that they can be better. As long as the young are angry, there is hope.

Clifton, Karachi
10 April 1995

CHAPTER 1

THE EARLY YEARS

In the seventies the BBC showed a serial on the Raj and it was
followed by a spate of books about those who ran it—Virginia
Woolf's chivalrous young men 'who negotiated treaties, ruled
India, controlled finance';[1] or in the words of Philip Mason, 'the
imperial ruling class of public school boys trained on classics,
cold baths and bodily exercise.'[2] There were reprints of diaries
or letters written by British officials or their wives, biographies
and works of social history, coffee-table books describing and
illustrating a glamorous world of hunts, tiger shoots, fancy dress
balls and languid love affairs. There were snapshots of sahibs on
polo ponies, memsahibs in picture hats, flaxen-haired *babas* in
the arms of inky-hued ayahs, of gingerbread bungalows with
rolling lawns in front of trellised verandahs. Not all these people
were upper class, but in the cantonments and civil lines of dusty
district towns, they lived a pastiche of English upper class life, to
which was added more than a touch of oriental flamboyance. A
memoir of the mid-nineteenth century lists the titles and duties
of fifty-four servants employed in a typical household—*khansamah*,
sirdar, *mashalchi*, *punkha-walla*, water-carrier, cook, grooms, syces,
etc.

But of course the bright young men and public school boys
did not rule India by themselves. They laid down the 'steel frame'
and saw to it that the 'feckless native' did not run things off the
rails. Those who actually administered the Raj on a day-to-day
basis were the scores of thousands of Indian officials, high and
low—deputy collectors, sub-judges, superintendents of police,
income tax officials and excise inspectors; they ran it, as the *kazis*
and *munsifs* and *daroghas* and *faujdars* had administered the far-
flung Mogul empire before the British came. This was the
workaday Raj without whose collaboration the Empire could not

have functioned nor perhaps lasted as long as it did—the Brown Raj, unglamorous, unsung, ambivalent and perhaps a little shame-faced. Some of the higher Indian officials affected English lifestyles and maintained households with butlers, nannies and uniformed chauffeurs. We too learned to 'drop cards', mix Martinis, serve sherry with soup and port after dinner. In the afternoon ayahs took the brown *baba log* to the public park where mustachioed up-country *jawans* of regimental brass bands blew tunes by Sousa and Elgar and Handel at uncomprehending ears. The parody of a pastiche!

'Society' in the district consisted of the collector, at the apex, and then in descending order, the sessions judge, the police superintendent, the executive engineer, the civil surgeon and the bank manager. In the beginning these were all British, but gradually Indians entered the hallowed circle and towards the end, in some districts all of the high officials were Indians. The local gentry, the great landowners, prominent lawyers, eminent doctors and journalists, were not a part of it and probably did not realize that they were being left out. At a lower level of officialdom were deputy collectors, sub-judges, excise inspectors and income tax officers—posts held by Indians and not considered very chic. They were never asked to dinner parties and only went to mass affairs like tea parties and 'At Homes' when some great panjandrum like the revenue commissioner or the governor came touring. In district headquarters, all would be bustle and excitement for days before the Governor came from far-off Bombay in his gleaming white train. Public buildings were whitewashed, fresh straw was spread on the dirt roads to prevent clouds of dust rising around the motorcade, and the whole town was spruced up. In places like Larkana and Sukkur, the senior-most officials togged themselves up in morning coat and in white tie and tails for the functions held in honour of the visiting dignitary.

My father came from a conservative Muslim family of Sindh but was impressed by things English and in particular, had a profound admiration for British orderliness, self-discipline, and professional integrity. At home this meant among other things that we had to gag on porridge, cold mutton and boiled turnips. Anglo-Indian nannies taught us table manners and to speak chi-chi English. And when the 'cold' weather came to places like

Larkana and Sukkur and temperatures plummeted to around 60 Fahrenheit, we had to wear flannel knickers and woollen hose and swallow a spoonful of cod liver oil in the mornings. One doubts that even Macaulay had meant things to be carried to these lengths.[3]

My maternal grandmother, a no-nonsense woman of strong will and decided views, was completely unimpressed by my father's attempts at 'Anglification' and nagged and ridiculed him for bringing up the children as *feranghis* and heathens. Occasionally we spent the school holidays in the country on my grandfather's farm and she seized the opportunity to try to iron the foreign wrinkles out of us. There were Koran lessons in the morning and regular prayers, and eating off a *dastarkhan* spread on the floor.

East is East and West is West, but somehow we moved without trouble or soul-searching, back and forth from one lifestyle to another. We lived in a sort of colonial limbo-land between the British and the Indians, between the rulers and the ruled and— at least on the surface—between Hindu and Muslim. We were counted as one of the 'respectable' families of Hyderabad in Sindh; respectable meaning townsmen exercising professions— lawyers, *kazis*, *hakims*, teachers—but people without land or money; that is, prominent but penniless.

I grew from childhood to boyhood in the tumultuous decade of the thirties, the decade of Hitler, Mussolini and Franco and the gathering clouds of war. In India the movement for Independence was gaining strength and tension between Hindus and Muslims was on the rise, culminating in the demand for the partition of India. However we were a rather apolitical family and I don't remember that a great deal of politics was talked about at home. Father was of the view, which is axiomatic among the Muslims of the subcontinent—a view which persists to this day, but is impossible to prove or to disprove—that all would be well with Muslims and every problem of theirs would be solved, if only they would became 'Muslims-in-the-True-Sense'. He looked upon the Indian National Congress as a lot of Hindu agitators. Although he was not the least bit communal-minded and had many Hindu friends, he spoke despairingly of the 'Hindu mentality' as if it was some sort of incurable disease. So, rather curiously, did the family on my mother's side, though they were only second generation converts from Hinduism, and kept up with their Hindu relatives. Among these was my grandmother's uncle, Acharya Kripalani, who became President of the Indian National Congress after Abul Kalam Azad. I met him when he paid a brief visit to Hyderabad soon after Partition, and found him very angry about the creation of Pakistan. 'You people are cutting your nose to spite your face!' he said to me in the course of an argument on the subject.

My mother's side of the family had a subversive bent of mind and were almost congenitally resentful of authority, or perhaps they were simply envious of people in authority. Sheikh Abdur-Rahim, my maternal great-grandfather, and among the first members of the family to convert to Islam, had been mixed up in the so-called 'Silk Letter Conspiracy'[4] against the British, but escaped being arrested by jumping off a train and disappearing. Another great-uncle, Shaikh Nur Mohammed, quit India on the ground that it was 'Dar-ul-Harb' (a Muslim land ruled by infidels) and therefore not a proper place for a Muslim to live. After getting a medical degree, he wandered through the Soviet Union to Berlin and then turned up in Afghanistan where he became personal physician to King Nadir Shah and then to King Zahir Shah, and spent a good part of his life in Kabul.

Sindh was a political backwater. It had been separated from the Bombay Presidency and set up as a Muslim majority province in 1936, a move strongly opposed by Sindhi Hindus for communal reasons. Nothing else of any great consequence, or that mattered much in the rest of India, happened there. There were no nationalist uprisings, no communal riots, nor was Sindh visited often by famines or floods or cyclones. Only a handful of Sindhi Muslims played a prominent role in Indian politics; there were scarcely any Sindhis in the All-India services, and none at all in the armed forces. Even years after Independence, this remained the case. When I told the wife of the French Ambassador to Pakistan that I came from Sindh, she exclaimed in mock disbelief, 'Really? I did not know that *anyone* came from Sindh!'

Sindh had dacoits then as it still does. My father who was a judge, sentenced one particularly notorious one, Abdul Rahman by name, to a public hanging in order to make an example of him for all times to come. This was more than sixty years ago, and as today dacoity is still prevalent, it shows that spectacular punishments are not the deterrent some people expect them to be. The dacoits at that time were rural folk, often driven to the wall by misery or injustice. In legend they were Robin Hood types who robbed the rich, but whether they gave anything to the poor is a moot point. Romantic indeed some of them were, hiding in woods, defying the police, and fighting it out to the death when cornered.

I heard an account of one such encounter (in the adjoining Seraiki region of the Punjab), from a police officer who was involved in it: Mohammad Khan a notorious outlaw, with forty-eight robberies and killings to his account and a price on his head, swaggered into the telegraph office of a remote desert outpost late one evening. He asked the operator to send a telegram to President Ayub Khan stating: 'Janab President, your police can never catch me. Do not waste them on me. But if you will excuse (sic) me, I shall come to you and surrender.' He did not really expect a reply and the message was an act of bravado meant to taunt the police. But they now knew where to begin looking for their man. The encounter took place two days later in a boulder-strewn ravine. Abandoned by his companions, Mohammed Khan fought on alone until disabled by a bullet. The police rushed him to a hospital in Rawalpindi where surgeons were standing by for blood transfusions and other ministrations, exactly as for a VIP. He was happy that fame and recognition had come his way at last, even if it was all going to end on the gallows.

The old time dacoit had conducted himself with panache, sending messages to his victim to be ready on a set date with the stated amount of cash, or else. He was gallant towards women and did not harm children or old people. There was no kidnapping for ransom. Dacoity was a cottage industry with the human touch of homespun things, and sometimes with a bit of romance. There was a couple who were lovers and did their brigandage together, and wrote poems when they had the time—as they did when they got a long spell in jail. Pakistan has not produced a woman dacoit so far, like India's Phoolan Devi; as in many other things, in this field of endeavour too we are a little behind India! However today's Kalashnikov-carrying thugs, toting walkie-talkies and moving about in jeeps, are another matter—the harbingers of high-tech to an otherwise still mediaeval rural life.

The Hur rebellion of 1940 employed the same old-time techniques but was a very serious affair and aimed at nothing less than the overthrow of British rule in Sindh. The Indian National Congress, glad of any helping hand in their struggle against the British, tried to give the Hur movement the colour of a national revolt, but it was nothing of the kind. The Pir of Pagara had launched the movement on the strength, it is said, of a Nostradamus-like Sindhi prophecy that when the British were driven from the land, he would inherit the crown they had snatched from the Talpur Mirs. The Hurs had launched a similar rebellion in 1890 and actually set up a parallel administration. This time, with the British at war, the prospect looked more favourable and indeed it took the government five years, using armoured vehicles and even aircraft, to bring the situation under control. The Pakistan Army has been more astute in incorporating the Hurs into a militia unit, known as the Mujahid Force.

Sindh was the first among the Muslim majority provinces to support Partition through a resolution passed by the Sindh Legislative Assembly. However, as was the case also with the other Muslim majority provinces, the Pakistan Movement was not particularly strong or vocal among the Sindhi political classes. Muslims in Sindh had complained about Hindus crowding them out of government services, professions and business, but the sense of grievance was confined to the relatively small urban middle class. The agricultural majority, whether land-owners or share-croppers, were not bothered much about business or services, which they considered beneath their dignity (or over their heads). Generally speaking, the feeling that existed between Muslims and Hindus in Sindh was that of a mild and reciprocal and almost affable contempt. Muslims scoffed at the Hindus' supposed lack of manliness, their money-grubbing and penny-pinching ways; Hindus saw the Muslims as dissolute, spendthrift and boorish. But there did not exist between the two communities in Sindh the white-heat hatred that pitted Sikh against Muslim in the Punjab; or the rancorous animosity and intolerance that festered in the Hindi-Urdu regions of India.

Karachi was a clean and orderly city with a population of about 300,000 at the time of Partition—an ethnic patchwork of Bohris, Ismailis, Makranis, Kutchi Memons, Parsees, Goanese, Anglo-

Indians, Hindus, Muslims, and others. Sindhi Muslims were even then a minority in the city, but did not feel excluded or threatened as no one was required in its cosmopolitan atmosphere, to measure up to any particular ethnic, cultural or religious norm. The ethnic diversity was not a motive for conflict or rivalry except of a relatively innocent sort, when, for example, the Pentangular[5] cricket matches pitched various communities against each other. Karachi enjoyed the somewhat patronizing title of the 'Cleanest City East of Suez'. As a matter of fact, the Karachi of those days would have compared favourably in cleanliness with many of today's cities west of the Suez. It had a brisk and efficient British air that blended pleasantly with an unhurried oriental tempo. Traffic policemen in starched uniforms, did a precision drill, stomping their feet as they did right and left turns, and threw their arms out stiffly to direct traffic. They had time enough to perform these evolutions for there was not much car traffic and scarcely any trucks and buses; people who did not have cars got around in wobbly looking hansom carriages known as Victoria *gharries*. Merchandise was transported in carts pulled by camels—aloof and responsible-looking creatures that went about their way in a dignified manner unlike the bumptious and noisy Suzuki vans that have replaced them.

On 'Elphie', (the Zebunissa Street of today) the main shopping street, named after a long forgotten Commissioner Elphinstone, there were smart shops—Beaumont the tailor, Haydn's for music, Bliss the chemist with its clean, astringent smell; English Cold Storage for kippers, marmalade, English biscuits. On Victoria Road there was Café Grand with its potted palms in huge brass planters, iced coffee and lemon tarts; Pereira the baker on another sidestreet prepared bread and vanilla biscuits the like of which seem to have disappeared from the earth. If I could find one to eat again, perhaps, like Proust's *Madeleine*, the taste might bring back in a rush the vanished flavour of old Karachi; for there was indeed such a thing and one sensed it already at Thatta, eighty kilometres out in the desert, in the clean, salt smell of the sea air and the sight of tree trunks bent leeward by the prevailing wind. Sometimes even today, something elusive may bring the old flavour back fleetingly—a fisherman's accent, the musty smell of some

surviving high-ceilinged house with wooden floors, the image of
Frere Hall seen across the thin Karachi rain and drooping fronds
of bottle palms, the ramshackle wooden balconies of some of the
older houses. Karachi was a small sleepy place but somehow it
seemed more 'urban' than today's sprawling network of slums,
nameless residential 'blocks' and unconnected settlements that
make up one of the largest and most crowded agglomerations in
the world.

Sindh was the last of the British conquests in the subcontinent
and was taken for no rhyme or reason from its Talpur rulers,
although they had faithfully observed the terms of the treaty
which the British had imposed on them. The action was
rationalized by Charles Napier the conqueror, 'as a useful bit of
rascality' in that it put an end to the alleged misrule of the Mirs.
In the book *Kurrachee*,[6] by Alexander Baillie, the British had a
bone of another sort to pick with the Mirs in this regard:

> The Bombay Government having collected information regarding
> the armies and fortresses of Scinde, when the occasion arrived,
> despatched a force capable of coping with a determined resistance
> but no such resistance was offered; the Mirs continuing to the last a
> policy of chicanery and subterfuge, and trusting perhaps that the
> treaty under discussion with Col Pottinger would put an end to all
> differences, had made no preparation against attack and when the
> British Commander summoned Manora to surrender, it possessed no
> means of resisting the imperative demand and [thus] a very pretty
> little piece of practice in the operations of a naval force against a
> land fortress [has] been lost to the scientific profession, owing to the
> negligence and remissness of the Amirs in not providing Manora
> with suitable artillery and matchlocksmen when H.M.S. *Wellesley*
> anchored off that point.

The vanquished Mirs received shabby treatment at British
hands and their case did not even get a hearing though they sent
a special emissary (described by Alexander Burnes in his *Travels
to Bokhara*[7] as a 'wily Akhund') to plead their case at Queen
Victoria's Court. The Hyderabad Mirs were exiled to Calcutta for
losing the war, but in due course, were allowed to return. On
return they built themselves a huge rambling mansion near the
river at Giddu Bandar, an exact replica of the one on the Hooghly
in which they had spent their years of exile and detention.

The British set about putting things right in Sindh but not much more than was strictly needed for their own purposes, and left largely untouched the feudal land-ownership system. They built an extensive irrigation system, and the port and city of Karachi, discovered the mysterious ruins of Mohenjo-Daro (and used up a good many of the 5,000-year old bricks as ballast for a railway track!) and constructed some fine stone buildings. On the whole they ran a good, clean administration, more honest and less bossy than in some of the other provinces of the Indian Empire.

It was from Sindh too that some of the last British troops quit the soil of the land they had ruled for a couple of centuries. Trevor Royle in his book, *The Last Days of the Raj*[8] gives a colourful description of the ceremony: Men of the 1st Battalion of the Black Watch regiment with colours flying, bayonets fixed and pipes and drums playing, marched through the city between vast, cheering crowds to the Governor-General's House and presented the Royal Salute to Quaid-i-Azam. At the Keamari docks, their own pipes and drums silent now, the Battalion presented arms and with the massed bands of the Baloch and 16th Punjab Regiments playing, the colours were slow-marched up the gangway and on board the ship. The last set to be played jointly by the bands was 'Will ye na' come back again?' It is doubtful that the Pakistani bandsmen knew the words or significance of the Jacobites' farewell chorus for the vanquished Bonnie Prince Charlie—or that the cheering crowds wanted the British to come back! But these farewell ceremonies, in India and in Pakistan epitomized the ambivalence of the relationship between the British and their Indian subjects.

Years later, wandering about in the Murree Hills, I came upon a little greystone church overlooking the blue foothills, beside which was a cemetery overrun with weeds and bearing inscriptions going back a century or more. A sense of desolation hung over the forlorn 'English' atmosphere of this little corner of the Punjab hills, with the church clock striking the hour over the emptiness and the names of the long-forgotten dead. Many had died as children, or young corporals and subalterns or civil servants and lay there abandoned in death with perhaps no one left now that even knows who they were and in what far corner of the earth they lie buried. What had brought them here and taken them to other far-flung corners of the earth—money, adventure, glory?

I thought about it while listening to a speaker on the BBC in a programme called 'About Britain'. He was poking gentle fun at things British, in a tweedy, pipe-smoking, avuncular voice. It was a civilized talk exuding common sense and moderation. Here was a genteel descendant of the generations of adventurers, brigands, pirates and soldiers of fortune who had put red on the map of half the globe; planted the Union Jack over steamy jungle settlements, Arctic wastes, the mud forts of the North-West Frontier and remote mountain outposts; created flourishing port cities; brought to their colonies the rule of law and a simulacrum of democratic institutions; cricket and Shakespeare; separate loos for Europeans and natives; Fabianism, fish and chips and 5 o'clock tea.

Much has been said and written about the British in India— why they came, and what, for good or ill, they accomplished there. The view of those who ran the Empire—the guardians— was that they did their duty by their wards and when it was done, went their way, happy in the knowledge that they were leaving behind them a working machine and successors who had learned how to run it. It is an idealized picture but not without some truth in it that ought to leaven the anti-colonialist view of the Raj as a system purely of exploitation, domination and racism. With the passage of time indeed many of us have forgotten the rough edges of the Raj and there are moments when its orderliness, honesty and style are recalled with something bordering nostalgia.

How should one evaluate the impact of British rule over the subcontinent, measure the impact of Britain's encounter with the complex and ancient societies over whom it ruled, and analyse the nature and extent of the British legacy? Nearly fifty years after they left our shores it is perhaps still too soon to make an objective appraisal of these things. In Britain the Raj is now forgotten except as a subject of nostalgia and in the not very welcome presence of a large number of the former subjects as fellow Britons. But for us the British period is not yet in the past—it is still all around us and present in our language, food and manners; the way we dress and speak; the games we play; the chrysanthemum shows and the regimental pipe bands in their tartan; and possibly, to some extent still, even in our modes of thought. In a very perceptive analogy, Zulfikar Bhutto whose own attitude towards the British was ambivalent, compared the British stamp on India with the imprint left by Moorish rule on Spain. However the Moors were in Spain for eight centuries whereas the British period from the Battle of Plassey to the departure ceremonies in Bombay and Karachi, spanned a little more than two hundred years.

When the Catholics reconquered Spain, they set about systematically extirpating every sign and symbol of Islamic rule. They did not fully succeed of course, and there remain in the Spanish language, manners and morals, vestiges of the Arab connection. Here there was no such vindictive wiping of the slate when the British departed. In Pakistan, something even of the Englishman's 'petty apartheid' was allowed to survive the end of the Raj. The Sind Club in Karachi continued to deny membership to 'natives' for a number of years after Independence, and opened its doors to locals only when the club could no longer be run on the fees paid by the remaining white members. Somehow no one seemed to mind or notice this bit of cheek. In India the statues of British monarchs, viceroys and other dignitaries were taken down as unwelcome reminders of a period of subjugation. Pakistan followed suit after some time, but for theological rather than nationalistic reasons. In Pakistan there remains the bitterness of Mountbatten's perfidy over the Radcliffe Award[9] and his connivance with India's grab of Kashmir.

The British period was a brief period in the subcontinent's history, but it was extraordinarily fecund and it laid down roots that have gone deep into the soil of our history. The new empire provided, by and large, not only justice and good administration as the best of the Moguls had done, but created institutions and systems and fostered attitudes of mind designed to sustain and ensure good administration. A British innovation were the ideas of self-rule and of the Rule of Law. Both ideas are implicit in Islam's emphasis on equality and justice, and the ruler's responsibility before God. But whereas the Islamic ruler is answerable to his conscience before God, the British gave the rule of law statutory force and institutional form.

There is no question that the idea of democracy and the introduction of institutions of self-rule were the most important

contributions of British rule. The conventional wisdom on the
subject is that the British 'gave' us democracy but we have not
been able to run it. One cannot quarrel altogether with this
criticism. But one must take into account the fact that, in practice,
the British dispensed democracy in small doses, on the ground
that the subject people needed to be prepared for the
responsibilities of self-rule. What the British actually bequeathed
us was diarchy, Section 144, the Sedition Act, Public Order
Ordinances et al.,[10] and what they inculcated was the attitude of
mind implied in the notion of the 'White Man's burden'. This
was that non-White people are not fit for freedom, but must
undergo a certain tutelage in order to learn how to govern
themselves. Accordingly, the British established pseudo-
parliamentary institutions, legislative assemblies, executive
councils, local boards, etc., that were democratic in appearances,
form and procedure, but operated on a somewhat make-believe
basis, anything of importance remaining subject to the
supervision and veto of the British rulers. The idea was that the
'natives' needed to learn democracy by playing at democracy—to
use a flippant analogy, something like learning about real estate
transactions by playing *Monopoly*. This pseudo-democracy is the
system under which Pakistan has, in fact, been governed for much
of its brief history, with the British over-lord replaced by the
Chief Martial Law Administrator. Along with flawed democracy,
the idea that the people were not fit to govern themselves came
to us as part of the British inheritance. The military rulers who
seized power from time to time justifed their action in terms that
were versions of 'White Man's Burden'—for Ayub it was 'basic
democracy', for Ziaul Haq it was 'Islamization'. Moreover, the
concept of democracy as the rule of the majority, is something
that we have always understood; but that democracy is also, and
above all, the right of the minority to dissent, is a concept that
has not yet taken root.

The Raj was not colonialism in the same sense as British rule
was in other parts of the far-flung Empire. In the perspective of
history, it can be seen as forming a continuum with the Mogul
empire which it had replaced. For the common people one *sirkar*
had taken the place of another, and would be judged by its
performance in the primary functions of a ruler—that is,
providing security and economic well-being. What would have

happened if the British had not been there to pick up the pieces as the Mogul empire began to fall apart? Would it have broken up into many separate entities—dynastic, linguistic and ethnic— as did Western Europe after the death of Charlemagne? Would it all have come together again as Europe is doing today on the basis of common economic interests and other pragmatic grounds? This is an interesting field of speculation.

The idea of self-rule was also the most unsettling legacy of the British rule for implicit in it was the concept of nationalism. It gave rise to the notion that India—vast, diverse, multitudinous— was a nation state like Italy, France or Japan. The concept was at best an abstraction based on the administrative unity imposed by foreign rule—first of the Moguls, then the British. The idea of national self-rule combined with the democratic principle of majority and minority, could not fail to lead to another abstraction—that of Muslims as a nation.

NOTES

[1] Virginia Woolf, *To the Lighthouse*, Vintage Books, London, 1992, p. 5.

[2] Philip Mason, *A Matter of Honour, an Account of the Indian Army, its Officers and Men;* Holt, Rinehart, Winston; New York.

[3] In his famous minute of 1835 on Indian education, Lord Macaulay, President of the Board of Education, wrote that its purpose must be to create 'a class of persons Indian in blood and colour but English in tastes, opinions, in morals and intellect.'

[4] Because secret messages were exchanged wrapped in bolts of silk.

[5] The five competing communities being: Hindus, Muslims, Parsees, Christians and the 'Rest'. Who these were I do not know—possibly atheists or Communists!

[6] Alexander Baillie, *Kurrachee*, Thacker Spink & Company, Calcutta, 1890.

[7] Alexander Burnes, *Travels to Bokhara*, reprinted by Oxford University Press, Karachi.

[8] Trevor Royle, *The Last Days of the Raj*, Michael Joseph, London, 1989.

[9] British lawyer Cyril Radcliffe was chairman of a joint India-Pakistan commission, and in view of the deadlock between the two sides, laid down the alignment of the boundary between partitioned Punjab and Bengal.

[10] Laws and regulations that restrict or prohibit political activities.

CHAPTER 2

PAKISTAN

In Pakistan people sometimes debate the so-called two-nation theory as if the right of Pakistan to exist had still to be established. An eminent colleague ascribed this phenomenon to the 'haunting sense of illegitimacy' felt by Pakistan at having broken away from the centre. Even Shivaji (before he became the arch rebel), he affirmed, had recognized the suzerainty of Delhi by accepting the title of raja conferred on him by Emperor Aurangzeb. The concept of 'the centre', the all-powerful *sirkar*, fountain-head of legitimacy, dispenser of justice, guarantor of order and security, is a very powerful one in the history of India.

Was Partition inevitable? Was it the only solution to the communal problem? To many older Pakistanis the question would smack of heresy. To the younger generation it may seem meaningless. Certainly the question is academic now. One could say that the answer is provided by the rise of Hindu fundamentalism in India, the destruction of the Babri Mosque in 1992, the fifty-year old freedom struggle of Kashmiri Muslims, and the general condition of Muslims in India. Yet it is a question that a man of my generation is likely to have at the back of his mind. Jinnah, seen as the ambassador of Hindu-Muslim unity in the beginning, himself came to the Pakistan idea fairly late in the day.

On the very eve of Independence and at a time when the demand for Pakistan had gathered irresistible momentum, Jinnah agreed to the confederal plan[1] proposed by the British Cabinet Mission. It is a moot point whether the complex three-tier federation would have worked in practice, given the deep-seated rancours and suspicions that had been stirred up and held sway on all sides. Would the three-fold grouping have squared the circle of the Congress party's concept of a monolithic Indian nationalism and the equally strong urge of the Muslim community to affirm its separate identity? It would have required an act of faith on each side and commitment to an overriding common goal. These were precisely the elements that were missing. In the words of Raj Mohan Gandhi, the Mahatma's grandson, 'An honourable compromise was neither the Congress' nor the League's pursuit in 1946-47. The greatest anxiety of each side was to avoid being out-manoeuvred by the other.'[2]

At any rate, Jinnah was willing to give compromise a try. The Cabinet Mission Plan was based on a denial of outright Partition and was in effect a negation of the sovereign and independent Pakistan demanded by the Muslim League, even though the Plan contained a provision that allowed provinces to opt out of the union after a trial period of ten years. The Quaid was prepared to take things on trust and postpone Pakistan for ten years (which, given the state of his health, meant perhaps indefinitely). What he sought was an equitable share in political power for the Muslims of India and an arrangement that would protect them from being swamped by the Hindu majority, enable them to preserve their identity, and ensure for them a fair share in the administration and the economy. In accepting the Cabinet Mission Plan, Jinnah indicated that Partition was a means to that end and that he was not irrevocably committed to it if the end could be attained by other means. In his autobiographical *India Wins Freedom*[3] Maulana Abul Kalam Azad leaves no doubt that at that critical juncture Partition could still have been averted and that if the opportunity was missed, the fault lay not at Jinnah's door, but with the Congress leadership and in particular, with Pandit Nehru.

It was Pandit Nehru who made Pakistan inevitable by going back, in effect, on the Congress party's acceptance of the British plan. What the Congress had given with one hand, it started almost at once to take back with the other by starting controversies over what this or the other article of the Cabinet Plan really meant—a now familiar Indian negotiating technique. Even the Cabinet Mission's own authoritative interpretations failed to resolve these controversies. Then Nehru threw a spanner in the whole works by declaring that whatever the Congress party may or may not have agreed to in accepting the plan, the Constituent Assembly was a sovereign body that was free to decide anything as it pleased. This gave the Congress party, which had an absolute majority in the Assembly, the power to go back on everything to which it had agreed!

Why did Nehru with an almost studied casualness, take a position that amounted to a sabotage of the compromise so painstakingly worked out by three British Cabinet Ministers in many months of negotiation? It is hardly possible that Nehru did not realize the effect that his words would have at that fateful turning point when everything hung in the balance.

There can be two possible explanations. Nehru dreamed of India as one of the four global powers which, along with the United States, the Soviet Union and China, would dominate the post-war world. He was, moreover, under the spell of the Soviet model of development and put his faith in a 'strong centre', believing that only under a highly centralized state, that could make five-year plans for the whole country, build heavy industry and impose social reform, could India rise from its abjection and assume its rightful place as a world power. He may have decided that it was better to have a smaller India with an effective centre than a powerless confederation, and that if it had to be, then so be it, let Jinnah have his Pakistan and let us be done with it. Secondly, in the prevailing atmosphere, the Congress leaders no doubt saw the Muslim League's acceptance of the Cabinet Mission's Plan as the thin end of the wedge and as the first stage in the eventual establishment of Pakistan—a Pakistan made up of the two Muslim groups of the Cabinet Mission's Plan would be a third of the size of India and would include the large Hindu majority areas of Bengal, including Calcutta, and of the Punjab as well as the whole of Assam. 'Assam is the soul of India!' Gandhi had cried out at the prospect.

The Congress accepted Mountbatten's Partition plan because there was no other choice at the time. Nehru saw Pakistan as a feudal, obscurantist anachronism that was economically unviable. He and other Congress leaders were convinced, and said it out aloud, that Pakistan would soon collapse under the weight of its own intrinsic irrationality and would return to the fold. They did not see the creation of Pakistan as an honourable settlement of the age-old Hindu-Muslim conflict, but as a necessary evil, as a bitter pill to be swallowed, in order to attain India's independence. Their policy was animated not by a search for compromise, but for ways of creating conditions that would hasten its inevitable demise, of adding in every way to the difficulties that the new country would face.[4] Nehru's sabotage of the confederal plan was surely not an impulsive act, nor could it have been the work of one man. Not a single member of Congress' Executive Committee that had approved the compromise with the Muslim League raised his voice to disclaim the significance of Nehru's words. The Congress leaders were perhaps encouraged in their cavalier attitude on the matter by the Viceroy's own hostile approach to Pakistan and to the Muslim League and by his partisan attitude and actions. Mountbatten's personal and fateful decision to advance the date of Independence by ten months may well have been influenced by similar considerations.

The Congress rewarded Mountbatten for his partiality by asking him to stay on as Governor-General of independent India. In Britain he was lionized as the man who had accomplished the feat of bringing India to freedom, organizing the partition and keeping the two new countries in the Commonwealth. Recent accounts have revised the assessment of the personal role played by Mountbatten in this crucial period. When a definitive history of the event is written, the last Viceroy cannot escape his responsibility for the bloodshed and chaos that overtook the subcontinent at the time of Independence, and for the legacy of war and contention that has followed.

It was a greater misfortune and indeed one of the ironies of history that there was such a gulf of incomprehension between Jinnah and Nehru, the two key men at the juncture, for both were secularists and had a parallel, though not common, vision of the future of the subcontinent. Nehru, proud of his Hindu heritage, was certainly no Hindu chauvinist. His cultural background was a mixture of Hindu, Muslim and English elements. Jinnah, for his part, was very far from sharing the revivalist views of some of the Islamist parties, most of which indeed opposed the establishment of Pakistan and for whom *he* was the adversary. The Quaid's concept of Pakistan was of a country that would include the whole of Bengal, the Punjab and Assam as well, and would therefore have a very large Hindu minority. In his concept, the fair treatment of the Hindu minority in Pakistan would guarantee similar treatment of the large

Muslim minority that would remain in India. This was described as the 'hostage theory' but it was something more subtle, a sort of symbiotic link between twin countries that would constitute a definitive settlement of India's age old Hindu-Muslim problem. Jinnah did not visualize the two states as religious monoliths. By all contemporary accounts, he was shaken and grieved by the mass displacement and transfer of populations that took place following Partition. The creation of Pakistan was meant to solve the Hindu-Muslim problem and to ensure an honourable place for the Muslim minority in India. Pakistan was not meant to be, nor could it possibly offer a home to all the Muslims of India. The two-way movement of population at Partition further thinned out the proportion of non-Muslims in Pakistan that was already much reduced by the partition of the Punjab and Bengal. Pakistan lost its 'hostages' and the theory could not be put to the test.

At all events, when 14 August 1947 dawned the country was free, and there was Pakistan where there had been British India. In place of the Union Jack, a new green and white flag fluttered over the house of the Collector of Hyderabad—the district's most important official and person. We felt proud and expansive and full of extravagant hopes and ideas for putting everything right. India's Independence came at midnight because astrologers had declared the fourteenth an inauspicious day for the purpose. The secular, sceptical Pandit Nehru turned this bit of superstition to advantage with a fine piece of eloquence at the transfer of power ceremony in the Indian Parliament: 'At the stroke of the midnight hour while the world sleeps, India will wake to life and freedom.'

But violence hung over the land like a pall that summer. Up-country, specially in the Punjab, there was communal rioting on a massive scale—murder, rape, looting and arson. I had to go up to Lahore in October, and took the train. Soon it began to fill up with people who were either fleeing from trouble or simply taking a free ride in the general confusion. Many rode on the roofs of the wagons, clinging precariously to whatever handhold they could find. A man was killed when he stood up as the train was passing under an over-bridge. As the train moved northwards, occasionally one saw in the far distance, like a frieze on the horizon, long lines of refugees moving in one direction or the opposite, fleeing their ancestral homes to find safety in a strange land. I saw no dead bodies in Lahore, but a pall of smoke hung over the city from buildings and shacks that had been set on fire.

What is the nature of the Hindu-Muslim conflict? On a hilltop complex in Kathmandu one can see Hindu and Buddhist temples coexisting peaceably side by side. But it was not always so, and in the early period as much blood had flowed between Hindus and Buddhists as does today between Hindus and Muslims or Hindus and Sikhs. Why, after 800 years of coexistence and cross-cultural interchanges, has no such equilibrium come to exist between Hinduism and Indian Islam? One ponders the question, only to get contradictory answers.

Hindus and Muslims as such are not two different races. Within each group one finds a variety of races and ethnic strains and these sometimes cut across the religious divide. The Hindus of Balochistan, for instance, do not differ in physical appearance and bearing from Balochi Muslims, but are as different from Madrassi Hindus as peas from potatoes. A large proportion of Indian Muslims are Hindu converts. This fact was used by the Congress party as an argument against the two-nation theory. But race is not necessarily the basis for nationhood, for if it were, Europe would not be divided into so many states.

One very hot summer afternoon as I stood at the door of an uncle's house in my home town of Hyderabad, a little old Hindu woman, looking exhausted and parched, stopped to ask me for a glass of water. I quickly went in and got it for her. But as she was about to raise it to her lips, her doubts were aroused, and she asked, 'You aren't a Muslim are you?' When I said that I was, she handed the glass back and shuffled away, hot and thirsty, but spared from being polluted! One can illustrate the Hindu-Muslim problem by such anecdotes. Or, by the antithesis between their practices: Hindus venerate the cow, Muslims eat it.

The Hindu-Muslim problem is not really 'religious' like the conflict between the Protestants and Catholics in Ireland or the wars between Christianity and Islam in the Middle Ages. Hinduism is so different in cosmology, social organization and moral beliefs from Islam, that there is little scope for a doctrinal dispute between them. Emperor Akbar attempted to bridge the gulf between the two religions by creating a new religion, the Deen-i-Ilahi, amalgamating what was considered the best in each.

But this doctrinal synthesis was politically motivated—a tactic of 'unite and rule' in place of the classical 'divide and rule'. It did not work and could not have worked precisely because it was synthetic. At the popular level, Sufi influence worked towards some kind of syncretism but it was a synthesis of popular superstitions and faith in holy men rather than a true melding of cultures.

In religious matters as such there was indeed considerable tolerance. Despite the accusations that Islam was spread by the sword, or by the fiscal duress of the *jizya*,[5] not much active proselytizing could have taken place, otherwise surely after 800 years of Muslim rule, Muslims would not have been a minority in India. Muslim rule in India was not always benign, but there was no systematic persecution of Hindus, as for instance, of Jews in Tsarist Russia. Even Aurangzeb, the most orthodox of the Moguls, had a Hindu Prime Minister and a Rajput bodyguard.

In general, Islamic society and rule have not been marked by religious intolerance. The case of Spain offers a striking example of the comparative tolerance of the Islamic state, for under the Moors (whose reign in Spain also lasted eight centuries) Muslims remained a minority in Spain, but when the Moorish rulers were driven from Spain by the Catholic 'reconquest', Muslims and Jews were forced out unless they accepted baptism.

The Quaid declared that Hindus and Muslims differed in everything—from the food they ate, the clothes they wore, and the way they lived, to their music, art, architecture. This is true, but there are differences in all these matters also within each community, between Punjabi Hindus and Madrassis; between the Muslims of Punjab and those of Bengal. On the other hand, there is also a great deal that is common between Hindus and Muslims of South Asia in all these fields that sets them apart from the rest of the world—cuisine, music, dance, architecture.

Over the centuries there has been much interweaving between the two cultures and peoples. The Taj Mahal and the Badshahi Mosque are indubitably Islamic but they are in their proper place on the banks of the Jumna and the Ravi. It is hard to visualize them standing on the banks of the Nile or the Tigris. There was no intermarriage between Hindus and Muslims, but conversions had created an ethnic mix. Upper class Hindus adopted the customs and etiquette of the Muslim courts, and families such as the Nehrus and Saprus were highly Islamized in culture, even as today the upper crust Indians and Pakistanis tend to be westernized. North Indian Hindus of this class spoke Urdu rather than Hindi. In Sindh, Hindu Amils, who were the Talpur rulers' trustee civil servants, spoke Persian and wore the Muslim Talpur dress.

Perhaps the fault lies in history, which Paul Valéry calls the most dangerous concoction of the chemistry of the mind, for it 'intoxicates people and sets them dreaming, keeps old wounds open, inspires men with megalomania or the persecution complex and makes nations proud, bitter, vain and insufferable.' These words came to mind, when Mrs Gandhi, after the surrender of Pakistani troops in Dhaka, is said to have exulted, 'We have wiped away the sorrows of a thousand years!'

But in the end India broke up not only because of the religious, cultural and other differences between Hindus and Muslims, nor by the opposing pull of history, but simply because the leaders failed to solve the problem of federalism.

Speaking to a visiting parliamentary delegation from Britain in 1976, Bhutto said that the main problem of the subcontinent throughout its history—a political problem of fundamental nature—had been that of regulating relations between the central authority and provinces. Under the Moguls the problem erupted in the form of rebellions and was settled by punitive wars. Under a constitutional regime it could only be resolved through compromise or partition. Nehru wanted to be the Great Mogul with the communal roles reversed. So Partition it had to be. But, then, the problem did not disappear with the Partition of British India, nor with the secession of Bangladesh.

To revert to the little old woman, I was not offended that she had rejected my glass of water, nor even surprised really. In railway stations, schools and other public places, separate urns provided *Hindu pani, Muslim pani* (Hindu water, Muslim water). I felt a little sorry in fact, as I saw the bent old figure disappearing around the street corner, that I had not fibbed to her for her own good. Yet it was an unusual experience for me personally for communal discords and animosities had not touched the lives of my family and myself and we had grown up with friends from all communities.

It is not that we lived in a cocoon, isolated from reality. Outside small circles such as ours, everything fell into the communal mould, from drinking water in public places, to schools, clubs and cricket matches. Yet one lived in the belief, or hope, that with education and economic development, all this would get sorted out and everybody would become integrated like our small, non-communal, somewhat Anglicized band of friends. In other words we were Utopian rationalists. But rationality could not prevail over reality. I still do not believe that the reality of the subcontinent is an immutable, fundamental and irreconcilable chasm between the two communities. But the reality of the time and circumstances, of how the leaders on all sides dealt with issues and reacted to each other, of the way people as a whole came to see things, led inexorably to what now seems to have been a predestined end.

The forties were a period of intensifying tension—between India and Britain and between Muslims and Hindus. Gandhi launched the Quit India Movement in 1942 when Japanese forces were knocking on the doors of Assam. At the time I was a student in the Sindh College in Karachi, where the accent was on sports and social activities rather than on politics. Some of the students organized demonstrations and the government disbanded the University Training Corps and took away the antiquated and unloaded .303 rifles which we used for rifle drill. In doing so it manifested greater nervousness than was justified by the situation in Karachi. Most students kept away from the agitation; to me it seemed that the Movement had been launched when Britain's defeat by Japan seemed inevitable and imminent, and this was an attempt to take advantage of their predicament. It seemed hardly likely that the British would just up and leave because they were being asked to quit. Personally I saw more point in Subash Chandra Bose's straightforward move to join the enemy's enemy in order to win the country's freedom, though the Japanese no doubt had ideas of their own about India.[6] It might even have made sense to have accepted the Cripps plan and made the best of things until the end of the war.[7] The Congress and the Muslim League might possibly have reached an equation by working in a coalition government, and the evolution to Independence would have been more orderly.

The idea of Pakistan was making headway, indeed it was spreading with the rapidity of a force of nature. I heard the Quaid-i-Azam speak on the subject at a students' rally in Aligarh

1. The Raj, *c.* 1895. Bridge under construction on the Indus at Sukkur.

2. The inauguration.

3. 'The Brown Raj', c. 1920.

4. The pioneers, Aligarh, 1940. (Author is in second row standing at extreme right.)

5. Moorish cavalry escort Pakistan ambassador to present credentials, Madrid, 1952.

in 1940. The Lahore Resolution had then just been adopted. He spoke with conviction and passion, using reason and cold logic as well as irony and humour to score points, and he aroused the vast audience to a state of intense enthusiasm and fervour. I too was stirred by the power of the Quaid's eloquence, by his sense of mission, by the evident truth of much of what he said about the differences that divided Hindus and Muslims, the refusal of the Congress to compromise, and indeed by the rationality of his vision of separate homelands for the Hindus and Muslims in India. Yet a doubt remained that there could be no other solution to the communal problem except the partition of the country.

However, gradually the idea of Partition took hold even among the sceptics and those who had believed in the possibility of a genuine multi-faceted Indian nationalism. If Partition was not the best, it now seemed like the inevitable solution to the Hindu-Muslim question that was fanaticizing India's body politic. It was thought that perhaps the radical surgery of Partition was the only means left to rid it of the virus of bigotry and communalism; when each side had its own space in which to express its identity, the suspicion and hatred of the other would subside. But like the vision of India as a great, united, multi-cultural nation, this too turned out to be an illusion. Partition had been visualized by the Quaid as a solution to the communal problem, with the two countries living side by side in symbiosis, and the minority community in each living with honour and enjoying full rights of citizenship. That was the meaning of his unambiguous and much-quoted speech to the nation on keeping religion separate from politics.

Now the battle seems lost, at least for the present generation, in both India and Pakistan. Bigotry and political opportunism, seen at their worst in the demolition of the five hundred-year old Babri Mosque in India and the mindless reaction to it in Pakistan, and the myriad frustrations of poverty and backwardness, have overtaken India's original commitment to secularism. In Pakistan India's secularism is derided as a sham and hypocrisy. The charge is not false. India has had Muslim presidents and ambassadors, but relatively few Muslims can find jobs as policemen, teachers or civil servants. All of India's national rituals and emblems are inspired by Hindu history and mythology. Indian radio and television have dropped everyday Hindustani in favour of highly

Sanskritic Hindi. (Urdu, alas, has met a similar fate in Pakistan at the hands of zealous pedants.) But however flawed it may have been in practice, secularism was genuinely the aspiration of leaders such as Nehru, and is surely the best protection for the minority communities, and in particular for the Muslims of India.

Jinnah too had visualized Pakistan as a secular state and said so plainly enough in the speech of 11 August 1947: 'You may belong to any religion, caste or creed—that has nothing to do with the business of the State...we are starting with the fundamental principle that we are all citizens, and citizens of one State.' He was speaking at the opening session of the Constituent Assembly of Pakistan that had just elected him as its president. The speech was not a manifesto, but one can take its words as a profession of his faith as a man and as the leader of a country that almost single-handedly he had brought into being. The speech was remarkable also for the absence of triumphalism and exultation at his achievement, and for its introspective tone. It was almost as if he was thinking aloud, when affirming that partition was the only solution to India's constitutional problem, he added, 'Maybe that view is correct, maybe it is not; that remains to be seen.'[8]

It was clear from much else that he said and did that he saw Pakistan as a liberal democracy where all citizens would enjoy equal rights, regardless of religious or other differences. This is what secularism means in practice and it is the basic principle of the Pakistan Constitution. There is also another meaning of secularism—and it relates to European history—that is, the primacy of the State over the temporal powers of the Church. In Islam— there being no church, infallible pope or ordained clergy—the question of a clash between State and religion does not arise. Nevertheless, the question of secularism versus Islam has been a matter of debate in Pakistan from the start. To some it is a carry-over of the pre-Partition polemics in which Nehru vaunted the Congress party's secular policy as against the Muslim League's allegedly theocratic approach. In Pakistan it is a debate in which the terms are not defined and, on the face of it, everyone seems to be on the same side. All major political parties claim to stand for an Islamic state and to be striving for an Islamic social order in the country, but the different political parties give diametrically opposite meanings to these concepts.

The Islamist parties are clear enough about what they want. They proceed from the position that Islam is not just a matter of personal faith, but a complete code of life by which a Muslim should regulate his life and according to which Islamic society must be organized. They hold it to be the duty of an Islamic state to enforce the Islamic code, and to that end, demand that all organs of State, including the legislatures and the judiciary must be placed under the superintendence of a body of religious scholars who alone are qualified to determine whether or not the actions and decisions of these organs are compatible with the tenets of Islam. Islamists do not really believe that democracy is compatible with Islam, wherein according to them, there can be only two parties—the party of God and the party of Satan. They favour a system under which governance would be in the hands of pious and God-fearing men who would discharge their duties with honesty, wisdom and justice. It is an attractive idea, but like Plato's 'philosopher king' the problem is how to find such paragons of virtue and rectitude and to keep them on the straight and narrow path. In practice such a system would give a group of hand-picked men the authority to overrule the will of the people and place all power in the hands of the person who appoints them. (In Pakistan a step in that direction was taken when Ziaul Haq gave the Federal Shariat Court the power to strike down any law it holds to be un-Islamic.)

On the liberal side, decades of political double-speak concerning Islam has clouded the issue in a fog of 'political correctness' and equivocation. The policies of the main political parties—whatever they might say in their manifestos—are in effect based on secular premises (equal rights for all, and 'no' to theocracy). However the rulers who succeeded the Quaid found it expedient to make one concession and then another to the religious parties. This despite the fact that the electorate in Pakistan has throughout denied support to the religious parties and continues to do so. The Jamaat-i-Islami is a political party with possibly the best grass roots organization in the country and it does a good deal of social work. Its members are highly motivated and its leaders are not given to changing views for the sake of office. Yet the fact remains that it has been consistently rejected by the electorate, never polling more than three per cent of the popular vote in any election. The Ziaul Haq dictatorship was the heyday of the Islamist approach. What the voting public thought of Ziaul Haq's Islamization was demonstrated by the virtual boycott of the referendum he held on the subject in 1984. The evident conclusion is that the Islamist agenda does not have very broad support among the people and that the voters are concerned with more down-to-earth and specific issues. On matters of this kind—education, health care, jobs, economic policy—the religious parties have little to offer or to say. Meanwhile Ziaul Haq's Islamization has left behind a legacy of Draconian laws that are used to harass and tyrannize ordinary people, and worse still, has let loose the demons of sectarianism, intolerance and obscurantism in the country. At times it has almost seemed as if, despite itself, the country is being made over in Pandit Nehru's bitter portrayal of it as feudalistic, theocratic and bigoted, and a country destined to disappear. But Nehru proved wrong at least in the last respect. Pakistan has survived every challenge from within and without and has prospered; and it may yet attain to the vision of its founder.

NOTES

[1] The plan envisaged a central government with very limited powers heading three sub-federations made up of two groups of provinces: in the north-west and north-east with Muslim majorities, and a third in the south made up of the Hindu majority provinces.

[2] 'Partition: who was to blame?' *Express*, 11 June 1989. The article was a review of H. M. Seervai's *Partition of India: Myth and Reality*, Emenem, 1989, Bombay.

[3] Maulana Abul Kalam Azad, *India Wins Freedom*, Orient Longman Ltd., 1988, Hyderabad.

[4] Thus the sudden exodus of Hindus from Sindh, where there was scarcely any communal rioting, was generally believed to have been instigated by the Congress in the belief that it would lead to the collapse of the administrative and public services that were largely manned by Hindus.

[5] A poll tax that may be imposed on non-Muslims in Islamic countries. It was sometimes justified on the ground that non-Muslims were exempted or excluded from military service in these countries.

[6] Bose, who was President of the Indian National Congress at this juncture, rejected Gandhi's non-violent approach, and fleeing from detention by the British, set up the Indian National Army which fought alongside the Japanese in the Far East.

[7] Proposed by Cabinet Minister Sir Stafford Cripps, it would have transferred all powers except the conduct of the war effort, to Indian hands. The Congress rejected the plan because it left open the possibility of Partition.

[8] *See* Appendix A.

CHAPTER 3

THE FOREIGN SERVICE

Around the time of Partition I got a job as Deputy Collector in the Sindh Civil Service. A Deputy Collector's main job was to collect government revenue—namely, a tax on agricultural produce, that was at the time, the mainstay of the provincial budget. A Deputy Collector also had a variety of other functions as well as magisterial powers that included imposing fines and jail sentences. In the ordinary course, it took years to climb up the ladder to the position of Deputy Collector, but the Sindh government had decided that a small number of these high-level posts would be filled directly by recruiting young college graduates in order to introduce fresh blood and a new outlook into the system. The old-timers were not amused and called the new recruits 'the Boy Deputy Collectors'.

For training, I was attached to one of the old-timers whom I accompanied on tours and learned to survey crops, read revenue manuals, the Criminal Procedure Code and other such forbidding material. That was the pre-Pajero epoch, and most of the touring was done on horseback and it took a full day's ride to reach some remote villages and outlying areas. The Sindhi horse does not trot or gallop, but taking short quick steps it can maintain a rapid pace over long distances. The rider does not post or move in any way, but sits straight up and lets the horse do the rest. When I toured on my own, people came to see me with petitions and grievances of all kinds, but I did not know what to do with these as I was under training and had no specific functions or powers at that point. Moreover, I did not make petitioners wait outside my 'camp office' for long hours, and instead offered them chairs to sit on when they came in. Such things were not done by the old-timers who knew how to inspire awe for the majesty of their office in the minds of the people by making them feel as uneasy and abject as possible. The petitioners themselves did not know quite what to make of my approach and probably concluded that I was not to be taken seriously.

Those were the days that older people now recall as the 'good old British times' of orderly procedures and respect for law. However, then as now, the power of officialdom over the lives of people was immense and was often abused by officials at various levels. I saw a man in a lock-up who had been there for eleven months without having been charged with anything or being produced before a magistrate as required under the law. Probably, he had been put in at the behest of a local bigwig, or because he had got on the wrong side of a local official, or else someone had an eye on his wife. During another tour with my senior Deputy Collector, there was an alleged prison riot. At breakfast we heard the sound of rifle shots and went over to see what was going on. Two prisoners were lying wounded on the floor, in a courtyard enclosed within iron bars. One had a bullet through his head and bits of his brain were lying spattered around on the floor; another had a bullet wound just below the chest. Astonishingly both were still alive, though not for long. The man with the chest wound was still able to speak. He said they had been shot by the guards after some wrangle. The guards alleged on the contrary, that the two prisoners were dangerous mutineers and were shot 'in self defence' as they were reaching out across the iron bars to seize rifles kept on a shelf on a nearby wall. It was a highly improbable story, but the Deputy Collector accepted it at face value. No one thought of summoning a doctor to attend to the dying men; anyway none was near enough to be able to arrive in time.

When Pakistan was created, the new country set about at once to establish and create the symbols and tools of national sovereignty—flag, anthem, passports, postage stamps and a diplomatic service. The interim government led by Pandit Nehru had already set up quasi-diplomatic offices in some major capitals. With the country's partition some of these too were split up, and a number of Pakistani missions came into being in London, Washington, and at the United Nations in New York, staffed by diplomats who had opted for the new country. I took the first competitive examination for the various Civil Services in Pakistan that was held in 1949, and was selected for the newly established

Foreign Service. A grubby grey telegram arrived one day, informing me of this, and asking that I report for duty at the Foreign Ministry.

As children we had been prepared from time to time by our parents to go to England, but for one reason or another the travel plans never got beyond poring over brochures of shipping companies—Anchor Lines, Ellerman's City Lines, Messageries Maritimes, Italy's Lloyd Triestino. Now it was all within grasp, the romance of travel to far-away places and the glamorous world of diplomacy.

For Indians, England was a sort of El Dorado at the time. Having been there was considered an accomplishment in itself and conferred on the person concerned a reflected glory, and he was regarded, at least by himself, as just short of being an Englishman. Persons who had travelled there were known as 'England-Returned'—and got a higher rating, for instance, in marital advertisements, in the same way that Green Card holders do today. But the England-Returned or the merely Anglicized was also a figure of fun and was held up as a warning to all in cautionary Indian movies. He would be depicted as someone who disdained native dress, traditional ways and old friends; who affected foreign airs and kept company with fast women (creatures who wore lipstick and high heels) in preference to the prim and proper lifemate selected by his mother. He was shown as pursuing those evil ways while his old mother cried her eyes out. Then he would come to the brink of a sticky end when some traumatic experience befell him, usually a motor car accident (that he could have avoided if he had also picked up a little English road sense!) and he would emerge from the hospital a reformed man reverting to the ancestral ways of eating with his fingers, wearing a *dhoti* and a hangdog expression.

The expression England-Returned is an example of 'Indicisms' that are more than simple linguistic innovations, but offer an insight into the subcontinental psyche and sociology. What matters is not getting something done but having made an attempt at doing it, or even just going through the motions, like the Delhi sweeper-woman whom Naipaul witnessed with bafflement, moving the dirt from one end of the floor to the other. 'But I have *swept* the place!' she protested, not understanding what else she was expected to do. Thus there exist not only 'matriculates' but also the 'matric-failed', that is, those who have attained the academic heights from which they could attempt to take the exam.

There was no antonym of England-Returned to describe the teeming millions who had not visited England. We just listened in wonder and dumb envy as the England-Returned recounted tales of the marvels they had seen. 'Roses the size of cabbages! I saw them with my own eyes. Shall we ever grow such flowers in *this* country?' The question was rhetorical for the speaker plainly implied that people of this country were genetically incapable of performing such feats or indeed of doing anything else that was worthwhile. I knew of England from such accounts and from school books in which it was extolled as the home of the *sahib log*, a very superior place; and from glimpses of it in picture books as a lovely land—all green and clean and inhabited by apple-cheeked milkmaids with golden tresses, handsome square-cut cattle and pert looking donkeys. When at last I myself made it to the fabled Vilayat (as the locals called it), I found all that and much more besides. But what impressed me most was on the drive from the airport to London, when the driver of the High Commission's staff car stopped the car at a traffic light—in the middle of the night and on a perfectly empty road! East is East and West is West, I thought, and the twain had better not meet at a traffic light in our parts. And even in later years, negotiating traffic in the streets of New York, Madrid, Beirut, Karachi, sometimes I still see in my mind's eye, the figure of the English chauffeur waiting, serene and self-possessed, for the Pavlovian traffic signal to turn green, and I feel that the true divide between people, the real 'clash of civilizations', is not based on race or religion or ideology, but on the way people drive.

It was my first visit abroad and my first experience of flying. At the airport there wasn't the bustle and excitement when the boat-train from up-country arrived at the Keamari docks, with memsahibs in trim suits and starchly uniformed servants looking to mountains of luggage—cabin trunks, hat boxes, and pets in baskets; country-boats under towering sails lurching crazily across the bow, and the gleaming brass and polished teak of the ship. This was 1949 and the plane was a KLM Constellation carrying a boisterous load of Dutch ex-colonials going home from newly-independent Indonesia. I had always dreamed of flying, but was turned down for a war commission in the air force on account of poor eyesight. Although now one flies as one takes a bus, I have never got over the sense of wonder and excitement I felt on that first flight as I watched the wheels of the plane leave the ground. The plane however, developed engine trouble as soon as it was airborne and after circling around for an hour or so to jettison fuel, returned to Karachi for repairs. This took the whole day and the flight couldn't be resumed until the next morning. Passengers were not allowed to leave the airport as they had already gone through immigration and customs and were more or less confined at the KLM's Midway House hotel. A French fellow-passenger, an Agatha Christie character, rotund and dyspeptic, a cigarette hanging from his lower lip, kept grumbling, *'Ce n'est pas amusant!'*

Mine was the first batch of officers that entered the Pakistan Foreign Service through competition. The training programme arranged for us was elaborate but eclectic. Some went for academic terms at Tufts' Fletcher Law School or the London School of Economics, but I shied off more schooling and opted instead for France to learn French. This was followed by a joint training course at the British Foreign Office for Foreign Service probationers from both Pakistan and India. My overseas training ended with a course at the State Department's Foreign Service Institute in Washington, DC. Europe had still not quite emerged from the aftermath of the war. There was rationing in England and in the French city of Tours, there remained extensive areas that had been bombed out during the liberation. Americans were fighting in Korea under the UN flag. Our lecturer on International Law dwelt a great deal on how admirably and effectively the United Nations was acting there on the world community's behalf to thwart aggression and enforce respect for the UN Charter. However even at that early stage, his eyes glazed over when one asked him whether the UN would show the same vigour in enforcing the Security Council resolutions on Kashmir.

Then we all returned to Karachi for further training in the Foreign Office and other concerned ministries and departments including Commerce, Defence and Information. In musty offices, superintendents perched on chairs, sipped tea and gave us to read piles of dog-eared files tied with raggedy pieces of tape, that looked as if they had not been opened in living memory.

Generally this part of the training was useful largely in showing how a government should *not* be run. The Foreign Office batch was evenly divided between East and West Pakistanis and a tour of the country was included in the training, with the East Pakistanis doing the West Pakistan provinces, and vice versa. During their tour the former found to their surprise that Urdu was not understood in many rural parts of West Pakistan and that it was not a West Pakistani language as such. Already there were interminable arguments between the two groups about Urdu being declared the national language.

My early postings were of brief durations and selected more or less at random. My French was reasonably fluent by now, and I thought I might be posted to Paris but that is not how things work in government. I had to wait thirty years before I made it there. My first post was Ottawa in 1951, under Mohammed Ali Bogra as High Commissioner; then Madrid the following year, when a family friend, Syed Miran Mohammed Shah, was appointed ambassador there. Spain was still ruled by Generalissimo Franco and in economic indicators such as per capita income, road network, electricity production, it was not too far ahead of Pakistan at the time. But its literacy rate was higher, and it had good educational and research institutions, and left Pakistan way behind a long time ago. The diplomatic highlight of the post was the presentation of credentials—to which the ambassador and I were taken in separate gilded coaches, escorted by units of Moorish guards in their blue and crimson uniforms with sabres flashing in the sunlight and mounted on caparisoned horses. The guards were not the only reminder of Spain's North African and Muslim connection. The relics of Spain's Islamic period are to be found not only in the gardens of Alhambra, the mosque at Cordoba and other monuments, but also in the language, manners and morals of the people.

In The Hague in 1954 I had the privilege of serving under Begum Liaquat Ali Khan. She made a great impact on the Dutch as a woman ambassador from a Muslim country. Moreover a newspaper noted that she was a woman envoy accredited to a woman, Queen Juliana, by another woman, Queen Elizabeth (Pakistan had not become a republic yet). A year later, I did a stint in Jeddah—viewed at the time as a punishment post—my offence being that I had sent a rude reply to a rude letter from the Joint Secretary Administration. Jeddah had only one paved street at the time, not more than a couple of kilometres in length. I had taken a sports car there which could get up to one hundred miles an hour within a few seconds flat, but the paved part of the street was not long enough to get the car into top gear. But the place had a Lawrence of Arabia charm—trellis-fronted white-washed houses with carved wooden balconies and oriel windows hanging over narrow, winding streets. When I returned there recently, that Jeddah had vanished; instead there is a sort of Houston-on-thé-Red Sea, with high-rise blocks along broad avenues lined with trees and strips of grass planted at astro-nomical expense, arabesque houses designed by Scandinavian architects, and a brightly-lit skyline that glitters like a diamond in the clear desert night.

After six years abroad I came back to the Foreign Ministry in 1956 and after a spell at the China desk (where we were already working on a draft of the Border Treaty that was signed in 1962) was posted as Foreign Minister Malik Firoz Khan Noon's Private Secretary. He was of the breed of public men who had been loyal servants of the Raj and made their careers in it. He was, for all that, a patriot and a gentleman of the old school, and would never have thought of abusing his office for personal aggrandize-ment.

When the time came to move again, I went with General Sher Ali to set up Pakistan's High Commission in Kuala Lumpur. Malaysia was still grappling with a Communist-led insurgency and the British Army was present in strength and was conducting the operation. Bob Thompson, an Englishman, was the Defence Secretary and he was later asked to advise the Americans on conducting an equally successful anti-guerrilla war in Vietnam. He tried, but it did not work. The essential difference between the two wars was that in Malaysia the insurgents were almost all ethnic Chinese and the government could count on the support of the Malaysian majority in hunting them down. In Vietnam the Vietcong were able to disappear in the sympathetic population like Chairman Mao's fish in water.

Tunku Abdur Rahman was a prince from the ruling house of Perak state, the first Prime Minister of independent Malaysia and the country's father-figure. One of the images I have retained of

Malaysia is that of the Tunku and his wife, sitting by themselves at an open air café at a charity fair in Kuala Lumpur, with no policeman in sight, no fawning courtiers around them, and no mob of supplicants and petitioners crowding around them.

CHAPTER 4

KASHMIR

Flying at 30,000 feet from Dhaka to Lahore, across the breadth of the subcontinent, far away to the north, aloof and above the haze, one can see the white Himalayas lie suspended in the sky, their snowy wastes and pinnacles like a celestial bastion guarding a forbidden and privileged land against the drab and dun-coloured plains stretching away below with their squalor and teeming multitudes. In a fold of these ramparts lies Kashmir. It is lovely as are many other corners of the world; but the beauty of Kashmir seems to be touched by a special magic, made more poignant and vulnerable by the contrast with the baking plains and low scrub-covered hills through which one comes to it. Climbing up the dizzying hairpin bends of the Pir Panjal range to the 9,000 feet high Banihal Pass—which even in midsummer can have snow on it—and driving through a tunnel at the top, as one emerges from the darkness, the Valley opens up before one's eyes like a revelation, a secret world unveiled—fields of saffron and poppy, poplar-lined waterways, green meadows and forests of pine. But the beauty of Kashmir is also touched by sadness, the sadness seen in the eyes of a people living in poverty and oppression in the midst of so much beauty and natural bounty, and who have known nothing else in their lives and the lives of their fathers.

We had spent occasional summer holidays in Kashmir, staying in houseboats in Srinagar, tent camps in Pahalgam, chalets in Gulmarg, and going on week-long excursions into the upper reaches of the Valley, at altitudes of ten to thirteen thousand feet above sea-level, by mountain lakes at the foot of glaciers. Our last holiday in Kashmir was in 1944. On the way up from Sindh, during the train's halt at Lahore, the railway station was suddenly filled with the sound of cathedral bells ringing out. I heard an

English voice cry out, 'It's over, it's finished! We've won!' It was VE day—victory in Europe. It was not our victory but one shared in the excitement of the moment because the war was ending and for India too a new era would begin. The sense of change was already in the air everywhere. The Quaid was in Srinagar that summer, staying across the river from where our houseboat was moored, in a double-storeyed houseboat called *Victory*. His own victory was closer than he could have thought at the time. The Muslims of Kashmir, from everything one saw and heard, were totally and unequivocally in favour of Pakistan, but when Pakistan came into being three years later, Kashmir would be lost to it.

Who lost Kashmir? The answer one receives in Pakistan depends on the politics of the person who responds to the question. For some it was lost by Ayub at Tashkent; others blame Bhutto for signing it away at Simla. In another view, that was aired in a series of articles in a Lahore newspaper, Kashmir was lost to Pakistan because the leadership of the times (that would include the Quaid) rejected, or did not take seriously, an offer said to have been made by Sardar Vallabhai Patel, the Indian minister dealing with the princely states, to swop Kashmir for Hyderabad. General Sher Ali, former Chief of General Staff of the Pakistani Army, and Syed Wajid Ali, a Lahore businessman, both told me of having brought such a message to Pakistan. I myself received an oblique confirmation of the story from an Indian source. In 1964, when the Kashmir question was being discussed in the Security Council, I ran into the Indian counsellor Krishna Rasgotra (who later became foreign secretary) in the delegates' lounge of the UN building. Referring to the Council's proceedings he asked, 'What exactly do you people want out of this meeting?'

'Kashmir,' I replied.

'It's too late now, my friend, to ask for Kashmir,' he twitted me. 'Pakistan should have taken it when it was offered a deal in the beginning.'

Assuming that an Indian offer of some kind was made at the time, some doubt must remain about its nature and purpose. Was the offer seriously meant or was it designed only to lull Pakistan and demoralize the Nizam of Hyderabad who was looking for ways to make his state a sovereign and independent entity? Indeed other rulers besides the Nizam, for example the Maharajah of Travancore, were flirting with the idea of independence. And so, of course, was the Maharaja of Kashmir. It is hard to imagine Pandit Nehru wanting to give up Kashmir for anything in the world, but it is not altogether far-fetched to suppose that Sardar Patel, who did not share Nehru's emotional attachment to the place, may have seen merit in using Kashmir as a bargaining counter to secure all the other princely states, and in particular, to see that Hyderabad did not slip away. Policy differences between Nehru and Patel were common knowledge at the time and could well have included the matter of Kashmir. But there is no hard evidence to substantiate the stories of a specific Patel offer, and indeed such a common sense approach was not at all in evidence at that time, on the smallest India-Pakistan issue.

At any rate, Nehru had set his heart on keeping Kashmir in India by hook or by crook, and appeared to have won the active sympathy (to put it politely) of Mountbatten in the enterprise. The first sign of what was afoot came when the boundary arbitrator, Cyril Radcliffe, split the Muslim majority district of Gurdaspur in order to award to India some *tehsils* (sub-units) which had a marginal Hindu majority. Without this small sliver of territory, India had no access to Kashmir and there could be no practical possibility of the state acceding to India. It is now widely recognized that Radcliffe carried out this gerrymander at Mountbatten's inspiration, in order to take care of this little difficulty.[1] No less a person than the Soviet Foreign Minister Andrei Gromyko, alluded to this matter during the Tashkent discussions. 'Perhaps it is this very method,' he said to Bhutto who was arguing in favour of mediation or arbitration on Kashmir, 'that led to the problem we are discussing today.'

The award of Gurdaspur to India should have set the alarm bells ringing in Pakistan, and no doubt they did. For, with India's land access to Kashmir assured, even if Pakistan had taken up Sardar Patel's alleged offer, there was not much that it could have done to force the Maharajah to sign up with Pakistan. Nehru (and Mountbatten) would have seen to it that he did not. To a considerable extent Pakistan's hands were tied by the Quaid's own formal stand that unlike the procedure for the British-governed provinces, in the case of the princely states, there would be no consultation with the people and it was to be left to the ruler of each state to decide its future affiliation. The Congress had taken the seemingly more democratic stand in holding that where there was doubt, the decision must be made by the people of the State. Nehru no doubt believed that with Sheikh Abdullah's help, the popular vote in Kashmir could be swung in India's favour. This was of course a mistaken assumption in view of the prevailing sentiment in Kashmir, as Nehru realized soon enough.

The Quaid justified his stand on legalistic grounds: the princely states were independent entities whose rulers were in treaty relationship with the British Crown, and this relationship of paramountcy could not be transferred without their consent to third parties. What were the underlying reasons or considerations that led him to make this departure from the principle of Muslim self-determination on which was based the whole concept of Pakistan? The question has never really been discussed in Pakistan. It is a fair assumption to make that the Quaid was anxious to make it possible for the Nizam of Hyderabad, and possibly other states such as Bhopal, to choose the option of Independence if they wished, or at least be able to negotiate reasonable terms with the Congress Government for accession to India. It has also been suggested that some Rajputana states had shown an interest in acceding to Pakistan and sent feelers in this regard to the Quaid-i-Azam. This may well have been so as perhaps they hoped to receive better protection of their princely rights and prerogatives from Pakistan than from India.

It may seem odd and contradictory that after agitating for the separation of Muslim areas from India, the Quaid should want to bring Hindu majority states into Pakistan. The answer may lie in Jinnah's concept of Pakistan. In seeking the partition of British India, the Quaid had not spoken in terms of a complete rupture between Hindus and Muslims. He wanted to redress a situation in which Muslims would be a permanent political and cultural minority in India. The creation of Pakistan was to be not simply the creation of a Muslim territorial entity in the subcontinent, but a guarantee of fair treatment for the large Muslim minority that would continue to live in partitioned India. In this perspective, the accession of Hindu majority states to Pakistan would not have been a contradiction of the Pakistan idea. In such a scheme of things, what would have emerged was a subcontinental patchwork, with two large countries, independent and sovereign but tied to each other by the presence in each of a substantial religious minority and a number of semi-independent princely states, some with rulers professing a religion different from that of their subjects, maintaining a variety of relations with one or the other of the two major states or with both. A very untidy arrangement it may have been, but with the merit of sublimating the Hindu-Muslim polarization within a network of trans-communal relationships—somewhat like those fostered by the great Moguls. Whether or not any such specific design was in the Quaid's mind, something of the sort would have resulted from what he was trying to bring about. In actual fact, it is more likely that Muslim League leadership, taking the accession of Kashmir to Pakistan for granted, was at that stage motivated by a more immediate concern, which was to bolster the position of the Muslim rulers of Hindu majority states, in particular the Nizam of Hyderabad and the Nawab of Bhopal, who both had close personal connections with the League leaders and had been supportive of the Pakistan Movement.

Then came the tribal incursion into the State. Who authorized the venture, how was it organized, what were its objectives, and who was in command? All these questions have to this day not been clearly answered. India described the event as an attempt by Pakistan to take Kashmir by force. In view of India's chicanery with the Boundary Award, the use of force was not unjustifiable in *realpolitik* terms. However everything else was against it. The control of Pakistan's Armed Forces was still in British hands, and through them Mountbatten effectively had a veto on how they might be used. The attempt was botched because it was undertaken with the help of undisciplined tribal levies who failed to secure or disable Srinagar Airport though they were within sight of it. As a Gulf ruler put it when I went to brief him in 1990 on the Kashmir situation, 'There would be no Kashmir problem if your men had reached Srinagar Airport on time.' When at long last the Pakistan Army did move into Kashmir, it was too late for it to do anything except prevent the Indians from over-running the whole place. It is said that when the cease-fire mediated by the UN went into force, the Pakistani forces were on the verge of launching an offensive that might have dislodged the Indians from Poonch and greatly improved Pakistan's strategic position. But the government ordered our troops to hold fire for fear that it could lead to a general war and imperil the existence of Pakistan itself. If the story is true, it prefigured in some ways what happened during the 1965 War.

The Kashmir story is well-enough known not to need detailed recounting. But it is nearly a half century since the dispute was taken up by the United Nations Security Council—on a complaint by India of alleged Pakistani aggression—and in such a long span of time the simplest facts tend to become opaque and to appear complex. However the facts are simple enough, the complexity comes mainly from the fact that India is in possession, and too strong and too influential to be dislodged either by military means or by diplomatic pressures. Briefly to sum up the history of the dispute that has gone through several well-defined phases: in the first phase, which lasted about two years, the United Nations' involvement in the matter was active and positive.[2] It sent a Commission, (UNCIP)[3] which arrived on the scene in July 1948, and after months of shuttling between Delhi and Karachi, brought about a cease-fire, established a UN supervised cease-fire line (CFL), and obtained the agreement of India and Pakistan to a plebiscite in the disputed territory, to be held in conditions that were clearly spelled out, and under the authority of a UN plebiscite administrator (Admiral Chester Nimitz of the US Navy). The signal accomplishment of UNCIP was that it obtained the agreement of both India and Pakistan to the proposed settlement which was endorsed by a resolution of the Security Council.[4] In January 1949 a cease-fire went into effect. The principal condition, and the rock on which foundered the UN-mediated settlement, was the withdrawal of forces by both sides from the state so that the population could express its wishes freely in the plebiscite. But at the end of two years, the UN Commission was compelled to report to the council that it had failed in its efforts to arrange the stipulated withdrawal of military forces. The differences between the two countries in this matter related to almost every aspect of the question.[5]

Who was to blame for the impasse? Each side blamed the other, but when Pakistan proposed to put the matter to arbitration or to adjudication by the World Court, India rejected the idea. A joint appeal in 1949 by Prime Minister Attlee of Britain and the US President Harry Truman met the same fate.

The UN itself refrained from laying down the law on how the troop withdrawals were to be carried out. Instead in the next phase which lasted some eight to ten years, the Security Council sent a succession of eminent international personalities—General McNaughton of Canada, Judge Owen Dixon of Australia, Gunnar Jarring of Sweden, and Dr Frank Graham of the United States— to try to resolve the issue. The specific question at issue was the creation of conditions, notably by the reciprocal pull-out of troops, that would permit the proposed plebiscite to be held in impartial conditions. But the real problem, as it soon became apparent, was India's refusal to contemplate the possibility of letting go of Kashmir.

The mediators in fact went beyond the plebiscite idea in seeking a solution. McNaughton mooted the idea of Partition by suggesting that the plebiscite be held on a regional basis.[6] The following year, Owen Dixon tried his hand at removing the obstacles to the holding of a plebiscite, but faced with India's opposition to any genuine popular consultation, decided to look beyond the plebiscite idea to other ways of resolving the dispute. The essence of his proposal was to partition the State of Jammu and Kashmir between the two claimants and he suggested two ways of doing this: (1) an overall plebiscite should be held but various regions be disposed off in accordance with the result in the region concerned. Thus Jammu and Ladakh would presumably go to India; Poonch and Baltistan to Pakistan. (2) Alternatively, the outcome could be anticipated for areas such as the above and the territories allotted accordingly to one or the other country, leaving only the fate of the Kashmir Valley to be decided by plebiscite. Nehru apparently showed some interest in the latter idea, but in the end nothing came of Dixon's proposals because Nehru would not agree to his stipulations for ensuring that the Valley plebiscite would be really free and impartial. Nehru no doubt saw the Dixon proposal only as a way of partitioning Jammu and Kashmir along the cease-fire line.

In 1953, some exchanges took place between Pandit Nehru and Pakistan's Prime Minister, Mohammed Ali Bogra, in Delhi, in the course of which the two leaders circled around the idea of partition. Nehru took the position that the plebiscite must not cause any large-scale shifting of population from one side to the other. This could be ensured, he suggested, by providing that certain regions in which the poll was overwhelmingly in favour of one side should be allocated to that side irrespective of the overall result. Boundaries of such regions should be demarcated with due regard to geographical, economic and other considerations and satisfy the requirements of an international boundary. He also asked that Admiral Nimitz be dropped as plebiscite administrator and another individual chosen from a smaller power. Mohammad Ali Bogra proposed the following pre-requisites of a truly free and independent poll: (1) neutralization of the Kashmir administration; (2) exclusion of the troops of both sides from the plebiscite area; and (3) vesting the plebiscite administrator with all necessary powers.[7] Bogra also asked that the proposed 'regions' in question should be defined in advance in order to remove ambiguity and any scope for subsequent misunderstandings. When the Indians got back to Pakistan it was with the reply that our Prime Minister had not correctly understood Mr Nehru who, they explained, had never suggested regional plebiscites; what he had proposed was that an overall plebiscite should take place and the results thereof be examined by the two prime ministers with a view to ensuring that no unfortunate migrations from, or disturbances within the state took place, and that in arriving at a decision in the matter, due regard should be paid to geographical, economic and other factors. As for Pakistan's proposals to ensure the freedom and impartiality of the plebiscite, Nehru merely said that these matters had already been disposed of by UNCIP. What India really wanted was a formal partition that would legitimize her hold on Jammu and Ladakh while leaving her free to manipulate the plebiscite in the Valley. The truth of the matter was stated bluntly by Owen Dixon when he concluded that there was little likelihood of India agreeing to any conditions which would ensure an impartial vote.[8]

In the years that followed Pakistan threw in its lot with the West, joining United States' sponsored military pacts against the Soviet Union and partly as a result, India was able to firm up the Soviet Union's veto for its case. During an official visit to India in 1956 Khrushchev decided to go the whole hog and declared the Soviet Union's support for the Indian claim that Kashmir was an integral part of India. (A nuance of at least academic interest in the Soviet position, was that it was based not on the Maharajah's accession, but on the assumption that the people of Kashmir had already decided in favour of joining India.) The upshot was that the last of the UN mediators, Dr Frank Graham of the United States, never got the opportunity even formally to present his report to the Security Council. However the next twist in the plot was the Sino-Indian border fighting that broke out in 1962. This set off a great flutter in London and Washington on the prospect of winning over India to the Western side. In Pakistan on the other hand, it raised hopes that India would now see reason, or be made to see it by the Western powers.

But the Western powers' first impulse was to tell Pakistan to forget about Kashmir, at least for the duration, and to join India in facing the 'real' danger from China. On 28 October, John Kennedy wrote a letter to Ayub Khan to this effect recalling that Ayub himself had, not long before, proposed joint defence between India and Pakistan and suggesting that he now send a private message to Nehru that Pakistan would make no moves against India's frontiers.[9] But of course Ayub's offer had called for, and was conditional on, a settlement of the Kashmir dispute. He still considered that the subcontinent faced a common security problem, but in the situation created by the Sino-Indian border clash, he wanted Western aid to India to be 'used as a club' to bring about a settlement and open the way to a joint defence arrangement. But the United States was not at all disposed to allow Pakistan, as Kennedy had made clear enough, to use American power to achieve its aims in Kashmir. However the Western powers realized that something would have to be done to mollify Pakistan which was threatening to queer the pitch by turning to China.

Accordingly British Foreign Secretary, Duncan Sandys, and the US President's advisor, Averell Harriman, were sent to the subcontinent, and in November 1962 they were able to stitch together an agreement between Ayub and Nehru 'to make a renewed effort to resolve the outstanding differences between their two countries on Kashmir...and to start discussions at an early date with the object of reaching an honourable and equitable settlement.'[10] The Western mediators had hardly left Delhi when Nehru made a statement in the Lok Sabha on their mission, in the course of which he asserted that 'anything that involved an upset of the present arrangement' would not do at all. This seemed to nullify the sense of the agreement that had been reached. Duncan Sandys who was in Karachi to announce the good news of the agreement, was greatly embarrassed and cancelling his flight to London, flew back to Delhi to straighten things out. All he managed to get from Nehru was a rather airy-fairy denial that he had meant to go back on the terms of agreement. At any rate the outcome of the Western efforts was that a series of meetings was held between the foreign ministers of the two countries over a period of six months, alternately in Pakistani and Indian cities to negotiate a Kashmir settlement on the terms of the agreement.

The first meeting, held in Rawalpindi from 27 to 29 December 1962, was overshadowed by the signing of the Sino-Pakistan Border Agreement.[11] In India there was a great hue and cry about Pakistan's 'perfidy', with sidelong glances at the West for moral support. The State Department muttered about the 'unfortunate breach of free world solidarity' but left it at that. Bhutto called for a plebiscite under the UNCIP resolutions. Swaran Singh spoke of the danger of introducing religious factors into the issue, heightening the risk of a renewed exodus of minorities and of a political upheaval in India. A joint communiqué issued at the end of the meeting appealed for a friendly atmosphere to resolve outstanding differences on Kashmir and put off further discussions to the next round.

This took place in Delhi about two weeks later and probed further into the matter of holding a plebiscite. Swaran Singh reiterated the dangers of stirring up communal feelings and said that Pakistan should not ignore the developments that had taken place in the fifteen years since the UNCIP resolutions were adopted, the several elections held in Kashmir and the democratic government established there as a result.

Bhutto, while formally reserving Pakistan's position on the matter of a plebiscite, agreed to consider any alternative solutions that India wished to propose. Swaran Singh said that any solution should take into account the relevant geographical and administrative considerations and be such as to cause the least disturbance to the life and welfare of the people. Bhutto affirmed that the factors especially pertinent to a just settlement were the composition of the population, defence requirements, control of river waters and the wishes of the people. Partition had not yet

been specifically discussed, but clearly even on the matter of
partitioning the State, the parties were poles apart. In meetings
with the British High Commissioner, Paul Gore-Booth, and US
Ambassador, John Galbraith, Bhutto urged the need for third
party mediation if the talks were to come to anything.

The third session of the talks took place in Karachi three
weeks later. At this session India came up with a 'working paper'
on partitioning the State. The substance of it was that India
would concede Pakistan's possession of Azad Kashmir and in
addition cede to it some areas to the west and north of the
Kashmir Valley, such as the Tithwal forest and the area around
the Kishenganga River—altogether about 3,000 square miles.
Pakistan, proceeding on the basis of the criteria Bhutto had
enunciated at the previous session, proposed a partition that
would leave India with some parts of the Jammu district while
the rest of the State would go to Pakistan. In view of the
irreconcilable positions of the two sides Bhutto put forward an
alternate proposal. This was for a phased approach that would
leave aside for the time being the 'heart of the dispute', namely,
the Kashmir Valley, and would focus on reaching an agreement
on a partition line through the rest of the State. The question of
the Valley would be settled later but India would have to
recognize Pakistan's 'interest and involvement' in the area. Maps
were exchanged and they showed that the gulf between their
positions was scarcely bridgeable, but to the Press Swaran Singh
still talked about the mutual desire for an amicable and
acceptable solution.

A month went by before the conference reconvened in
Calcutta. At this session discussions focused on topics such as the
Sino-Pakistan Border Agreement, the Rann of Kutch, the
expulsion of Muslims from Assam and Tripura, and not much
was said about Kashmir. When the negotiations resumed in
Karachi, after yet another month, the British and US envoys had
to intervene to save them from immediate breakdown. Bhutto
said that if India recognized Pakistan's claim to the Kashmir and
Chenab valleys, Pakistan would be willing to allow Indian troops
transit rights to Ladakh. India rejected this offer and Nehru
scoffed at it in the Lok Sabha saying that Pakistan wanted the
Indians to shed their blood to defend Ladakh in order then to
hand it over to Pakistan!

The last round of talks was held in Delhi. Bhutto made yet another proposal. This was to the effect that there should be an interim period of six months during which Indian troops in the State would be replaced by third country forces and the Valley placed under international administration; at the end of the six months, the wishes of the people would be ascertained. India rejected this and proposed instead a declaration that neither side would use force to alter the *status quo* in Kashmir.

Speaking in the Lok Sabha on the negotiations, Nehru described partition as an extremely harmful idea, and withdrew the offer that Swaran Singh had made to Bhutto in the course of the negotiations. On Pakistan's side, Bhutto also rejected 'categorically and without equivocation', the idea of partitioning Kashmir.

Thus ended the attempt, the only one made up to then and since, to resolve the dispute through face to face negotiations. At one stage the United States and Britain took a hand in the matter and communicated to both sides their view of the elements that might go into a settlement. The main elements were a partition of the State in such a way that India and Pakistan should each have a substantial position in the Valley and assured access through it; India's interest in Ladakh and Pakistan's in developing water storage in the Chenab would be recognized; and there would be clearly defined arrangements with regard to political freedom, free movement of people, development of tourism and the economy of the State. Both countries rejected the idea of partitioning the Valley but Ayub was prepared to consider 'other' solutions which preserved the unity of the Valley, gave the inhabitants a voice in their own affairs and provided for the defence and economic needs of all parties.

The failure of this effort at a bilateral settlement was a forgone conclusion for a number of reasons, not the least of them being the failure of its Western sponsors to back it up with the required diplomatic pressure. In fact, while the negotiations were still under way, the United States announced that the military aid it had promised to India was not tied to a successful outcome of the negotiations. Before the fifth and final round, Nehru—after meetings with Harriman and Sandys—declared that he had received assurances that a settlement of Kashmir was not a condition for continued Western military aid. No less important, perhaps, was the unilateral cease-fire declared by China in the border conflict, for it indicated that her aims against India were limited in nature.

Then followed a most turbulent year in Kashmir and in the relations between the two countries. India speeded up its moves to integrate Kashmir fully, in substance as well as in symbols, into the Indian Union, in violation not only of the UN resolutions but the Maharajah's Accession Agreement on which rested India's whole case for being in Kashmir. The unrest and tension caused by these moves was brought to a head by the theft of a relic from the Shah Hamadan Mosque at Hazratbal. The motive of the theft was obviously political, and India accused Pakistan of being behind it. Pakistan accused India of having arranged the incident in order to come down hard on the anti-Indian agitation that had the territory in its grip. The State now went virtually out of the control of the authorities—roads in and out of Srinagar were sealed, government offices ceased to function as officials were scared to stir out of their homes, and the administration was paralysed or rather, went into the hands of an Action Committee that had been conducting the agitation against India. Then, suddenly, the relic—a hair of the Holy Prophet—was found and authenticated as genuine by a committee of *ulema*.

All this woke India to the precariousness of its position in Kashmir and the risks of pushing ahead with the integration of the State. The case against Sheikh Abdullah was withdrawn and upon release from goal, he called for self-determination and proceeded to Delhi to meet his erstwhile friend, Jawaharlal Nehru. A month later, with Nehru's approval, he went to Islamabad to meet Ayub Khan whose agreement he obtained for a meeting with Nehru in June. But Nehru died on 27 May, and with his death also died the little flicker of hope raised by Abdullah's tentative attempt at mediation.

Matters went downhill, and in the following years Pakistan and India stumbled into war again—the second war over Kashmir. I have dealt with the war and its aftermath in separate chapters and shall conclude the present one with a brief description of the renewed attempts after the 1965 War to settle the Kashmir dispute and to deal with the whole India-Pakistan tangle.

The Tashkent summit served to restore the *status quo ante bellum* with a commitment by the two countries to seek peaceful settlement of their differences. Kashmir was discussed throughout the conference but it found only oblique mention in the Tashkent Declaration. The India-Pakistan meeting held in Islamabad to implement the Declaration went round in circles— the Indians refusing to commit themselves to 'meaningful' negotiations on Kashmir.

Then in October 1966, during the annual session of the United Nations General Assembly, India's Swaran Singh made the following proposal to the Pakistani Foreign Minister for resuming the effort to resolve India-Pakistan problems:

(1) that 'technocrats' of the two countries meet in Geneva to hold talks on Kashmir, arms reduction, the Farraka Dam problem, economic co-operation and also to reach an agreement on rotation of candidatures in UN elections beginning with Pakistan's support for a Security Council seat for India that year. In return India would support Pakistan for the seat to be vacated by Japan the following year, and

(2) that meetings should be held in complete secrecy.[12]

What did all this signify? Was it a sudden change of heart on India's part, or the result of prompting by the United States? Very probably it was the latter. In Islamabad US ambassador Locke had already visited the Foreign Office, and put in a suggestion that 'trusted representatives' of the two sides should get together quietly to negotiate an arms control agreement. The offer of secret talks was received by Islamabad with scepticism and reserve. India was, in all respects, in a strong position after the 1965 stalemate, and wanted perhaps to renew attempts to impose a settlement along a marginally adjusted cease-fire line, with the support of the United States and the Soviet Union. Both powers desired to isolate the subcontinent from China's influence or threat, and the proposal was designed perhaps to sow doubts in China's mind about Pakistan's intentions. On the other hand, we could not very well reject something that Pakistan itself had first proposed. At the post-Tashkent meeting in Rawalpindi in March, Foreign Secretary Aziz Ahmad had suggested to the Indian side the idea of holding meetings on Kashmir in secret in case it wanted to avoid problems with public opinion. President Ayub had indicated to Mrs Indira Gandhi that if India was shy of holding open talks on Kashmir, Pakistan would consider any other procedure that India might suggest. For Pakistan, the

channel of secret talks offered the opportunity not only of
exploring the shape of an eventual settlement, but of redressing
the situation in occupied Kashmir and halting India's creeping
annexation of the territory.

Hence it was thought that secret talks on Kashmir might begin
as an exploration of intentions rather than as a full-fledged
negotiation between plenipotentiaries. If it was found that India
was serious about reaching a settlement regarding Kashmir, talks
could be held on the same basis simultaneously, on other matters
like arms control and reduction; the Farraka Dam problem that
concerned East Pakistan; as well as trade, joint projects and other
such subjects. Agreements in principle reached on the various
specific issues would not be put into effect until there was a
whole package that could be used to tempt or press India into
making concessions on Kashmir.

Accordingly, High Commissioner Arshad Hussain was
instructed to seek a meeting with Sardar Swaran Singh in order
to try to gauge India's intentions and to ascertain whether the
offer signified a shift in her position on Kashmir. It became clear
soon enough that this was not the case. Swaran Singh said that
when talking to Foreign Minister Pirzada in New York, he had
received the impression that as long as talks were held on
Kashmir, other issues could be raised by either side and settled.
India, he said, was ready to talk about Kashmir but settlement of
other issues should not be contingent on progress being made
on any one issue. The High Commissioner tried to correct this
impression and affirmed that the general relationship between
the two countries depended very much on a settlement of the
Kashmir dispute; also while Pakistan appreciated that the Kashmir
dispute could not be resolved in a few meetings, it would need
some tangible token of India's intention to resolve it if comprehensive talks were to be held with any hope of success. To this
end the High Commissioner proposed that India might consider
making a public statement of its intention to seek a compromise
solution acceptable to Pakistani, Indian and the Kashmiri people.
Swaran Singh said that the very principle that a settlement must
take into account the wishes of the Kashmiri people was not
acceptable to India, but he felt sure that once other issues were
settled and friendly relations established, the two countries would
be able to find a way out also on Kashmir.

In the beginning of 1967, speaking at the Institute of International Affairs in Karachi, Ayub Khan suggested that India and Pakistan would do well to agree on a mutual reduction of their armed strength. Taking this up, the new Indian Foreign Minister, Muhammad Ali Chagla, wrote to his Pakistani counterpart Sharifuddin Pirzada, proposing talks on the subject. Pakistan responded by asking for simultaneous talks on Kashmir, a reaction that cannot have surprised India. The Indian Foreign Minister treated it as a rejection of his proposal, but declared nevertheless that India was ready 'to discuss all questions between India and Pakistan, including the Kashmir question, at any time and place mutually convenient.'

The High Commissioner met Chagla to pursue the matter, but they got stuck on the wording of a joint declaration—demanded by Pakistan—defining the scope of the proposed talks. Chagla proposed the following wording:

> Talks would be earnest and meaningful and on a confidential and continuing basis. A sincere effort would be made by both sides in a friendly spirit and in conformity with the Tashkent Declaration to seek solutions of various problems existing between the two countries including Jammu and Kashmir which Pakistan regards as a basic dispute between the two countries.

The High Commissioner instead suggested the following:

> Talks would be earnest and meaningful and on a confidential basis. A sincere effort would be made by both sides to seek a solution of various disputes and problems existing between India and Pakistan including the basic dispute regarding Jammu and Kashmir, in a friendly spirit.

This formulation the Indians were unwilling to accept and the discussions came to an end. Was this an opportunity lost? It may seem that the distinction between describing Kashmir as a 'problem' or a 'dispute' was a quibble, but against the background and history of India-Pakistan negotiations on the subject, these were code words that indicated whether India was prepared to negotiate a settlement of the dispute or merely hold a general discussion on the issue. It is another question whether we were right in linking the subject of arms reduction with that

of Kashmir in this way. My own view was and remains, that arms
reductions and control is a goal that should be pursued in its
own terms, and agreement on it would be of immense benefit to
people on both sides.

On returning home from his meeting with the Indian Foreign
Minister, High Commissioner Arshad Hussain heard on All India
Radio a statement that the Minister had recorded before the
meeting. This was to the effect that Kashmir was an integral part
of India; friendship with Pakistan could not be purchased by
yielding any part of India; and that Pakistan was in illegal
occupation of Azad Kashmir!

So ended another episode in the tussle over Kashmir: the
Indian offer proved to be a feint and India had opened a door
that, in Pakistan's eyes, led into a maze. No one was greatly
surprised. Then followed a lull with regard to Kashmir that lasted
for almost a quarter century. It was a blood-stained period in the
history of the subcontinent—the Bangladesh War, the Sikh
insurgency in India, Bhutto's rise and fall and liquidation, the
Afghan War, the assassinations of Mujibur Rahman and Indira
Gandhi and then of her son, Rajiv. Throughout these upheavals
and ups and downs in Indo-Pakistan relations, the Kashmir issue
remained strangely quiescent.

It had been last mentioned between the two countries at Simla.
The Simla Conference was not about Kashmir but about
retrieving as much as was possible of what General Yahya Khan's
military adventure in East Pakistan had cost the country—its
name and honour, territory in West Pakistan, and 90,000 men in
POW camps. As to Kashmir, there was at the time the fear that
India would use her decisive military victory to settle the issue on
her terms once and for all. That she did not make the attempt,
was due no doubt to the fact that the great powers—the United
States as well as the Soviet Union—did not want any further
messing about with the *status quo* in that part of the subcontinent.
Bhutto's adversaries accuse him of having given up in the Simla
Agreement, Pakistan's right to ventilate the Kashmir dispute in
international forums. This is, of course, factually incorrect since
Pakistan has from time to time raised the issue in various
international forums.

When Bhutto spoke at the UN General Assembly's 1973 session,
he referred to the Kashmir question in the following words:

I say therefore without unfriendliness or hostility, but in all seriousness, that the important issue of self-determination for the people of Jammu and Kashmir to which the United Nations and both India and Pakistan are committed, will have to be faced and honourably resolved for the good of all of us in the subcontinent. In asking for sanity and justice in the relations between India and Pakistan, in asking for the settlement of disputes on the basis of the principles enshrined in the UN Charter, Pakistan is taking a position entirely in accord with the evolving international situation.

Bilateral negotiations and international action are not mutually exclusive options. Insofar as Kashmir is concerned, the difficulties arose not at Simla, but almost as soon as the UNCIP resolutions were adopted. The remarkable thing about Simla was that at a time when all the cards were stacked against Pakistan, Bhutto was able to include in the Declaration a reference to Kashmir and to obtain a commitment from India to negotiate a peaceful settlement of the issue—a commitment which implicitly contradicted her assertion that the subject was foreclosed.

A hiatus of a quarter of a century since the Simla Agreement had the effect of making the world almost forget that there was such a thing as a Kashmir problem. Some powers have come to take the view that the UN resolutions of nearly fifty years ago are no longer capable of being applied. In the minds of others, the principle itself of self-determination arouses misgivings and they feel that it should be tempered by pragmatic considerations, otherwise states composed of different ethnic, linguistic, religious or racial groups would be threatened with dismemberment or possibly extinction. Against the background of the renewed Balkan upheaval, one cannot dismiss such considerations out of hand. And yet the idea that some nations can be free, while other people should have their freedom abridged in the name of stability, is even more dubious and could open the way to a new kind of colonialism. The pragmatic answer to the dilemma would seem to be that whereas the right of self-determination is unqualified in itself, how it is applied in different situations may vary from case to case. In the former Federation of Yugoslavia, the failure of national consensus led, not to an attempt to seek a new concord, but provoked the resurgence of a primitive and atavistic Serbian nationalism that tried to expand by suppressing the right of self determination of other nationalities. As against this, there are the examples of Belgium and Canada where too the pull of ethnic and linguistic affiliations seems to threaten the larger national loyalty, but where the efforts to reconcile the two have not been altogether unsuccessful.

Pakistan itself came into being on the basis of the principle of self-determination. Though Partition was accomplished in bitterness and bloodshed, the fact remains that the emergence of the two independent and sovereign states of India and Pakistan was the result of a historic compromise between the representatives of the two major communities of the subcontinent. It was designed to put an end to their age-old rivalry and contention. The fact that the bitterness remains, and in Kashmir the bloodshed continues, is due largely to the fact that the compromise was vitiated by the denial of the principle in the case of the state of Jammu and Kashmir whose population continues to be denied the right to decide their future in freedom.

However, in considering this issue the question unavoidably comes up whether the Kashmiris' right of self-determination is circumscribed by the partition arrangements and the UN resolutions, or goes beyond to encompass the right to full independence. On one occasion when the Kashmir question was being considered in the Security Council in New York, a sort of 'rap session' developed among some Pakistani delegates in the presence of Bhutto who was leading the delegation. In what might be called the 'absolutist' view, Pakistan could not very well advocate self-determination for Kashmiris, but deny them the right to go their own way if that was what they really wanted. Moreover, on the plane of practical politics, it was argued that by conceding the 'third option' Pakistan would strengthen its case before the bar of world opinion. The opposing view was that allowing the creation of a third independent and sovereign nation in the subcontinent could lead to the balkanization of both India and Pakistan and that therefore the option of independence for the princely states had been implicitly excluded in the partition and independence arrangements worked out between the British government, the Indian National Congress and the Muslim League. Bhutto himself said that in principle, if we were willing to let Kashmir go to India in a plebiscite, then we could surely live with an independent Kashmir. But he too was of the view that in terms of practical politics the independence option would not be in the interests of either India or Pakistan, or indeed of the Kashmiris themselves. An independent Jammu and Kashmir, he felt, would not cease to be a bone of contention between India and Pakistan, with various Kashmiri factions and regions looking to one or the other country and being manipulated by them; nor, in the triangular cold war that prevailed at the time, could Kashmir avoid becoming the playground for the designs and ambitions of the surrounding world powers.

The question is of course academic. The pertinent question for fifty years has been not whether a third option should be given to the Kashmiri people, but whether they are to be allowed any option at all. During these years India has tried everything to secure and make permanent its shaky hold on Kashmir and to create a semblance of popular approval for it. At first she had the support of Sheikh Abdullah, the popular 'Lion of Kashmir'. A Constituent Assembly dutifully endorsed the Maharajah's accession. From time to time elections were staged in the State. India has spent vast sums of money in Kashmir—most of it to maintain the forces of occupation, but also on economic development—in order to win over some political support. Nothing has worked, and over and over again India has had to return to repression and brute force. Sheikh Abdullah was put in jail where he languished off and on, for fifteen years. The hand-picked Constituent Assembly's decisions were held to be devoid of validity by the UN Security Council.[14] The elections were all rigged; only three per cent of the electorate went to the polls in the most recent of these, held in 1989, provoking what has become a full-fledged revolt against the Indian occupation. Yes, India has done everything it could in Kashmir except draw the obvious conclusion: Kashmir is not at home in India.

Kashmir has shaped the foreign and security policies of both India and Pakistan. It has kept alive the bitterness of Partition and prevented the healing of wounds. In Pakistan there is deep frustration and a sense of betrayal that the United Nations has failed to enforce the settlement set out in its own resolutions. In India too there is emotion over Kashmir but of a different kind, based on memories of ancient wrongs. The idea that keeping Muslim majority Kashmir in India strengthens India's secular polity is hardly tenable if the link has to be maintained by force.

The liberal argument that Kashmir's opting out of India would have an adverse effect on the position of Indian Muslims is not necessarily insincere. But one can argue the contrary thesis that, to a considerable degree, the festering conflict over Kashmir is what fuels the continuing Hindu-Muslim animosity in India. Fifty years of argument and bickering have made the settlement of Kashmir look like a zero-sum game. One side cannot win without the other feeling that it is losing. This attitude has not only ignored the interests of the Kashmiri people, but has sacrificed those of the people of both countries.

The situation in Kashmir has reached a stage where a solution has become a historic inevitability as was the independence of Algeria, the end of apartheid and peace in the Middle East. This does not mean that it is within reach or that there is a simple formula for achieving it. A just and final settlement of the Kashmir dispute is not a matter of one side triumphing over the other, but of finding a way by which Pakistan and India can live with each other in peace and co-operation and finally close the bitter chapter of Partition.

NOTES

[1] A recent account of this sordid business is given in Alastair Lamb's *Kashmir: A Disputed Legacy*, Roxford Books, London, 1991.

[2] For the pertinent UN resolutions *see* Government of Pakistan Kashmir Documents—texts of main resolutions adopted by the Security Council and the UN Commission on India and Pakistan, Karachi; 1962.

[3] The United Nations' Commission on India and Pakistan (UNCIP), was made up of five members, Argentina, Belgium, Columbia, Czechoslovakia and the United States.

[4] Security Council Resolution number 47 of 1948 'noted with satisfaction that both India and Pakistan desire that the question of accession of the State of Jammu and Kashmir to India or Pakistan should be decided through the democratic method of a free and impartial plebiscite.'

[5] *See* Government of Pakistan 'Reports on Kashmir by United Nations Representatives', Karachi 1958.

[6] Ibid.

[7] In a spirit of accommodation, Pakistan agreed to Nehru's demand to drop the American Admiral as the Plebescite Administrator, but no one else was ever appointed in his place.

[8] Ibid.

[9] Ayub Khan, *Friends not Masters*, Oxford University Press, Karachi, 1967, pp. 140-41.

[10] Ibid., p. 149.

[11] Keesings Contemporary Archives; 27 July-3 August 1963; p. 19543.

[12] However, another Indian Cabinet minister, Mr Sanjiva Reddy took the position that if negotiations were to be held on the Kashmir dispute then both sides should have the courage to say so publicly.

[14] *See* Government of Pakistan Kashmir documents—texts of the main resolutions adopted by the Security Council and the UNCIP; Karachi 1962.

CHAPTER 5

THE UNITED NATIONS
1961-1964

In 1961, I was transferred from the High Commission in Kuala
Lumpur to the Permanent Mission at the United Nations. I
arrived there just after the New Year in time for one of the
longest spells of sub-zero temperatures in New York's history.
But coming from Malaysia's steamy year-round summer to snow-
bound New York was not merely a change of climate; the nature
and scope of the assignment, as well as the size, make-up and
mode of work of the mission, were very different. The permanent
mission to the United Nations is one of our largest diplomatic
offices and here relationships and procedures are far more
complex than in the little family outfits like Madrid, The Hague
and Kuala Lumpur where I had served previously. Prince Aly
Khan, whom Malik Firoz Khan Noon had appointed as
Permanent Representative to console him for being passed over
by the late Aga Khan as his successor, had been killed a short
while before in a car accident near Paris. Though there were
mutterings in Pakistan about a 'playboy' ambassador, he was by
all accounts, an effective representative, respected and liked by
all sides in the UN. He ran a very stylish embassy and threw
glittering parties for which guests flew in from Paris, Rome,
Hollywood. When I arrived, the reception rooms of the Mission
were still furnished with French antiques, Gobelin tapestries and
nineteenth century paintings, but all this alien and borrowed
finery was removed shortly afterwards by the decorating firms
who had lent them to the Prince. Chaudhri Zafrulla Khan, who
followed a year or so later, was elected President of the UN
General Assembly in 1963, and brought great distinction to the
role. Indeed he established a unique reputation by doing

something which no one had been able to do before or has done since, that is, start the Assembly's sessions on time. His method was daring but simple: punctually at 10.30 a.m. he ascended the podium, settled into his chair and banged the gavel. After some initial dismay, delegates caught on and not a single meeting started a minute late, not even the long-awaited ceremonial meeting at which the delegation of newly-independent Algeria was admitted to the United Nations. The only trouble this time was that the Algerian delegation itself had not yet shown up! Undeterred, Chaudhri Zafrulla banged his implacable gavel and the Assembly was about to play Hamlet without the Prince of Denmark, when the Chief of Protocol rushed in at the last minute, huffing and puffing, with the Algerian delegation in tow.

At the United Nations it was India's heyday. It seemed that nothing occurred there in which India was not involved and no major decisions were taken without India being consulted. A UN peace-keeping force that did not include Indian contingents was almost inconceivable, and often these forces were led by Indian officers. India had come to acquire the status of a quasi-world power as the leader and spokesman of the non-aligned group, and was treated as such by Western powers. The fact that India ceaselessly nagged, chided and lectured these powers, specially whenever Defence Minister Krishna Menon arrived on the scene, seemed only to make them more eager to curry favour with her. There were a number of factors for India's pre-eminence at this stage. Her great size and large population were the more evident reasons. But India had also given proof of her diplomatic acumen during the Korean War, first by giving accurate warning to the United States that China would intervene if American forces crossed the Yalu River, and then by helping to resolve the tricky prisoners of war issue.[1] Moreover, Nehru's personal charisma and international standing, combined with Mahatma Gandhi's credo of non-violence, had created an image of India as not only a world class power but one that was devoted to peace and peaceful ways. India's invasion of Goa in 1961 gave the Western countries a jolt but all they did was to growl about double standards. The American Press took it out on Krishna Menon, and coined the term 'Goa-Constrictor' to describe the Indian Defence Minister who had a lean and somewhat serpentine appearance. As for Kashmir, India's Western apologists were quite prepared to believe that if India was flouting UN resolutions and holding on to the State by force of arms, it was in the worthy cause of consolidating Indian secularism and promoting national unity. The myth of India's cultural and historical predilection for peace is so ingrained in the West that even when in 1974 India carried out a nuclear test, her admirers could only chide her gently for not being true to her own peaceful instincts.

A workaday reason for India's active role in the UN was that Indian diplomats were proficient in English officialese and clever at drafting resolutions. These are indispensable skills in the UN paper factory. But all this was beginning to change. For one thing, the primacy of the English language was somewhat affected by the influx into the organization of a large number of France's African colonies to whom de Gaulle had granted independence all at one go.[2] For the French-speaking Africans, the nuances and subtleties of English drafting lost a lot in translation. What is more, many African delegations were led by fiery young militants who found India's position a bit too pragmatic, if not equivocal, on matters that were all-important to Africans, such as the question of comprehensive sanctions against South Africa or the setting of a target date for the independence of colonial territories. Thus in an Afro-Asian meeting, Ambassador Quaison Sackey of Ghana, advised those who were doing so (referring to an Indian proposal on sanctions, though he did not mention the country by name) to refrain from putting forward 'tame and spurious drafts' that only confused issues and impaired Afro-Asian solidarity. In any case the Africans were now a very large group and soon broke off from the Afro-Asian group to set up a separate one of their own. Members of the Asian group rarely agreed on anything and this too narrowed the base of India's influence. India for her part was now trying to distance herself from the rhetorical extravagance that had become the accepted style of speech in UN debates. At the non-aligned summit held in Belgrade in 1961, Pandit Nehru declared that the world stood at a turning point between war and peace before which 'anti-colonialism, anti-imperialism, anti-racism and all that...' were things of secondary importance. This was not a point of view that the militant leaders of newly independent countries could accept, and Belgrade only papered over the controversy regarding it.

The watershed in India's position at the United Nations and the world at large, was the Sino-Indian border conflict. In the West there was alarm not unmixed with jubilation and a good deal of 'I told you so'. For years there had been talk of an ideological and economic competition between a democratic India and a totalitarian China for the hearts and minds of the uncommitted Third World. Now it all seemed to be coming true. Indian spokesmen entered fully into the spirit of the thing, and some, like brown reincarnations of Colonel Blimp, were even carried away into speaking of China as the 'Yellow Peril' However, the Third World, unconcerned at the battle for its heart and mind, tended to look askance at India's veering to the Western camp and this affected India's influence in the UN to a certain degree. Also, regardless of the rights and wrongs of the Sino-Indian border dispute, India's military humiliation at China's hands could not but undermine her claim to be a world class power in her own right.

Pakistan's position and standing in the United Nations at the beginning of this period was an odd and uncomfortable one. The delegation's general brief was to play a role that 'should be moderate and rational and not designed merely in pursuit of popularity'. These were perfectly sound instructions, but the problem was that as a West-leaning country, Pakistan's moderation was liable to be seen as subservience to the Western camp. Pakistan, because of its membership in Western military alliances, was lumped together with a marginal group of camp followers of the West, like Liberia, Thailand and the Philippines. We found it galling that this should be so despite the fact that unlike some of the other pro-Western countries, Pakistan did not hesitate to play an active role and take anti-Western positions on issues such as decolonization, apartheid and Palestine. Matters were not improved by the occasional obsessiveness of some of our delegates towards India and all things Indian, which led us sometimes to play into the hands of Pakistan's Indian detractors. This happened on the question of Portuguese colonies, with regard to some of which, such as Angola and Goa, Portugal took the position that they were not colonies at all but were overseas parts of Portugal itself. To counter this fiction, the Africans every year moved a resolution, listing by name all of Portugal's colonial possessions. To this resolution Pakistan regularly moved an amendment proposing that Goa and other Portuguese territories in India should be excluded from the list. Year after year the African resolution was carried and Pakistan's move was rejected. Everybody realized of course, that Pakistan was trying to get at India, but few could understand exactly what our 'bizarre' amendment (as one delegate described it) was supposed to achieve. Then, for many years and until Pakistan itself decided to join the movement, Pakistani spokesmen were constantly deriding the 'hypocrisy' of neutralism. Again they were tilting only at India, but managed also to irritate Indonesia, Egypt, Yugoslavia, and other important non-aligned countries. Besides, this Pakistani echo of the John Foster Dulles doctrine on the immorality of 'neutralism', served to reinforce India's propaganda that Pakistan was a Western stooge.

The first and major phase of decolonization had begun with the gentlemanly Independence ceremonies in Delhi and Karachi, and closed with the end of the bitter and bloody war of Algerian independence. In a sense the Algerian War was the last truly anti-colonial war. There were of course vast tracts of Africa still under colonial rule in Rhodesia (now Zimbabwe) in South-West Africa, and under the Portuguese. The Indo-China trouble was at an incipient stage and war was yet to come. These struggles would become confused with the cold war tussle between East and West. Perhaps without the cold war factor, independence might have come sooner and less painfully to many of these territories. The wars in Vietnam, Angola, etc., started as anti-colonial struggles, but became proxy wars in the ideological contention between Communism and the so-called free world. The world stage was occupied at that time by charismatic and militant leaders— Nasser, Sukarno, Nkrumah of Ghana, Sékou Touré of Guinea— who had attained international eminence as leaders of the fight against colonialism in their own countries. They brought to international politics the fervour and vehemence with which they had fought those battles. Their representatives in the United Nations were young, able, and articulate men picked up from all milieux: Ashkar Maruf, a dancer from the Guinea National Ballet, who had impressed Sékou Touré with an eloquent speech he made at the end of a performance for the President; Quaison Sackey, Barrister-at-Law, who wore dark suits and stiff collars, looked rather like a black Rampole!; Diallo Telli, the son of a

Muslim religious leader who later became Secretary-General of the Organization of the Islamic Conference. They carried the political style of their leaders—agitation and street demos—into the international organizations whose staid debating halls now rang ceaselessly with censure and denunciation of the colonial powers.[3] It was a Manichaean world at the UN in which the ex-imperialist West were the bad guys and the Soviets the good guys. It was not that there were any illusions about the motives of the latter, but they supported anti-colonial moves; indeed the more 'extreme' these were the better the Soviets liked them.

Underlying the anti-colonial agitation in the UN was a struggle for influence and domination among African countries themselves. Due to Nkrumah's personality and international standing, Ghana was at this time seen as the leading African power and the flag-bearer of anti-colonialism and African unity. But when Nigeria became independent and joined the UN, she made it clear that she would not countenance any such pretensions on the part of Ghana or any other country, and indeed was not in favour of attempts to 'unify' the whole continent. When Nigerian Prime Minister Tafawa Balewa visited the United Nations in 1961, he addressed a homily to the Afro-Asian group in terms that were not usually heard in that body. 'We should put our own house in order instead of always blaming colonialism, imperialism and other scapegoats for our shortcomings,' he exhorted the startled audience. A lecture that may have gone down better with the many one-party regimes represented in the Afro-Asian group, was delivered by President Ayub during his visit to the United Nations at the same session of the General Assembly when he spoke to the group of the unsuitability of 'Western democracy' for developing countries, and recommended that they find a system 'suited to their genius'.[4]

The Ghana-Nigeria rivalry surfaced during the Congo Crisis in which each country backed a different policy and different local contenders for power. The stakes were high, for the Congo is a country as big almost as the Indian subcontinent, and is endowed with enormous natural resources. The contest was won, in the end, by the CIA and the Belgian mining giant, Union Miniére, under whose aegis the senior-most Congolese military officer, a sergeant Mobutu, took over power and after more than thirty

years, still rules the country which is now known as Zaïre. The
Congo operation was the first, and so far still the only truly
military operation conducted by the United Nations as such. The
Korean War of the fifties and the UN operation against Iraq forty
years later, though both conducted under the UN flag, were
really American wars fought for essentially American purposes.
The Congo Crisis broke out in the midst of the country's
independence ceremonies that the Belgians had wanted to model
on the British precedent in India and Pakistan. King Baudouin
had come down from Brussels to preside personally over the
transfer of power to the Congolese. But the Congo had not been
run like the steel-framed Raj. There were few trained
professionals of any kind, and only a handful of university
graduates. The senior-most Congolese military personality was a
sergeant. The choice for prime minister fell upon a postal
employee, Patrice Lumumba, who had been active in the fight
for freedom and had suffered imprisonment. In the middle of
the speeches and flag hoistings, he suddenly burst forth and
poured insults and invective at the dumbfounded King. In the
next few days chaos threatened to overtake the whole country. A
UN peace-keeping force was hastily put together and sent to the
spot under a Security Council mandate. The Indian contingent
was the largest, but Pakistan too contributed a contingent, albeit
a non-combatant unit which looked after signals and communications. (The United Nations operation in the Congo was always
described by its French initials as ONUC, as the English acronym
UNOC could make it the butt of ribaldry!)

I represented Pakistan on the Secretary-General's Advisory
Committee on the Congo (made up of countries with military
contingents in the peace-keeping force) and got the opportunity
to observe Secretary-General Hammarskjöld at work. An austere,
unsmiling, rather aloof man, he brought to his job an activist
and missionary conception of what the organization should be
doing, and of his own role as Secretary-General. The conception
was visionary but quite unrealistic. The United Nations was not,
and is not today, a supra-national body with an agenda and
responsibilities of its own. Notwithstanding a veneer of
parliamentary structures and procedures, it is at bottom a
conference of sovereign states. Hammarskjöld got the
opportunity to put his concepts to the test during the Congo

Crisis, and the attempt very nearly wrecked the organization. When the Congo peace-keeping operation was launched he had foreseen that it would involve 'a kind of interference' in the internal affairs of the country. Interference in domestic affairs was in fact the very aim and purpose of the operation. It was not a peace-keeping operation in the proper sense since there was no war or external threat. It was a 'fire brigade' operation mounted hurriedly in the face of a total collapse of internal law and order and the administrative structures of the country. At one time the interference went to the length of UN troops preventing Prime Minister Lumumba—at whose invitation they were there—from addressing his countrymen on the national radio. The action was quite clearly contrary to the UN Charter and could be justified only in the light of the anarchy prevailing in the country and by the UN command's fear that Lumumba's words might push it into the abyss. However, later the UN forces did not interfere when Lumumba was seized and put on a plane and taken to the headquarters of his bitter foe Tshombe in the breakaway province of Katanga; on the way there he was beaten almost to death, and on arrival at the airport, shot dead on the spot. These events provoked great contention in the UN and created a storm of indignation within the African group. But Hammarskjöld was able to weather the storm because the Africans were divided among themselves and even the militants among them did not suspect him of acting for the West. Indeed the African and Third World countries were the mainstay of Hammarskjöld's support when he found himself and his office under attack from the Soviet Union.

The Soviets took the line that Hammarskjöld was playing the Western game and that in any case he was trying to assume independent policy-making powers in the Congo. They broke with him totally and definitively, refusing to deal with him or acknowledge his presence in any way, declining even to accept official notes or letters sent by him. The Soviets went too far however in proposing to replace the existing structure of the UN Secretariat with a 'troika' of three secretary-generals representing the Socialist, Western, and non-aligned groups respectively. The proposal was a non-starter and found few takers even among the pro-Soviet Third World countries, but it gave the West some anxious moments. When Hammarskjöld was killed in an air

crash—whether by accident or design, it will never be known—
the Soviets brought up their troika proposal but it was quickly
scotched by the election of the Burmese Permanent
Representative U Thant, as Secretary-General.

U Thant was a man of few words and complete integrity, and
did not entertain grand ideas either about the UN's role or his
own mission. He was slow, cautious and pragmatic, but did not
hesitate to take decisions that were not 'politically correct'. Thus,
when the independence of the Belgian colonies of Rwanda and
Burundi[5] showed signs of deteriorating into Congo-like disorder,
he requested Belgium to leave some troops in the territories for
a transitional period even though hard-liners in the Afro-Asian
group were pressing for their complete and immediate
withdrawal.

Contrary to accepted stereotypes, it was Dag Hammarskjöld
from 'materialistic' Europe, who was a mystic and a visionary. His
oriental successor was practical-minded and thoroughly scrutable,
a man who, a British colleague said to me, would make a perfect
headmaster of an English public school. But if Dag
Hammarskjöld's approach was that of a moralist, U Thant's words
and actions were no less inspired by idealism. In his last annual
report to the UN in 1961, Hammarskjöld had addressed to the
members a homily on 'the failure of the world community...to
co-operate in order, step by step, to make the charter a living
reality in practical political actions as it already is in law.' U Thant
faced them with a paradox. Speaking of the UN's success in
stopping the fighting in such places as Kashmir, Palestine and
Cyprus, U Thant said, 'It may well be true that the existence of
UN peace-keeping operations and the feeling of security that
goes with its effectiveness, reduces the sense of danger and
urgency about the continuing disputes, thus relieving the
pressure on the parties to seek a settlement.' He went on to
suggest, 'There is room for imaginative and forward-looking
initiatives [by the Security Council and the General Assembly] to
seek ways to...settle disputes instead of trying merely to stop the
fighting.'[6]

The moral or idealistic approach to international problems to
statecraft in general, suffers from the disadvantage that its success
depends on bringing about a fundamental change in the motives
and springs of action of nations and their governments. It is

optimistic to base the effectiveness of the world organization on the hope that member states will sacrifice immediate national interest and work for an undefined 'common good'. The lofty rhetoric of the cold war, the appeals to moral values, the practice of describing national policies in terms of eternal categories such as peace, justice, freedom, equality—or in Pakistan's context, of Islamic brotherhood and the bonds of the *ummah*—cannot conceal the fact that states are not in themselves or by their nature, moral entities guided by philosophical considerations.

It would not be right to suggest, however, that conscience and idealism have no place in relations between states; there is indeed such a thing as 'world opinion' and by and large, it does tend to come down on the side of justice and fairplay. In the crisis in Bosnia it was popular outrage and demand for action in Western countries that finally goaded their governments into taking effective action to stop Serbian aggression. The fact that some of history's greatest tyrants have found it necessary to put forward a philosophical justification of one kind or another for their acts of tyranny, testifies to the intangible power of moral considerations. Machiavelli recognizes it in his own way when after enumerating all the many qualities that an ideal ruler must possess, he goes on to say, 'A prince will not actually need to have all the qualities I have mentioned but he must surely appear to have them.'[7]

The cold war was at its height in the sixties. Khrushchev had come to the General Assembly's summit meeting in 1960, and in a belligerent speech promised that communism would 'bury the West'. Even then these words sounded vainglorious and boastful, even to the Third World delegates whom they were intended to impress. President Kennedy in his inaugural speech in January 1961, too made a pledge in terms of thoughtless bravado: 'Let every nation know, whether it wishes us well or ill, that we shall pay any price, bear any burden, meet any hardship, support any friend, oppose any foe, to assure the survival and success of liberty.' The resounding words reflected a frame of mind that may have led the United States into the Vietnam misadventure.

One felt the chill wind of reality blow through the halls and corridors of the United Nations during the Cuban Missile Crisis of October 1962. As Soviet ships carrying nuclear missiles sailed towards Cuba, American naval vessels were taking up positions off the coast with orders to prevent them from reaching their destination. Hourly and then half-hourly bulletins kept members informed of the shrinking distance between the two fleets, and between peace and holocaust. Drama was added to the events because the day was United Nations Day, celebrated all over the world as a homage and invocation to peace. In a preternatural hush, delegates gathered in the great hall of the UN General Assembly to listen to the Leningrad Symphony Orchestra which had come from the Soviet Union to celebrate the event. It was hard to believe that Armageddon was scheduled for that very afternoon. In the delegates' lounge there was something forced about the jokes, and the humour was gallow's humour.

The late Dag Hammarskjöld had blamed the ills and inadequacies of the world community on the gap between law and political reality—the gulf between the ideal and the actual, the word and the intention. The fact is that the United Nations is not the worlds' Parliament, but a world-wide diplomatic forum, where the claims of justice must be adjusted against the prerogatives of power. This is nowhere more so than in disputes and issues involving the less powerful members of the world community. It is the reason why the international organization is often unable to act in time, and when it does step in, it is most often only in order to stop the fighting rather than, as U Thant had suggested, to find ways of settling disputes before they lead to war. Power has a sort of inertia, and powerful states have a tendency to see virtue in the *status quo*. In a UN committee (one of the many set up from time to time) charged with considering these questions, one delegate asserted that the number of armistice and cease-fire lines that the UN was supervising, showed the organization's increasing effectiveness. There is coming into being an 'international law of the cease-fire line', he affirmed, and cited the Kashmir and Palestine cases as examples. Here indeed was a vindication of the doctrine of 'might is right', and the negation of what the United Nations had been set up to achieve.

The Kashmir question came up at the Security Council twice during this period; the first time in 1962, and then in 1964. Both times it was taken up at Pakistan's request and in the face of great reluctance of, if not in direct opposition to the superpowers. By 1961 the Kashmir case had been dormant in the UN for four years and the Council had not met even to receive the report submitted in 1958 by its own representative on Kashmir, Dr Frank Graham. The ostensible reason for this state of affairs was that Dr Graham had recommended that the two countries hold direct negotiations to resolve their differences on implementing the UN resolutions on a plebiscite. The real reason was that no one knew how to break the Kashmir deadlock, and in any case, any proposal that India did not like was liable to be vetoed by the Soviet Union. Meanwhile the prospects for a peaceful settlement were becoming dimmer with every passing year as India continued to tighten its legal and constitutional grip on the State, nibbling away at the autonomous status guaranteed to it by the Accession Agreement. Sheikh Abdullah was in jail and the general situation in the occupied territory was tense though well in India's control.

India's annexation of Goa, had humiliated NATO member, Portugal, and stirred anger and resentment against India in the Western powers. (India's action did not go down well with all the Africans either, many of whom saw it as a bad precedent for a continent with many disputed borders.) We expected therefore some reactive sympathy for the Kashmiris' plight and considered the moment opportune to re-open the question in the Security Council. Chaudhri Zafrulla Khan devised a procedure which he thought might help us get around the Soviet veto. Its essence was that there would in fact be no debate in the Council, but that the President—after consulting members—would make a statement to the effect that they would like to invite Dr Graham to update his report and submit it to the Council along with his own suggestions on how the UN resolutions on Kashmir might be implemented. As the move was procedural in nature, it would not be necessary to table a resolution and thereby risk a Soviet veto; upon receipt of Dr Graham's report and suggestions, the Council could hold a substantive meeting. It was an ingenious scheme in legal terms but politically disingenuous, and did not work. Dr Graham himself was willing enough to proceed further with his mission on the proposed basis, but Council members were not.

In January 1962, I accompanied our Washington ambassador, Aziz Ahmad, on a lobbying mission to the two Latin American members of the Security Council, Chile and Venezuela, where we got a mixed reception. Chile's thirty-one year old leftist Foreign Minister, Carlos Martinez, said the question of procedure would be left to his Permanent Representative at the United Nations. He did not rise to the Goa bait and was generally very circumspect. At one point when the Spanish interpreter from a sense of courtesy, tried to put something of a gloss on the minister's plain words, he whispered to her (in Spanish, which I happen to speak), 'Mind how you interpret what I have said. I don't want to give any sort of commitment on Chile's behalf!'

In Venezuela they were more forthcoming and promised full support for self-determination in Kashmir. But here we were faced with a snare that is common enough in multilateral diplomacy: the morning after we arrived, a Caracas newspaper reported that the purpose of the visit was to seek Venezuela's support on Kashmir in exchange for Pakistan's backing to Venezuela's claim on British Guiana. This was the first we had heard about this matter, but I soon received a call from the head of the Foreign Ministry's International Affairs department who took me out to lunch and explained what it was all about. The claim went back to the time when Spanish rule ended over that part of Latin America. Venezuela had claims to some 50,000 square miles of territory that had come under British control. The matter went to an arbitration tribunal, headed by a Russian judge. The tribunal awarded only 5,000 square miles to Venezuela and she had no option then but to accept the award. But lately, new documents had come to light indicating that the British government had made a deal with the Tsar conceding some Afghan territory to Russia in exchange for Russia's support to British claims in Guiana. Venezuela proposed to take the matter to the UN's Special Commission on Colonialism and now asked for Pakistan's support in the matter. It was not an unlikely story, but there was not much chance that the commission in question would take cognizance of the claim at a time when Guiana was about to become independent and enter the United Nations. However Venezuela's case for going back on an agreed territorial settlement was in the same spirit as Afghanistan's questioning of the Durand Line, and one could see the Afghan delegation jumping in to grind their axe. We could not very well support the Venezuelan thesis, but could hardly say this in so many words while we were seeking their support on Kashmir. We therefore did what one does in the UN in such predicaments: vigorously upheld the principle at stake, offered vague words of sympathy, and hoped in our hearts that the problem would somehow go away. This fortunately it did, as Guiana's Jagan Cheddi had many friends in the Special Commission and they talked the Venezuelans out of the attempt.

When the Security Council took up the Kashmir question, Krishna Menon, representing India, made a five-hour long statement in his characteristic style: sneeringly self-righteous, and mostly besides the point. In Pakistan, they have basic democracy, he said, but in India democracy is basic! On Kashmir itself, he said that by virtue of the instrument of accession signed by the Maharaja, the state of Jammu and Kashmir had become an integral part of India. He said that the Kashmiris had endorsed the decision in several elections and Pakistan had no *locus standi* in the matter. For the first time India was openly repudiating its commitments under the UNCIP resolutions. Zafrulla Khan responded with a six-hour presentation that not only beat Krishna Menon's performance by an hour, but scored on legal points and thoroughly demolished India's case. However when it came to the crunch, there was not enough support for the proposal to revive the Graham mission nor, in view of the threat of a Soviet veto, for the tabling of a draft resolution. We were having difficulties in finding a member willing to table a draft in the Council. In the end it was the Americans, though they had strongly urged Pakistan against going to the Security Council, who came to the rescue when President Kennedy made a personal phone call to the Irish President to request the Irish delegation to move a resolution on Kashmir. This was a mildly worded resolution, both in text and intent, not going much beyond asking the parties to hold bilateral talks on the dispute, but the Soviets vetoed it nonetheless. The Egyptian delegation abstained, explaining that as Egypt had friendly relations with both India and Pakistan, it would vote only for a resolution that had the support of both countries. I was watching the proceedings from a seat on the side of the Council table, sitting between an Egyptian and a British delegate. The latter did not want to miss the occasion and leaned across me to say to the Egyptian, 'I am sure you would like us to bear your principle in mind when the Arab-Israeli question comes up next!'

The following three years witnessed increasing turmoil and tension in the subcontinent. The outbreak on the Sino-Indian border in 1961 brought about a shift in the strategic balance in the region. Eager to bring about a united subcontinental front against China, and to assuage a Pakistan aggrieved by US military aid to India, the United States and the United Kingdom sponsored India-Pakistan negotiations on Kashmir. The negotiations, conducted by Zulfikar Ali Bhutto and India's Swaran Singh, were held over a period of several months, alternately in the two countries. These were the only direct substantive negotiations on the subject ever held between the two countries, but as recounted in the previous chapter, they came to nothing.

In 1964, Pakistan took the Kashmir case back to the Security Council. Again the Americans were not pleased that we were doing so, and doing it without consulting them. The Western powers as a whole did not consider the time opportune for the question to be aired again in the Security Council, and in any case did not favour the tabling of a resolution. The United States representative, Adlai Stevenson, suggested that instead of pushing for a resolution that was certain to be vetoed by the Soviet Union, we should settle for a statement, by the Council President, to be drafted in consultation with Pakistan and India, setting out the views of the Council on the Kashmir issue and calling on the two governments to enter into direct negotiations. The Americans said that the procedure would give Pakistan the substance of what it sought on the matter of self-determination, whereas a resolution, no matter what it said or how many members voted for it, had no value if vetoed. In discussions with other members of the Council, we found them all holding a similar view—a view that was not unreasonable in itself. When Foreign Minister Bhutto arrived to lead the delegation, the representative of the Ivory Coast, Ambassador Arsene Usher, called on him with a draft text which he admitted was given to him, and in fact was authored by the United States. Mr Bhutto pressed the case for a resolution, but not having an answer to the problem of the Soviet veto, entered nevertheless into a discussion of the text brought by Ambassador Usher and pointed out the various respects in which it was unsatisfactory from Pakistan's point of view. Thus although we kept asking for a resolution, discussions took place throughout on the text of the so-called 'consensus' statement. India for her part, objected even to the rather oblique reference made in the text to the wishes of the people of Kashmir. At this point nine members of the Council, other than Czechoslovakia and the Soviet Union (the Council had only eleven members then) began informal consultations to find appropriate wording for a 'consensus' that would give Pakistan more or less what it was seeking without running into the Soviet veto—in other words, a text that would be acceptable also to India. Four of their members, Brazil, Ivory Coast, Morocco and Norway, were given the task of negotiating with Pakistan, India and the Soviet Union with a view to drafting an agreed text.

The mediatory group shuttled between the Pakistan and Indian missions with an occasional detour to the Soviet mission, in pursuit of its task. After several days of intensive negotiations they produced a new draft modified to accommodate some of Pakistan's concerns. Thus the document was drawn up in the format of a resolution with a preambular part and an operative part setting out the Council's appeal. As to the substance of the case, its reference to the UN resolutions on Kashmir said merely that 'these resolutions stand', adding however that most of the Council members believed that 'ascertaining the will of the people concerned' was still the appropriate way to resolve the issue. It called on Pakistan and India to resume their negotiations and, if they considered it useful and appropriate, to seek, in consultation with the UN Secretary-General, the good offices of a country or statesman of their choice, to assist in the negotiations.

Mr Bhutto objected that while Pakistan was being asked to give up its demand for a legally-binding resolution, the document proposed was not only legally weaker but deficient in substance. The ambassador of Norway demurred that it was a considerable improvement on the Irish draft that the Soviets had vetoed two years previously. After very intensive discussions and negotiations over the next three days, the mediatory group produced a draft that had been further amended. The Norwegian Ambassador who brought it over late in the evening after a last exhausting effort at the Indian mission, strongly urged Pakistan to accept the 'consensus'. He held that it contained the substance of what Pakistan wanted that is, reference to the Council's past resolutions; a call for negotiations; a role for the Secretary-

General; and moreover it had the great merit of having the unanimous approval of the members of the Security Council, including the Soviet Union and Czechoslovakia. Bhutto acknowledged the force of some of these points, but explained to the ambassador that an agreed text that was so vaguely worded as to be capable of contradictory explanations, was capable of being construed as a new agreement superseding the one laid down in the UN resolutions.

In a delegation meeting held at night at the mission after the Norwegian envoy left, Bhutto sounded out opinion on the question and found that it was divided. On the one hand there was concern that the pertinence of the existing UN resolutions might be diminished; and on the other, the pragmatic view that a 'consensus'—particularly one that favoured Pakistan on major points and had been evolved by nine Council members—would be better than going back empty-handed. Accepting it would gain us the goodwill of these countries at a time when India's obduracy had irritated everyone.

We went round and round these points in the ambassador's poorly-lit, wood-panelled, smoke-filled office, and at midnight the discussion was petering out, but there was still no clear cut conclusion. Nor was it clear which way Bhutto himself was leaning in this internal debate. Bhutto had conducted the negotiations with consummate skill. He was firm but did not give the impression of being unyielding; he reasoned, and did not argue, and where he felt a concession could be made, he made it promptly and gracefully, without haggling.

It was decided to sleep over the matter and take a final decision the next morning. As we were going down the grand stairway of the mission's entrance hall, Bhutto said to me, 'Nothing is going to come of all this, I know, but if we do accept this paper we can put the Indians on the spot, for the moment I get back home, I shall ask Swaran Singh [India's Foreign Minister] to start the negotiations under the "consensus".'

However when the delegation met the next morning, I sensed a change in mood. Agha Shahi wore a glum expression and Bhutto turned to him to ask what was troubling him. Shahi reiterated the legalistic argument in stark terms. He said that once a 'consensus' was on the books, the UNCIP resolutions would become a dead letter and the foundations of Pakistan's case would be eroded. On the other hand, G. Ahmad, our ambassador in Washington, pressed strongly for acceptance of the 'consensus'. He pointed out that as the move had really been fathered by the United States, the Americans would see to it that it was implemented in letter and spirit. A rather rosy-eyed proposition in my view! Our permanent representative at the UN, Syed Amjad Ali, was also in favour of accepting. I thought that both sides were tending to overstate their case and felt that what Bhutto had said to me on the stairway the previous night was perhaps the best way to go. But I also sensed that underlying the conflict of opinions on the question was another, undeclared conflict—that of policies, interests and personalities. Since taking up the portfolio of Foreign Affairs, Bhutto had been trying to change the pro-American direction of our foreign policy and give it a non-aligned and pro-China orientation. China's war with India, and US military aid to the latter had strengthened his hand. But he faced powerful opposition from influential individuals and circles who were against having truck with any Communist country whatsoever. But there was more to it than ideology. There was opposition to Bhutto as a person and to anything that might reinforce his position or increase his influence. Adoption by the Security Council of a US sponsored 'consensus' would work for the pro-Americans in the establishment, whereas if Pakistan came back empty-handed from the Council the case for a pro-China policy and the influence of its proponents would be strengthened. The country was under the one-man rule of Ayub Khan and the disputation within the delegation over the seemingly procedural matter of the form that the Security Council's decision should take, was really a battle for Ayub's heart and mind.

So that morning, the argumentation swirled back and forth in the delegation meeting, and in the end the decision was neither to accept nor to reject the 'consensus', but to ask for an adjournment of the Council on the ground that more time was needed for reflection. Members agreed to the adjournment, with surprise at the abruptness of the request, but no doubt also with relief. The four mediators who had laboured long and hard to produce a 'consensus' may have felt chagrined that their efforts had come to nothing. The Western members were incensed when it was learnt that Bhutto had hurried away from the UN in order to meet the *bête noire* of the Western world, Premier Zhou Enlai of China. Thus when the Council resumed substantive consideration of Kashmir in May, Bhutto got a rather cool response from these countries; the 'consensus' had dropped out of sight and there was no attempt by the Council to resume its mediation.[8] The Council President summed up the proceedings with a statement that asked both parties to refrain from any acts that might aggravate the situation and expressed the hope that they would resume their contacts with a view to settling their disputes, 'particularly that centering upon Jammu and Kashmir'.

These were meagre pickings for a debate that had stretched over several months and had mobilized the efforts and good offices of so many members of the Council. The meeting was not however entirely fruitless for Pakistan. New member countries, particularly African countries, were made aware of the facts of the Kashmir case for the first time. The sympathy it evoked among African countries surprised and impressed the United States. Another notable feature of the debate was that though the Soviet bloc continued to support the Indian case, they did so without attacking Pakistan. Indeed they tried to distance themselves somewhat from the more extreme Indian positions. Thus comparing the Kashmir dispute to the territorial disputes that erupted among Latin American countries after the end of the Spanish Empire and in central and eastern Europe after the end of the First World War, the Czech representative said, 'We simply cannot ignore all these territorial disputes and act as if they do not exist.'

In retrospect the importance of the 1964 meetings of the Security Council on Kashmir lies also in the fact that this was the last time that the Council took up the Kashmir question as such.

NOTES

[1] At issue was the question whether all North Korean soldiers taken prisoner by the UN forces would be handed back to the North Korean government, even if some of them did not wish to go back, and were in effect seeking asylum in the West or South Korea.

[2] A passing side effect of the influx was a sort of 'Africa-chic' in New York society. A local gossip column declared that it was quite the done thing to include one or two African delegates at dinner parties. The United States Permanent

Representative, Governor Adlai Stevenson, running into a dark-skinned delegate in a UN corridor, made a deferential bow, but looked a bit cheated when the gentleman introduced himself as a member of the Pakistani delegation!

There was other evidence of people trying to climb on the African bandwagon. Thus during the tussle between Indonesia and the Netherlands over the future of Dutch New Guinea (now Indonesia's West Irian), delegations received a little poem, purportedly from the people of the territory:

> *O Virgin Island in the East—*
> *New Guinea, land of sun and rain,*
> *Our Negroid people have increased,*
> *As those of the African domain.*
> *We have the same rights as they—*
> *The right to live and grow....*
> *In our own way.*

However the next stanza gave a hint as to the muse behind these poetic sentiments:

> *The Netherlands shall be our guide,*
> *Our friend for all the world to see...*

[3] Many of them, including those named above, fell foul of their rulers and ended their days in dungeons or on the gallows.

[4] Author's notes.

[5] These two countries were among the new entrants to the UN in 1961. Under Belgium they had been administered as one entity. A Belgium-sponsored delegation from the territory argued long and hard against its being split into two, but failed to convince the General Assembly's fourth committee. Walking out of the committee room after their motion had failed, the incensed leader of the delegation paused at the door, and before kicking it shut behind him, turned to the members and shouted, 'Bunch of cannibals! You will be sorry for what you have done today.' Perhaps he was right.

Belgian Foreign Minister, Paul Henri Spaak, who attended the meetings on behalf of the colonial power, later played a leading role in bringing about the economic union of Belgium, the Netherlands and Luxembourg, known as Benelux, and dubbed by one local newspaper as 'Spaakistan'.

[6] Secretary-General's report to the twenty-first session of the United Nations General Assembly.

[7] *The Prince,* Chapter 18,'In what way Princes should keep their Word'.

[8] Meanwhile the Indians got up to a bit of bazaar-bargaining with the Bolivian delegate who was the Security Council's President for the month. Bolivia, a land-locked county, had a conflict with Chile, its coastal neighbour, over its claim to sovereign right of passage to the sea through Chilean territory. Taking advantage of the inexperienced Bolivian's anxiety to use his position to get some benefit for his country, the Indian Commonwealth Secretary, C.S. Jha, cut a deal with him promising support for Bolivia against Chile in return for his help on Kashmir in the Security Council. Both sides were foolish enough to put this down in writing

in an exchange of letters, copies of which were swiped from the Bolivian's desk and brought to me by a counsellor of the Chilean mission. It did not occur to the gullible Bolivian to wonder how India, a maritime power that rejected Nepal's claims for access to the sea, could possibly support the Bolivian claim. On the contrary he entered into the deal with such gusto that in the opening meeting of the May session, he proposed to rule the agenda out of order on the ground that the Kashmir question was an internal affair of India! As soon as the Council debate was over, India officially repudiated the deal, declaring that Mr Jha had merely said that India supported the legitimate demand of all land-locked countries for access to the sea.

CHAPTER 6

WAR—1965

The years 1964-5 were fateful years for Pakistan. They marked a turning point in its brief history and set in motion forces that would shake the foundations on which the country had been established. Ironically, at that time Pakistan's self-esteem and its standing in the world's eyes were at a high level. President Ayub's position appeared unassailable at home and, thanks to a foreign policy skilfully pursued with the assistance of Foreign Minister Bhutto, he had acquired the stature of a world statesman, of an Asian de Gaulle, who could keep the relations of his country on an even keel with all three contending world powers and who got economic and military aid from each. On the other hand, rival India, Pakistan's standard yardstick of comparison, was facing a multitude of troubles and, in the aftermath of Nehru's death, appeared leaderless and without many friends in the world. India's border conflict with China, provoked more by Pandit Nehru's hubris than any irreconcilable difference between the two countries, ended in military humiliation and loss of international standing for India. The event gave Bhutto the opportunity to untie Pakistan's foreign policy from its traditional pro-Western moorings and persuade Ayub to venture into the unfamiliar waters of non-alignment and Third World diplomacy.

In the autumn of 1964 I returned to the Foreign Ministry and was put in charge of the India desk, an important desk but not a very lively one at the time. Much of the work consisted of sending and receiving protest notes to and from the Indians. It was humdrum work, concerned with juggling words of remonstrance and reproof, warning and threat. Through repetition, the hackneyed verbiage and stock phrases of diplomacy had lost their impact and only befogged the reality of the crisis that was building up. The despatches on the conditions in India that we were receiving from High Commissioner Arshad Hussain in Delhi painted a picture of gloom and disintegration. Much of what he wrote was confirmed by reports of foreign observers (including for the first time, Soviet political commentators) and by India's own newspapers. Nehru's death had left a political vacuum that appeared all the greater on account of the nondescript personality of his successor, Lal Bahadur Shastri. The Indian Press had at first damned Shastri with faint praise but was now more and more openly critical of his failure to give a lead. This was not quite fair, for many of the problems that were now coming to a head had been left to simmer in Nehru's time, whose prestige and authority had been used not to resolve the issues, but to keep the lid on the pot.

India's third Five-Year Plan was in trouble and it was only thanks to monthly gift shipments of American grain, that the country was warding off hunger, perhaps even famine. Anti-Hindi demonstrations had led to Vietnam-style self-immolations in South India. Many of the leaders of the post-Nehru generation were 'homespun' men with their roots in local politics who could not rise above their regional, communal or caste milieux. The notion that the Chinese border attack had strengthened national unity was not fully borne out by facts. The Chinese threat had receded and the Chinese bogeyman, while it served the ends of Indian diplomacy, was no longer a national rallying cry.

There was talk of the Indian union coming apart and in Pakistan there was a good deal of wishful speculation on the subject. In truth there was little likelihood that things would go that far. There existed many factors in favour of keeping the Indian union in one piece—the common interest of the industrialists and businessmen in a united market; the armed forces and the highly centralized civil service Establishment; the interlinked economy, and simply the inertia of things. It was not likely either that the United States and the Soviet Union would stand aside and watch India fall apart. Nevertheless it was symptomatic that every political agitation or movement in India at that time, whether it was the anti-Hindi movement in South India, or those launched by the Sikhs, Nagas or Mizos, reflected a centrifugal trend.

There was danger for Pakistan too in the situation, for the one matter on which Indians in general seemed to be of one mind, was in their hostility towards Pakistan. The bellicosity that is the normal state of affairs between Pakistan and India was aggravated by the growing stridency of right wing parties in the post-Nehru India, by Pakistan's *rapprochement* with China and by India's growing military edge over Pakistan. The volume of American and British military aid to India was not really overwhelming, but its psycho-political effect was great and quite out of proportion for Pakistan on account of the fact that we had put all our eggs in the American basket. Pakistan felt aggrieved, betrayed and isolated. India, on the other hand, felt more confident in pursuing its Kashmir policy and did not seem greatly troubled by the American assurances to Pakistan of support against possible Indian aggression. 'Aggression' is difficult to define, and in any case the American assurances did not cover whatever India might do on her side of Kashmir. For the United States Kashmir was a secondary matter, and in the evolving circumstances, the US had come to identify its interest with the *status quo* in Kashmir and did not see any possible interest in trying to upset it.

In August 1963 Ayub had reasoned with US Ambassador MacConaughy that the Indian military build-up constituted a serious threat to Pakistan. He assured him that Pakistan was not involved in China's policies and actions and urged the United States not to drive Pakistan, for the sake of survival, to courses it did not wish to take. 'We need you and you need us...do not put us against the wall,' he pleaded.

A month later Assistant Secretary of State George Ball came to Pakistan, (as he put it, 'to visit old friends') bringing assurances. He explained that US military aid to India was a limited programme that would not affect the military balance between the two countries. Speaking to the Press, he declared, 'Then there is the US assurance to Pakistan to come to its assistance [in the event of an attack by India]. We do not make promises lightly. We keep them.' Ayub was not convinced and said to his 'old friend': 'We urged the United States, please don't compromise our position. You *have* compromised it. We are a poor people but a proud people. Do not drive us to the wall.'

On the ground there was an air of unrelieved tension and belligerence; civil strife continued in occupied Kashmir, and violations of the cease-fire line were frequent and increasingly serious. Gratuitous acts of provocation were committed by both sides and these intensified the sense of crisis. One such incident took place over Dahagram and is worth recounting as an example of the bizarre complexity of the India-Pakistan relationship. Dahagram is an eight square mile patch of territory belonging to what was then East Pakistan, but separated from the mainland by 150 yards of Indian territory, and situated inside the Indian state of Tripura. There were 123 such Indian enclaves on East Pakistani territory and 74 East Pakistani enclaves on Indian soil. The origin of this curious state of affairs lay in a long-forgotten battle that took place in the eighteenth century between the troops of the Mogul emperor and those of the Maharaja of Cooch Behar. The fighting ended inconclusively and a truce was concluded under the terms of which each side retained the bits and pieces of territory that its troops happened to hold at the moment, pending a permanent settlement or a more decisive battle.

Neither thing happened and this crazy patchwork survived through the British period. When the subcontinent was partitioned, East Pakistan inherited the Mogul enclaves and India got the ones that had remained with Cooch Behar. The sensible thing would have been to exchange the enclaves at Partition and in fact there was an agreement that this should be done, but it was not. Now some Indians had intruded into the Dahagram enclave, burnt huts and caused the inhabitants to flee. The trouble had started at the local level for purely local reasons, but angry protests were exchanged between Delhi and Karachi and troops were deployed. The whole thing went on for several months and then one night, under cover of darkness, the Indian troops withdrew and India affirmed that they had never gone there at all. The incident was then considered closed and it had all been quite pointless.

The Rann of Kutch incident may have started in the same spirit of thoughtless malice. One morning in April 1965, Counsellor Kaul of the Indian High Commission asked to see me urgently and came over with a protest note. It was, he explained, about an intrusion into Indian territory in the Rann of Kutch area by a Pakistani patrol. The Government of India took a serious view of this violation of its territory, he said, and called upon Pakistan to cease and desist or bear the consequences.

The Rann is an 8,400 square miles stretch of land that was described by a nineteenth century English traveller as 'of a nature peculiar to itself...alternately a dry sandy desert and a muddy inland lake...the wild ass its only inhabitant.'[1] Apparently the Rann had been a navigable body of water until an earthquake in 1819 closed off the inlet from the Indus delta, and even now it is sometimes flooded during heavy monsoons or by high tides. The area, uninhabitable and economically without value, is situated between Sindh and the Indian state of Gujarat but the boundary here had been left undefined and undemarcated by the Partition arrangements. The dispute over its status goes back to the year 1762 when Ghulam Rasul Kalhoro, the ruler of Sindh occupied its northern half, dispossessing the Maharao of Kutch who had exercised some sort of authority over the wasteland. In 1819 the Maharao signed a Treaty of Alliance with the British which guaranteed the integrity of his territories but it was not clear whether these included the whole of the Rann. At the time of Partition all concerned had other more pressing boundary matters in mind and left the future of this abode of wild asses to be settled at a later stage.

Some years later Indian border troops overpowered a Pakistani police unit, and seized a place called Chhad Bet, where herders from Sindh traditionally grazed their flocks.[2] Pakistan lodged a protest but left the matter on the back-burner to be resolved at some undefined future date when the Rann dispute as a whole would be taken up. We therefore did not attach unusual importance to the note brought by Counsellor Kaul and sent it to the Ministry of Defence with the usual request to furnish 'material for a reply'. However within days the situation had blown up into a major diplomatic crisis and soon into armed clashes that threatened to escalate into war. In a rapid strike Pakistani forces moved forward up to Biar Bet and Ding, points a good way inside the Rann, and established posts there. Indian troops pulled back in disorder and quite a few were taken prisoner. There was nothing, except good sense, to stop Pakistani troops from marching forward to the 24th parallel and taking over the whole of the Rann. Good sense prevailed, and the Pakistani troops were ordered to stay put at Biar Bet.

The situation brought American and British mediators scurrying to Karachi and Delhi in order to avert the worst. The United States protested to Pakistan at the use of American equipment in the fighting. US Ambassador MacConaughy in a meeting with the Foreign Secretary Aziz Ahmad, refused to be drawn into discussing the merits of the Rann case and said that the US role in the issue was that of a 'fire extinguisher' and no more. However he warned that the United States was unwilling to permit the use of American military equipment by either side in the Rann hostilities. The warning was emphatic though he sought to soften its impact by explaining that it referred to the specific situation in question and was not to be taken as a general interdiction on the use of US supplied military equipment for defence purposes. Ayub reacted testily to these remonstrances, declaring, 'If Pakistan is attacked, we can't be expected to put our weapons in cotton wool.'[3] The British took the lead on this occasion and managed to bring about an agreement between the two countries to restore the *status quo* on the ground and put the boundary dispute to arbitration.[4]

In some subsequent assessments, the importance of the Rann incident has been minimized as a minor skirmish fought between militia and border forces that were on the scene. In fact it was a fairly substantial engagement involving armour and aircraft and a good deal of sound and fury off-stage. India brought up troops to the Pakistan borders from far-away cantonments and added to the drama by staging a combined exercise in the area in the course of which, among various other moves, India's aircraft carrier, the INS *Vikrant* sailed up the Arabian Sea off the Kutch coast. It may have been a mini-war, but its impact went far beyond the size and type of forces that took part in it.

For India this was her second military humiliation after the débâcle against China a couple of years before. It sent a shock wave through the country and there were demands for retaliation. Angry words were spoken in the Lok Sabha and elsewhere. Defence Minister Chavan threatened that India would 'become the graveyard of Pakistan';[5] the Socialist leader Ram Manohar Lohia urged the government to teach Pakistan a lesson by hitting at East Pakistan.[6] In May, Prime Minister Shastri promised the Lok Sabha that India would strike back at Pakistan 'at a time and place of India's choosing'. For Pakistan the Rann of Kutch episode was a great morale booster and there was a good bit of chest-thumping. It created a quite misplaced euphoria that was not confined to the popular level, for in retrospect and in the light of subsequent events, the victory can be seen to have been something of a mirage. The easy win in the Rann misled everyone, including Ayub Khan, as to the country's relative military capability. What is more, we were inclined to see in the episode a model for a Kashmir settlement—a local military gain followed by mediation by alarmed superpowers, and the affair ending in a peaceful settlement through arbitration or similar means. This was of course wishful, as we found out in due course. Finally, and most importantly, the adventure put India on its guard. She had brought up a large number of troops to forward positions during the crisis, and though they moved back after the Rann agreement, they did not go back to their peacetime stations. Thus when the fighting came to Kashmir, the Pakistan side lacked the advantage of strategic surprise.

The flicker of hope raised by Sheikh Abdullah's mediation had died with the death of Nehru. It was, in any case, probably an illusion. Lal Bahadur Shastri, soon after he succeeded Nehru, made a stopover at Karachi Airport at Ayub's invitation, and at their meeting he agreed that a mutually satisfactory solution of the Kashmir dispute was necessary. However, he said that personally he did not feel strong enough to do anything about it for the time being. That was all very well, and Pakistan agreed that he needed time to prepare the ground for a settlement. But in actual fact his government was doing nothing of the sort and on the contrary, accelerated the measures that were under way to bring about the complete merger of Kashmir with India.

Sheikh Abdullah who was still at liberty, raised his voice at home and abroad against these moves to extinguish Kashmir's autonomy. Speaking at a mammoth protest rally in Srinagar in January 1965, he declared to the Kashmiris: 'You cannot achieve freedom by imploring anybody. In view of India's present attitude, you have to think how to face her effectively.' The implication of his words was not hard to understand. He was quite explicit in a letter he wrote to President Ayub around this time stating that the use of force was now the only way left to end India's occupation of Kashmir. He then went on a tour of the Middle East and Europe, and while in Algiers had a meeting with China's Premier Zhou Enlai and accepted his invitation to visit China. The meeting was supposed to have been 'secret' and arranged through Bhutto's good offices—all of this only added to its sinister significance in India's eyes. India's fury knew no bounds. Abdullah was accused of treason and as soon as he returned, he was taken off to detention once again.

That meeting, and the whole idea of Sheikh Abdullah making a triumphal progress though various Islamic and European capitals (where he was received like a visiting Head of State) was perhaps a tactical error. In fact nothing was achieved by a face to face encounter between Abdullah and the Chinese Premier that could not have been obtained by indirect contact. It was a case of a public relations gain taking primacy over policy objectives. The move was based on the illusion that a Kashmir solution would be facilitated by mobilizing international pressures. What it did undoubtedly do was to give India the pretext to lock up Abdullah and many other front-rank leaders, and eventually, militant workers and activists of the Kashmiri resistance right down to the grass roots level. Thus when the Kashmir action started, there was no resistance infrastructure and no local leaders to support it and the commandos had to operate in a political vacuum.

After the failure of the bilateral negotiations of 1963, and given the Security Council's passivity and the Western powers' apparent acquiescence in the Kashmir *status quo*, thinking in Pakistan was moving in the same direction as Sheikh Abdullah's letter to Ayub suggested. It was given added urgency by the knowledge that India was building up its military muscle and could soon leave Pakistan altogether behind. It was GHQ's estimate that India's military preponderance could become 'absolute' by as early as the year 1968. At a briefing that I attended at the Directorate of Inter Services Intelligence in June, the prevailing position was explained with the aid of maps and charts. Briefly, the assessment was that while the race was likely to go to India in the future, for the moment, while the new Indian formations were not yet fully trained and were still using their old equipment, Pakistan had an edge in offensive weapons, specially in armour. 'Our tanks will cut through the Indians like a knife through butter,' a young, gung-ho staff officer said to me at the briefing. The conclusion reached was that if there was to be war, then this was the window of opportunity. At the end of June, the C.-in-C. submitted a threat assessment along these lines to the President and asked for the raising of two more infantry divisions as well as some units of light armour and territorial brigades. The President, wary of the war party's fervour, asked a committee of Federal Secretaries to examine various aspects of the matter, and determine whether the country had the money to spend and what assistance, if any, might be expected from foreign powers. The C.-in-C.'s request for raising more troops did not get past the financial hurdles.

Meanwhile in response to Pakistan's representations against US military aid to India, the United States had conveyed the following: (1) India would not attack Pakistan; (2) if she did, the United States would come to Pakistan's help; and (3) precautions had been taken to ensure that American military equipment given to India would be used only against China. However nobody, least of all Ayub, had any illusion that these stipulations would hold good in the event of an action in Kashmir. His own assessment was that as time went on the United States would become more and more lukewarm towards Pakistan.

Eventually the President came around to the view that military action had become inevitable and could be undertaken with hope of success. Afterwards, the Foreign Ministry (Bhutto, according to his detractors) was held responsible for having led the country into war by assuring Ayub that India would not attack Pakistan across the international border. Indeed in a letter to the President on 12 March 1965, Bhutto had said, 'India is not at present in a position to risk a general war of unlimited duration for the annihilation of Pakistan.' This was a reasonably accurate assessment. It certainly could not be taken to mean that India would not counter-attack across the international border if her position in Kashmir was endangered. General Gul Hassan, who was Director of Military Operations at the time, states in his memoirs that his office had warned the government in unambiguous language that the country should be prepared for an Indian attack across the international border in reaction to the fighting in Kashmir.[7]

It is more reasonable to suppose that the operation was launched on the basis of the GHQ's reasoning and in the belief that things would go more or less as they had done in the Rann of Kutch. A Cabinet decision in June stated laconically that the course of action to be taken by the armed forces in the event of an Indian attack had been decided, and it would under no circumstances be such as might lay Pakistan open to the charge of aggression. In July, a meeting was held at which the President, the C.-in-C., the Foreign Secretary, the Director of Intelligence, and General Akhtar Malik were present. General Malik presented his plan to 'thwart Indian designs in Kashmir' which was approved by the President on the understanding that it would not provoke a general war. The plan, code-named Operation Gibraltar, was aimed, according to General Musa, at sabotage and disruption of communications, and in the longer term, at initiation of a guerrilla movement in Indian-held Kashmir.[8] The Indians published a captured document that purportedly sets out General Malik's instructions to the men sent across the cease-fire line:

> I visualize that India will be forced to pull out if a sizeable threat is posed in their rear.... You will infiltrate across the CFL to operate behind enemy dispositions in the Tangdhar-Tithwal area and cause maximum attrition of enemy potential...you will not undertake set-piece attacks and tie down our troops unnecessarily, thereby causing casualties. The pattern must be to concentrate on pre-selected targets at a fixed time, carry out raids, inflict maximum casualties, cause maximum damage, and disperse in different directions. The principle to follow is not to attach importance to ground features, but aim at shock actions and create maximum possible pressure in the area through concerted and continuous offensive actions against the enemy's defence HQ and lines of communications....[9]

The crossings took place on 5 August along the whole 470 mile length of the cease-fire line. About 8,000 men were involved and they entered occupied Kashmir in groups of fifty to one hundred. The main body converged on Srinagar with the aim of proclaiming its take-over on 9 August which happened to be the twelfth anniversary of Sheikh Abdullah's imprisonment. They were not able to do this, but some fighting did take place on the outskirts of the city. On 8 August a clandestine radio station calling itself the Voice of Kashmir went on the air and declared that an armed revolt had broken out in occupied Kashmir and a Revolutionary Council had been set up to direct all out war against Indian occupation. It directed that no one was to pay any taxes to the Indians and warned that anyone collaborating with India would be shot. The station, instead of using a mobile transmitter, was broadcasting from the frequency of Radio Azad Kashmir, so no one was in any doubt about what was what. Moreover the 'revolution' scenario, dreamed up by some bright

public relations mind, unfortunately did not correspond to the
reality on the ground. Foreign journalists reported from Kashmir
that they had seen no signs of a revolt. The Indians claimed that
Kashmiris were denouncing the infiltrators to the authorities. In
fact the Indians were making much of some isolated cases in
which Gujjar herdsmen, illiterate and impoverished rustics, had
betrayed some commandos to the Indians. Ayub himself took
this matter greatly to heart. In the course of one discussion when
some reference was made to Kashmiri public opinion, he flared
up, 'Don't talk to me about Kashmiri public opinion! These
people have sold their souls to the devil.' This was not a well
considered judgement. The commandos could not have gone
across a cease-fire line guarded by three Indian divisions deep
into heavily-policed territory, fought pitched battles with Indian
troops, reached the outskirts of the capital, and survived as long
as they did, unless they had the support of the local population.
In some areas local administrations had been set up and it took
considerable Indian effort to dislodge them.

But there was no sign of the uprising that had been expected
and that had figured in the Information Ministry's imaginative
scenario. An important reason why there was no sign of revolt
when the action began, was that all those who might have led
one had already been locked up as a result of the turmoil and
political agitation that had preceded the launching of Operation
Gibraltar, and the arrest of Sheikh Abdullah after his meeting
with Zhou Enlai. General Musa rightly points out that the fault
really lay in the lack of co-ordination of the military, political,
diplomatic and other aspects of the operation.[10]

On 8 August, the Indian Cabinet's Emergency Committee held
a meeting at which the Indian C.-in-C. was present. The meeting
went on till midnight. The next morning the Indian High
Commissioner called on President Ayub to express his
government's concern at the large-scale infiltration that was
taking place in Kashmir. On the following day he met Bhutto to
warn that 'the most serious consequences' would follow if the
infiltration was not stopped at once. The High Commissioner,
Mr Kewal Singh, spoke fluent, literary Urdu, and recited verses
of Ghalib and Iqbal to make his points, and he did so with
exquisite courtesy. He had presented his credentials to President
Ayub only three days before and remarked upon the great

sincerity with which the President had spoken of the need to improve relations between the two countries. He complained that the occurrences on the cease-fire line constituted an unhappy and retrograde step at a time when the Rann of Kutch settlement had raised hopes that other questions at issue would gradually be tackled. Earlier, the High Commissioner met Foreign Secretary Aziz Ahmad—a man not given to making his points in Urdu couplets. Aziz Ahmad told Kewal Singh bluntly that Indian actions in Kashmir had virtually destroyed all hope of settling the Kashmir dispute and that if the people of Azad Kashmir decided to cross the cease-fire line to go to the help of their brethren on the other side, the Pakistan government could not be expected to use force to stop them. Moreover, as they were moving about in their own country, albeit divided by an artificial line, they could not be considered as 'infiltrators'. For good measure he added, 'Besides infiltrations are occurring both ways and people from Indian-held Kashmir have also crossed into Azad Kashmir.' Kewal Singh smiled at this and said with mock sympathy, 'So I see, we are facing a common problem!' He treated the whole interview as an exercise in irony and dismissed Aziz Ahmad's disquisition on the Kashmir situation as something he was not qualified to speak on, saying, 'I have been instructed to say that the Government of India takes the gravest view of the events and is bound to react.'[11]

· A few days later, Indian troops crossed the cease-fire line and captured two posts in Kargil. These were the same posts they had taken in May and had vacated a month later after the intervention of UN Secretary-General, U Thant. The posts were situated at an altitude of 13,000 feet and were important to India because they dominated the Srinagar-Leh Road. This time the Indians simply walked in as our own people had not re-occupied the posts after the earlier incident for the reason that they had not been cleared of mines laid by the Indians in their earlier incursion. In the week that followed, the Indians captured a number of other posts on the Pakistani side of the cease-fire line in Tithwal, Uri and the Haji Pir Pass.

Pakistan hit back on 1 September in the Chhamb sector, and in three days the momentum of the offensive had carried the Pakistani troops to the banks of the Tawi River and just six miles short of Akhnoor. Akhnoor was the key point of the whole operation, for its capture would cut off the large Indian force along the cease-fire line and make the Indian position untenable in the whole area. The Indians were caught completely off balance and retreated in haste leaving much equipment and many prisoners in Pakistani hands. A distraught American Embassy Counsellor said to me, 'Next thing, the Pakistan Army will be at the gates of Delhi! The United States is not going to allow this to go on, you better believe me.' The atmosphere was electric with tension. The Indian move across the cease-fire line had been stopped at the Haji Pir Pass, the two air forces had clashed and in a dogfight, Pakistan had downed seven Indian aircraft.

The Chinese Foreign Minister, Marshall Chen Yi, was in Karachi on 4 September when the fate of the whole enterprise hung in the balance. Bhutto, accompanied by a few officials, went to meet him at the State Guest House where he was staying. The meeting held around the dining table, with maps of the battle area laid on it, went on all morning in an atmosphere of suspense and anticipation. All eyes and ears were focused on the outcome of the battle that was going on in Chhamb.

Bhutto outlined the developments that had led to the crisis saying that Pakistan had tried every peaceful avenue but India had refused to negotiate—refused even to recognize that a dispute existed—while on the other hand, the Security Council too had failed to act. He declared that in the circumstances, if Azad Kashmiris had gone to the help of their brethren across the arbitrary line that divided Kashmiri from Kashmiri, Pakistan could not be expected to stop them. He said that India was the first to send her troops across the cease-fire line, three weeks earlier, but no one had stirred a finger then; now when Pakistan had retaliated and was advancing in the Chhamb sector, the Western powers, the Soviet Union as well as countries such as Egypt and Yugoslavia, were making *démarches* to Pakistan and U Thant had summoned a meeting of the Security Council to call for a cease-fire. A cease-fire had existed in Kashmir for years, Bhutto pointed out, and it had not brought about a settlement. He said that the answer was not another cease-fire but self-determination to settle the dispute.

Bhutto was cautious in broaching the subject of Chinese help: 'We don't want to be a burden on our friends. We realize that

China has its own difficulties at the moment.' He recalled the
many times in the past he had discussed with Premier Zhou
Enlai, President Liu Shaoqi, and Chen Yi himself, the sort of
eventuality that had now arisen. At the present critical juncture,
he was fortified by the knowledge of the mutual understanding
that they had reached in those meetings. In the present conflict,
it was Pakistan's objective to confine the fighting to Jammu and
Kashmir, and he wanted the Foreign Minister to consider how
China could help Pakistan keep the fighting localized.

Chen Yi, a stocky, jovial man, had followed Bhutto's exposition
with animated attention, interjecting occasional exclamations and
comments. Speaking in reply, he thanked Bhutto for his lucid
account of the background of the crisis and of Pakistan's aims.
He fully agreed with the Foreign Minister's analysis and affirmed,

> China stands firmly beside Pakistan not only out of friendship, but
> also for the sake of world peace. We must not let India's expansionist
> designs succeed. If she succeeds in its violations of the cease-fire line
> and intrusions into Jammu and Kashmir, there will be no limit to her
> designs.

He said that the Indian ruling class, emboldened by Soviet and
United States' aid, believed that it was free to pursue its limitless
ambitions and that it could solve India's internal contradictions
by attacking Pakistan. Chen Yi believed that those calculations
were wrong, and that India was mistaken in assuming that China
would remain silent in the face of the India-Pakistan situation
because Chinese forces were engaged in Vietnam. He stated that
China would not abandon its friends and would support Vietnam
as well as Pakistan and would not be deterred even if the United
States landed its forces on Chinese soil. He felt that India's
purpose in provoking the present conflict was to demonstrate to
her two patrons—the United States and the Soviet Union—that
China would remain a helpless spectator in the face of the attack
against Pakistan. 'Such a thing shall not happen,' Chen Yi
declared.

The Marshall said that China agreed with Pakistan's immediate
objective of limiting the area of the fighting and preventing
general war. Such a policy was 'very clever' and would be the
basis of Pakistan's victory, he said. 'You fight but keep calm. We

have great admiration for your caution and limited objectives.' Chen Yi said that different contingencies could be visualized, even the worst case scenario in which with India's help, the Vietnam War was extended to Chinese soil along the Sino-Indian frontier. But he understood that there was no need for immediate participation by China in Pakistan's limited action against India for which Pakistan was capable of relying on its own strength.

'To achieve your objective,' Chen Yi advised, 'you must annihilate India's massive forces along the cease-fire line at one or two points where action against them would be most effective.' This is what China had done in its action against India and as a result there was tranquillity on that front. The South Vietnamese population had inflicted defeats on superior US forces by using similar tactics. If the day should come, Chen Yi said, when the United States extends the Vietnam War into China, the only way China could deal with the situation would be by the massive annihilation of American forces.

Chen Yi also agreed that Pakistan should not withhold help from the Kashmir freedom fighters. He presumed that at that stage Pakistan was against a cease-fire and would not fall in with any suggestion for negotiations that the Western powers might put forward. 'This is the moment to strike hard to disable and eliminate the massive forces of India.' The lesson China had learnt from her fight against Japan was that it was not necessary to destroy physically the enemy in large numbers. Holding up his hand with the fingers splayed, Chen Yi made a sharp cutting movement at the little finger: 'Knock them out at Akhnoor. That will help the freedom fighters and also guarantee the security of East and West Pakistan. With the little finger gone, the whole hand becomes useless!'

The Marshall went on:

But we will not push Pakistan into war, nor sacrifice your interests to ours. China and Pakistan are brothers and comrades-in-arms. The idea does not exist of leaving Pakistan alone to pull the chestnuts out of the fire. We are prepared to do all in our power, to consider doing anything you suggest, that would help you to contain the fighting.

He appreciated that for the moment Pakistan was relying on its own strength. He could promise political and diplomatic support straight away; if Pakistan needed any military equipment from China, it would be given immediately. As for taking some actions along the Sino Indian border, he would submit the matter to Premier Zhou Enlai. China feared nothing but whatever action China took must be 'appropriate' and such as would help Pakistan's objective. China had no purpose of its own to pursue in the matter. He added, 'If the conflict is enlarged, we will need another consultation to consider further measures, in the political, economic, even military fields.'

Chen Yi said that before he left for Karachi, Chinese leaders had held a high-level meeting in Beijing to examine the India-Pakistan conflict and its international repercussions. Their assessment was that neither of the superpowers would welcome an enlarged conflict in the subcontinent. His own political analysis of the situation was that the United States, the United Kingdom and the Soviet Union were not prepared to support India in a war against Pakistan and if Pakistan were to defeat India (in Kashmir) it was inconceivable that any of these powers would directly intervene on India's side to restore the *status quo ante*. So, the Marshall advised, this was the best moment for Pakistan to achieve its limited objective, and he reverted to the importance of destroying the enemy's forces. Jabbing a finger at a point on the map, he said: 'If India's best forces are concentrated here you need not send your best forces there. A headlong collision is not the best way to prevail; it will cause you also to suffer heavy casualties.' He urged again, 'Concentrate on Akhnoor and give the Indians a crushing blow there. This is the crucial moment for you.'

Bhutto thanked the Defence Minister and said that if Pakistan was to succeed in annihilating Indian forces the limited co-operation that was sought from China 'must be effective and come at the right time.' Chen Yi said he fully appreciated the need for timely action and would immediately transmit the substance of the morning's talks to Beijing. He was confident that there would be a prompt response to the need to create some pressure on the Indian forces in the north. If any action became necessary in the border areas, China had sufficient troops there and would not need to bring up more from elsewhere. China had lodged a strong protest with India over Sikkim and that should be helpful to Pakistan. Although one should not create an impression of collusion between China and Pakistan, if there were to be general war then China would come to Pakistan's assistance and would do so as an ally.

In Chen Yi's opinion, India had made a great mistake in refusing negotiations on Kashmir, for these could have dragged on for another eighteen years. Her attack along the cease-fire line had actually created favourable conditions for solving the Kashmir question. In his view, Indian leaders had no clear strategy and Indian forces would retreat if they got a beating. '*This* is the moment for Pakistan!' Marshall Chen Yi urged once more.

During the course of the meeting which went on all morning, I was sent to the phone a number of times to get news of the front and find out whether Akhnoor had fallen. The news did not come that day, nor on the next, and Akhnoor never fell. Our troops were within reach of it and the Indians in retreat. The arrow in full flight suddenly stopped in mid-air and dropped to the ground. Why and how this happened, why the commander of advancing troops was suddenly relieved of his command, the full and true story of that may never be known. There was much speculation that some ulterior motive was at work. In his book General Musa says that the change of command had been pre-planned and General Akhtar Malik himself as well as General Yahya who took over from him were aware of it. But what was the logic of a plan for a change of command in the heat of battle and at a time when the momentum of the battle was at its height? The only explanation General Musa offers is that General Akhtar Malik's 'return to his main operational HQ was an imperative operational necessity...'[12] In short, General Akhtar Malik was needed for some more pressing task at the precise moment when the offensive he had launched was in full force and whose momentum seemed unstoppable not only to the Pakistanis but also to the Indians who were in retreat before it. Morrice James the then British High Commissioner in Pakistan, has asserted in his memoirs that Akhtar Malik was removed from this command because Ayub gave in to an American warning and no longer wanted the offensive to go forward.[13] This seems as implausible as General Musa's rationalizations. General Sarfaraz Khan in an impassioned defence of the performance of Pakistan's generals in the war, asserted: 'The change of horses in mid-stream was a pre-planned conspiracy with a political motive rather than a tactical necessity.'[14] I once asked the late General Fazle Haq why the change had taken place and he replied in one word: 'politics'. But what politics, who conspired with whom, for what purpose and to what end? As General Gul Hassan said: 'There is more to it than meets the eye and I don't think we shall ever learn the truth.'[15]

Marshall Chen Yi's emphasis on the importance of Akhnoor was confirmed by what happened next. The fighting moved beyond Kashmir as Indian forces moved into Pakistan proper with a three-pronged thrust against Lahore in the early hours of 6 September and some days later in the Sialkot sector. In revisionist post-war accounts produced in Pakistan, the attack on Lahore was depicted as the beginning of an all out attempt to undo Partition, or at least, to take over Pakistan's part of Kashmir as well. But even at the time, it was plain that the Indian move was aimed at relieving pressure on Akhnoor and putting the Pakistan forces on the defensive. Explaining that the Indian attack on Lahore was not intended to capture the city but to divert the pressure from Chhamb, the Indian C.-in-C. General J.N. Chaudhri said:

> The Pakistan thrust on Chhamb could not have been contained by action inside Kashmir alone with the limited number of troops and tanks there and reinforcements a long way off. For Pakistan access to the Chhamb sector was easy. Pakistan's advance on Akhnoor would have bottled up all the Indian troops in Kashmir and achieved the political objective that the infiltrators had failed to achieve.[16]

The attack did not, or should not, have come as a total surprise, for two days earlier the Pakistan High Commissioner in Delhi, Mian Arshad Hussain, had informed the Foreign Office by cable of an emergency meeting of the Indian Cabinet at which the decision was taken to hit at Pakistan.[17] It was not to be imagined that India would not react with all it had, while Pakistan was going for her 'jugular' in Kashmir. However the Indian offensive caught Pakistan unprepared for it appears that mines had not been laid at the border crossing points as elementary prudence demanded. The Indian forces were held at both places by sheer human effort and valour. But the character of the war had changed and the initiative passed from Pakistan's hands. The key premise of Pakistan's strategy had failed to hold. The war was no longer confined to Kashmir and could not be fought on Pakistan's terms. Of course, it was not over by any means. Men at the Lahore front fought like tigers to hold and even push back the Indian attackers and in Sialkot a tremendous tank battle was fought, such as had not been witnessed since the desert campaigns of World War II.

Then Pakistan launched its armoured offensive in which all hopes had been placed. So great was the confidence in its success that some arrangements had been visualized for administering the East Punjab areas that might come under Pakistan's control and preventing undue harm coming to civilians, in particular to the Sikhs. Instructions were sent to our diplomatic missions on how to project the Pakistani occupation of Indian territories to foreign governments and media. The offensive commenced promisingly on 11 September with 225 tanks of the 1st Armoured Division pursuing Indian infantry in retreat. But after a rapid initial advance to, and the capture of Khem Karan, a small town some fifteen kilometres inside India, the whole move bogged down. Bridges that had not been recced, collapsed under the weight of the tanks; the tanks themselves got mired in fields inundated by the Indians; those that did break through to points near Amritsar had to turn around and come back because they were not followed by infantry that could consolidate the gains. A large number of our tanks were destroyed or captured.

'Such is the fog of war!' says a rueful General Musa describing the débâcle in his book.[18] Ayub, who had conceived the operation himself, also tried to take things philosophically. 'These things happen in war,' he said later in the course of an informal discussion. But it was not just one of those things—a simple botch up. It was the end of the war.

Meanwhile on 27 August China had sent a stiffly-worded protest to India accusing her of acts of aggression and provocation along the Sikkim and Ladakh borders. This was followed by a warning on 8 September and orders were issued placing Chinese border forces on alert. On the sixteenth, China sent India a three-day ultimatum to dismantle military works she was alleged to have constructed at the border, and on the eighteenth India reported some Chinese troop movements at the border. In Oldi Daulat Beg, they were reportedly brought forward to within 500 meters of the border. But on the nineteenth the Chinese ultimatum was extended by three days upto the midnight of 22 September. This was also the time and date by which the two parties had to comply with the mandatory cease-fire decreed by the UN Security Council. The coincidence was not fortuitous, for no doubt China had learnt or been informed, that Pakistan was preparing to accept the cease-fire ordered by the UN.

The threat of Chinese intervention set the cat among the pigeons. Kosygin wrote to Ayub and Shastri on 20 August urging them not to do anything that would lead to a major conflict. On 4 September he appealed for a cease-fire and offered Soviet good offices, and on the seventeenth wrote again to propose a peace conference in Tashkent under Soviet auspices. The United States told Pakistan, 'the Chinese ultimatum makes it imperative that the Indo-Pakistan conflict be stopped.' The US Ambassador who conveyed this message to our Foreign Minister warned, 'If Pakistan encourages, or by failure to agree to a cease-fire, should create a situation that produces Chinese intervention, it will have alienated Pakistan from its traditional allies and associates.' Over and over again the Ambassador urged that Pakistan should, must, accept the cease-fire and do so 'today!' The United Kingdom also joined in the effort to prevent China's intervention. The British Prime Minister sent a message to President Ayub 'to consider the consequences of Chinese involvement' and proposed that the President publicly dissociate Pakistan from China's actions against India. On 21 September 1965, the British High Commissioner, Morrice James, had the following exchange with President Ayub:

High Commissioner: 'We feel that dangerous possibilities can be averted by an agreement to cease fire. Pakistan has everything to gain. Kashmir is now before the world. We and others are now determined to settle this question.
Ayub: 'Is that a firm promise?'
High Commissioner: 'Yes Sir! The United Kingdom will do all to promote a Kashmir settlement [once a cease-fire is established]. This is the pledged word of the British government. This I am asked to convey with all the emphasis at my command.'[19]

At an early hour on 6 September, I was woken up by Wing Commander Aziz, my contact at ISID, to be told, 'It's war!' There was a note of elation in Aziz's voice as he conveyed the news. My own first feeling was of release from the pent up suspense of the previous few weeks, and a feeling almost of exhilaration at the hope that at long last Kashmir and many other problems were to find a solution. At the Foreign Ministry later in the day, when I saw a dispatch-rider speeding off on a wobbly motor bike with his trousers flapping about his thin ankles, to deliver some important message, a thought fleetingly crossed my mind, 'What is there in it for him, and for the millions of other scrawny, ill-fed men like him, *what* is it Indians and Pakistanis are fighting about?' Was it age-old rancours, bigotry and hatred that set them at each other? Or, was it the second-hand imperialist dreams dreamt by men who had served as officials of the British Empire and now feel that their own time has come.[20]

For a moment the war seemed like a parody! But it was a fleeting thought, and one's heart filled with pride as, a few hours after Indian forces had crossed the Pakistan border, we listened to Ayub's stirring speech to the nation, 'We are at war and time has come to give India a crushing blow. The Indians will soon know what kind of people they have taken on!'

But on the thirteenth, two days after the Khem Karan fiasco, Ayub was saying, 'Pakistan is not against a cease-fire as such but it must be a purposeful cease-fire...' On the fifteenth he spoke to President Lyndon Johnson seeking the United States' help to stop the war.

The scene shifted to the United Nations where Secretary-General U Thant had shown concern at the Kashmir developments from the time it appeared that they might lead to war. He drew attention to deep penetrations into Indian-held Kashmir that had taken place from the Pakistan side since 5 August. Pakistan found this focus on its actions irritating, but on 3 September the Secretary General evened the scales by reporting to the Security Council that the Kashmir problem 'has again become acute and is now dangerously serious...a potential threat to peace not only between India and Pakistan but to broader peace.' He added that the differences over Kashmir were 'sharp, great and ominous' and must be resolved if peace in that area was ever to be secured. The Security Council adopted a resolution

calling for a cease-fire but two days later came India's attack on
the Lahore front, a turn of events that the Security Council
deplored in another resolution as something that had added
'immeasurably to the seriousness of the situation.'[21]

U Thant then flew to the subcontinent for a four-day visit
during which he had meetings with Ayub in Rawalpindi and
Shastri in Delhi. His proposal for a cease-fire did not get an
unequivocal response from either side; though, for evident
reasons, India was readier to accept a simple cease-fire than
Pakistan which wanted the cease-fire to be followed by steps to
hold a plebiscite in Kashmir. The Secretary-General convened a
Security Council meeting as soon as he returned to New York. At
his request the Council adopted a resolution under Chapter VII
of the Charter (decisions under Chapter VII have binding effect
and may be followed by sanctions against the party that does not
comply) ordering India and Pakistan to cease fire with effect
from 0700 hours GMT on Wednesday the 22 September, and to
withdraw troops to the positions they occupied on 5 August.[22] As
a sop to Pakistan the resolution also stated that when all this was
done, the Council would consider 'what steps could be taken to
assist towards settlement of the political problem underlying the
present conflict.' But the resolution studiedly avoided naming
the 'underlying problem' as Kashmir. The keyed up public mood
in Pakistan could be judged from the violent anti-Western
demonstrations that broke out on the adoption of this resolution.
In Karachi the diplomatic missions of the United States, the
United Kingdom, and of course India, were attacked.

Bhutto was to lead the Pakistan delegation to present
Pakistan's case at a meeting of the Security Council scheduled
for 22 September, the last day of the Council's ultimatum. A
statement had already been made in the Council a day before by
Law Minister S.M. Zafar who was at the United Nations for the
session of the General Assembly. But everyone was eager to listen
to Bhutto who had established his reputation as a fiery and
eloquent speaker; moreover, it was known that he was bringing
Pakistan's formal reply to the Council's cease-fire order. The
principal delegations must of course have known what the reply
was to be, but among the general membership there was a good
deal of suspense as to the direction events were going to take.
Would Pakistan defy the Council and bring sanctions upon

itself?[23] Would it pursue the war and by bringing China into it,
take the world to the brink of a wider conflict, perhaps a world-
wide conflagration? The suspense was heightened as the clock
ticked towards the Security Council's deadline and news came
that Mr Bhutto's plane had been diverted to Montreal because
the New York airports—and others nearby—were fog-bound.
There was speculation that Mr Bhutto might be taken by a special
plane to the nearest functioning airport and from there be driven
to Manhattan by car. This could take time and carry the meeting
beyond the cease-fire deadline. Despite the lateness of the hour
every seat in the Council chamber was taken and the delegates'
lounges were crowded and humming with speculation on these
and other such questions.

However, as in the script of a suspense movie, the New York fog
lifted in the very nick of time and Bhutto came from John F.
Kennedy Airport straight to the Security Council's chamber making
an entry worthy of the high drama of the occasion. He must have
been exhausted after his long flight and the tedious detour to
Montreal, but showed no sign of it. He was given the floor at once
and held forth very forcefully and comprehensively on the history
of India's perfidy regarding Kashmir, the usurped rights of the
Kashmiri people and the justice of Pakistan's case. Then at the
crescendo of his denunciations, with only minutes to go to the
cease-fire deadline, he stopped and reaching into the inside pocket
of his coat, pulled out a paper and read Ayub's message to the
hushed audience. It stated that Pakistan considered the Council's
resolution of 20 September to be unsatisfactory, but in the interest
of international peace and in order to enable the Security Council
to evolve a self-executing procedure which would lead to a just and
honourable settlement of the root cause of the present conflict, 'I
[Ayub] have issued the following order to the Pakistan Armed
Forces: They will stop fighting as from 12.05 West Pakistan time
today. As from that time they will not fire on enemy forces unless
fired upon, provided the Indian government issues similar orders
to its armed forces.'

Thus, in anticlimax, the war came to an end. Bhutto concluded
his own statement with a rhetorical flourish:

We have decided to give the United Nations a last opportunity to
determine what it can do towards a purposeful, peaceful and lasting

settlement of the Kashmir problem. We shall give the United Nations a time limit. If within a certain period of time the Security Council is not able to act in accordance with its responsibilities, then Pakistan will have to withdraw from the Organization.

The cease-fire was broken by skirmishes at the local level to improve held positions. The Security Council had to adopt another resolution to reiterate its call for an 'effective' cease-fire and also to reaffirm its resolution of 20 September 'in all its parts', an oblique allusion to the settlement of the 'underlying problem' which, we were allowed to suppose, was the unnamed Kashmir dispute. Secretary of State Dean Rusk answering a pressman's question in Washington reaffirmed the United States' 'historic position that a plebiscite in Jammu and Kashmir should be considered as part of an over all settlement of the differences between India and Pakistan.' However, the American Permanent Representative, Arthur Goldberg, told the Jordanian Representative in the Security Council that the United States would join the Soviet Union in vetoing any draft that tried to spell out specific measures to resolve the problem. The United States was very much in India's tow during those debates, a position that seemed to be personified when the stubby Mr Goldberg was seen hurrying in and out of meetings behind India's tall Foreign Minister, Swaran Singh, and trying to keep up with his longer stride.

The war had been short, an affair of three weeks from beginning to end, but it had been in the making for a long time—almost from the moment the two nations achieved Independence in bloodshed and violence twenty years earlier. For close to two decades Pakistan had prepared for it and India had waited for it. While it ended in anticlimax, neither side gaining a decisive advantage over the other, for Pakistan its consequences and repercussions were far-reaching. Pakistan was of course not defeated and the people stood united and showed remarkable self-discipline in the face of the Indian attack. The armed forces gave a good account of themselves in terms of valour and personal sacrifice. But Pakistan failed to achieve the objective which was the liberation of Kashmir from India's clutches. Neither did the war serve to mobilize effective diplomatic support for a peaceful settlement of the dispute. This

6. Governor-General's Ball, Ottawa, 1951. Author with High Commissioner Mohammad Ali Bogra.

7. Begum Liaquat Ali Khan, The Hague 1953. (Staff members accompanying her are Military Attaché Col. Khaleeli, author, and Commercial Secretary Saadullah.)

8. Ambassador Miran Muhammad Shah presents author to Generalissimo Franco, Madrid, 1952.

9. Author presenting credentials to President Gamal Abdel Nasser, Cairo, 1968.

10. 1965 War. Foreign Minister Zulfikar Ali Bhutto addressing UN Security Council.

11. Tashkent Conference. President Ayub Khan, Prime Minister Shastri and Soviet leaders, January 1966.

failure put the Kashmir dispute on hold for the foreseeable future; it ignited conflicting emotions and unleashed a backlash, the first victim of which was Ayub himself. A few years later it led to the break-up of Pakistan.

How were things brought to such a pass? The immediate reaction was to pass the buck. Some blamed Bhutto for misleading Ayub about India's intentions or the Finance Ministry, for denying funds to raise more infantry divisions. Many said that Ayub had lost his nerve. Almost everyone felt that our allies had let us down. And so it went. Defeat is an orphan. On the other hand, the Establishment simply declared victory and set about re-making the war to its desires. Thus, the war had not been over Kashmir. It was an Indian war of aggression to destroy Pakistan, and victory was ours because we had prevented India from taking Lahore. This was the line taken in a paper prepared in the Foreign Office under Foreign Secretary Aziz Ahmad's supervision. However in a separate note to Ayub Khan, Aziz Ahmad took a different line. The despatch of 7,000 trained commandos into Indian-occupied Kashmir, he wrote, was a major military undertaking that had in it all the makings of escalation; the Foreign Office had not been consulted about the political implications of the move. In another note he said that he himself learned about the commando crossings from the newspapers.

It was some twenty years before there was a public discussion on the whys and wherefores of the war when a Lahore daily, ran a series of articles on whether Pakistan won or lost the war.[24] It was an academic question, to say the least, but the polemic cast an oblique light on the motives and considerations that had guided the decision makers. What was also brought to light were our own egregious blunders including the failure to mine the border near Lahore, to cancel army leaves, and the inexplicable change of command in mid-battle. The then Air Chief, Noor Khan, revealed that there was no plan for a joint overall conduct of the war nor for the replenishment of equipment and ammunition.

The layman's judgement was that the war was valiantly fought but was poorly led. I am not qualified to speak authoritatively on military questions, but one thing was clear. Those who had conceived the war did not bear in mind one of the cardinal principles enunciated by Clausewitz: 'No war should be commenced...without first seeking a reply to the question, what is to be attained by it?' The 1965 War was planned in a confusion of aims and affected the way it was conducted. The confusion was rooted in the belief that Kashmir, lost on the battlefield in 1948, could be won back by diplomatic means. The means we had in view was international pressure on India—specifically Western pressure—to comply with the UN resolutions on Kashmir. After nearly two decades of knocking at this door it should have been clear that this was not going to happen. Yet an unstated purpose of the 1965 War was to demonstrate that the Kashmir problem was a threat to international peace and hence to persuade the superpowers that it should be resolved on the basis of the UN resolutions.

The venture therefore fell between the two stools of Pakistan's Kashmir policy, the first being to mobilize diplomatic pressures for imposing the settlement laid down in UN resolutions; and the second, to seize important Indian territory and then exchange it for Kashmir. Perhaps the Rann of Kutch case misled Ayub into believing that the two could be combined.

Thus the period before the outbreak of fighting was given over to creating an environment of tension and belligerence where cease-fire violations multiplied and Sheikh Abdullah made highly publicized international tours culminating in a provocative 'secret' meeting with Zhou Enlai. All this served admirably the cause of bringing the Kashmir question to international attention and drawing attention to its dangerous potential. But this diplomatic and public relations success was won at the price of alerting the Indians to what was brewing and thereby warning them and giving them the time to take counter measures. If war in Kashmir was in the works, then there should have been no dress rehearsal in the Rann, no heating up of the cease-fire line, and no Abdullah-Zhou meeting. If we were going for the 'jugular' then we should have kept at it even if it meant that there might be fighting around Lahore.

What the superpowers did in fact was to move swiftly to put an end to the war, and by stopping supplies, eliminate Pakistan's capacity to continue the fighting. The war also raised a larger question and one which remains unanswered and has not yet been dispassionately considered: Can war be a solution to the fundamental difference that divides India and Pakistan?

NOTES

[1] Alexander Burnes in his *Voyage on the Indus*, John Murray 1834; reprinted by Oxford University Press, Karachi, 1973.

[2] *Bet* is the Sindhi word for island, and recalls the maritime antecedents of the Rann. The *bets* in the Rann are in the nature of oases in an arid expanse where some grazing for camels can be found in the rainy season.

[3] *The New York Times*, 10 June 1961.

[4] In simplified terms the Indian stand was that a defined and partially demarcated boundary already existed and it needed to be demarcated fully. Pakistan's position was that the boundary between Sindh and Kutch had never been agreed and that, the Rann being an inland sea, it should follow the 'thalweg' or median line. There was evidence in support of both positions but the arbitration tribunal taking a pragmatic line, gave Pakistan the Chhad Bet area that had been forcibly taken over by India some years before, and drew the boundary along markers set down in the previous century.

[5] *Hindustan Times*, 15 March 1965.

[6] *Dawn*, 30 April 1965.

[7] Lt. Gen. Gul Hassan Khan, *Memoirs*, Oxford University Press, Karachi, p. 181.

[8] General Mohammad Musa, *My Version*, Wajidalis, Lahore, 1983, p. 35.

[9] Keesings Contemporary Archives; 4-11 December 1965; p. 11203.

[10] General Mohammad Musa, op. cit.

[11] Author's notes

[12] General Mohammad Musa, op. cit., Chapter 3.

[13] Sir Morrice James, *Pakistan Chronicle*, Oxford University Press, Karachi, 1993.

[14] *The Nation*, Did the Generals Fail in the '65 War? Lahore; 30 October 1987.

[15] Lt. Gen. Gul Hassan Khan, op. cit., p. 187.

[16] Keesings Contemporary Archives; 4-11 December 1965; p. 21108.

[17] In the polemics on the subject it was suggested that the Foreign Office (implying Bhutto) kept this telegram from Ayub. This was not so, as all cipher messages are automatically marked and immediately delivered to the heads of state and government.

[18] General Mohammad Musa, op. cit., p. 67.

[19] Foreign Office minutes of the meeting.

[20] *See* K.M. Pannikar, *Future of India and South East Asia*, Allied Publishers, Bombay 1945. 'Unless distant bases like Singapore, Mauritius, Aden and Socotra are firmly held and the naval arms [give] protection to these parts, there will be no security and safety for India...what seems to be required in the light of experience of the present war, is the reconstitution of the old Indian Empire on a new basis.'

[21] Security Council Resolution 210, 1965.

[22] Security Council Resolution 211, 1965.

[23] The United States and Britain had let it be known that they were working on a draft imposing sanctions on the country that rejected the Council's cease-fire order. This was obviously directed at Pakistan as India had already signalled its readiness to accept a simple cease-fire. (France stated that she would veto such a draft).

[24] *The Nation*, October 1987.

CHAPTER 7

TASHKENT

Pakistan went to Tashkent against the background of the anticlimactic events traced in the preceding chapter, and in some confusion of motives. On the eve of departure for the conference, I noted in my diary: 'We will pretend to be tough, the Indians reasonable and the Soviets judicious.' In fact none of the parties lived up to these roles. Pakistan was not uncompromising. Bhutto, unable to be 'tough', was argumentative, but his attempts to put up a bold front were sapped by the pragmatism of Ayub who was all too keen to put the misadventure of the war behind him. It was little Shastri, meek and mild and mumbly, who was hard as nails. The Soviets did not even try to be impartial. In the previous year or two a change had come about in the tone of their statements on India-Pakistan questions, but not in their support— enunciated by Khrushchev in 1956—of India's basic position on Kashmir (that the State is an integral part of India). They had invited India and Pakistan to a peace conference when the war was in the initial stages and not going well for India, the threat of some kind of Chinese involvement was in the air, and the outcome of the whole adventure was liable to be unfavourable to Soviet interests in Asia. Even then the Soviets had suggested not that the proposed conference would try to resolve the Kashmir issue, but only restore peace in the region. Four months later the situation had stabilized, a cease-fire was in effect, and the Kashmir issue was more than ever deadlocked. Now they were interested only in the 'success' of their bold diplomatic initiative, that is, to conclude the conference with an agreement—any agreement that could be had—between the two belligerents. It was clear that in the circumstances that prevailed, an agreement could only be based on some kind of ambiguous verbal formula. The Soviets bent all their efforts to this end, and from the first were firm in side-tracking Pakistan's attempts to make Kashmir the centre piece of the conference.

Waiting at the Peshawar Airport from where the President's flight was to take off, was Averell Harriman veteran diplomat and presidential advisor, who had flown across specially from Washington with a personal message from President Lyndon Johnson, expressing his good wishes for the success of the conference. It was a signal of American endorsement of the Soviet initiative, but no doubt was also meant to keep the United States' hand in the game. China, although wary of Soviet intentions, did not object to Pakistan's accepting the Soviet initiative. Indeed the Chinese Ambassador in Islamabad expressed a view that was in substance not in conflict with that of the other great powers. Tashkent, he affirmed, 'could be of use to Pakistan in order to gain time to prepare for a political struggle, instead of a military one, to protect the rights of the Kashmiri people to self-determination.'

At Tashkent Airport, Ayub was received by Premier Kosygin who was accompanied by Foreign Minister Gromyko, Marshall Malinovsky, as well as the members of the Uzbekistan government. The road to the city was lined by crowds who clapped and cheered as the motorcade went by. Many of the faces in the crowd appeared to be Russian faces, but Uzbeks stood out in their long *chogas*, turbans and boots and Uzbek bands blowed on great horns and banged on kettle drums. This was a touch of local colour as was the presence of the Uzbek ministers in the airport receiving line.

The Tien Shan mountains, their snow-clad peaks gleaming in the winter sun, overlook the city with its broad tree-lined boulevards and avenues. Most of the buildings were low-slung with yellow stucco façades and mullioned windows but there were also a good many modern blocks with glass fronts. All this was in the Russian part of the town. The old city was a huddle of white-washed houses behind high blank walls, enclosing tranquil courtyards, glimpsed briefly through open doorways as one drove past. It could have been a Pakistani city, except that it was spotlessly clean. On the outskirts of the city we saw work in progress on a complex of high-rise residential blocks, that were considered symbols of progress in socialist countries. Our Uzbek guide pointing out the buildings said, 'But these are being built for *them.*' It was clear to whom 'them' referred, and so was the underlying hint of racial segregation—not formal or regulated as in European colonies, but present nonetheless.

The two delegations were put up in different parts of town with separate villas for the two heads of government. There was also a 'neutral villa' for joint meetings of the two delegations but as things turned out, this facility was very little used. The Indians and Pakistanis met face to face only on the opening day and for the closing ceremony; the rest of the time the Soviets met them separately, shuttling back and forth from one villa to the other with bits and pieces of paper, that emerged at the end as the Tashkent Declaration.

The Soviets were not playing a mediatory role and did not claim that they were doing so. More than once Kosygin and Gromyko said that they were not speaking for India and held no brief for the Indian delegation.[1] However, on all major points at issue there was little difference between what the Indians wanted and what the Soviets proposed. This became apparent at the very first meeting between Ayub and Kosygin when, after escorting Ayub to his villa and then receiving Shastri at the airport, Kosygin returned to pay a formal courtesy call on Ayub. 'How would you like the Conference to proceed,' he asked Ayub. But when the latter suggested that to begin with the two sides must agree on what they are to talk about, that is, set up an agenda, Kosygin demurred that any attempt straight away to discuss 'specific issues' would take the conference into troubled waters. 'As soon as the Kashmir problem is taken up,' he said, 'all sorts of complications would arise.' He proposed therefore that the more immediate questions be taken up first and among these the foremost, in Kosygin's view, was the withdrawal of troops of each side from the territory of the other and the re-establishment of the frontier, followed by the exchange of POWs, and restoration of diplomatic relations.

At this first meeting Kosygin also brought up India's long-standing proposal for a no-war pact between the two countries and expressed his own conviction that such an agreement would not only eliminate the danger of war in the subcontinent but could also show the way to a settlement of the Kashmir dispute. 'A no-war pact between India and Pakistan would be an inspiring example that others also might follow,' he urged.

President Ayub agreed that the disengagement of troops should be the first thing to be settled. As for a no-war pact, he recalled that Pandit Nehru had put forward the idea nearly ten years earlier and Pakistan had accepted it on condition that the pact should provide also for means for the peaceful settlement of disputes between the two countries. A no-war pact now without any agreement on a settlement of the Kashmir dispute would be putting the cart before the horse; if he were to agree to such a thing, Ayub Khan said, the people of Pakistan would consider that he had sold the country's interests down the river.

Later in the evening Foreign Minister Gromyko called on Bhutto and hammered away at the same points as his Prime Minister. A no-war pact was something from which both sides stood to gain whereas Kashmir was a controversial subject. The Soviets did not think that the two things were comparable or should be mixed up. Gromyko advised Pakistan to give up the thought of setting up a formal agenda (in other words, of negotiating Kashmir) and instead talk to the Indians about troop withdrawals and renouncing the use of force. Pakistan, he asserted, had more to gain from troop withdrawals than India, and that was why the Indian side found the Pakistanis 'keen on withdrawals'. Bhutto replied heatedly that that was simply not the case, India had as much, if not more, to gain from troop withdrawals. The Soviets kept coming back to this subject and talked as if the withdrawal of troops would be a particular boon for Pakistan. In the end President Ayub got quite fed up and said, 'Well then let the Indians keep the pieces of our territory that they are holding and we shall retain the Indian territories that our troops have taken.' Pakistan had actually taken rather more square miles of Indian territory (including the important Chhamb salient in Kashmir) than it had lost to the Indians. But the truth of the matter was that India's gains included a salient in the Punjab that put them uncomfortably close to Lahore, and we would have been glad see them out of there as soon as possible.

Whereas Kosygin had been deferential when speaking to Ayub, the tone of Gromyko's meeting with Bhutto was unceremonious and blunt. This may have been a reflection in part of the personalities of the two men, but I felt that it went beyond that. As the discussions proceeded, the Soviet leaders made it clear

that (like the Americans) they would rather deal directly with
Ayub. They evidently found Bhutto's general approach to India-
Pakistan questions uncongenial and demagogic. No doubt they
also shared the Americans' misgivings about his pro-China
leanings. They may have had a shrewd suspicion that Bhutto
could use the failure of the Tashkent negotiations to further his
personal ambitions. Throughout the next morning's meeting,
Kosygin addressed, and directed his gaze at Ayub alone,
acknowledging Bhutto's presence only by a bantering remark
once or twice: 'We shall ask your young and clever Foreign
Minister to sit with Gromyko and draft an acceptable formulation
[for a no-war reference]; that is why we have Foreign Ministers,
even if they themselves don't always understand the meaning of
their clever drafts.'

At another meeting Bhutto started to read out from a Foreign
Office brief, an academic, long-winded paper on the history of
no-war pacts—Locarno, Kellogg-Briand, etc.—in support of his
argument that the renunciation of the use of force remains
without effect if it is not backed up by peace-making procedures.
Gromyko cut in, speaking in a sharp admonitory tone to rebut
Bhutto's point. Kosygin also joined in to chide him: 'What is
needed is a solution to the present impasse, not arguments,' he
said, 'if Pakistan uses the kind of arguments Mr Bhutto is putting
forward, the issue will certainly not be resolved.' What riled the
Soviets was that Bhutto's arguments spoilt their case for an
unconditional no-war pact. Bhutto was taken aback by Gromyko's
vehemence and after the meeting was over asked me why I
thought the Russians had lost their cool. I said 'I suppose it was
because no one likes to lose an argument.' As the French saying
goes, 'It is very wrong to be always right'![2]

Next day it was Bhutto's turn to be vehement and he was
sounding off forcefully about India's record on Kashmir.
Gromyko, who for a change was in an affable, almost jolly mood,
raised his clenched fists to his temples and shook them as if to
say, 'Temper, temper!' An almost theatrical demonstration of
how things stood came at a decisive stage of the discussions when
Kosygin and Gromyko were employing every stick and carrot to
get Ayub to agree to the declaration they had set their hearts on
getting for India. In the heat of the argument and counter-
argument, Kosygin addressed a question to Ayub. Ayub hesitated

a moment and seemed to be searching for words, and it was Bhutto who made as if to reply to the query. In a spontaneous movement both the Russians half rose from their seats, arms extended to shush him into silence: 'No, no! Let the President speak, let the President reply!'

The situation was ironical for it was Bhutto who had broken the ice with the Soviet Union and flown to Moscow when he was Minister of Industry and Natural Resources, to sign an agreement on oil exploration. He had done so in the face of bitter opposition and all manner of obstruction from the Establishment and entrenched oil interests and perhaps, Ayub Khan's own doubts about giving the communists a foot in the door. It was no less ironic that though the aims and policies of the Soviet Union and the United States in South Asia were antagonistic, at this juncture their policies ran in parallel grooves, not merely in their distrust of Bhutto, but on Kashmir and on the India-Pakistan relationship as a whole. This parallelism continued until the end of the decade when the United States began to revise its view of China.

The terms of the Tashkent discussions and the nature and limits of the Soviet role therein, were set in the first day of the meetings with the Soviet leaders. The talks and negotiations that followed in the next six days were intensive and the involvement of the Soviet Prime Minister and Foreign Minister was constant, direct and personal throughout. But the discussions simply kept going round and round and round the points made in these preliminary 'informal' meetings, without the slightest change taking place in the Indian or Soviet positions. The Soviets, unwilling, or perhaps unable to mediate, remained unwavering in their aim which was to bring the conference to a conclusion with some sort of peace declaration between the two warring parties.

On the second morning, the Indians and Pakistanis met at the 'neutral' villa, which had separate wings and even separate entrances for the two delegations. The proceedings began with an 'informal' meeting between the two heads of government and their close advisers, with Kosygin presiding. When we entered the Indians were already in their seats except Defence Minister Chavan and Foreign Minister Swaran Singh who bustled in when the meeting was nearly halfway through.

Shastri, a diminutive man, looked even more tiny when he came forward to shake Ayub's hand.[3] As the two adversaries stood there, hands clasped for a moment, it seemed a personification of the age-old Indian stereotype—the bluff, simple, soldierly Mussulman and the frail *bania* full of wiles. However, the stereotype—as superficial as they tend to be—was not quite apt in the present case. Both men had risen from modest backgrounds and each in his manner had fought his way to the top. It was Ayub who had shown a gift for political machination and a capacity for creating and seizing political opportunity. He had left his modest origins a long way behind in every way. Immaculately dressed, crisp and military in manner and mien, but moderate in action and speech, he inspired confidence and projected the image of an urbane, dynamic and progressive Pakistan. His personality helped to put a gloss on the seething passions and dangerous weaknesses of Pakistani society and politics.

Shastri was a poor man's son and it is said that as a child he sometimes swam across a river to get to school because he didn't have money for the ferry ticket. He had acquired no external patina of success or power, and along with his white shirt, *dhoti* and sandals, wore a look of diffidence, almost of unease. He kept to his rural manners and orthodox ways. The story goes that on his first official visit to Cairo, he scandalized his Egyptian hosts by cooking his own meals in the presidential suite of the hotel where he had been put up. He too personified an image of India—not at all in accord with reality, but firmly fixed in Western eyes—the image of an other-worldly nation, wedded to peace and non-violence, wise and unchanging. But Shastri too cannot have been a simple personality to have come to the top over the heads of powerful and more prominent contenders. No doubt the choice of the Congress party hierarchs fell on Shastri precisely because of his apparent insignificance and his lack of a strong personal following in the party. He must have seemed to them— with his vapoury, unambitious personality—just the sort of person to fill the vacuum left by Nehru's death—a stopgap arrangement until various claims and rivalries could be sorted out and a natural successor emerged. When after the signing of the Tashkent Declaration he quietly died, it seemed like the ultimate act of self-effacement. Yet, what stores of will, determination and ambition must have propelled him forward to a position from where he ruled over 800 million people and dealt with the mightiest of the world. As Shastri's appearance belied his inner qualities, so in its own way did Ayub's. Shastri's frail and tiny frame concealed a firmness of will and clarity of purpose which he displayed when he led India into war 'at a time and place of India's choosing', exactly as he had threatened to do. The same tenacity would be in evidence in the way he conducted the negotiations in Tashkent. Ayub Khan, on the other hand, once his war plans fell to pieces, showed indecisiveness and irresolution both on the battleground and during the Tashkent negotiations. He seemed anxious only to get the country—and himself—out of the predicament into which they had fallen.

The informal meeting was a brief affair. Kosygin opened it by welcoming the two leaders and lauding their statesmanship and desire for peace. He made a verbal offering of sorts to Pakistan by affirming that every problem must sooner or later be solved and that conditions now existed for resolving the India-Pakistan disputes. Shastri spoke then, never looking directly at Ayub but darting glances at him from the corners of his eyes. He suggested that discussions proceed simultaneously on the 'broader aspects' of India-Pakistan relations between the two Heads, while ministers and officials concerned tackled the various specific problems arising out of the war. He also suggested that after the formal opening session scheduled for later in the afternoon, President Ayub and he meet by themselves to discuss 'the general principles of the improvement of relations between the two countries'. Ayub went along with the proposal but suggested that at some stage an agenda would need to be drawn up. This led to a whispered consultation between Shastri, Chavan and Swaran Singh, after which Shastri proposed that the question of agenda could be taken up by the two Heads in their tête-à-tête. The 'question of agenda' was code language for the question of Kashmir; it was symptomatic of the post-1965 situation that the issue now was not how, when, and in what conditions the dispute might be discussed, but whether it could figure at all on the agenda of India-Pakistan negotiations.

The formal meeting opened at 4 p.m. in a flurry of whirring TV cameras, popping flash bulbs and the milling around of newspaper reporters who had come from all corners of the globe.

Kosygin, welcoming the two delegations, spoke of the Soviet Union's friendship for both countries and expressed the hope that their meeting in Tashkent would prove a turning point in their mutual relations. Naturally, he cautioned, one should not expect to find a solution for all problems in the course of one conference and added 'but when governments coolly and objectively consider outstanding issues, taking mutual interests into account, not only are conflicts ended but the source from which they spring is also largely eliminated.' Each delegation was left to make what it wished of this Delphic advice.

There was no arrangement at Tashkent for simultaneous interpretation, and every statement was translated sentence by sentence as it was delivered, by interpreters stationed behind each leader's chair. Shastri who spoke after Kosygin, kept sitting down after each sentence and after it was translated, rising to deliver the next. With his studious mien, all this bobbing up and down made him look like the school know-all, rising up with the answer to every question. 'The only justification for the use of force in international relations is to repel aggression. Our assurance to each other not to use force would mean therefore that each side has agreed to respect the territorial integrity of the other,' he affirmed. 'Once this has been accepted, the whole character of Indo-Pakistan relations would be transformed...' In view of India's claim that Kashmir was an integral part of India, this assertion did nothing to allay Pakistan's opposition to the proposal that followed—the old Indian chestnut of a no-war pact. Such an agreement, Shastri said, would pave the way for resolving the differences existing between them, for many differences, he conceded, did exist though he did not want to enumerate them.

The curious thing was that when it was his turn to speak, Ayub too shied away from mentioning Kashmir by name but spoke instead of the 'basic problem' lying at the root of Indo-Pakistan differences. The omission did not pass unperceived, specially by the Indian Press which saw it as signifying a shift in Pakistan's position. Pakistan, Ayub declared, was ready to sign a no-war pact with India once the 'basic problem' confronting them was resolved. The two countries, he said, had managed to reach an agreement on sharing the Indus waters, and had submitted the Rann of Kutch dispute to arbitration, so why should they avoid discussing this 'basic problem' that was the cause of conflict between them. It is not clear what impelled President Ayub to avoid referring to the Kashmir dispute by name for everyone knew that that was what the war had been about. In Pakistan opposition politicians and those newspapers who could get up the nerve, hinted at an Ayub sell-out and other dark doings. There was no truth in this nor was there a 'Tashkent Secret' to be revealed. Kashmir was at the centre of all of Ayub's and Bhutto's discussions there. Perhaps the President's reticence was motivated by a sort of courtesy towards his Soviet hosts who were anxious that the conference get off to a good start and not immediately descend into polemics and recrimination.

At any rate, when the formal session was over and Ayub and Shastri went into their one-to-one meeting, Shastri wasted no time and words in telling Ayub how things stood with regard to Kashmir: 'Mr President, it will annoy you of course to hear this, but we cannot give up Kashmir.'[4] They were by themselves for no more than thirty minutes; meanwhile, members of the two delegations stood around in the lounge sipping tea, exchanging courtesies and even some banter. When the two leaders emerged, Shastri went off with his people to the Indian side of the villa and Ayub gathered us all around a conference table and told us Shastri's news.

The next morning the two chiefs had another tête-à-tête, this time in a dacha set aside by the Soviets for the purpose. Ayub found Shastri in a somewhat more amenable mood than the previous evening. In response to Ayub's exposition of the Kashmir case, he conceded that 'something will have to be done about it,' and pleaded, 'but you too must help.' He said that the Rann of Kutch incident had queered the pitch for the peaceful settlement of disputes between the two countries. Ayub said that he still could not understand why they had come to fight over the place and questioned what good the fighting had done to either. He suggested that to prevent the sort of situation that had sent things out of control in the Rann, they should think of setting up a high-level machinery to discuss and settle disputes.

The meeting in the afternoon between the two Foreign Ministers was tense and unavailing and bereft of the niceties and lofty generalities about peace and friendship that had lightened the morning's formal proceedings. Swaran Singh, the Indian Foreign Minister, rattled off a list of items for discussion—return of nationals and seized properties, restoration of communications, border problems in East Pakistan, even post-Partition financial questions; everything except our 'basic problem'. The basic question for India, the Indian Foreign Minister emphasized, was whether the two countries were prepared to eschew the use of force against each other. If they had come all the way to Tashkent, he went on, it was because of the war and not to debate the Kashmir question. 'We have debated the question in other forums and many places and we know quite well each other's position,' Swaran Singh said to Bhutto, 'just because we are now in Tashkent doesn't mean that the issue can be resolved.'

Bhutto must have been seething inwardly but tried to maintain a calm front and to moderate his language and tone of voice. The two countries had come to Tashkent, he urged, to break the deadlock between them, not to perpetuate it; they must find a tangible and lasting basis for good relations and 'not be content with a web of thoughts and wishes and semantic artifices'. War had occurred because India had closed all doors to a peaceful settlement. He pointed out that under the UN charter, member states were already committed to refraining from the use of force; reiterating the principle in Tashkent would in no way add to the weight or effectiveness of the commitment. Anyway, he said, the Kashmir dispute was to be discussed by the two heads of government; the Foreign Ministers had been asked to draw up an agenda for the conference.

Swaran Singh said that nobody could stop the heads of government from talking about whatever they wished, but the Indian position on Kashmir—of which he said the Pakistan Foreign Minister was fully aware, as he himself was well aware of Pakistan's position on the subject—needed no reiteration. Legally and constitutionally, the state of Jammu and Kashmir became a part of India in accordance with the procedures laid down in the Act of Independence by which India and Pakistan had themselves become independent and sovereign states. He reminded Mr Bhutto that the two of them had thoroughly discussed all aspects of the subject in a series of meetings in 1963-4. Had it been possible to settle the dispute they would have done it then. Indian sovereignty over Kashmir was not negotiable, he said, and no useful purpose would be served by going 'round and round' the subject all over again.

In the evening, Bhutto met Gromyko to put him in the picture about his fruitless meeting with Swaran Singh and the latter's refusal to admit that Kashmir could even be a subject of discussion at Tashkent. Gromyko was affable but unhelpful. Shrugging his shoulders he said to Bhutto, 'It is for the two of you to agree on how to proceed, we can try to help but we cannot decide things for you.' Then, speaking in English throughout, he started hammering away at the no-war pact idea again. Logically, he asserted, such a proposal should be coming from the weaker country but in the present case it was the stronger one that was pressing for it; Pakistan would be conceding nothing by reiterating what was already in the UN Charter and in return it would get concrete agreements on a number of issues, 'perhaps even' the withdrawal of Indian troops from Pakistani territory. The alternative was nothing—no treaty, no agreements, no progress on any matter. Both sides would be the losers from such a situation and Pakistan would not lose the least. 'Take this as coming from a friend,' Gromyko urged and he did so in a friendly way but there was an undertone of warning. Bhutto was quick to point out that Pakistan did not have a unilateral interest in troop withdrawals and Gromyko back-tracked to assure him that for the Soviet Union, withdrawals meant real and full withdrawals by both sides from the areas occupied by each (this was in the context of demands that were being made in India to retain the three Kargil area passes).

Next morning Ayub paid a return call on Kosygin. This time Kosygin entered into the substance of the Kashmir dispute and asked what precisely was meant 'at present' when one said that the Kashmir dispute must be resolved. He said he wished to examine various possible ways of resolving the dispute, bearing in mind the 'co-relation of forces' both internal and external. 'You are telling Mr Shastri that he must resolve the Kashmir dispute,' Kosygin said to Ayub, 'but how is he to do it?' as behind Shastri stood the Indian Parliament and the whole group of people who had raised him to power. Could he go back and tell them he had given Kashmir away to Pakistan? Kosygin asked. 'Noble sentiments,' Kosygin said, 'cannot solve problems between states; one must take into account the objective possibilities...You and I may have one thought on the subject, the people of Kashmir may have an entirely different view.' Kosygin went on,

'Who indeed can say what the people want in a territory where tribes and languages differ from valley to valley!' The idea of independence from both India and Pakistan might appeal to Kashmiri nationalists and intellectuals but it would not be in the interests of either country, the Soviet Premier affirmed. An independent Kashmir would inevitably fall under the influence of third parties, he asserted, and asked Ayub, 'You *are* aware, are you not, that there are parties that seek such an outcome in Kashmir? Nationalist sentiment is like a match, light it one place and the fire will spread all over.' Kosygin warned, 'Let us therefore cross out the idea [of an independent Kashmir], let us rule it out altogether.'

Explaining that he was only voicing his personal views and thoughts, Kosygin then referred to the possible alternatives to the accession of the whole of Jammu and Kashmir to Pakistan and asked Ayub about the feasibility of some alternative solution. When Ayub asked whether he was thinking in terms of partitioning the State, Kosygin replied, 'What I am asking is whether a radical re-carving of the territory is possible, whether any fundamental change at all in its present status is feasible in the present circumstances.' To him, he went on, it seemed that looking at the situation in all its aspects, the only practical course was to restore the cease-fire line, conceding to the people on both sides some sort of self-government. The world had learnt to live with more complicated problems than Kashmir, he said; Germany was divided into two parts though the Germans were one nation.

Despite Kosygin's bleak analysis, the tone of the discussion was civil, almost conversational. At one point he leaned forward and said to Ayub, 'Mr President, if I am saying things that you find unpleasant, please don't hesitate to say so.' He said that he preferred to speak with complete frankness but he was not trying to suggest or propose or impose any ideas. In point of fact he *was* trying all the time to suggest, propose and impose one thing and that was for Pakistan to sign some sort of a joint declaration with India. 'You must find a solution based on compromise, Mr President,' he pressed, 'you must not leave Tashkent without reaching such a compromise.'

Ayub kept his cool, letting Kosygin do most of the talking, and refrained from taking him up on every point. When Kosygin's dialectic on Kashmir led him to the conclusion that 'no fundamental change at all was possible' in the *status quo*, Ayub merely said: 'You mean that there are areas of agreement and areas of disagreement between the two countries; settlement should be reached on the former and on the latter, the two sides would agree only to disagree.' Kosygin had no difficulty of course with this conclusion, but when he came back to see Ayub in the evening after a meeting with Shastri, he made another pro forma attempt at discussing the Kashmir issue. The cease-fire line, he proposed—with perhaps some modifications, perhaps in Pakistan's favour—might become the international frontier between India and Pakistan, with provision for autonomy within each part of the State. He said: 'Everybody would be happy with such a solution, even, with appropriate guidance from Pakistan, the Kashmiri nationalists.'

Ayub reminded Kosygin that the proposal he was making had been made by Mr Nehru many years ago and had been repeated by India from time to time. Pakistan had rejected it out of hand. The people of Pakistan would not accept it, the people of Kashmir would not consent to be divided and neither he nor any one else could make them do it. 'That is definite, Mr Kosygin!' President Ayub declared in order to put an end to further argument. Then he went on to say that rather than discuss it further he would leave the Kashmir dispute 'in suspense' for the present. Later in order to remove any misunderstanding, Ayub made it clear that he had proposed to 'suspend' the discussion on Kashmir only at the present meetings in Tashkent. Bhutto said that there could be no renunciation by Pakistan of its stand on the issue and no abandoning of the Kashmiri people. Kosygin said that was precisely how he understood the position. The Soviet Union did not expect Pakistan to renounce its claims; if he had thought that Pakistan could forget Kashmir, he would not be arguing the way he had been doing.

At any rate, for the Soviets the way was now clear to concentrate on the matter of the proposed declaration and no-war pact. They had tried from the beginning to pass this off as a 'compromise solution'—Pakistan would renounce the use of force and India would give back territories taken by its troops in the recent fighting, including the three Kargil posts. On this matter however, Ayub was clear and firm: if Mr Shastri was having difficulties with the Lok Sabha on the matter of withdrawing troops from the Kargil Pass area, then let the Indian troops stay there and Pakistani troops too would remain where they were across the cease-fire line. Mr Shastri could please himself! On this question the Soviets supported Pakistan, not wanting either side to make territorial gains from the war.

Kosygin next turned to Pakistan's demand that a no-war pact should provide for some peace-keeping machinery to settle outstanding disputes. 'Let us suppose for argument's sake, that a settlement machinery is set up. What would be the practical consequences? Pakistan would keep saying one thing, India another, and it would all lead nowhere.' As for arbitration, India was categorically opposed to it and Kosygin did not think that in the case of 'great states like India and Pakistan', arbitration was a practical or appropriate idea or in consonance with their national honour and prestige. Who, he asked, would enforce the arbitrator's award if one of the sides refused to accept it? If the two countries were willing to accept an award by a third party, surely they were capable of reaching agreement by themselves. In reply Ayub Khan pointed out (and perhaps he was not thinking only of India) that politically, arbitration offered the advantage that it made it easier for a government to make its people accept an unpopular solution proposed by an impartial arbitrator than to impose it itself. Gromyko intervened to say that perhaps it was this very method which, through the Radcliffe Award, had led to the problem that was being discussed.

The withdrawal of troops coupled with a non-use of force agreement, Kosygin said, was the one and only thing that could be achieved at this stage. It could be the starting point for better relations between the two countries and he could not conceive that for the sake of a few words Pakistan would break up everything. 'In the construction of boats,' Kosygin went on, 'a screw is always fully tightened first, then loosened by half a turn, for if a screw is left on too tight, it could break. Let us be guided by this analogy!' Kosygin urged Ayub, who could very well have given the same counsel to the Soviets.

Kosygin commended Shastri as a good man, a man of integrity, with whom it was important to have the right approach. 'Please have a long meeting with him,' he pressed Ayub, 'have a real heart-to-heart talk and not just say a few words for the sake of saying them and then come away.' He urged Pakistan not to reject out of hand any proposals that the Indians might put forward; instead Pakistan should try to suggest alternative wordings or formulations, propose amendments of its own, or at least undertake to think over India's proposals. 'Please do not refuse point blank even to discuss Indian ideas,' Kosygin pleaded—in short, sit down with the Indians and start drafting the text of a declaration.

And that is how things went for the remaining three days of the conference. Bits of paper were bandied about; draft texts were exchanged. The Pakistani texts tended to be terse and to the point; the Indians went in for a lot of padding concerning peace and friendship and culture and so forth, and kept coming up with elaborate, treaty-like documents, covering every aspect of the relations between the two countries. A particular formulation which was considered indispensable by one side was completely unacceptable to the other; whole paragraphs were eliminated or sentences, phrases or words were lopped off; amendments were amended and revisions, revised. But like crustaceans that regenerate amputated limbs, they would sprout in another place or reappear in the disguise of a paraphrase or euphemism or synonym. Everything would come full circle and appear to be winding down and then somehow things would be set in the groove and round and round we would go again. This was diplomacy of the age of mass communications and mass media, of joint communiqués and manifestos and declarations, when governments negotiate with each other but address wider, sometimes conflicting audiences. It can be a rather gratifying game for people who are clever with words and can turn them inside out without touching the underlying intent. Both Indians and Pakistanis tend to be good at this game and seem to revel in it all the more because they play it in a foreign language. At Tashkent the task was to clothe in language of accord and friendship a deep and fundamental difference, and to do so without running counter to the war-like mood to which public opinion had been aroused on both sides.

It was a tedious and frustrating job. In the end it boiled down to a question of words. Kosygin could not understand why, when Pakistan was prepared to say that disputes should be solved 'peacefully' or 'by peaceful means', it would not say the corollary. He could of course have asked the Indians the opposite question, but I don't suppose that he did. The Soviets may have suspected that the Chinese, who at the time were propagating the Maoist thesis of peoples' war, were behind Pakistan's seemingly doctrinaire refusal to renounce the use of force. There exist 'external forces' Kosygin said, who would be glad that there should be war between India and Pakistan in order to prove that disputes between states could only be solved by war. He himself was convinced, Kosygin said, that Pakistan had no such intention, even though it may find it expedient at times to strike up a bellicose pose and to make 'loud noises'.

The fact of the matter was that the inconclusive outcome of the fighting had given India a *de facto* no-war situation; in insisting on getting a formal declaration on the subject, what the Indians were seeking was a *de facto*, implicit renunciation by Pakistan of its claim to Kashmir. Kosygin however professed to see a more immediate tactical reason for the Indian position: the three Kargil positions taken by Indian troops were important for the security of India's link with Ladakh, and when Shastri stood up in Parliament to explain why he had given them back, he would have the no-war pact to show in return. But there were reasons of no less substance on Ayub's side to deny to India this victory of form and not to sign away the option to settle the Kashmir question by all available means.

Bhutto battled hard on this behalf but the only weapons in his armoury were arguments. Ayub supported him of course, but his heart was not in this wordmongering. One morning, in an unscheduled tête-à-tête with Shastri, he went so far as to add the taboo phrase '...and will not have recourse to force' to a round-about formulation which the Pakistan side had worked out precisely to avoid having to say this. Ayub Khan was a big enough man to admit in a subsequent delegation meeting that he had made a mistake in doing so. But it was a mistake only of tactics. In terms of words it was a quibble and it made no great difference what formula was used. In the end we settled for one that said, 'They affirmed their obligation under the UN Charter not to have recourse to force and to settle their disputes through peaceful means.' This had the merit of allowing the Pakistan side to say that settling disputes by peaceful means under the Charter meant having recourse to the methods set out in its Chapter VI, that is, negotiations, good offices, mediation, arbitration et. al.

The denouement came at the Pakistani banquet for the Soviet leaders. The President's chefs had been brought with the delegation and they had come fully equipped and provisioned to prepare a grand Mogul feast. However Kosygin and Gromyko were more than an hour late for the dinner and the rest of us milled around hungrily in the rising aromas of *biryani*, chicken *korma*, etc. The Soviet leaders had been held up by a long and difficult—or so they said—session with the Indians. At that point everything else had been agreed upon and there remained only the first paragraph with its controversial reference to the non-use of force. Kosygin said to Ayub, 'Now if we cannot find an acceptable text for this paragraph, then there is only one thing left for me to do—hang myself from this chandelier!' He was spared this tragic end and went on to accomplish vastly more significant things than the Tashkent Declaration, including signing a 'Friendship Treaty' with India under whose military cover India used force to bring about the birth of Bangladesh a few years later.

The one who died was Lal Bahadur Shastri, only a few hours after signing the Declaration and the grand gala hosted by the Soviet leaders to celebrate the occasion. The signing took place amid much clapping and hand-shaking. By mutual agreement, no speeches were made for fear that some loaded word or phrase might bring the whole verbal house of cards tumbling down—only the text of the Declaration was read out in English and Russian before it was signed. The Soviets wore the triumphant look of a midwife emerging from the delivery room to announce, 'It's a boy!' The Indians looked smug, the Pakistanis grim.

Not that Pakistan lost anything at or through Tashkent that hadn't been lost already. We had gone there with no particular expectations other than to end an inconclusive war, and to whatever extent possible, neutralize Soviet support for India's position on Kashmir. The exercise brought us face to face with the realities of the situation. For long years our diplomatic efforts had been deployed to mobilize international support for the Kashmir settlement set out in the UN resolutions of 1948-49. We assumed that if it could be demonstrated that the dispute could lead to war, then the great powers would intervene to remove the danger by enforcing a settlement along those lines. This might possibly have been the result if the war had ended favourably for Pakistan, had our troops broken through to Akhnoor or made headway in East Punjab. It is a moot point. As it was, the United States and the Soviet Union bent all their efforts to stop the fighting, to prevent it from spreading, to keep China out of it, and to restore the *status quo.* The only recognition we could get for the Kashmir dispute in the Tashkent Declaration was a mention that it was discussed and that the two sides had put forward their respective positions.

Rather than accept such an unsatisfactory result, Pakistan could have threatened to go back without a declaration of any sort and thereby deprived the Soviet Union of the diplomatic success they desired, particularly *vis-à-vis* China. But then what? No doubt the Soviet Union attached a great deal of importance to this, their first mediation effort in the Third World, and in a region which had been the traditional preserve of Western influence. A successful outcome meant a lot to them in their quest for equality of status with the United States and in their effort to curb China's growing influence not only in Pakistan but in the rest of the Third World. It was not for nothing that the Prime Minister and Foreign Minister of the world's second most powerful state, put aside their other concerns and preoccupations for nine whole days in order to engage in a drafting exercise with Pakistan and India. Failure of the conference would have been a considerable setback for the Soviet Union and they were prepared to do whatever they could to prevent it. So of course they put pressure where it was likely to work—on a Pakistan whose options seemed, for the moment at least, to have been exhausted and who was being required, after all, only to make some verbal concessions. The Soviet Union's ability to impose a settlement on India or to compel it to accept arbitration, was limited, and moreover it had no national interest in doing so.

The Pakistani side often cited the Rann of Kutch settlement as a precedent. Swaran Singh argued that the two cases were altogether different; in the Rann the question was where the boundary between the two countries lay, whereas in the case of Kashmir, Pakistan wished to put India's sovereignty to arbitration. This was very specious reasoning against the background of the case: Pandit Nehru's categorical assurances concerning a plebiscite, the United Nations' resolutions, India's commitments thereunder, etc. What was to be arbitrated was not India's 'sovereignty' but the differences that had prevented the agreed solution of a plebiscite from being implemented. The real difference between the two cases was that in the Rann, Pakistan had gained a military advantage, however limited and localized it may have been, whereas the September War had ended in a draw and a draw leaves things where they are.

NOTES

[1] All references and quotes in this chapter are based on the author's notes of the meetings.

[2] *C'est un grand tort d'avoir toujours raison.*

[3] The Russians made fun of Shastri's small size. An official told us a joke on the subject: noticing that the applause on Shastri's ride from the airport was not very loud, Kosygin guessed that the crowds lining the streets couldn't see him and suggested, 'Mr Prime Minister, maybe you should stand up on the seat.' To this Shastri replied, 'But I am!'

Soviet mid-level officials regaled us with disparaging stories about the Indian delegation—how Indian pressmen were pestering them for free TV sets and other expensive gifts, the problem of arranging accommodation with seven different WCs for the seven different castes in the delegation, etc. I supposed this was Pakistan's consolation prize in place of the political support that was reserved for India.

[4] *'Aap yeh sun kar khafa zuroor hongay, lekin hum Kashmir nahin chhor saktay.'*

CHAPTER 8

INTERREGNUM

At Tashkent Premier Kosygin said to President Ayub, 'Let us do what can be done today. Who knows what tomorrow may bring.' And what could be done at that point was to get both sides to square one. That was the one specific result of the Tashkent effort. Both countries carried out the mutual withdrawal of forces from territories occupied during the war. India shilly-shallied over vacating some points in the Kargil area claiming that these were important for preventing a repetition of Pakistani incursions. But on this matter the Soviets were not prepared to go along with India, and were firm in their position that withdrawals must be total, and carried out by the agreed deadlines. The diplomatic representatives of the two countries resumed their posts—a metaphorical move since they had not actually left their respective capitals. Propaganda in Pakistan's state-controlled media was switched off by a phone call made from Tashkent by the Information Secretary as soon as the Declaration was signed.

The Indians tried to make much of the Tashkent Declaration and invariably included references to the 'spirit of Tashkent' in their statements and joint communiqués. They proposed a joint celebration when the anniversary of the signing came around. Pakistan politely declined. In Pakistan the Declaration was badly received. The fact that an agreement was reached at all had come as a surprise to the general public. The Pakistani media, force-fed on 'press advice' and official briefings, had not followed the ups and downs of the negotiations and were, until the last hours, saying that the conference was heading for a breakdown. When, instead, it ended with a full-fledged Declaration, people were suspicious that Ayub had knuckled in under American pressure. The fact that Ayub helped to carry Shastri's coffin at

Tashkent Airport, a gesture of ordinary civility in the circumstances, did not go down well with many people. When Ayub's flight arrived at Chaklala Airport, the usual flag-waving crowds had not been mustered to greet him and there wasn't even the long line of diplomats, officials and notables who are normally present at Presidential departures and arrivals. At a reception that Ayub gave for the delegation that evening, I didn't hear one good thing said about the Tashkent Declaration. In Pakistan Tashkent was soon to become a bad word, used by Opposition politicians to revile and embarrass the government. The practice was started by Bhutto when he began a movement against Ayub, with dark hints about a 'Tashkent secret' that would be revealed at the proper time. The practice continued until Tashkent was replaced by the Simla Agreement in the lexicon of Pakistani political invective.

There were protest demonstrations in a number of towns— street signs were uprooted, public property damaged, and buses were set on fire by the very people who have to stand for hours every day to catch one. I happened to get caught in the tail-end of one such demo outside the Shezan restaurant in Lahore. The street was littered with brickbats, broken glass and miscellaneous debris. A group of students, street urchins and sundry patriots were pelting lampposts with stones. The mood of the crowd was derisive and mocking rather than violent or aggressive. One individual was carrying part of a billboard advertising an exhibition of captured Indian weapons. A little soldier suddenly turned up around a street corner and a cheer went up from the crowd. The army was adulated and admired then unlike what was to happen in the subsequent war. The astonished warrior, probably a supplies or signals clerk, was hoisted on someone's shoulders and carried about for some distance amidst patriotic slogans. Askew on his wobbly perch, the hero tried to acknowledge the plaudits with a nervous wave of the arms. Then, the crowd's attention being diverted by something else, he was put down unceremoniously and left to go his way. The demonstrators were expressing frustration at the disappointment of the hopes that had been aroused rather than calling for a renewal of the war. The manifestations petered out in due course. There was, for a while, talk of a second round, but this too died down in time. But it was a disquieting sign of the country's mood that some of the protest marches were led by widows and orphans of military officers killed in the fighting. The agreement was badly received by the Establishment which was the base of Ayub's system and the principal source of his strength.

Ayub had tried to rise above it all, saying little about Tashkent himself and leaving it to Bhutto to do the talking and explaining. Bhutto was better at the cut and thrust of public debate but, more to the point, Ayub may have wanted also to tie him down to the defence of the Tashkent Declaration and pre-empt any idea he may have had of making an issue out of it. Bhutto had not actually opposed the signing of the Declaration, but was unhappy and frustrated at the way negotiations had been conducted and the situation had evolved. He had chafed at the weakness of Pakistan's position and Ayub's readiness to compromise. On the flight back from Tashkent, Bhutto sent a steward to ask me to join him in a vacant seat next to his. In a whisper that was not so low that Ayub, sitting a couple of rows in front, could not hear if he lent an ear, Bhutto criticized 'our', namely Ayub's, pusillanimity in the war. He said bitterly, 'We are taking the rap from the Americans for cosying up to China, but when it came to profiting from the relationship, we lacked the guts to do it.'

By the end of January, Ayub could no longer disregard the cloud of criticism, rumour and innuendo that continued to swirl around the Tashkent Conference. He decided to speak up or was advised to do so. A 'select' group of intellectuals and concerned citizens—that is, government officials and the semi-elected local counsellors known as Basic Democrats—were brought together for the purpose. Ayub spoke cogently and with irrefutable common sense about the hows and whys of the war and of the Tashkent Declaration; he described in detail the disparity between India's military strength and ours and the Soviet Union's support for India. He concluded with a remark that is hard to forget: 'I simply don't understand what all the fuss is about!'

Although the group was 'select', there was at least one forthright question. 'Sir,' a mild-looking individual rose to ask, 'you have spoken of the disparity between our strength and India's and other such facts. But this situation prevailed also on the fifth of August...' A hush fell upon the gathering. For on

that day was launched Operation Gibraltar. Ayub waited,
seemingly for the man to finish, and then said, with a touch of
impatience, 'Well go on man, ask your question; don't be afraid!'
In a small voice the man replied, 'The question is self-evident,
Sir!' Later over tea and cakes, while the President sat in a corner
with the Assembly Speaker and some ministers, the room buzzed
with malice and gossip against him. Ayub was the scapegoat for a
failure that was not his alone but the cumulative result of the
many errors and illusions of the past.

In East Pakistan not much was said one way or another about
the Tashkent Declaration, for there grievances of another sort
altogether, and of more vast consequence, were beginning to
come to a head. They had been simmering for a long time but
the way the war had been fought and had ended, brought to the
fore the unsettled question of Muslim Bengal's place in Pakistan.
In East Bengali eyes the war had disproved the doctrine that the
defence of the eastern province lay in the plains of the Punjab. If
it was the threat of China's intervention that had kept the Indian
Army out of East Pakistan, then what do we need Pakistan for,
the Bengalis began to ask.

The spring session of the National Assembly was, as usual,
held in Dhaka. Ayub had given Bhutto the task of speaking about
the war and explaining and justifying the Tashkent Declaration.
On 14 March Bhutto opened the two-day debate on foreign affairs
by reading out the speech he had asked me to write for him, his
heart not being in the task. He read it in a resigned monotone
and without much conviction. A member of the Opposition
taunted him for having to read out his speech from a prepared
text, something he didn't normally do, and insinuated that he
was being kept on a leash. The *Morning News* the next morning
described the statement as 'bald' (but I was flattered that the
paper saw in the baldness a sign of the growing maturity of
Pakistan's foreign policy!). However on the following day,
winding up the debate and speaking extempore, Bhutto let
himself go and put on one of his brio performances. In the guise
of explaining and justifying the Tashkent Declaration, he recited
a chauvinistic ode to the glory of a war fought to uphold justice.
The performance thrilled the galleries, subdued the derision of
the Opposition and left the treasury benches in bewilderment.
In any case, the small Opposition made up, but for two members,

entirely of Bengalis, focused its attention on other matters altogether: democracy, adult franchise and socialism. The criticism was wholly along provincialistic lines for these were code words for ending West Pakistani domination of the government, and for a greater share in the country's economic resources and the loaves and fishes for East Pakistan. At the end of a day of bitter debate, as we sat reviewing events, Bhutto asked me whether the government of Pakistan would not be duty bound before the judgement seat of history—if it came to it—to use force to keep East and West Pakistan together, a question that foreshadowed the tragedy and misfortune that were to come. I thought that if matters ever came to such a pass, the game would already have been lost.

A co-ordinating committee of federal secretaries of the various ministries concerned, was established to follow up on the Tashkent Declaration. I was the committee scribe. In the very first meeting the lines were drawn between the hawks and doves. Foreign Secretary Aziz Ahmad led the hawks and S. M. Yusuf, who would succeed him shortly, was the most vocal of the doves. Aziz Ahmad, who said he knew the Hindu mind and what would count most with it, wanted to retain seized properties as a means of putting pressure on the Indian delegation. I said to Agha Shahi after the meeting, 'Surely Aziz Ahmad doesn't really think that we can swop Faletti's Hotel for Kashmir!' Shahi said that the real purpose was to put a spanner in the works for some deal that was allegedly being worked out in Washington for normalizing India-Pakistan relations. Aziz Ahmed himself was a man of integrity but the remark was revealing of the equivocal and shadowy position Pakistan's bureaucracy had acquired in the country's politics. A Civil Service that had lost the moral courage to press unpalatable advice upon the President and was unchecked by the fear of public opinion, had split into factions and cliques, and was finding recourse in the classic and time-honoured subterfuges of bureaucracy—mislead, hamper, obstruct and undermine—to attain its ends. Underneath the pseudo-politics of Ayub's Basic Democracy there had grown up a crypto-government of senior Civil Servants.

The co-ordinating committee's proceedings were also revealing of the way the government operated. On the one hand was the hard, objective, concrete situation of fact and circumstance; on the other, the committee represented the pulling and tugging of factions and vested interests, of special lobbies and demands and of wishfulness and self-justification. Public opinion was frequently invoked in support of this or that course of action or proposal, invoked by people who enforced censorship and connived at misleading the public and were only too prompt in stifling dissent and discussion.

I was given the job of drafting a summary for the President which would: recommend that the talks with India not be broken off in any circumstances, but at the same time the world was not to be given the impression that Pakistan had acquiesced in the *status quo*; our own people were not to feel that the government would agree to the normalization of relations without a Kashmir settlement, while the world was not to think that Pakistan was dragging its feet on the Tashkent Declaration! The Indians arrived on 1 March for a two-day visit. It did not take long before C. S. Jha the Indian Commonwealth Secretary, was saying, 'I hope I am mistaken in the impression that if Kashmir is not discussed, you will not discuss anything at all.' He rather confirmed Aziz Ahmad's reading of the 'Hindu mind' by exhibiting acute anxiety on the matter of the return of seized properties and the resumption of transit trade through East Pakistan. Both issues were of *absolute* importance and must be discussed, he affirmed. No such thing was going to be done of course, and the day's discussions were spun out to no conclusion. Next morning it was the foreign ministers' turn to do the same thing, but Swaran Singh allowed that the Kashmir 'problem' should be solved and solved to the satisfaction of both countries. Then the ministers went into a tête-à-tête along with the foreign secretaries after which the latter held an officials-level meeting to draft a communiqué. When the secretaries got stuck over the proposed reference to Kashmir, the problem was referred to the 'ministers level'. It was an odd little see-saw characteristic of the Indo-Pakistan negotiating make-believe. When the ministers ran into a dead-end over something, they pretended that it was a matter of detail to be settled by officials, and when the latter reached a deadlock on precisely the same issue, it was agreed on all sides that the difference must be submitted to the ministers to decide at their superior political level! So the Indians flew back to Delhi, nicely wined and dined, but with nothing in their pockets. One of them said wryly that of their twelve working hours in Pakistan, they had spent more at the dining table than around the conference table!

Gradually the temperature of relations between the two countries again rose to its normal fever-pitch. Mrs Indira Gandhi, India's new Prime Minister, alternated bellicose condemnations of Pakistan with assurances that India was ready to talk to Pakistan any time, about anything, at any level.

The Americans now took a hand in the matter. Ambassador Goldberg had pledged that the Security Council resolution of 20 September would be America's 'Bible'. But Kashmir, the so-called 'underlying problem' mentioned in it was nowhere to be found in the proposals brought back by Finance Minister Shoaib from a World Bank meeting in Washington in May. These were in the shape of five conditions for the resumption of United States' aid to Pakistan: (1) peace in the subcontinent; (2) a reasonable ceiling on defence expenditure to be determined and adhered to by India and Pakistan; (3) economic co-operation between the two countries; (4) an end to 'overt' condemnation of United States policies in Asia and (5) elimination of the more 'aggressive features' of Pakistan's China policy. Whatever the Americans had in mind with regard to Kashmir was subsumed in the portmanteau first item—in all probability some kind of an autonomous Sikkim type of status for Indian occupied Kashmir but leaving untouched India's formal control. This was a non-starter for Pakistan, and I dare say the Americans knew it. Their real objective was to put some sort of constraint on Pakistan's developing relations with China—as spelled out in item (5)— and also through the proposed limit on defence spending.

Pakistan's assumption had been that in order to prevent renewed fighting in the subcontinent, the United States would do all they could to resolve the root cause of war—the Kashmir dispute. But the Americans seemed to have decided that the simplest way of maintaining peace was to limit the striking capacity of Pakistan which alone had the motive to start a fight over Kashmir. The only hurdle in the way was Pakistan's ability to have recourse to China.

Of course, the idea of putting a ceiling on defence spending had much merit in itself and thought had been given to it in GHQ, the Foreign Ministry and other concerned agencies. That the money spent on defence could be more productively used otherwise was a truism that the leaders of both countries constantly commended to each other's attention. The situation after the 1965 War was that the United States had cut off all military supplies to both countries. This was hurting Pakistan more than India because for lack of spares we couldn't even maintain our existing equipment, US-supplied for the most part, leave alone keep up with India's defence build-up from its own industry and continuing Soviet assistance.[1]

Pakistan's relations with the Soviet Union had been improving for some time and the Tashkent exercise gave them a further boost. The Soviet Union had indicated a willingness to supply military equipment to Pakistan and did give some. However we were well aware of the limits within which Pakistan-Soviet relations could develop. The Soviet Union's main pre-occupation at this stage was the challenge from China. Its cold war rivalry with the United States in the subcontinent was now a secondary consideration and indeed an unspoken, if limited and tactical, 'alliance' against China had come to exist among the two superpowers and India. The purpose of Soviet aid to Pakistan was the exact opposite of what we wanted—a viable military balance with India. What the Russians wanted was to stabilize the military and political situation in the subcontinent in order to set a limit to Sino-Pakistan collaboration in these fields. There could be no question of Pakistan making any fundamental shift in its relationship with China; to do so would imply in fact, a fundamental change in our Kashmir policy and at the same time entail a loss of the flexibility which the Chinese relationship gave us in our dealings with the other two superpowers. For Pakistan the importance of the Soviet Union's role in this matter lay not in that it would help to redress the military imbalance with India, but that the Soviets had it in their power to make it worse.

In January 1967, in the course of a speech at the Pakistan Institute of International Affairs, President Ayub Khan called for an agreed reduction of their defence expenditures by India and Pakistan. This brought a prompt response from India in the shape of a letter from India's Foreign Minister, M.C. Chagla, proposing talks on the subject between officials of the two countries on a 'quiet, continuing and confidential basis'. The ensuing correspondence got bogged down straightaway over the question of whether or not there would be simultaneous and serious discussions on Kashmir, and the whole thing ended in the usual polemics. Matters were not improved by Mrs Gandhi's declaring around the same time that Kashmir belonged to India and there was nothing to be negotiated with Pakistan over the matter. Earlier Defence Minister Chavan had declared that there could be no question of India reducing its force levels. When Pakistan remonstrated against such statements, the Indian High Commissioner said to our Foreign Secretary that statements made in public by Indian leaders did not reflect the real position of the Government of India! He held that once the process of negotiations began, some way leading to a mutually acceptable solution of the Kashmir dispute would be discovered.

In fact neither side was really serious about arms control, and both were responding to pressures from the United States which had its own aims. The American Press was talking of America's 'bold new plan' for an arms limitation arrangement in the subcontinent that would provide also for autonomy for Indian-held Kashmir and enable India to shift her armed forces to the Chinese border. In Pakistan there was not the least doubt that whatever agreement might be reached India was bound to cheat and there were also misgivings about US intentions. Dean Rusk had made it clear to our Ambassador that there was no longer a special relationship between the US and Pakistan. The Americans were incensed with Pakistan over the war, and when things started going badly, Dean Rusk twitted the Pakistan Ambassador in Washington: 'You didn't consult us at the take-off, now you want American help for the crash landing.'

Pakistan also had to bear in mind the reaction of China which was now Pakistan's only dependable source of arms. The Hsinhua, China's official news agency, put forward the view that the United States' efforts to promote Indo-Pakistan co-operation and arms control was the first step in uniting the subcontinent against China. China had also expressed some disquiet at Pakistan's growing relationship with the Soviet Union. However on objective considerations, the supply of Soviet arms to Pakistan, if it redressed the Indo-Pakistan military imbalance and caused some attenuation of Indo-Soviet ties, would probably not have been unwelcome to China. The United States for its part would not object to the Soviet Union and China acting as rivals in Pakistan if this served to exacerbate Sino-Soviet-differences. The arrival of a Soviet supplied helicopter to help in building the Chinese-assisted Karakoram Highway, symbolized the intricacy of the triangular power relationship and rivalry in the subcontinent.

The truth was that China did not want a new war in the subcontinent any more than the two superpowers did. China assured us that in case of an all out Indian attack on Pakistan she would come to Pakistan's assistance, but she did not consider that such an attack was a serious possibility at that juncture. On the other hand, clearly she did not wish Pakistan itself to embark on an adventure that might embroil China in a conflict with America or Russia. When Pakistan expressed a desire for a closer military relationship between the two countries, China did not go beyond suggesting joint operational planning by the two armed forces; this too may have been with an eye on moderating any rash impulses on Pakistan's part.

Nevertheless, all things considered, an arms control negotiation, even if no agreement emerged, would have been advantageous for Pakistan. It was not a convincing argument that arms control could not take place unless there was a Kashmir settlement since reciprocal and balanced reduction of forces would not affect the relative military strength of the two countries. Moreover, it was not simply a matter of logic; as long as Pakistan's force level depended to the extent that it did on US military supplies, the United States government was in a position, in co-operation with the Soviet Union, to enforce on India and Pakistan more or less the military ratio that they considered reasonable. Indeed there was a section of opinion in the United States that favoured allowing the natural disparity between India and Pakistan to assert itself.

On the face of it, even if India's motives were in doubt, there was something to be said for taking up arms control on its own merits, irrespective of a Kashmir settlement. India was prepared, Chagla said, to discuss without preconditions and pre-commitment, all questions at issue between the two countries, including Kashmir, in confidential talks. Both the United States and the Soviet Union supported this position. Taking a long view, the situation offered opportunities that might have been exploited to our advantage. But the public mood was not for a common sense approach; the Ayub government had suffered a loss of self-confidence and Pakistan's diplomacy was not headed, at that point, by a person with the skill and insight needed to carry out the sort of delicate balancing act that the situation demanded.

Sometime before these developments, Bhutto's welcome had run out in the Ayub government. In June, Ghafur Hoti one of Ayub's confidants, told me that Bhutto's fate had been settled and sealed and the date of his exit fixed for 15 July. In the event the thing happened even sooner. On 19 June a terse announcement was issued from the President's House stating that Mr Bhutto had been granted long leave on medical grounds and that the President wished him good health and Godspeed. He also assured the country that this would not result in a change in foreign policy. This rather gave the game away, for why should the foreign policy change if a Foreign Minister is taken ill? Bhutto himself had known that his dismissal was coming. A month or so earlier he had asked me over one evening to his house for a chat and told me that he had decided to resign in July. He was becoming tired, he said, of Ayub Khan's petty persecutions and jealousies—vetoing his overseas visits, discouraging the holding of welcome receptions during his tours within the country, and so on.

At the Foreign Ministry's farewell for him on 20 June, Bhutto had tears in his eyes as he spoke of the 'romance' that had attracted him to the field of foreign affairs and of his regret at leaving it when challenges were mounting before the country. 'I am a man of the desert,' he declared, 'I have a personal equation with every one of you, from the Foreign Secretary down to the section officers; I have dealt with you not as a Minister but as a *Wadera.*' In his farewell speech, Foreign Secretary Aziz Ahmad paid him a tribute:

It is little more than three years since you came to this office. These have been momentous years in the life of this nation, years of change and movement, marked by historic events and by a new dynamism in our foreign relations...You brought to your task a clarity of vision free of sentimentality, an acuteness of perception unencumbered by wishfulness and an understanding of Pakistan's rightful place in the world that have given to Pakistan's foreign policy its new direction.

In October when he returned from his overseas 'health trip', he stopped for a few days in Rawalpindi and I spent a good deal of time with him. He told me that a message had been conveyed on behalf of the President, warning him that he was free to attack India, Imperialism, or America to his heart's content, but he must lay off the President—or else. He was advised also to bide his time which, it was hinted, might well turn in his favour again in due course. He asked me what I thought of all this. I suggested that he should take the advice to lie low for the present and in my opinion, also lay off the Americans, Imperialists and the lot. But a low profile was not Bhutto's style, and soon he was going all over the place stirring up things. By December, Ayub was losing patience but took the advice to give Bhutto a chance—first persuasion, then warning and only if he didn't take it, pressure and harassment and finally, if nothing worked, jail. I met Nusrat Bhutto in 'Pindi around this time and told her of the danger of Bhutto being detained. She said, 'But that is just what he would like to happen right now.'

Bhutto had been succeeded at the Foreign Ministry by Sharifuddin Pirzada, a constitutional lawyer who had come to Ayub Khan's notice when he helped to prepare Pakistan's case on the Rann of Kutch dispute. It was a choice that surprised everyone, for Pirzada had neither any experience of foreign affairs nor any particular aptitude for it. But now Ayub's own time was running out. He had been in the saddle for ten years and the end came rather unexpectedly and in the midst, ironically, of the celebrations of his decennial—'The Decade of Progress'—a gimmicky idea thought up by PR men in the Information Ministry. Public relations is no substitute for policy but in Third World countries with news media under their control, public relations has been the opiate of the ruling classes. In truth Pakistan had indeed made a good deal of progress under Ayub—in the economic field, in the matter of women's rights and family planning. Ayub had placed economic and social issues clearly at the top of the national agenda. The Indus waters dispute with India had been settled and work started on the Tarbela Dam. In the field of foreign relations he had allowed Bhutto to re-orient relations with the great powers in such a way that Pakistan was on equally good terms with China, USA and the Soviet Union.

Why then did his rule and his system suddenly collapse? This is well-trodden ground and I shall only enumerate the various reasons. The failure of the 1965 War no doubt had something to do with it. His family's dabbling in business and his own failing health were other reasons for the erosion of his standing and authority. Paradoxically, the dismissal of the ambitious and troublesome Bhutto also undermined Ayub's position, for it removed from the government its most popular member, and provided the Opposition with a leader around which it could rally. I was ambassador in Cairo at the time and when I went to brief President Nasser on the situation, he said that he was sorry that Ayub had fallen out with 'Zulfikar' and was sure that the Americans were behind this rift. 'Such men,' he added, 'are best kept inside the system where they can be useful and their actions can be more easily checked.'

The discontent with Ayub's rule had been building up steam for a long time and when the lid blew off, there was no way of putting it back on again. The trouble that had started over the price of sugar or some such thing, took on the shape of a country-wide revolt against authority. In Lahore, for a while students were controlling traffic, fining speeding drivers and dispensing justice in 'People's Courts'. In Dhaka Information Minister Shahabuddin's house was burnt to the ground.

Ayub tried the conciliatory approach, making concession after concession. To pacify students, the minimum marks required to pass an examination in the second division were reduced from fifty per cent to forty-five per cent. Government's medical service was upgraded to become a Class One service. But like Bhutto's 'Islamist' measures a decade later, all this had little relevance in the prevailing situation and only accentuated the impression of the waning of Ayub's authority. The Round Table Conference he had called reached agreement on holding elections on the basis of adult franchise and reverting the country to the federal, parliamentary system, but it could not agree on the question of provincial autonomy and the undoing of the One Unit in West Pakistan. These were issues on which the opposition parties were sharply divided among themselves. Jamaat-i-Islami zealots fought it out in the streets with Bhutto's party. Some Opposition leaders feared Bhutto—who had kept out of the Round Table Conference—even more than they distrusted Ayub. But the revolt was against Ayub himself for he had become the target of the decade-long grievances that had come to a head—East Pakistan's against the Centre, that of the smaller West Pakistan provinces against the One Unit, and generally against the indifference, inefficiency and corruption of the administration. It was suggested to Ayub that he should obtain the people's verdict by holding a referendum. He is said to have replied that what was going on in the country at that point was referendum enough. Ayub consulted the service chiefs about re-imposing martial law but got an ambiguous response.

On 21 February Ayub threw in the towel and announced his 'final and irrevocable' decision to quit. In a melancholy valedictory over the radio, he said:

> My dear countrymen, we should now forgive and forget. I hope that we shall all have the courage to do so. May God bless you. You have never hesitated in making any sacrifices for the sake of the country. In this lies the secret of Pakistan's strength and solidarity. Office and power are transient things. Pakistan will hold for ever.

Ayub had seized power on the ground that the people were tired of too much politics and needed a system 'suited to their genius'. The fact, on the contrary, was that Pakistan had not had enough genuine politics. No general election had been held in the country since Independence. Provincial elections had been manipulated and rigged by the Establishment. The first general election was about to be held in 1958 when Iskandar Mirza abrogated the newly enacted Constitution. Bureaucrats had pulled strings more and more openly and became ever more powerful under Ayub. His system institutionalized the intervention of the military-bureaucratic-feudal-business complex in politics and aggravated the alienation of East Pakistan from West Pakistan, the smaller western provinces from the Punjab, the rich from the poor, and the people from the rulers.

On 25 March, General Yahya Khan, the Chief of Army Staff, took over power and the country was placed under martial law again. In due course he made himself President on the ground that 'a country must have a President after all'. In May he summoned to Lahore a conference of envoys from the major countries and explained with seemingly disarming *naiveté* how he came to be in the President's chair: 'I happened to be the senior-most officer.' He said that the reason why the country was under martial law was 'because that was the only Constitution the armed forces know.' But he assured the ambassadors that he was there only to hold the fort and to hold elections; it was for the politicians to agree among themselves and make up the ground rules. However behind this façade of *bonhomie*, Yahya's people were already at work preparing the ground to consolidate his personal position. He himself dropped a broad hint. In assuring the envoys that he had no desire to stay on as Martial Law Chief a day longer than he had to, he added, 'But many politicians are asking me, "Sir, where do you think you will go after the elections?"'

No one could have foreseen at that time the abyss into which the man was going to lead the country.

NOTES

[1] In Tashkent, Bhutto had mildly complained about this to Gromyko, who denied it and waxed indignant. But as it happened, Bhutto had in his pocket the text of a contract signed only a few days previously for the supply of Soviet aircraft to India, but wisely, he decided not to confront Gromyko with it.

CHAPTER 9

CAIRO—1968-1971

In June 1967, Pakistan's government-controlled media acting on official 'Press advice', were publishing news about the Middle East War taken only from official Arab news agencies—breathtaking stories of scores of Israeli planes downed by the Egyptian Air Force, of Syrian troops advancing on Tel Aviv, and a variety of other triumphs bordering on the miraculous and spelling Israel's impending doom. At a lunch in Islamabad, I turned to a senior army officer seated next to me and remarked upon the marvellous progress made by the Arab forces in the decade since the Suez War. He gave me a quizzical look as if to see whether I was joking and said, 'The marvel would be if they last out a week!'

The point of the story is not the Pakistani general's prescience but the use and abuse of bluff in diplomacy. The Six-Day War was never meant to be. It ended in the worst military defeat suffered by the Arabs at Israel's hands and from the consequences of which they may never fully recover. It came about as the result of a particular turn in the disputation that was endemic at the time among Arab states. Egypt and Jordan for some reason had been indulging in a war of words and Radio Jordan, among other things, had taunted Nasser for being faint-hearted in supporting his Syrian brothers against Israeli threats. Nasser's war-like words and moves, while they were addressed by name to Israel, were actually directed at Jordan for the benefit of Syria, which nominally remained part of the United Arab Republic. But there was also the Soviet Union's rather odd role in the affair for it was Soviet Ambassador Sergei Vinogradov who had woken up Nasser in the middle of one night to warn him of an imminent Israeli attack on Syria. Some Egyptians believed that the Soviets had thus deliberately pushed Nasser into taking actions that provoked an Israeli attack, thereby nipping in the bud an incipient Egyptian *rapprochement* with the United States—a rather far-fetched thesis.

At all events, whoever was bluffing whom, when Nasser closed the Straits of Tiran to Israeli ships and started talking about throwing Israel into the sea, he was not expecting Israel to call his bluff. In a public statement in Cairo a year after the war, he said that in asking Secretary-General U Thant to remove UN troops from the cease-fire line, it was not his intention that they should be pulled out of the whole area.[1] He had certainly done nothing to prepare the country or the armed forces for the eventuality of an Israeli attack. On the contrary, in order to lend credibility to the tough words he was addressing to Israel, he moved substantial forces across the Sinai desert to the Israeli border where they were an easy target for Israeli aircraft and armour, and were picked off like flies when the fighting started.[2]

I was posted as ambassador to Egypt in 1968 after four years on the India desk in the Foreign Ministry—a desk where all the action was during those years. But now the excitement was over and things were beginning to pall. Cairo presented a new challenge in the aftermath of its Six-Day War with Israel. I accepted the posting—my first as head of mission—with some trepidation because it had usually been filled by men with established reputations and greater experience than I, and also because Cairo was a capital with which Pakistan's relations had not always been of the happiest.

Beirut—where we stopped *en route* for a couple of days of rest and recreation—was at the time like an extension of the Côte d' Azur with luxury hotels and smart boutiques, girls in bikinis lining the beaches and pool sides, crowded casinos, and a sophisticated night-life. At night the city's skyline was lit up brilliantly; there was not the slightest sign that this was the capital of a country officially at war. Beirut was boom town at this period; the playground of the oil-rich Sheikhs from the Gulf. However money was pouring in not only from the Arab oil countries but had been brought in, along with their business acumen and varied skills, by Palestinian refugees. It seemed a long time back to 1958 when American marines had landed on the beaches to save the Chamoun government from a Nasser-inspired overthrow. There were few signs to indicate that all was not as it seemed and a civil war was to overtake all this in a few short years.

Cairo is one of those world cities, like New York or Venice, that have been shaped by their geography as much as by history and whose form and physical shape reflect a distinctive, almost legendary quality. Squeezed between the sands of the desert with the Nile snaking through it, with the silent pyramids brooding over a hundred minarets and domes, modern high-rise towers and Louis XVIII mansions, arabesque façades and latticed windows, the city is at once Islamic and Pharaonic, European and African, modern and ageless. In spite of its Third World hurly-burly and the socialist slogans scrawled on walls, there was still a turn of the century elegance about the city. Many of the famous hotels and restaurants—Sheapard's, the Mina Palace, Groppis—and the beautiful opera house built by Khedive Ismail for the inaugural celebrations of the Suez Canal, were still there, evoking a bygone age of pashas and khwajas and imperial proconsuls. It was curious that this should be so, for Nasser's revolution was to some extent aimed against the Egypt that these things and names represented; an Egypt in which Egyptians had played a subordinate role and the fellahin counted for nothing. In fact the revolution had not made a clean sweep but, in keeping with the temperate national character, settled for the middle ground in many things. Thus the very exclusive Gezira Club was allowed to stay, but was partially proletarianized by having it open its doors once a week to the general public. The club's polo ground was turned into a football field; on the other hand, the golf course suffered only a reduction in the number of its holes from thirty-six to twenty-seven.

In Cairo itself there was little evidence of wartime tension—no signs or sense of defeat, no heightened alertness. Black-outs were in force but were observed in the breach. Even when Israeli air raids took place on Cairo, no sirens blew and at night the city continued to be brightly lit up. Everyone went about his daily business unconcerned. It was a sign of fortitude but there was in it a part of apathy and a feeling that Egypt's fate was once again in the hands of others. But there were also undertones of bitterness and anger. At an embassy dinner an Egyptian town planner said to me: 'Egypt lost 20,000 men in the war. What have we given them? A minute's silence on the war's anniversary. The night-clubs, the bars, the restaurants, the lights, everything is on as if Egypt had not suffered its worst defeat!' It was a curious paradox that things came to a head not during Nasser's time nor against Nasser who was the author of the Arab disaster, but against Sadat who had started to undo some of its consequences.

In 1952 when King Farouk was overthrown, Nasser had stayed in the background at first and only slowly did he come to the forefront as the man behind the Egyptian revolution. In the years since, he had come to occupy the centre of the Third World stage, by the side of figures like Nehru, Sukarno and Tito. Like many younger Arabs he admired Gandhi and Nehru for their fight against British imperialism. Nehru himself valued what the friendship and support of this charismatic and progressive Muslim leader meant for India in its disputes with Pakistan. Initially Pakistan too had welcomed the revolution in Egypt but relations had soured on account of Nasser's pro-Indian leanings.

When I paid my farewell call on President Ayub before leaving to take up the post in Cairo, he cautioned me not to overdo the Islamic angle in Egypt. 'They are a very nationalistic people and a bit arrogant,' he said to me, 'they won't be taken in by talk about Islamic brotherhood and all that.'

Things had changed since the Six-Day War. When I presented my credentials to Nasser there was no sign of arrogance about him. A tall man, he appeared less imposing and looked older than I had expected. He had tired eyes—the eyes of a man living with disillusionment. But when he laughed his whole expression changed to almost boyish gleefulness. He had an unassuming manner and was a genuinely unassuming person. He spoke of Pakistan in a friendly way and told me on another occasion that he had relatives in Pakistan through his Iranian-born wife. Here was a man who had stood up to the mightiest in the world, shaken Egypt out of its torpor, and swept through the Arab world like a tornado. But now he had lost it all and this time there would be no Eisenhower to pick his chestnuts out of the fire.[3] He knew that he was living on borrowed time.

But he was still there, and so was his regime with all its institutions and repressive machinery—intelligence agencies, secret police and Press censorship. In the immediate shock of defeat, Nasser had resigned his office but had been induced to withdraw the resignation as a result of mammoth popular demonstrations begging him to stay on. He had pledged thereafter to change everything: to bring in free elections, the rule of law and personal liberties; to end Press censorship; to curb the intelligence agencies and the secret police; and to free the economy. None of this happened or was going to happen. Nasser tried to fulfill his promises by reshuffling the pack and taking some bright young new ministers into his government. A decree was published abolishing the right of the military to arrest and question people for political offences. New elections were being held to the National Assembly but Vice President Hussein el Shafei told me with a self-congratulatory air, that they had made sure that only 'good people' would be elected. It was considered a great advance when the daily *Al Ahram's* powerful editor, Hasnain Haikal, published a criticism of the Director of Intelligence for the arbitrary and unjustified arrest of a senior official on an absurd and untenable charge. These piecemeal and hesitant steps towards liberalization served only to emphasize how arbitrary and overwhelming had been and still was, the exercise of power by the State.

In November 1968 there was a serious outbreak of student trouble. It had started in a small way in the provincial city of Mansoura, the seat of an important religious college. Students of this institution were held responsible for giving a political and violent turn to the protests that began over a new regulation concerning promotion examinations. This was an early manifestation of the role of the religious factor in Egyptian politics that would later lead to Sadat's assassination and assume larger dimensions. But the disturbances spread to Alexandria's secular engineering faculty where also there was violence. For several days Alexandria was like a city besieged—students rampaged through the streets destroying everything in the way. Shouts were heard of 'Where are you, O Dayan!' The Governor of the city was manhandled when he went to reason with the demonstrators. In Cairo, helicopters circled the city, educational institutions were closed, and faculty members were among the many arrested as a precautionary measure. One got news of these happenings not from the local Press but from the BBC which made the point that whereas popular demos in Arab countries were generally directed against Zionism, Imperialism, etc., this time the Egyptian regime and its leaders were themselves the targets; moreover, the students' anger was directed not against unnamed 'centers of power' or their direct boss the Interior Minister, but at Nasser himself.

It so happened that Miangul Aurangzeb of Swat and his wife Naseem (who was President Ayub's daughter) were visiting us in Cairo during those very days and Nasser had invited them and my wife and me to tea *en famille*. He was relaxed and smiling and showed not the least sign of being under strain of any kind. A short time earlier, President Ayub had been facing troubles of his own in the streets of Lahore, Karachi, and other cities, and the first thing Nasser said to us was, 'You were having trouble last month and now its our turn!'

Six months later, after Ayub's resignation, he said more on the subject when I delivered to him Yahya Khan's letter explaining the Pakistan developments. Nasser was surprised at the sudden explosion of discontent and violence in Pakistan and expressed particular concern on account of Pakistan's 'difficult geographic and political' situation—a reference, I supposed, to the possibility of India making trouble. He praised President Ayub's 'generous and large-hearted nature'.

He said that he had advised President Ayub to give social content to his policy and to organize his political movement on the basis of a social programme. 'It is never wise to arrest students,' he said, 'but equally unwise to let them off easily once they are arrested. One should preferably not use force against people of this kind, but if force has to be used, it must be used effectively.'[4] He recalled that in 1954 the growing differences between the 'Revolutionary Council' (that is, himself) and Naguib, the nominal head of the regime, had come to a head. A million people were out in the streets, demonstrating against the regime and crying for Nasser's blood. President Naguib was haranguing the crowds from the balcony of the Abedin Palace, promising all things to all men—democracy, social justice, Islam—and was enjoying every minute of it. In fact Naguib was being used as a pawn by the Communists and the Ikhwan ul Muslimeen who had joined hands for the sole purpose of ousting Nasser. He said that he then went to Naguib and warned him that if his harangues did not stop at once, he would resign there and then and leave him to face the music: 'I told Naguib that the crowds who were now cheering him would then be after *his* blood.' It was touch and go Nasser said, for he had withdrawn all units of the army and police from the city. 'Not to appease the crowds,' he said candidly, 'but because I was afraid that they too might join the movement.' Fortunately Naguib funked and by this time, he said, the 'workers' who were still with him—whom his Intelligence Services had no doubt infiltrated into the crowds—got to work breaking up pro-Naguib groups, telling them that he would bring back all the old pashas and corrupt politicians and feudal lords. From then on Naguib went downhill and his wings were clipped little by little and eventually he was divested of all power and position. Naguib, Nasser said, knew nothing of politics or government and had been put at the head of the revolutionary regime only because it was felt that Egyptians would not like the idea of being ruled by a young man of thirty-three. Nasser said that there were still elements in the country hostile to him and his regime. These were people who had lost power, property or positions as a result of the revolution. 'We know exactly who they are,' he said, 'and after 300 or so of them are locked up things would go back to normal.' He said that he was under pressure from both the far left and the far right. However in the case of the current student troubles he seemed to blame the religious elements. He could not understand why this was so for he had already released 500 out of the 800 Muslim Brotherhood people who were in detention. At one time, he added, he had no less than 18,000 of the Brotherhood locked up! The Ikhwan had been receiving help, he said, not only from Saudi Arabia but the United States and West Germany.

Nasser recalled how some years earlier, a member of the Ikhwan had fired eight shots at him at a public meeting in Alexandria. People standing near him had been hit but he himself escaped unhurt. His daughter broke in to recount how Tahir, her youngest brother, had leapt up and pulled Nasser down to the floor of the platform as soon as the first bullet was fired. In the general mêlée, Nasser continued, the top of a red-ink fountain-pen he was carrying in his breast pocket came off and red ink leaked all over his shirt. Those who saw this thought he was mortally wounded and there was consternation and panic for a while.

The Ikhwan has a long history of political struggle and martyrdom. They are single-minded men dedicated to their cause and fired by zeal. Arrests and executions had weakened neither their resolve and will to power, nor their organization. The factors on which a party of this type flourishes had not disappeared—

quite the contrary. In adversity one tends to turn to religion for solace. In Egypt too there was a certain resurgence of religious feeling and observance. On the political plane, after long years of being fed on socialist slogans, people were tending to swing away from the left and if some stopped half-way at liberalism, many went all the way to the extreme right.

Not that the Nasser regime was socialist in the 'godless' Marxist sense. Nasserism was an ideology of the Third World—populist, bureaucratic, anti-Western and basically a cover for one-man rule. Nasser and his comrades had little tolerance for Communists, so much so that some of them were opposed to seeking Soviet help in building heavy industry and the Nile High Dam for fear that it would bring in Communist influence. Nasser had kept large numbers of Egyptian communists in jail until the Soviets interceded on their behalf after the June War.[5]

The place and role of religion in the Nasser regime was somewhat curious. Among the first things the Revolutionary Council did on seizing power in 1952, was to abolish the Shariat laws that had prevailed in the country (side by side with the Code Napoléon), because the overthrown feudal regime had used them to suppress and exploit the people. But Egypt was not in a formal sense a secular country since Islam remained the state religion and the imams and the sheikhs were all on the government's payroll. Many of the revolutionary officers were devout Muslims and some, like Anwar Sadat, had been members of the Muslim Brotherhood. Nasser himself was a religious person and told me that as a young army captain he had read all the works of Maulana Maududi. 'But,' he added, 'religion is sometimes misused for political purposes.'

The issue of religion was raised in a meeting of the Arab Socialist Union by a member, Sheikh Ashur of the Abdul Abbas Mosque in Cairo. He blamed the prevailing malaise in the country on the decline of religious values, the wearing of miniskirts, drinking of alcohol and the general prevalence of Sin. He said that the blame for the 'religious vacuum' should be laid not only at the door of students but of the members of the National Congress as well. He said he once attended a symposium on socialism to which the main speaker had arrived in an air-conditioned Mercedes car worth 7,000 pounds wearing a diamond ring on his finger, and had lectured the gathering on the need for austerity. Nasser who had joined in the laughter when the venerable Sheikh mimicked a girl walking in a miniskirt, said,

> I consider our country to be in the forefront of those that adhere to religion as universally recognized. The revolution also worked for religion and I can tell Sheikh Ashur and his colleagues that it is also their job to teach religious values, for which they get paid...
>
> At the outset of the revolution I was called upon to take a number of steps in regard to religion, on the ground that what could not be achieved by the exhortations of the Koran should be enforced by the authority of the State. But we could not concede these demands because that would have restricted all the freedoms to which we are accustomed in this country and from which we have not retracted. As for miniskirts, if a law is enacted banning the dress, it would give the police the power to stop every girl on the street to check whether she was wearing a miniskirt or not...It is for the family itself to see to such things...One may ask how we learnt our religion. We learnt it from our families. Our fathers taught us what is good and what is evil.

Ten days after the student riots, Nasser explained matters to the National Congress of the Arab Socialist Union. His statement was a mixture of reproof and apology, with a refrain of 'I don't understand' running through its length. But he put things in perspective at once by stating that the changes he had promised had already been made. As an example he mentioned the debate about to begin in the National Congress 'within the sight and hearing of the whole country'—this, he claimed, was something 'new, positive, singular and healthy'. Laws concerning arrest and detention had been amended. 400 Muslim Brothers had been released and only 400 were still detained—anyway, he said, the purpose of detention was to 'enlighten' the person and then release him; new elections were to be held to the National Assembly; student demands had been met; economic and fiscal reforms were under study and the Press was provided with the greatest amount of liberty and freedom! Then he warned that open society did not mean open capitalist society, but open revolutionary society. Neither the Press nor anyone could be given the freedom to express or conduct counter-revolution.

At the time of the student riots the Paris daily *Le Monde* wrote that though he still had some chance, his regime and institutions had none. Indeed the Nasser era that had signified so much to the world, one way or another, was over and Nasser himself was on trial. The defeat had thrown everything into question—Egypt's position in the Middle East and its policy towards the great powers; the usefulness of non-alignment; the price of Egypt's adventures in places like Lebanon and Yemen; and the merits of socialism. Linked to the answers to these questions were questions regarding the legitimacy of Nasser's regime and its institutions and his own position.

As long as Nasser's gambles had paid off, the Egyptian people had gloried in the pride and dignity he brought to the country. They did not notice or had overlooked, the hardships inflicted on many by the arbitrary, vindictive and whimsical manner in which the state's authority was exercised in the name of socialism. Not that the regime had brought no material benefits to the ordinary people—bread was cheap; education was free at all levels; medical facilities were much improved; industry and employment were created; and the High Dam was built.

But the mood of Egypt in those difficult years alternated between bouts of fervour and apathy. The morrow of the war and defeat had seen Nasser being acclaimed as a hero; now the feeling had changed to frustration and pent up anger at promises unfulfilled or betrayed. After years of being fed on slogans about socialism, people in general did not have the stomach for more of it. The presence in Egypt of hordes of intrusive and overbearing and thrifty Russians, and, possibly, also the invasion of Czechoslovakia, had soured the attitude towards the Soviet Union.[6] Socialism, in Egypt as in most Third World countries, essentially meant the rule of the bureaucracy. The Arab Socialist Union was a make-shift ideological façade for one-man rule, whose real sanction lay in its control of the armed forces, the secret police, and intelligence agencies; in short, the apparatus of state power.

In his book *The Philosophy of the Revolution*,[7] written in his days of glory, Nasser had spoken of Egypt as a hero in search of a role. The role Nasser was required to play at present was not of a heroic mold and he seemed oddly unfit to play it. When Nasser addressed crowds now, mechanically repeating the old indictments and denunciations, his voice was low-pitched and slightly querulous, his manner schoolmasterly; the applause he received was mechanical and orchestrated. When he said that the enemy's first target was he himself and his revolution, he was not wrong. But Israel was not the sole adversary of Nasser. There were many among the Arab fraternity—King Faisal, Bourguiba of Tunisia and probably the Syrians too—who would not have minded seeing the last of him. The Anglo-Americans of course would have been glad to see him go but were not sure who or what might come in his place. However none of this seemed to create the martyr's halo around Nasser's head or bring back the old fervour.

He was right in saying that he was under attack from both the extreme right and the extreme left. This had been the case from the beginning. What was changed, and this is what he did not want to recognize, was that the people in the middle, the ordinary people who had idolized and followed him, were no longer inclined to do so. When the new National Assembly opened in January, it was, as Hussein el Shafie had promised, an assemblage of 'good people' selected from various classes and conditions— *tarbooshes*, *galabiyahs* and skull-caps were scattered amidst dark business suits. Nasser spoke in stirring words, from a prepared text: 'We shall not let go of an inch of our soil. We shall fight for every grain of sand. We shall fight for every green stalk that grows on our plains and in our valleys and on our cherished mountains.' He uttered these Churchillian phrases in a nasal monotone, the words falling like stones in a pond, raising automatic ripples of applause.

The Egyptian people were dispirited and tired of glory. They wanted nothing but that the weight of bureaucracy be taken off their backs and the burden of constant tension lifted from their minds. But Nasser seemed to have become a prisoner of his own preconceptions and institutions, and was clearly understating his problems in saying that things could be put right by sending some more people to jail. Of course Nasser was by no means reduced to the position where he could not control events. If he was no longer a hero, if his popularity was diminished, his image remained untarnished as a man of unquestioned personal integrity, who continued to live in the simple house of the Colonel he was when he had launched the revolution and who, above all, had stood up to those great powers who had for nearly a century dominated and derided Egypt. Most Egyptians saw

Nasser not as the man who had led them into the wilderness, but as the one who could still rally the people and lead them out of the maze.

The most important change wrought by the Six-Day War, was of course in the overall relation of Egypt and the other affected Arab countries, to Israel. What had been implicit and latent uptil then, was now explicit and actual: peace in the Middle East would be made on Israel's terms and the dream of restoring a Palestinian entity in some shape or form, was now more difficult to realize than ever, if indeed it had not become altogether unattainable. The Arabs had reacted to the situation with defiance and the Arab League summit held shortly after the war in Khartoum, decreed the three negatives *vis-à-vis* Israel: no recognition, no negotiation, no peace treaty. The declaration was made in a spirit of proud defiance, a refusal to accept Israel's—and America's—terms for peace. But it was based on a complete misreading of Israel's scarcely concealed intentions. The idea that Arab recognition, a peace treaty, etc., were prizes that Israel coveted above all else, may have been true at one time, but time had moved on and entirely new prospects had opened up before Israel as a result of its 1967 victory.

Israel knew that any settlement with the Arabs would be a settlement imposed by outside powers or by circumstances, and it had been Israel's policy throughout to create such circumstances. Israel was of course interested in diplomatic recognition and peace treaties, but as the peripheral consequences of Israeli domination. This could be ensured not by Arab acceptance but by the proxy power of the United States. Thus Israel participated in the UN's mediatory efforts and other peace-making initiatives mainly to the end of gaining time in order to 'create facts' that could not be undone. The Arab reluctance to negotiate face to face with Israel, their refusal to sign a peace treaty and other such formalistic considerations, served in fact to further this Israeli purpose.

In truth the Khartoum Declaration was aimed as much at Egypt as at Israel, for it was feared that Egypt might make a separate peace and leave the other affected Arab parties—Jordan, Syria and the Palestinians—to fend for themselves. This is what Egypt did in fact do some years later when Sadat signed the Camp David Agreement. Sadat paid with his life for doing so. However the truth is that Nasser himself had come to the bitter conclusion that the Arab cause was lost and that Egypt would now have to come to terms with the realities, going it alone if necessary.

In public Nasser often declared, 'What was taken from us by force can only be regained by force.' Hasnain Haikal wrote every week in *Al Ahram* about the coming 'Battle of Destiny', analysing brilliantly but wishfully, how Egypt need not actually win a war but only a battle, in order to achieve its ends; such a limited military success, Haikal held and many Egyptians believed, would suffice to bring home to tiny Israel its tininess and the fact that it was surrounded and out-numbered. Israel was of course only too well aware of these handicaps and had brilliantly designed a policy to neutralize them. It had managed to harness Western, and in particular United States' diplomatic and military power to its own ends.

Sometimes the Egyptian reading of the situation relied on a sort of logic of despair. Dr Mahmoud Fawzi, a seasoned diplomat of the old school, and at the time President Nasser's Adviser on Foreign Affairs, once explained matters to me in the following terms: if there was another war and the Arabs were gaining the upper hand, the US would intervene immediately to stop them in their tracks; the US would then impose a settlement that would not please either side, but it would guarantee Israel's security and ensure peace and stability in the region for perhaps fifty years; if on the other hand, Israel won and acquired more Arab territories, it would cease to be the Jewish homeland. So, he concluded, Israel would win by losing and lose by winning.[8]

It sometimes seemed as if the Egyptians wished events to take matters out of their hands and let fate and history settle things for Egypt as they so often had in its 7,000-year history. The fallacy in Dr Fawzi's line of thought was that there was no reason why Israel should embark on further territorial conquests. If the Israelis perceived a military threat from any Arab country, they would see to it that the threat was destroyed without having to take over the offending country. This is precisely what the United States would do for Israel a quarter of a century later when Saddam Hussain's adventure against Kuwait demonstrated the potential of danger from Iraq.

The oracular Mr Haikal's euphemism to describe Egyptian policy was: 'refusal to disengage from battle'. In a war of attrition, he said, the Arabs could overcome Israel's technological superiority by raising the enemy's losses beyond the point he could endure. Arab manpower could sustain the loss of 50,000 men, he affirmed, but if Israel were to lose 10,000 men out of its small population, it would be forced to sue for peace. Furthermore the Arabs could force Israel to seek terms merely by extending hostilities beyond the period—approximately three weeks—during which Israel could maintain the total mobilization of its manpower and resources.

Nasser himself took a realistic view of the military situation. Speaking to me on the subject in 1969, he said that on the ground Egyptian forces had the latest artillery, ground-to-ground missiles and other advanced equipment. They had succeeded in destroying the Bar Lev Line[9] so that they now could and did cross the Suez Canal at will. Sinai no longer offered any substantial targets and in order to make an impact Egypt must hit from the air at Israel proper. But Egypt was weak in the air, he said. The Egyptian Air Force had received top-of-the-line Soviet aircraft but the pilots had learned only to fly them and not yet to use them as weapons. He said that some of his advisers thought that defence was the most effective tactic for the Arabs but he himself felt that defence without deterrence would be ineffective and that Egypt must think in terms of hitting back at the Israeli home base. However, he was aware of the risks: it would amount to another defeat for Egypt if the exercise had to stop after making one or two raids. That is why he had resisted pressure from his people to launch retaliatory raids against Israeli attacks.

Rather curious in this context was Egypt's reaction to reports that began to appear around this time about Israel's nuclear capability. I asked Dr Fawzi why so little had appeared in the Egyptian newspapers about a story that was making headlines in the world Press. He said that Egypt had decided as a matter of policy, to play down this question in order prevent the creation of unnecessary alarm among the people. He did not say what Egypt would do if it were established that Israel had made a nuclear bomb. Nasser was asked about the matter in an American TV interview and said that if Israel produced nuclear weapons, Egypt had the technicians and would do it too. But actually Egypt did not even have a functioning research reactor at the time and the Russians were sure to thwart any Egyptian attempt in that direction. Anyway nothing further was heard on the matter.

Haikal's rationale of Egypt's stand was revealing:

> ...refusal to disengage from battle with the enemy was and remains a continual warning to world public opinion, drawing its attention to the gravity of the crisis in the Middle East. If the Cease-Fire Lines become stabilized there would be no justification for keeping the Middle East crisis on the top of the international agenda—it would be put away in the 'mammoth refrigerator' of the world's unresolved problems.

In other words, the booming of guns across the Canal was not a prelude to war but a substitute for it. (I was struck by the parallel between this policy and the thinking underlying Pakistan's Kashmir policy.)

But in any case there was a limit to what could be achieved by such a 'Battle of Destiny', at best, a separate peace for Egypt; and this was what Egypt obtained as a result of the 1973 War. 1973 also demonstrated the limits of American even-handedness in the Middle East—the United States would *not* allow Israel to be defeated; the United States could not maintain real pressure on Israel on almost any matter that Israel considered vital to its interests or ambitions.

In reality Egypt was not seriously thinking of war and had come a long way since the 1967 War towards accepting the peace terms set by Israel and the United States. A conclusive, victorious war was never a real option for the Arabs. The Egyptians had given Israel a bruising in the firing across the Canal and the fedayeen had set off bombs in Tel Aviv. The Israelis had retaliated by bombing Cairo and carrying out commando raids and terrorist attacks of their own. There was no illusion in Egypt that the Israelis could be expelled by military force. It was not a question of the superior military competence or greater motivation of the Israeli compared to the Egyptian—these were transitory factors whose importance was exaggerated by the Western Press—but of geopolitical fundamentals. The Soviets had rebuilt Egypt's armed forces at great speed to the point that a few years after their destruction by Israel, they were among the most modern and best-equipped in the Third World. However the Soviets had made Egypt strong enough only to deter an Israeli crossing of the Suez Canal but not to allow Egypt itself to do so. In December 1969 a high-powered Soviet delegation visited Cairo in response to pressing requests to build up Egypt's offensive capability. The Soviets promised some aid but a Foreign Ministry official told me that they were more liberal with counsels of patience and restraint. Nasser asked them plainly what would be the Soviet attitude in the event that attempts to find a peaceful settlement failed and Egypt was forced to take up arms. The Soviets promised to stand by Egypt but said so in too roundabout a way to carry conviction.

Egypt looked for someone to pull its chestnuts from the fire and it relied on the cold war competition to provide the moving force. In the circumstances, paradoxically, the mediator could only be the United States. The Soviet Union was Egypt's great friend and ally at the time and its diplomatic and military support was indispensable to Egyptian policy. But Soviet support and aid to Egypt could not match what the United States was willing to give to and do for Israel. America's vast storehouse of weapons and its tactical intelligence were open to Israel to the extent of its needs (as would be seen in the 1973 War). But there existed also a qualitative difference in the attitudes of the two superpowers towards their respective Middle East clients: the US had come to identify its own strategic and economic interests with those of Israel; on the other hand, the peace settlement that the Soviets themselves were advocating was not so very different from what the Americans were proposing.

The United States and the Soviet Union were not in conflict in the Middle East, but in competition. The cold war in the region was not over the future map of the place but its alignment. The Soviets had no desire to see another war break out and to a considerable extent, they were in a position (surely to the satisfaction of the United States) to control events through the presence within the Egyptian Armed Forces of Soviet advisers in large numbers and at various levels. The Soviet desire to avoid a confrontation with the US and to resume the movement towards peaceful coexistence, was so manifest at that time that the periodical Arab predictions of a world conflagration over the Middle East did not carry conviction.

Though Soviet military involvement in Egypt had grown steadily since 1967, on the whole their influence was being exerted on the Arabs to recognize the 'realities' of the situation facing them. A year after the war, Foreign Minister Gromyko brought to Cairo a five-stage peace proposal which proposed that an agreement be negotiated through the UN mediator on 'secure and agreed' borders for Israel—hence, not necessarily the lines of 5 June 1967. During the PLO trouble in Jordan in 1969, the Soviets were a restraining influence on Iraq and Syria. At a dinner party at that time, I was seated between the Soviet Ambassador Vinogradov and the ambassador of Jordan, Hazim Nesseibah. Vinogradov leaned across and said to him, 'In principle we are anti-monarchist, but in Jordan we support the King. The Soviet Union would not like King Hussein's position to be weakened.' The Soviets had no time at all for someone like George Habash[10] of the PFLP, and considered him to be 'sold' to China; but even towards a moderate like Arafat their sympathy had evolved slowly. The Moscow monthly *Soviet Russia* wrote in April '69, 'The objectives which the Al Fatah and other Palestinian organizations have set themselves, i.e., the liquidation of Israel and the establishment of a democratic Palestine state, are not realistic. It would be difficult to undo history and recreate a Palestinian people consisting of Jews and Arabs.' When Nasser accepted the US Secretary of State Rogers' Peace Plan, the Soviets lauded the action and rebuked those who called for a prolonged war. Indeed the Soviet Union held that it was 'not admissible to seek "self-determination" for some at the price of completely denying national rights to other peoples'—a clear endorsement, it would seem, of the Jewish right to a homeland.

Yes, the peace that was available to Egypt could only be brought about by the United States. Yet Egypt's relations with the United States were marked by a peculiar and tortured ambivalence. On the one hand there was scepticism about America's willingness and ability to bring about a fair settlement. 'What American Middle East policy?' Foreign Minister Mahmoud Riad said to me. 'The views of the Rostow brothers!'[11] He went on to ask a rhetorical question: 'Can you really see the four great powers coming together to force Israel to withdraw from all occupied territories? And even if they agreed to do so, what means do they have of forcing Israel to accept?' Israel had military power on the ground and political clout in the places that mattered.

The Egyptian attitude towards the United States was a mixture of fury and hope, rancour and wishfulness. In Egypt the memory had not yet faded of the Suez War when Eisenhower had compelled three of America's closest allies and friends to step back and disgorge the gains of the war. I found an unspoken expectation at the popular level, and even among some officials, that despite everything, this time too the Americans would step in to redress the situation. When Nixon was elected as President in the 1968 elections, some Egyptian newspapers recalled wistfully that he had been Eisenhower's Vice President at that time. Despite their instinctive scepticism and ceaseless strictures against United States' policy, Egyptians were looking forward to Nixon's advent with a mixture of eagerness and anxiety, seeing signs of hope in the fact that American Jews had voted in general for the Democratic candidate, Hubert Humphrey, and in Israel's unhappiness at Nixon's win. Nasser wrote a very friendly personal letter to the President-elect in the hope of influencing his thinking. 'All that I remember of our meeting in Cairo in 1963 and all that you said to me at that time,' he wrote, 'leads me to believe that the trust that the American nation has placed in you will have an important bearing upon certain international situations.'

Nixon responded by despatching Governor William Scranton to the Middle East as his special envoy, and Scranton, speaking of 'a more even-handed' American policy in the region, created a bit of a flutter (not least of all, in the Israeli lobby in Washington who soon put him to rights). However the new administration's Assistant Secretary of State, Joseph Sisco, put matters in perspective again, saying bluntly to the Egyptian Foreign Minister, 'After all when you lose a war you must be prepared to pay a price.'[12]

Nasser was indeed prepared to pay a price and a high enough one—acceptance of the Israeli-American interpretation of Security Council resolution 242; minor border rectifications (of the West Bank-Jordan border; Egypt's own borders were not in question); recognition;[13] in due course, diplomatic relations; trade, etc. with Israel. Nasser would not make a peace treaty with Israel but was willing to sign a 'peace agreement'—a quibble. Before the idea of a separate Egypt-Israel peace was proposed in the Rogers' package, Egypt had agreed to it in accepting the

Gromyko peace plan of November 1968. Dr Mahmoud Fawzi told me then that Egypt was prepared to go ahead without Syria and take upon itself the onus of accepting a peaceful settlement with Israel. Then Sisco came to Cairo to press Nasser to break yet another Khartoum taboo: agree to direct face to face talks with the Israelis. Nasser said to him, 'You aren't really asking me to receive that old lady [Golda Meir] in this room!' The Turkish ambassador who told me this piece of diplomatic gossip, took it to imply that a meeting in another place or under other circumstances was not to be ruled out.

Yet it all came to nothing under Nasser, though the premise at the time was that only Nasser had the popular standing to be able to sell an agreement with Israel to the Arab people. Only when Nasser was dead and his successor sent troops across the canal and himself went to Jerusalem, that peace came and it was the same peace that Nasser had been prepared and eager to make—a separate peace on basically Israeli terms. Sadat did not make a break with Nasser on the matter of war and peace, but he changed many other things: he turned out the Soviets; he went to beard the lion in his den. Logic is not all in relations among men or states. In diplomacy, reasonableness is often viewed as a sign not of wisdom but of weakness. America may have seen in Nasser's new-found moderation an indication of his helplessness. Sometimes gestures may be all in diplomacy—Nasser had said all the right things, but Sadat made the two or three gestures that mattered. Even sending Egyptian troops across the Canal in 1973 was a gesture—a proving of Egypt's manhood, a warning to the world to do something about peace in the Middle East, and an assurance to Egyptian pride that he was making peace from a position of strength.

The three years between the 1967 War and the death of Nasser were nevertheless, a period of intense, almost non-stop diplomatic activity. Far from being frozen in the 'mammoth refrigerator' of the world's lost causes, the Arab-Israeli conflict, and in particular the Egyptian side of it, was at the centre of international concern during that time. First came the Security Council's mediator, Gunnar Jarring (who some years before and vainly, had tried his hand at mediating the Kashmir dispute).[14] Jarring's comings and goings served only to clarify that the gulf between the Arabs and Israelis would not be bridged by conventional diplomacy. Foreign

Minister Mahmoud Riad described as the 'Battle of the Ticker Tapes' the questionnaires Jarring cabled to one side and the other and the answers he received from each. Israel chose to see the Security Council's resolution 242 as an agenda of Arab-Israeli negotiations whereas for the Arabs it was a Security Council decision that had to be implemented. The resolution's language was interpreted by Israel to mean that 'it was reconcilable with a broad variety of solutions' (for example, on the matter of withdrawal from occupied territories and defining 'secure' borders).

Then Nixon's Secretary of State, William Rogers, came to Cairo himself and impressed those he met with his sincerity and honesty. However when he put forward his peace plan it was found to be not very different from the proposals made by his predecessor, Dean Rusk, in the Johnson administration's closing days. A Foreign Ministry official told me that the visit had been fruitful and added 'but fruitful does not mean satisfactory.' Secretary Rogers commended Egypt for its co-operative attitude; he acknowledged that Israel's replies to various peace moves had been deficient in that Israel 'had only indicated what it would not do but hadn't said what it *would* do.' However Rogers answered Egypt's questions with the three American Nos: No pressure on Israel; No halt in military supplies to Israel; No action through the Security Council. 'Pressure is an ugly word,' said the US Secretary of State, at a press conference before he left Cairo, betraying an unaccustomed fastidiousness.

The Americans did not budge an inch from the position they had taken from the beginning, despite pleas and threats, alarums and inducements:[15] an end to the state of war and belligerency against Israel; withdrawal from occupied territories, yes, but as the result of an agreement to be negotiated, preferably in direct talks; while the agreement 'cannot and should not reflect the weight of conquest', the 'secure and recognized boundaries' to which Israel would withdraw need not be identical with the lines held prior to 5 June 1967; the problem of Palestinian refugees should also be settled through negotiations (as to the number that Israel would take back);[16] and the Suez Canal should be opened to international navigation, including Israeli ships. What it boiled down to, in the view of Foreign Minister Riad, was that everything was made subject to negotiation and agreement (in other words, to Israeli approval) except two matters, that is,

Jerusalem and navigation through Arab waters for Israeli vessels. On both of these the Israeli position was conceded right from the start without benefit of negotiation or discussion. (On Jerusalem the United States managed to eat its cake and have it too, by refusing to recognize the city as Israel's capital while holding that it must not be divided again.) 'And what is America doing to bring about peace in the Middle East?' Mahmoud Riad asked, and answered his own rhetorical question: 'Negotiating the sale of Phantom aircraft to Israel!'[17] In the circumstances, he said, America's support for the Security Council's resolution had no greater value than that of Zambia's!

The 22 November 1967 resolution of the Security Council was far from meeting the wishes of the Arabs, and they had accepted it with reluctance and unhappiness considering it to be vague and ambiguous. But to its Anglo-American authors the merit of the resolution lay precisely in the 'constructive ambiguity' of its language. In other words, each side could interpret it to mean what they wanted it to mean. When it was being drafted, the Arabs had put up a stubborn fight to have the resolution call on Israel to withdraw from 'the' Arab territories it had occupied, in the belief that the definite article would carry the meaning that *all* occupied territories were to be evacuated. They lost the argument; it was perhaps an ill-advised point to insist on, for when it was lost, the omission of the definite article came to acquire a significance that in plain language it probably did not have. Thus for more than a quarter of a century an obscure and probably misconceived point of English grammar and usage became a key element in the search for peace in the Middle East. Such are the arcane ways of UN diplomacy and the pitfalls of working in a foreign language!

Now however the resolution had become the cornerstone of Egypt's Middle East policy and Egypt too could find some merit in its ambiguity. One of Nasser's problems in pursuing a policy of 'No war-No peace' was that he had to play to more than one gallery at the same time. Thanks to its ambiguity the resolution— which had not been accepted by the Palestinians, Syrians or Saudis—could be made to appear consistent with the position of the Arab hard-liners. (A rule of thumb, a cynical Egyptian friend said, was that the farther away you were from the battlefield and the less you had to lose, the harder the line you took.)

Opening the first meeting of the newly-constituted Palestine National Council, on 29 January 1969 Nasser declared:

> The Palestine resistance has the right to reject the 22 November resolution which may be sufficient for liquidating the consequences of the June 1967 aggression, but is not adequate for the Palestine destiny...I do not see in this attitude on the UAR's part any conflict with the UAR's acceptance of the resolution.

Neither Israel, nor the Palestinians saw matters in this bland light. A Palestinian said to *Le Monde's* Cairo correspondent, 'Our hope lies in the fact that Israel rejects peace in order to pursue her expansionist policy. We rely for our cause indeed on the nationalism of the Jews more than on the patriotism of the Arab leaders.' The Palestine National Council's manifesto issued in Beirut in the same month pledged not to launch struggles against any Arab state, but only on the ground that, 'One enemy at a time is enough!' However it asserted the Council's 'total and definite' rejection of political solutions and declared that the 'unique meeting place of resistance movements is the field of battle,' and that every Arab resource and capacity must be 'thrown into the crucible of revolution'. All this was a far cry from the line Egypt was following in its search for peace. For all his fiery speeches and heroic postures, Nasser was not the man for 'throwing everything into the crucible of revolution' or 'making the field of battle the unique meeting place'.

Things came to a head over the peace package put forward by Nixon's Secretary of State, William Rogers.[18] What it proposed in effect, was a separate settlement between Egypt and Israel, more or less on Israel's terms. Foreign Minister Riad's response to the basic American approach was sceptical. Nasser's own first reaction had been to say, 'Evacuation from the Golan must come even before the Sinai.' In the circumstances when Nasser suddenly turned round and gave a clear, unconditional and unambiguous approval to the American proposal, it came as a surprise to everybody—and to many as an unpleasant one. The Palestinians denounced Nasser's action in such strong terms that they were denied the use of Radio Cairo's transmitters and their movements in Egypt were ordered to be kept under close watch.

When Nasser announced his acceptance of the Rogers' Peace proposals in July 1969, King Faisal was in Algeria signing a joint communiqué which held that armed struggle by Palestinians was the *only* answer to the Middle East problem, and promised them all support. Haikal reflected Egyptian irritation by asking in his weekly column in *Al Ahram*, 'Are Arab states serving a common cause or each making use of it for its own ends?' But Arab states could surely ask the same question about Egypt's acceptance of the Rogers' plan, and indeed about Nasser's 1967 adventure.

Nasser was a hero to the Arab masses but almost all Arab governments were at odds with Egypt on account of his policies, his attempts to assume the leadership of Arab countries and his interference in their internal affairs. In my first meeting with Nasser, when I presented my credentials to him, he talked about the difficulties he was facing and said that all sorts of people, near and far, continued to attack and criticize Egypt. Mentioning Bourguiba in that context, Nasser tapped a finger on his temple and said, 'I don't know what is wrong with that man.' Bourguiba had not favoured the Khartoum Declaration and was pressing for a new Arab policy towards Israel and the United States based on a recognition of realities. In fact this was the direction in which Nasser himself was moving, but in a speech in the National Assembly he declared, 'Only a clear and overt agent of the USA could proclaim friendship for the United States in the Arab world.'[19] What really displeased Nasser was Bourguiba's attacks on him personally for having led Arabs into the 1967 disaster. Differences erupted into the open at an Arab League meeting in Cairo in September 1968 after the Tunisian delegate was cut off in mid-speech on the subject. He went outside and gave the text of his speech to the Press. It attacked Egypt for having brought misfortune upon the Arabs by taking unilateral actions, trying to assume the leadership of the Arab world, and employing sabotage and provocation against their governments. The incident was shoved under the carpet but many of those present couldn't have disagreed with a lot of this.

Before the 1967 War, Egypt and Saudi Arabia had been fighting a proxy war of their own in Yemen. Now behind the façade of the Khartoum Declaration, the state of affairs between the two countries (and at the personal level between Nasser and King Faisal) was still a prickly one. A story Nasser told me

indicated how things stood: when in the course of the Yemen
War the Saudis had sequestered Egyptian banks, Egypt had hit
back by taking over all Saudi properties in Egypt including a
palace owned by King Saud who was later removed from the
throne for ill health. When these decisions were reversed after
the Khartoum Conference, the palace was returned to ex-King
Saud who had taken up residence in Cairo after his destitution.
But now, said Nasser, King Faisal was insisting that the palace was
state property and should be given to the Saudi government
instead. Although relations with Saudi Arabia had improved and
Egypt was receiving financial assistance from the Kingdom, Nasser
said he refused to turn the ex-King out of a house where he was
living.

An Arab Summit held in Rabat in December 1969 to discuss
Arab strategy ended in accusations and counter-accusations and
complete confusion. The *Al Ahram* published an account
according to which Nasser said to the gathered Chiefs, 'Egypt
has made no request for funds but it feels that the responsibility
is of everyone, and this needs a complete pooling and marshalling
of the Arab potential...I want to know whether you are ready to
go into battle or not?' From a well-informed Western diplomat
who claimed to have seen the original minutes, I learned that
the discussion had been heated and acerbic. King Faisal said
bluntly that if there was to be a common struggle, then it should
be conducted by a joint command; he was not prepared to send
Saudi troops to fight under Egyptian command. Algeria too
supported this stand and recalled that there had been difficulties
on the Suez front between the commander of her contingent
and the Egyptian high command. On the matter of financial
assistance, Saudi Arabia made it clear that she preferred to give
it directly to the PLO. The sharpest differences were over the
question of Soviet influence in Egypt. King Faisal asserted that
Egypt was coming under Soviet domination and he was not
prepared to place Saudi troops indirectly under Soviet command
nor to contribute money to promote socialism. Faisal's suspicions
about Egyptian meddling in the kingdom's affairs were revived
by a recently discovered plot within the Saudi Army to overthrow
the monarchy. In *Al Ahram*, Haikal quoted Nasser as assuring the
King, 'We have not carried out any activity against the system of
government in Arabia since 1967. But it is true that before that

we had not been idle in this regard...' However one result of the failure of the Rabat summit to take decisions for joint action was that Egypt's freedom of action was enhanced. Nobody had risen to answer Nasser's question, but then neither did anyone question Egypt's right in the circumstances to proceed as it wished in order to liberate the territories lost in 1967, nor to pursue its efforts to reach a political settlement.

Later, under Sadat, Egypt's relations with Arab governments improved considerably but even so, speaking in the National Assembly on the occasion of May Day 1971, he said:

> In those black days of June 1967 there were many people—not our enemies but our relatives—who rejoiced and gloated at Egypt's misfortune. These kinsmen left us to struggle alone until we set up the first defence line on 23 November 1967. Then they started to draw up contracts with us to discuss prices, installments, repayment schedules.

However although Nasser's stature was diminished by the 1967 defeat and Egypt's claim to the leadership of the Arab world was no longer actively pursued, it would be wrong to think that Egypt had ceased to count in the Middle East or that Nasser himself was a spent force. On the contrary his was still a unique and dominant personality in the Arab world and his authority was still invoked in times of crisis. This happened in the troubles that erupted first in Lebanon and then in Jordan during the last months of his life.

In November 1969, Nasser's good offices helped to defuse the crisis in Lebanon between the Lebanese Army and the Palestinian fedayeen. The agreement, for co-ordination of action between them, did not resolve the roots of the Lebanese problem and did nothing to prevent the civil war that broke out a few years later. The aims of the Palestinian commandos and what the Lebanese Army was trying to do were two entirely different things. But Nasser's apparently successful intervention in a major crisis in the Middle East reaffirmed his stature in the Arab world and showed his new side as a moderate and constructive statesman. Even America must have noted that Nasser was a man with whom serious business could be done. (Israel however was not pleased at any of this and showed it by sending a Mirage to fly over Cairo roof-tops at supersonic speed, trying to frighten the inhabitants and breaking a lot of window panes.)

A more serious business was the outbreak in Jordan in September 1970—the 'Black September' of Palestinian annals. Used for two decades as pawns in the internecine rivalries of the Arab regimes, the Palestinians were now able to appeal to the Arab people over the heads of their governments, who had to reckon with the Palestine factor in their calculations of policy. The Resistance movement was now led by men of a very different calibre than the wordy and bombastic Shukairy[20] who had been succeeded by Yasser Arafat as Chairman of the Palestine National Council. These people rejected all ideas of accommodation, compromise and concession. Nor did they always respect the sovereignty or laws of their host countries. Wherever Palestinians were present in strength, they tended to act as a state within a state.

In Jordan trouble had been simmering for some time on account of these factors. Palestinians had always treated the Jordan monarch as an adversary. On the eve of the 1967 War, Shukairy was publicly urging the assassination of King Hussein as an essential first step towards meeting the Israeli threat. Now the King was thought to be moving towards a deal with Israel and suspicions concerning the King had been further inflamed when the Israeli Prime Minister, Levi Eshkol spoke of indirect contacts with Arab rulers through channels he would not disclose, but claiming that Arab rulers had heard 'interesting things' from Israel.

However when Nasser met King Hussein in August, he spoke to him with the utmost warmth. Egypt would not forget, he declared, how the King had put his forces into battle in 1967 whereas he could have stayed out and saved the West Bank and Jerusalem. With regard to the problem with his Palestinians, Nasser advised Hussein to show the patience of Job and avoid a showdown, but promised neutrality if trouble broke out. This was taken by the King as Nasser's tacit approval to any measures he might take to put it down.[21]

Nasser's support of the King was sincerely meant for if he were to fall or be weakened, Egypt would be left as the lone upholder of the Security Council resolution 242 in the Arab world. Nasser's public defence of Hussein had provoked

12. A ladies' iftar party, Cairo. (In the picture can be seen Jehan Sadat, Om Kulsum and Lala Akhund.)

13. President Nasser at home, 1969. (With him are President Ayub's granddaughter and Lala Akhund.)

14. Yahya Khan visits Cairo to condole Nasser's death, 1970.

15. 'There will never again be a Balkan question in the world...' President Josip Tito, Belgrade, 1971.

16. UN Secretary General Waldheim addresses Security Council, October 1976; author presiding.

17. An informal consultation among Security Council members. Author and permanent representatives of India and Romania, 1977.

mutterings among some Palestinian resistance groups. Nevertheless the Jordan action against the fedayeen was so forceful and ruthless that there was a great outcry and Nasser summoned an Arab summit in Cairo to consider the situation. It reached an agreement that provided for a cease-fire between the King's men and the commandos, withdrawal of the latter from Amman, and the setting up of the inevitable committee to square the circle of ensuring the continuity of guerrilla action from Jordan as well as respect for Jordanian sovereignty. Yasser Arafat the new PLO Chairman, played a restraining role in the conference whose proceedings were far from smooth. The King was in a defiant mood and asked Nasser: 'You accuse me of a war of extermination against the Palestinians. Why don't you talk about what your own soldiers and aircraft were doing in Yemen?' And turning to King Faisal, he asked, 'If even half a dozen men raised their voices against Your Majesty in Saudi Arabia, what would be their fate?'[22] The young Gaddafi was also at the meeting and looked very much the clean-cut subaltern he was before seizing power. His name was not yet a household word, but already he gave an indication of his maverick way of thinking and trenchant speech. The fault lay, he declared, neither with the king nor with Arafat, but with 'the extremism of the Arab left carried to the point of insanity, and acting as a puppet of the East and of the Arab right carried to the point of treachery, in the service of the West'.

The Western assessment at this stage was that after suffering grievous losses in Jordan, and witnessing the perfidy of Iraq and Syria's ineffectiveness, the commandos may have been brought around to taking a more realistic view of things. I asked the Jordanian ambassador in Cairo, who himself belonged to a prominent Palestinian family, about this. He said that this assessment was not too far off the mark; quite a few among the commandos had begun to believe that a Palestine entity should be established wherever it could be, and Israel itself left alone for the present. He elaborated his thoughts on the following lines:

No Palestinian organization would openly accept the 22 November resolution, but Nasser may be right in believing that he could persuade the PLO to accept a settlement on its basis because if as a result, Israel evacuated the West Bank and Gaza, not many would be left willing to continue the fight to regain the whole of Palestine.

During the Jordan fighting, Pakistan had come in for criticism for having helped to plan and carry out the operation against the commandos. It was alleged in particular that Jordan's response to the Syrian armoured intervention in the situation, known as Operation Jauhar, was planned and carried out by a Pakistani general of that name. I was approached by the PLO in Cairo with a complaint about the matter. I referred it to the government and was informed that there was no Pakistani officer by that name serving in Jordan. In fact the officer in question was General Ziaul Haq. The Palestinians brought the matter up again with Agha Shahi years later when he was lobbying at the Islamic Foreign Ministers' Conference in Dakar, Senegal, to prevent any pro-Bhutto moves at the Conference.

When Yahya Khan visited Cairo in October 1970, he himself raised the subject with Sadat and said that as Pakistan was being blamed for interfering in Jordan's internal affairs, he had written to King Hussein proposing to withdraw the Pakistani training contingent at least until the internal situation in Jordan settled down. President Sadat said that such a move would not benefit the Arab cause as a whole and urged President Yahya Khan to be patient. He said that the fedayeen had conflicts among themselves and Egypt itself was trying to help King Hussein to stabilize the situation. He said that it would be to the benefit of all the Arabs if the Pakistani military advisors continued to stay in Jordan. Nasser himself had said to me that he was grateful for Pakistan's help to Jordan, for Jordan's need was acute. He knew that a Pakistani pilot had shot down four Israeli aircraft over Syria in the 1967 War. While he didn't ask for military aid for Egypt, more than once he spoke of possible military co-operation between Pakistan and Egypt, particularly in defence production.

His moves over the Jordan events were Nasser's last diplomatic initiative in the Arab world, for shortly afterwards he died, leaving the scene with the same dramatic suddenness with which he had appeared on it eighteen years before. On learning the news, I drove out along with some members of the embassy staff, towards the President's residence. It was late at night and Nasser had been dead only a few hours, but a seemingly endless stream of people from all walks of life—students in blue jeans and bush shirts, women with scarves knotted over their heads, city workers in striped pajama suits, peasants in *galabiyas*—were already on the streets, heading towards the palace where the Rais' mortal remains had been removed to lie in state. For days from all corners of Egypt, people came in by train, car, bus, and donkey cart to pay tribute to their leader and to weep and pray together. The streets of the city were deserted, traffic was down to a trickle and the bustle of the noisy and teeming city was stilled. It was like a household deprived of its protector and breadwinner.

The funeral took place two days later amidst scenes of tumult and emotion rare in the life of nations. The coffin was brought by helicopter to the building where the original Revolutionary Council used to meet in the early years after King Farouk was overthrown. As the gun-carriage bearing the coffin and drawn by six black Arab chargers began to move between the troops lining the funeral route, cannons boomed and all broke down and sobbed like children, including stern-faced commandos and members of the honour guard, standing at attention with rifles reversed. Peasant women in black rent the air with the traditional ululation—a lamentation, half-pagan, half-Islamic that rose, so it seemed, from all Egypt to the skies. The cortege took nearly an hour to reach the end of the bridge, less than 500 yards from the starting point. When it was across the bridge, all semblance of order broke down; the crowd surged through the police lines to try to touch the coffin, and very nearly overturned it. Thereupon attempts to continue in solemn procession were abandoned, and using a certain amount of force, the police transferred the coffin to a military vehicle and sped it to the burial place. But there again a vast and agitated sea of humanity was waiting, and it was with the greatest difficulty that the Sheikh of Al Azhar said the funeral prayers and the burial took place. It was also with considerable difficulty that the foreign and other dignitaries were able to leave the Council building as it was situated on an island in the Nile and the bridges were blocked by the crowds. After a wait of several hours, with nothing to eat or drink, the increasingly restive guests were finally taken back in boats commandeered by the Protocol Department.

Anwar Sadat, who had taken over as acting-President and was receiving condolences from foreign dignitaries, collapsed at one point, apparently from exhaustion, but later the problem was diagnosed as a mild heart attack. As space in the modest Council building was very restricted and the place was packed with people, Sadat was just laid out on the floor. Until a doctor could come and proper attention be arranged, he lay there with people walking past, and at one point I saw a man simply stepping across the prone body of the Head of State. A rumour spread through the crowd that Sadat too was dead, and later it was suspected that it had been spread by one or another of the other contenders to Nasser's succession.

Kings and presidents, prime ministers and dignitaries of every kind had come from all over the world to attend the funeral. Conspicuous among those who did not come were Tito and Indira Gandhi. Pakistan was represented by Justice Abdul Malik who would the following year, preside over the last Pakistani administration of East Bengal.[23] President Nemiery who had just taken over the Sudan in a *coup* made himself conspicuous by weeping noisily throughout the proceedings. And when Sadat collapsed, Nemiery took it upon himself, along with Gaddafi and Yasser Arafat, to receive condolences from the other foreign visitors. Not content with this, he then called a meeting of the gathered Arab heads 'to assess what were the responsibilities of each in the situation created by Gamal Abdel Nasser's disappearance.' Egyptian officials, not very pleased by all this fraternal bustle, did not attend Nemiery's meeting.

Prime Minister Kosygin came from the Soviet Union and issued a homily in favour of continuing the search for a peaceful settlement. He signalled Soviet support for the Establishment by holding a meeting with the entire Egyptian Cabinet and then with Sadat and the Army Chief, General Fawzi. But he also wanted to make sure that the Egyptian Establishment would continue to be left-leaning and pro-Soviet and that persons who were not 'co-operative' would not find a place in the power structure. The United States was represented by Secretary of Health Elliot Richardson, who said nothing and sat modestly among the ranks of the ambassadors. But he had come with a strong delegation and they had a long meeting afterwards with the Acting-President Anwar Sadat (and also with Premier Kosygin). The Americans were trying to firm up the cease-fire agreement that had allegedly been violated by Egypt. The violations consisted of Egypt having moved some surface-to-air missiles into the stand-still zone, a charge Egypt denied (but was actually true, an Egyptian official told me in confidence). However the United States was making a quite disproportionate fuss over a relatively minor infringement of an ambiguous provision of the cease-fire agreement and had refused to attend further meetings of the four power talks on the Middle East until the question of the SAMs was sorted out. Foreign Minister Riad put it down to Zionist pressure at a time of congressional elections.

In fact the Americans at this stage were waiting and watching. Their main interest was to get an extension of the cease-fire and Richardson did manage to get a three-month extension from Sadat. I got an idea of Western thinking when the Canadian ambassador said to me that the hope was that the cease-fire situation might develop such a weight of its own that neither side would want to break it. The thing to do, he said, was to find ways of keeping talks and contacts going as a justification for prolonging the cease-fire. He laughed when I said, 'In other words, you want to do a Kashmir on the Arabs!' The West must have felt that they had got it right from the way Anwar al Sadat the new President went about the matter of the cease-fire, issuing ultimatums about ending it, ordering troop movements and trial black-outs, then at the last moment extending the cease-fire for another period. He added to the confusion by declaring, 'The end of cease-fire would not necessarily mean the beginning of war.' He said that 1971 was the crucial year during which the issue of war or peace should be decided. The year came and went and nothing was decided. He began to look like someone who was whistling in the dark. However, whether or not this was actually his purpose, these apparently empty threats and ultimatums worked like the perfect deception plan and lulled the Israelis and everyone else into taking Sadat for a loud-mouth whose words were not to be taken seriously!

Sadat had taken over as President quickly and smoothly. One of the remarkable features of the situation was the relative stability of Egypt. Nasser's death had not left the vacuum and uncertainty that many had expected. It gradually became clear that Sadat had no wish to take on Nasser's mantle. Indeed he began quietly to change the Nasser policies and take the Nasser system apart.

Egypt always thought of itself as the heart of the Arab land— which was well and good as long as Arabism meant Egyptian leadership of the Arab world. Now that the burden of leadership was beginning to weigh, the average Egyptian would be happier if the new leader concentrated his attention on Egypt first and last. The Egyptians were now tired of making sacrifices, and tired of fighting for the Arabs. They were satiated with the rhetoric about 'the Arab Nation' and began to distinguish themselves as Egyptians. Among the first things Sadat did on succeeding Nasser was to give the country back its name—Egypt—and drop the title 'United Arab Republic'.

Sadat's moves were popular, at least in the early period, and Sadat was able to put down without difficulty a brief challenge from the residual Nasserists in the regime. After dismissing Aly Sabri (rather unfairly known as the Soviet Union's man),[24] he had a number of others locked up—including the powerful Ministers of Defence, the Interior, Information—on charges of conspiracy. He went on the air to reveal in a theatrical statement ('You can hear me now in your cell, O Fawzi!') how the plotters had plotted and how he had foiled them. It was at root a contest for power, but these men were also advocating that Nasser's revolution be kept alive and not dismantled piece by piece as Sadat was doing; that a peaceful settlement should not be purchased at any price and that, at any rate, Egypt should not have placed all its cards on the table as Sadat appeared to be doing. The purge, besides removing a threat to his position, rid Sadat of all this nagging and carping and left him free to pursue his peace moves. Those who believed that Nasser alone was capable of delivering the goods on Egypt's behalf would also soon be proved wrong. In his interim peace initiative, Sadat went even further than Nasser had done in trying to come to terms with the United States.

In October 1970, shortly after Nasser's death, Pakistan's new dictator, General Yahya Khan, paid a visit to Cairo on his way to Washington. He told Sadat that on learning that he was stopping over in Cairo on his way to Washington, President Nixon had sent him a memorandum and, in reply to queries raised by Pakistan, another paper setting out and clarifying the US position on the Middle East. Nixon had asked Yahya Khan to convey these to President Sadat. There was nothing in these papers that the Egyptians did not already know, but Nixon's gesture—besides being a show of confidence in Pakistan—was meant to convey to

Egypt his keenness to bring about a settlement in the Middle East.

Sadat said that US support of Israel was complete and unconditional. American U2 aircraft keeping a watch on the region, were in fact taking photographs only of the Egyptian side and ignored what was happening on the Israeli side; Israelis were flying American supplied planes, using American made bombs and even American pilots (Israelis of American origin were allowed to hold double nationality). America had gone back on its promise not to give new military aid to Israel as long as the American peace initiative was being discussed.

President Sadat said to Yahya Khan, 'When you meet President Nixon, please ask him one thing: if Israel is sure of the backing of the United States for any and everything it does, why should it withdraw from Arab territories, why should it compromise?'[25] Sadat said that he had no confidence in America's good faith and that if there was no peaceful settlement, Egyptian forces which totalled 700,000 men, would take steps to liberate the occupied territories themselves. The United States, he said, was trying to create a situation in which a separate peace could be made between Israel and Egypt and the other concerned Arab countries. 'This,' Sadat asserted, 'we shall *never* allow to happen.' Famous last words! This was exactly what he would do at Camp David some years later. Indeed Nasser himself, when he accepted the Rogers' Plan, had implicitly agreed to go ahead with a separate peace. King Hussein also felt free to move in the same direction and held a series of secret meetings with Ygal Allon, an Israeli Cabinet member, and other Israeli leaders, with the knowledge and possibly the concurrence of Egypt.

In his review of the situation, Yahya Khan made two assertions which had an element of truth in them, but both were disproved by events: (1) time was working against Israel; and (2) in accepting the Rogers' Plan, Nasser had gone as far as it was possible for an Egyptian leader to go. The fact however was that the Arabs spent much time striking up postures of defiance and rejecting this and refusing that, while Israel was 'creating facts' on the ground that would not be undone easily or at all. Unable equally to make war or to concede peace, the Arabs had made piecemeal but substantial concessions only to find Israel continually putting up its price. Nasser had gone a long way, no doubt, to meet the substance of the Israeli-US position on the Security Council resolution 242, but Sadat went a good deal further on the broader issues that were of primary concern to the United States—that is, Egypt's 'revolutionary' actions at home and abroad, its connection with the Soviet Union, and indeed the whole future shape of things in the Middle East.

Nasser said the right things but Sadat did the things that needed doing to arouse the interest of the United States. He started to dismantle the Nasser system and turned out all Soviet experts and advisers. In showing the Russians the door, he served a double purpose: on the one hand, he took away something from America's argument that its aid to Israel was meant to counter the massive Soviet presence in Egypt, and on the other, with the Russian advisers and controllers gone, Sadat was able to plan and carry out his military moves in secrecy.

Of course all this took some time to unfold, but the Soviets had already smelled a change in the wind and they worked hard to keep the Soviet-Egyptian alliance on course. Kosygin had promised more and better military aid when he came for Nasser's funeral. President Podgorny came soon after and promised more advanced weapons. But Egyptian gratitude was not unmixed with mistrust and there were important people in the leadership who considered it as basically unsound that Egypt should be solely dependent on the support of one great power.

The occasion of the Soviet President's visit was the opening ceremony of the Aswan High Dam, the construction of which America had—rather peremptorily and inexplicably—refused to assist, and the Soviets had jumped in to build. It was an impressive project on which the Nasser regime had set its heart and hopes. Some years later an Arab guest visiting the opening of the Tarbela Dam in Pakistan was amazed at its size and said, 'To think that Nasser set the Middle East on fire on account of a dam not half as big.'

Podgorny came again in June and this time, signed a treaty of peace and friendship with Egypt. He described the treaty as 'a new blow' to imperialist scheming, that would cause relations between the two countries to 'rise to a higher degree and enter a specific stage'. In his response Sadat took a somewhat more prosaic view, and it was said that he had been more or less bullied by the Soviets into signing the treaty. However for Sadat the treaty did have one merit—it strengthened his position *vis-à-vis* leftists in Egypt and abroad, and he didn't have to worry too much about any harassment from that side while he went ahead with his search for a settlement. Whereas Podgorny had fumed against those (namely the United States) 'wearing false clothes of peace-makers', who had taken it upon themselves, unasked, to act as arbitrators, Sadat was pleading with the same United States to assume the role of mediator. When a couple of years later the time came for it, the treaty which had caused a bit of a flutter in diplomatic dovecotes at the time, did not prevent Sadat from bundling out all Soviet advisers. Oddly, there was no overt reaction to the move from the United States. A *New York Times* analysis, based apparently on a briefing by Assistant Secretary of State Joseph Sisco, concluded that a reduced Soviet presence in Egypt made an attack across the Canal less likely—a complete misreading of the situation. In fact the Soviet Union had throughout denied Egyptian requests for offensive weapons, though the Egyptians said they needed these not to start a war but only to neutralize Israel's diplomatic advantage. The Egyptian Permanent Representative at the UN, Esmet Abdul Meguid, said to me that the Soviet Union found it 'profitable' to allow the 'No war, No peace' situation to continue.

When, three years later, war broke out again, I was Permanent Representative at the United Nations. In May the Security Council considered a proposal to redefine resolution 242 in order to clarify precisely what the Arabs and Israelis respectively were required to do under its provisions.[26] In the words of the Egyptian Permanent Representative, the Council should 'spell out in basic English' what each of the parties was supposed to do. The move was opposed by the United States for exactly that reason. The Council must not, the American Permanent Representative urged, alter the 'substance and delicate balance' of the resolution—its 'conscious ambiguities'. But now Egyptian troops were across the Canal and ambiguity and balance and so forth would be put to the test of the sword. The UN was electrified with excitement. In Western circles, there was consternation as Israel's defences in the desert crumbled and the way lay open for Egyptians to sweep to the Mitla Pass. But the Egyptian Army paused and the tide of battle turned. The 'Battle of Destiny' ended with the Arab destiny more than ever in the hands of others.

Egypt perhaps was glad to let it be so. Sadat's visit to Jerusalem was an event of the highest drama. As I watched it on American television—the arrival in the lion's den, the accolades, the floods of eloquence on both sides—it was difficult not to share the emotion of the moment. Some years later in March 1979, Erik Rouleau of the Paris daily *Le Monde*, gave an account of how Sadat's historic initiative took shape: a suggestion by President Carter, followed up by Romania's Ceauçescu, and then a secret meeting in Morocco between Sadat's emissary, Hassan el Touhamy and Moshe Dayan in which the Israeli made an offer that if Sadat came to Israel, the Sinai would be restored to Egypt, and as for the rest 'everything is negotiable'. Sadat proposed, for form's sake perhaps, that the heads of state of the five permanent member countries of the Security Council go with him and stay on there until a global peace was achieved. But then he took the plunge and went to Israel by himself, taking much on trust.

Then followed Camp David and a separate peace with Israel, signed in Washington. Agreement was made possible only at the price of substantial concessions by Sadat. Even the return of the Sinai that he obtained, had been offered to Nasser years before without any of the conditions extracted from Sadat. The 'moderate' Arabs complained that by going to Jerusalem Sadat gave recognition to Israel without obtaining anything in return, and now once again without getting a full settlement in return, he had given Israel what it had sought from the beginning—a separate peace.

The other Arabs stormed and raged but could do little other than expel Egypt from the Arab League and pull the League headquarters out of Cairo. At the Havana summit in 1978 they tried to have Egypt expelled from the non-aligned movement. The move was spearheaded by Syria and the PLO and many others joined in to berate and revile Egypt. Yasser Arafat scored some telling points: 'Who is Sadat trying to kid? What war has been ended by Sadat's peace? I have come here from the battlefield, the hell of daily bombardment by Israeli forces from land, sea and air...Sadat has sold Jerusalem for the sands of the Sinai!' Foreign Minister Yazdi of Iran pronounced a poetic anathema: 'Pigeons flock together with pigeons, eagles with eagles fly. Egypt has chosen Israel.'[27] The Egyptians sat forlorn, abandoned and mute and no one spoke up for them. But Deputy

Foreign Minister Boutros Ghali returned a soft answer and carried the day. The sponsors of the move against Egypt had called a night meeting to take a final decision on the question. They intended perhaps to achieve their end by taking the committee by surprise, but succeeded only in irritating members who, at six in the morning, divided half and half and there was no consensus on suspending Egypt.

During a lull in the debate Boutros Ghali took me out for a cup of coffee in the lounge and complained that Pakistan as a big Muslim country, was not giving the lead it should in finding a solution to the inter-Arab differences, but was simply going along with the majority. He also said with a wry smile, 'Even our best friends [referring perhaps to India and Yugoslavia][28] are willing to help Egypt only from behind the scenes.' Boutros Ghali analysed the situation in terms of a parable that was revealing of Egypt's own frame of mind at the time: Egypt is like a woman, he said, still beautiful, but who has begun to fade and grow old and is tired of caring for her twelve difficult and balky children. Then suddenly a suitor appears, a tall, white, handsome *khwaja* (foreigner), and off she goes with him leaving her fractious, squabbling charges screaming with rage and fear at being left to fend for themselves.

My principal job in Cairo of course was to promote Pakistan's relations with Egypt. The relationship had not been a very happy one in the past. The reason for this was not very complex. Pakistan gave the Arab cause full and unconditional support, often even before they asked for it. The Arabs knew this, appreciated Pakistan's fervour, and in time came to take it for granted. But they did not always respond in kind. They tended to shy away from taking Pakistan's side against India; on the contrary, some of them looked up with admiration at Gandhi, Nehru and other Indian leaders who had fought the same imperialist enemy that they themselves were confronting.

This was not true of all Arab countries but it was certainly true of Egypt. Egypt, for centuries one of the main centres of Islamic civilization and political power, was not very pleased at Pakistan's attempts to take centre stage as the largest Islamic nation. King Farouk is said to have remarked sarcastically on the advent of Pakistan, that one would think that Islam was born on 14 August 1947! Thus from the start, there was a touch of irritation and perhaps a shade of rivalry, about Egypt's attitude towards Pakistan. But there was no direct conflict of interest, no bilateral question at issue between Pakistan and Egypt nor, in the beginning, was there a divergence of policy on any major matter. What caused the strain in mutual relations was the relationship of each with third countries—Egypt's with India and Pakistan's with the West.

The period between 1947-52 was marked by relative cordiality. Foreign Minister Chaudhry Zafrulla Khan's advocacy of the Palestine case (and of other Muslim causes ranging from Eritrea to Algeria) at the United Nations had earned for Pakistan a reputation as the Arabs' most staunch and vocal supporter. Nevertheless even then, though Egypt had voted along with other members in favour of the Security Council's Kashmir resolution in 1950, in the lobbies the Egyptian representative Dr Mahmoud Fawzi, was seen advocating the Indian thesis that the two countries be left to sort out the problem between themselves. After Nasser took over in 1952, the Pakistan Chargé d'Affaires, Syed Tayyeb Hussain, who had established close personal relations with Nasser and other leaders of the new regime, played a role in helping along Anglo-Egyptian negotiations for the evacuation of British troops from the Canal zone. But as Nasser's revolution gathered steam, the divergence between his socialistic and anti-colonial fervour and Pakistan's close relations with the West and its pan-Islamic vocation, became more and more apparent. These factors brought Egypt closer to India which was then following a left-leaning neutralist policy, more in line with the thinking of the new Egyptian leaders. The divergence of attitudes turned into hostility when Pakistan joined the Baghdad Pact.

The period from 1955 to 1964 was one of increasing ill-will and friction as Pakistan became more closely involved in pro-Western moves and policies, while along with Nehru and Tito, Nasser was one of the leading lights of non-alignment. This was a period of increasingly close co-operation in political and other spheres between Egypt and India. Pakistan's Prime Minister Suhrawardy annoyed Egypt by playing a somewhat equivocal role in the 1956 Suez Crisis[29] (a role that however was disowned and denounced in street demonstrations in Pakistan). In 1962 Egypt abstained on a Security Council resolution concerning a plebiscite in Kashmir.

In 1968, when I took over as ambassador at Cairo, relations were beginning to improve. Ayub had paid Egypt a visit and got on surprisingly well with Nasser. In the previous year's war, Pakistan had stood firmly—and even actively—by the Arab side. The shock of defeat had shaken Egypt's beliefs in the value of non-alignment and in the grandiose 'revolutionary' approach to foreign policy as well as social and economic problems at home. This had its effect on Egypt's relations with India. A joint Indo-Egyptian project to produce a supersonic fighter plane was dropped.[30] By 1968 India herself had become relatively passive on the Arab-Israeli question and was living on the capital of goodwill left over from the Nehru-Krishna Menon era. For its part, Pakistan had cooled towards its pro-Western alliances and impressed the diplomatic world with its ability simultaneously to remain in anti-Soviet Western pacts, enjoying an unofficial alliance with Communist China while receiving military aid from the Soviet Union.

But there were still minus points. Though Pakistan had eased away from its Western alliances, now its close relationship with China was not without its problems in the relations with Egypt. Maoist China treated the Security Council resolution and the four power efforts to mediate an agreement as a 'peace fraud' that was designed to confirm Israeli usurpation of Palestinian rights.[31] These sentiments found an echo in the heart of every Palestinian and added to the discomfiture of President Nasser who was having a hard enough time trying to reconcile Egypt's declarations of support for the Palestine cause with his search for a peace settlement with Israel. Pakistan's zeal in supporting the Palestine cause may therefore have had a questionable side to it in Egyptian eyes.

At any rate better Egypt-Pakistan relations did not mean that the shape of the Egypt-Pakistan-India triangle was any different. It remained an obtuse-angled triangle with the Egyptian line leaning towards India. Mohammed Riad, an old friend and the Foreign Minister's *chef de Cabinet* said to me that Egypt recognized the greater sincerity, as compared to India, of Pakistan's support to the Arab cause, and relations between Egypt and Pakistan were going from strength to strength, but Pakistan should not make Kashmir a touchstone of relations with other countries. I said to him that for Pakistan Kashmir came first and it was as important to us as the Palestine issue was to the Arabs; and, our friends should bear this in mind and consider whether it was advantageous in the long run to adopt one set of principles in one case and a different one in another.

But of course a double standard there was and no doubt about it. President Nasser is supposed to have said to a Pakistani ambassador: 'Your government is under popular pressure to support the Arab cause. I have no such compulsion with respect to Kashmir!' Whether he actually said this in so many words or not, it reflects fairly well the real situation and the position that Egypt, and many other Arab countries do in fact take on India-Pakistan issues. The way the Egyptians saw the matter was that Pakistan's support of Palestine and in general of Arab and Muslim causes was fired by religious zeal and therefore it was not subject to political vicissitudes. India's support was of great value to the Arabs for the opposite reason: that it came from a non-Muslim country of great size and influence, and was based not on sentimental considerations but on political calculation. Egyptian officials acted on the principle that Egypt had to try harder in order to retain India's support, precisely because it was not as sincere or spontaneous or dependable as Pakistan's.

The policy regarding news from India in Egypt's managed news media was 'bad news is no news'! So, when after the Six-Day War, Mrs Moshe Dayan visited India, nothing at all was allowed to be printed in Egyptian newspapers about the ecstatic public receptions, swords of honour, etc., she was receiving, or indeed that she was in India at all; the only snippet that appeared—to show that India's heart was in the right place—was that India had declined an offer of twelve scholarships brought by Mrs Dayan.

Director-General Ramzi, who headed the South Asian desk in the Foreign Ministry, had an interesting insight on the subject. When our troubles broke out in East Pakistan, he told me that India was threatening to review its Middle East policy if the Arabs did not come out clearly against Pakistani actions there. Then he said, 'But of course they won't do it.'

'And why not?' I asked.

He laughed and said, 'On account of Pakistan! Because they would be afraid that then Pakistan's position would gain in the Arab world.' Thus Pakistan's support was doubly useful to Egypt—for its own sake and in helping to keep India on track.

The same official, explaining why Egypt was opposing the proposal to set up a permanent secretariat for the Islamic conference said to me very frankly that the reason was that it might open the doors of the Conference to all kinds of bilateral disputes and grievances being brought up. Some of them, such as the Kashmir question, he said, were liable to affect the unity of the Arabs and strain their relations with both India and Pakistan. He wished to tell me quite candidly that while they were one hundred per cent confident of Pakistan's support at all times, the position with regard to India was rather more shaky, and he hoped Pakistan would understand their anxiety not to do anything at this stage that might cost them India's support.

Nasser himself said to me once that he was aware that the Indian Press was sympathetic to Israel, and Israelis were very active in India and that he realized that Pakistan on the contrary considered the Palestine case as its own and felt deeply concerned over the occupation of Jerusalem and the Al Aqsa mosque by Jews. I recalled what the Iranian Ambassador in Islamabad, General Pakravan, had said to me as I was leaving for Cairo: 'You people are too idealistic about Islamic solidarity. Egyptians do not believe in it at all. They are realistic and ruthless. Be yourself with them...'

In point of fact the Kashmir issue was dormant during that period and the matter was not put to the test, but it was clear that if it came up in some forum, Egypt would still prefer to sit on the fence. However perhaps now Egypt was not likely to take a position against Pakistan's interests, as it had in 1962 and 1950. Egypt did not of course formally recognize Kashmir as a part of India or accept India's thesis that the people of Kashmir no longer had the right to decide their future. Rather, like many others they wondered, as Nasser once said to me, shaking his head, 'Who is going to solve that problem!' When I answered that the people of Kashmir would have to decide their future themselves, he looked sceptical and asked, 'But how are they going to do it?' He said the British had created the Kashmir problem when they left behind the McMahon Line (confusing it with the Radcliffe Award). He added that he had offered his good offices on Kashmir at one stage but they were not accepted. Nehru, he said, was strong enough and should have done something about Kashmir in his lifetime; the Shastri government was too weak.[32] Shastri himself, he said, was a good man but he was afraid of the Opposition and the Press. 'It is really a pity about you and India,' Nasser added with another shake of the head, 'Indians and Pakistanis are really the same people, of the same race. You look the same!' He laughed when I said, 'So do the French and the Germans, and the Americans and Russians.'

All told relations were a lot better than they had been in the past. Still, there was the occasional hiccup. In his speech in the National Assembly in January 1969, Nasser gave thanks by name to various countries that were supporting the Arab cause, mentioning them in a sort of order of merit. The USSR came first of course, then France and de Gaulle personally. Both received (in the agitprop language of the times) 'prolonged and stormy applause'. Then came Tito and Indira Gandhi, each mentioned by name, and again there was applause, somewhat less prolonged and a bit less stormy. Next, African countries were mentioned as a bloc, and they too were good for a nice round of clapping. Finally Islamic countries 'such as Mauritania and Pakistan'. These names were received in stony silence that, in its own way, made an even greater impact than the thunderous accolades that had preceded it. These matters were of course carefully orchestrated in Nasser's Egypt. Thus during the ceremonies to mark the completion of the UNESCO's Abu Simbel project, the audience of illiterate fellaheen, trucked over from the countryside for the occasion, cheered wildly every time they heard the name Gamal Nasser mentioned, even when the speeches were in English or French, and even when the Minister of Culture said that President Nasser was sorry he could not come as he wasn't well.

So what was the meaning of the silence that greeted Pakistan's name? Was it a foul-up on the part of the Under Secretary General of Accolades and Applause, had someone forgotten to rescind standing orders from less friendly times, or was Pakistan unbeknownst to itself, still in the doghouse, or what? The affair caused some wagging of tongues in the Cairo diplomatic circle but no one could figure out the cause of Pakistan being offered this deliberate and gratuitous snub. It was not a matter on which one could lodge an official protest, but we made sure that Pakistan's bafflement and chagrin did not remain a secret from Egyptian officials. In Islamabad the Foreign Office also spoke to the Egyptian ambassador in 'sorrow-but-not-anger' about the matter.

In the following days, Egyptians made an effort to make amends. The President's Adviser, Dr Fawzi, asked me over for the sole purpose of showering quite extravagant praise on the Pakistan Foreign Minister for his statement on the Middle East at a recent Commonwealth Conference. My friend Mohammed Riad came over to the Embassy bearing lame excuses: Pakistan was mentioned last because it is considered a member of the family; Turkey, Malaysia and Afghanistan were not mentioned at all; (as if being given thanks for doing Egypt a favour was a system of awards like the Queen's birthday honours!). Anyway we decided to take it philosophically. On a previous occasion, Nasser had forgotten to mention Pakistan at all and its name had to be doctored afterwards into the text distributed to the Press; this time Pakistan had actually received mention. So there was progress!

A rather more awkward business was the imbroglio over India's attempt to join the Islamic Conference at the summit meeting held in Rabat in 1969. India had been lobbying hard for a long time to get into the Islamic Conference, on the ground that she had a large Muslim population. President Yahya at first had sort of agreed to let India come in, but when the Indian delegation headed by a Minister showed up in Rabat and started holding press conferences and jubilating, Yahya realized what India's admission into the Islamic Conference would mean in diplomatic terms and to public opinion in Pakistan. So he dug in his heels and threatened to walk out if India was allowed in. The explanation we offered for Yahya Khan's apparent volte-face was that he had agreed only to India's Muslim community being represented. Other Conference members were annoyed at the incident and at the diplomatic ineptitude exhibited by Pakistan. At any rate they could hardly afford to let Pakistan walk out, and with much wringing of hands and many excuses the Indians were persuaded to withdraw. Egypt took the whole thing very sourly— there were critical, even hostile newspaper comments about Pakistan and officials spoke to us in tones of reproof and remonstrance. A Cabinet Minister was despatched to Delhi personally to present Egypt's apologies to India.

The Islamic Conference was the occasion of yet more trouble with Egypt the following year when it met in Jeddah and the

Saudis moved that the Conference should have a permanent Islamic Secretariat. This time Pakistan was not directly involved though of course Pakistan lobbied strongly for the proposal. Egyptians saw it as a piece of one-upmanship by King Faisal that they found hard to swallow, but failed to carry the day against the move. They were now threatening to boycott the next meeting of the Conference which was to be held in Karachi. I went to see President Nasser to urge that Egypt's failure to participate in the Karachi meeting would be very unfortunate for our developing relations. 'I will speak to you frankly,' Nasser said, 'you know we have our difficulties with Saudi Arabia, although we do not say much about it in public.' King Faisal, he said, was going about in all kinds of ways to undermine Egypt and other progressive Arab regimes, and is trying to use the Islamic Conference for the same purpose. The king intends to use the proposed Secretariat as an instrument to erode Egypt's influence and ideology, Nasser said. The Secretariat idea was pushed through with this end in view, he added, in spite of the many practical objections that were raised against it. That is why Egypt had decided to reject it and so had the Sudan, Libya and Algeria. Together with Iraq, Syria and South Yemen (who did not attend the Jeddah meeting) more than half the Arab countries were out of it.

Nasser went on to say that he did not believe that religion should be mixed up with politics and Egypt did not decide its stand on various issues on the basis of religion. Thus Egypt had supported Christian Greece against Muslim Turkey in Cyprus, because it was in favour of removing British bases from Cyprus. These bases had been used for attacks against Egypt during the Suez War. In Nigeria, Egypt had supported the Muslim-dominated federal government against the Christian secessionist movement in Biafra, not for reasons of religious affinity but because the Biafra movement was instigated by imperialist intrigue and intervention.

Hassan el Tohamy[33] who had been one of Nasser's senior advisers and a 'closet Islamist' at the time, told me after Nasser's death, 'Now that the citadel of unbelievers has fallen, things are going to be different!' He said, 'Nasser had no time for Islamic co-operation. He used to sneer when the name of Pakistan was mentioned. Sadat on the other hand has great regard for Pakistan and believes in Islamic solidarity.' Indeed in one of his speeches after he became president, Sadat singled out Pakistan as the foremost among the countries supporting the Arabs. Under Sadat there was a change in Egypt's attitude as to the Islamic factor, but only in the sense that he decided to add the Islamic card to the others that he held—Soviet, non-aligned, Arab, etc.—in order to strengthen his hand. He believed in the solidarity of Islamic countries but with Egypt playing a central, leading role.

The change in Egypt's attitude towards Pakistan became apparent during the Bangladesh crisis. Egypt showed genuine concern at the threat to Pakistan's integrity and the Cairo Press were given official advice to take a 'balanced line' on the subject—that is, to soft-pedal the adverse news coming from there. *Al Ahram's* editor, Hasnain Haikal felt obliged to cry out, 'How can we remain silent in the face of the unprecedented massacres that are taking place in East Pakistan?' When India sent Minister Fakhruddin to Cairo to expound the Indian line, he got nothing much out of Egypt except advice that India ought to encourage Yahya Khan's current attempts at political compromise. In reply to a personal message on the subject from Mrs Gandhi, Sadat advised her that India's own good lay in helping Yahya Khan to overcome the crisis. When he received Admiral Muzaffar Hasan, the Pakistan Naval Chief of Staff (in his village home, seated on the ground) Sadat made the following three points: (1) whatever happened, Egypt was for the integrity of Pakistan; (2) he was aware of India's involvement in the situation; (3) he commended the wisdom of Yahya Khan's proposed plan to transfer power to the elected representatives.[34]

In the Afro-Asian Peoples' Solidarity Organization, the Egyptian delegation lobbied to defeat an Indo-Soviet move to condemn Pakistan. Egypt suggested that a group of ten Islamic, non-aligned and Commonwealth countries might be set up to help defuse the situation and induce the refugees to return. Pakistan did not pursue the idea actively and India had its own ideas for resolving the crisis.[35]

NOTES

[1] Perhaps the worst might have been averted by a little expedient prevarication by the Secretary General, but U Thant's hand was forced to some extent when India and Yugoslavia informed him that after Nasser's demand they could not allow their contingents to remain in the UN Emergency Force.

[2] General Hakim Amir, the Army Chief, was alleged to have killed himself on account of his responsibility for this disaster. The Cambodian Ambassador who lived in a house next to the General's, told me a different story about his likely end. According to him, hearing a hue and cry coming from the General's house, he went out on the terrace to see what was going on and saw General Amir being driven off in a black limousine by some hefty men while his wife and daughter were raising lamentations. Next morning came the official announcement of his suicide.

[3] When in reaction to the seizure of the Suez Canal, England, France and Israel invaded Egypt, Eisenhower took a very stern line and compelled all three countries to withdraw from Egyptian territory.

[4] Conversation with author.

[5] Mohsen el Aini, later Prime Minister of Yemen, found himself in a Cairo jail on suspicion of being a Communist. 'Can you see Yemen going Communist?' he said to me when I visited him in Sana'a some years later. 'All I was trying to do was to bring this country from the fifteenth into the eighteenth century!' Some years later I could have told him: Pakistan too is trying to get to the eighteenth century but starting at the other end!

[6] Not for 'liberal' reasons alone, but because it showed that the Soviet Union was not afraid of US reactions where its own direct interests were at stake.

[7] Gamal Abdel Nasser, *The Philosophy of the Revolution*; Public Affairs Press, Washington DC,1955.

[8] Conversation with author.

[9] Named after an Israeli general, the line was a series of fortified positions along the Israeli-occupied eastern bank of the Suez Canal.

[10] A Christian Palestinian of the Greek Orthodox Church, and graduate of Beirut's American University, he is a Marxist who heads the rejectionist and ultra-leftist Popular Front for the Liberation of Palestine.

[11] Walt Rostow, President Johnson's National Security Advisor, and his brother Eugene, were Jewish and Zionist sympathizers and powerful figures in the Democratic Administration of the sixties.

[12] Author's conversation with Foreign Minister.

[13] Hassan el Zayyat, the official spokesman put it thus on one occasion: 'After all, in a civilized society even an illegitimate offspring has the right to live!'

[14] One interesting idea of Jarring's, perhaps the fruit of his South Asian experience, was to take the Indus Basin settlement as a model for settling the Palestine refugee problem: they would be settled in various Arab countries and international aid would be mobilized to finance irrigation works and desalination plants that would provide jobs for them in those countries.

[15] An Egyptian journalist said to me, 'What do the Americans have to fear? They know that Muslim Egypt won't go Communist. As for oil, there is no danger

to US interests; Egypt's own new finds are being exploited by US firms.'

[16] Dr Mahmoud Fawzi told me that Dean Rusk wanted the Arab governments to actively dissuade them from choosing to go home, and to accept financial compensation instead.

[17] Conversation with author.

[18] The main elements of the peace plan proposed by Secretary of State William Rogers were: (1) a cease-fire for three to six months; (2) Egypt, Jordan and Israel to declare their acceptance of Security Council Resolution 242 and to nominate representatives who would discuss its implementation; and (3) a just and lasting peace to be based on recognition of the sovereignty and independence of all states in the region and withdrawal of Israel from territories occupied in the 1967 War.

[19] Kissinger once said: 'It is perhaps dangerous to become an enemy of the United States in the Middle East. But to pose as a friend of our country would surely prove fatal…'

[20] I used to see him, abandoned and forgotten, taking long walks around the disused Cairo racecourse. I recalled an earlier meeting with him in Madrid when in the guise of playing at the devil's advocate, he had argued against Pakistan's case both on Kashmir and 'Pashtunistan'.

[21] Author's notes on conversation with Jordanian ambassador, 27 August 1970.

[22] Author's notes based on a conversation with a participant in the conference, 29 September 1970.

[23] The airline had managed to lose his luggage and the embassy had to launch a big effort among the not very numerous Pakistani community in Cairo to find a *sherwani* that would fit him.

[24] Aly Sabri had some pseudo-Marxist ideas but Nasser said, 'This is only because he went to school with the Jesuits'!

[25] Author's notes.

[26] An amusing exchange took place between the Israeli and Indian representatives in the course of these meetings. The Indian representative, admonishing Israel for flouting the United Nations, advised it to follow India's ways in showing respect for the United Nations' decisions. Israeli ambassador Tekoah said in reply, 'But according to what the Arab delegations say, Israel in fact is precisely following India's ways, is it not?'

[27] Author's notes.

[28] However when the Conference adopted a resolution condemning Camp David by acclamation, India did not join the applause and remained conspicuously seated while members rose from their seats to give greater emphasis to the acclamation.

[29] The crisis arose over Nasser's abrupt move to nationalize the Anglo-French Suez Canal Company. Pakistan supported Egypt's right to do so, but the Suhrawardy government went along with a Western proposal to set up a Canal User's organization to run the Canal, a move that was rejected by Egypt as a back-door attempt by Britain and France to resume control over the Canal.

[30] The machine was based on combining an engine designed by an ex-Nazi German engineer in Egypt and a Soviet airframe built in Bangalore. A ceremonial test flight was actually staged with a lot of fanfare, but after a great deal of money had been spent, the engine and airframe were found to be incompatible.

[31] However the basic Chinese position was stated in a Security Council meeting in June 1973: 'We are not opposed to the Jewish nation and the people of Israel.'

[32] He recounted how Shastri, Sukarno and Zhou Enlai, on the way to attend the Afro-Asian Conference, had all arrived at the Cairo Airport at the same time, and he had to rush from one part of the airport to the other to receive each. He had wanted to bring Shastri and Zhou together but Shastri was not willing. So separate VIP halls had to be improvised and he put Shastri in one and Zhou and Sukarno in another.

[33] Tohamy was the man who opened the way for Sadat's visit to Jerusalem by holding secret talks with Moshe Dayan in Morocco.

[34] Author's notes.

[35] Ibid.

CHAPTER 10

BANGLADESH—WAR AGAIN

In March 1971 I was in Karachi on leave from the Embassy at
Cairo and under orders of transfer to Belgrade. The day on
which Yahya Khan sent the troops in against the Bengalis, I was
taken by friends to a *qawali* in the evening. Replete connoisseurs,
immaculate in white *kurta-paijamas* reclined against fat bolster
cushions on the floor, chewing betel leaf and uttering cries of
appreciation as they offered crisp banknotes to the singers.
Scarcely anyone said a word about what was happening in East
Pakistan and what it implied for the country. This was the West
Pakistani Establishment, the rulers and administrators. There
were some there who sympathized with the Bengali grievances
but many probably felt that Mujibur Rahman had got what was
coming to him. There was at that party no sense of crisis, no
premonition of impending catastrophe. Certainly no concern was
expressed for the population of Dhaka.

On his return from Dhaka Zulfikar Ali Bhutto declared,
'Pakistan has been saved!' However when I telephoned him the
next morning at his Karachi house, he sounded a bit subdued. I
asked him why Yahya Khan had banned all political parties since
only the Awami League was accused of treason. He said, 'Oh,
that is only for appearances' sake. You will see other developments quite soon.' It was not clear what he was expecting to
happen. Perhaps he had been led to believe by the military that
they would let him form an interim government and from a
position of strength, make a try at winning over East Pakistan by
political means. It became clear soon enough that anything of
that sort was the farthest thing from their minds. Nevertheless
Bhutto held his peace and only after several months had elapsed
did he speak out against 'the night of the long knives' and
condemn what the regime was doing in East Pakistan.

One can make what one wants of the might-have-beens of history. Many in Pakistan hold that Bhutto and Bhutto alone, was responsible for the tragedy of East Pakistan. This view is put forward specially by those who were in charge at the time and stand in need of a scapegoat. Many others feel that even though he cannot be absolved of his share of responsibility, had Bhutto been at the helm in those critical months, he might have steered the situation towards some political settlement and if this meant a break with the East, it might have been brought about without the carnage and havoc that took place.

In the embassy at Cairo and later at Belgrade, we settled down to business as usual. This now consisted mainly of trying to convince the officials, Press and people of the host countries that the horror stories coming out of Calcutta about the army action in East Pakistan were all fabrication and propaganda; that Mujib was a tool in India's hands; and that the people of the eastern province, barring some malcontents, were fully behind the government. I had a number of East Pakistanis on my staff in both places. They were circumspect and kept their thoughts to themselves though it was not difficult to imagine what was going through their minds. But I considered that the only proper and politic thing to do was to act as if we were all still on the same side and that nobody had any difficulty in believing the line Islamabad was putting out about what was going on and about the government's motives and intentions. I did not discourage discussion and debate on these matters and when I went to brief officials or the Press about the situation, I often took along one of my Bengali colleagues. This worked in the beginning by giving them the feeling that they were trusted and so attenuated tensions to some degree. But as time went by and the situation in East Pakistan became increasingly polarized, it was more and more difficult to keep up the façade.

The period that followed the night of 23 March when troops moved into the Dhaka University campus, and up to the last week of November when Indian troops entered East Pakistan in strength, was and remains a nightmare interregnum—a period of confusion and darkness, dark for the barbarities that were perpetrated as also in the sense that no one knew the exact truth and extent of what was happening. Some garbled reports of the initial horrors did manage to filter out but then a curtain fell upon the scene. Reality was concealed, on the one side by Pakistani censorship and the expulsion of all foreign correspondents, and on the other, it was smothered in exaggeration and invention. In Pakistan the controlled Press reproduced official stories of miraculously restored tranquillity, the village milkman making his daily rounds, of life going on peaceably. The rest of the world got its news about the situation via Calcutta from stories told by East Pakistani refugees and those made up by Indian propaganda. But even Pakistan's controlled Press could not avoid all reference to the increasingly frequent incidents between Pakistani forces and the so-called 'miscreants' and alleged Indian agents. Nor could the fact be denied that Bengalis were fleeing their homes in increasing numbers and seeking refuge in India.

Soon a world-wide storm of disapproval and condemnation broke around Pakistan's head as the facts and Calcutta fantasies began to receive publicity in the world media. In time the whole panoply of human rights organizations and ecologists, rock bands and the Beatles and Hollywood stars were galvanized in support of the Bangladesh struggle. In Pakistan this campaign was seen as an Indo-Zionist plot against Islamic Pakistan. India's involvement and strategic interest in the situation were of course plain for all to see. There was little doubt that she was given a helping hand by Israeli sympathizers who see in Pakistan a gratuitous adversary of Israel and were glad at the chance to pay it back in kind.

A meeting of Pakistani envoys in the major countries was held at Geneva, chaired jointly by Foreign Secretary Sultan Muhammad Khan and General Ghulam Umar, who was one of Yahya Khan's close confidants and advisers, to consider why Pakistan's image in the world media was so bad. We were asked in a reproving tone, 'What are our ambassadors doing about it?' The ambassadors in turn asked to be told exactly what was going on in East Pakistan and some ventured to answer back, 'What do you expect the image to reflect but the reality?' But such was the state of self-delusion in Islamabad that in the month of May, the Foreign office was telling Yahya Khan in a 'Summary for the President' that in the world there was 'overwhelming diplomatic support for our endeavour to put down the secessionists'. In fact Pakistan's name was by now in such bad odour that according to a report from our High Commission in Delhi at a dinner party, the wife of a foreign newsman had her place changed when she found herself seated next to a Pakistani First Secretary.

Meanwhile war was coming and many people could see it coming. London *Times* correspondent in Delhi, Peter Hazlehurst reported in the 13 July issue of the newspaper that the option of war was being considered in the most responsible circles in India. About the same time the UN Secretary General U Thant spoke to the Pakistan Permanent Representative of his 'increasing conviction that war between India and Pakistan could come in October or November'. He conveyed his concern also to the Security Council and suggested the need for finding a solution to the 'political aspects' of the East Pakistan crisis. Marshal Tito had gone on an official visit to Delhi in the summer of that year and on his return wanted it conveyed to the Pakistan government that he had come back 'with the most serious forebodings about the prospect for peace in the subcontinent'. In other words, he had found India getting set to go to war. In the joint communiqué issued at the conclusion of the visit, Tito backed India's position in asking Pakistan to reach a settlement with Mujibur Rahman. However he claimed that he also spoke in the strongest terms to Indira Gandhi against recourse to war to solve the issue. Later Yugoslavia also voted for a UN resolution calling on India to cease fire and withdraw from East Pakistan.

I was in Belgrade at the time and the official who conveyed to me the foregoing information also said that Tito was prepared to mediate if Pakistan would like him to. I believe that Tito meant this offer quite sincerely because he saw a parallel in the situation of his country and did not want India to set a precedent for humanitarian interventions in the internal affairs of sovereign countries. When I presented my credentials to him, Marshal Tito treated me to a homily on ethnic and nationalist conflicts and affirmed that it was wrong and futile to try to solve them by the use of force. 'Over here in Yugoslavia,' he declared, 'we have solved these problems once and for all. There will be no Balkan question ever again in the world!'

He could not in his worst imaginings have foreseen that his country would simply disappear from the world's map amid some of the most ghastly bloodshed and savagery ever seen. Indeed the Bangladesh War was hardly over when the first serious trouble broke out in Croatia, his home republic. And forgetting his sagacious counsels to Pakistan he did not hesitate to use military force to subdue it, before working out a political solution.

I cabled Tito's offer to Islamabad and a meeting between him and Yahya Khan was arranged to take place in Persepolis during the extravaganza the Shah was staging there to celebrate the 2,000 years of the Persian monarchy. A Yugoslav official who was with Tito at the meeting told me that it was a dialogue of the deaf. Tito could not get much of a word in and Yahya spent the whole time hectoring him about India's expansionism, duplicity, mischief-making, and so forth. The impression the Yugoslavs got was that Yahya Khan was not at all looking for a political settlement of any kind but only seeking to justify his action in East Pakistan. Indeed the Yahya regime ignored signs and warnings from all quarters and seemed to have become disconnected from reality. The government was receiving fairly accurate intelligence reports about what India was doing, and could hardly have failed to see the signs of approaching war; yet the regime seemed to be mesmerized into inaction by the very peril taking shape before its eyes. Our diplomatic efforts were wholly concerned with trying to expose India's machinations and demonstrate to the world India's ulterior motives. Our permanent representative at the United Nations did the best he could in this line and in one of his statements in the Council, took the members all the way back to the 1905 partition of Bengal to show how even then the Hindus had opposed the idea of a Muslim Bengal. What the bemused Council members made of all this, one does not know, but India herself took no great pains to conceal her intentions, and could count on the support of the Soviet Union and, at that point, perhaps also the benign neglect of the United States. The Indian representative took Agha Shahi's indictment in his stride. 'The Pakistan representative was moved while speaking of the break-up of his country,' he said, 'but it *has* broken up. Nothing on earth can stop it; it has happened.'

When the Indo-Soviet Friendship Treaty was concluded, it should have set the alarm bells ringing. The treaty had a military clause the object of which was quite clear: to deter any move China might think of making to neutralize eventual military action by India in East Pakistan. The Yugoslavs put the matter to me obliquely: 'Pakistan no doubt understands the limits on the

ability of its friends to help it this time.' But apparently this was
not the case. The Foreign Office made a *démarche* in Moscow and
received the bland assurance that the treaty was not directed at
Pakistan. Meetings were scheduled among the various ministries
and agencies concerned to examine the implications of the treaty,
but for one reason or another, kept being postponed and in the
end it seems that none was ever held. In its own analysis of the
treaty, the Foreign Ministry was content to observe that one could
only 'wait and see how the Soviet Union lives up to its assurances'.
No serious approaches were made in either Washington or
Beijing to counter the Soviet threat nor was any change
considered in the regime's strategy or tactics in East Pakistan.
The Foreign Ministry's own assessment, in keeping with the
prevailing complacency and obtuseness, was that the Soviet
support for India would stop short of letting her to go to war. In
fact the initial Soviet reaction to the situation was cautious. In
April Podgorny wrote to Yahya Khan in a friendly tone and he
was still speaking of 'the well-being of the entire people of
Pakistan'.[1]

On 21 November Indian troops dropped the shadow-boxing
and crossed the border into what to all intents and purposes had
already become Bangladesh. Such was the climate of international
opinion by now that the world reacted to this open invasion
without any expression of shock or disapproval and when China
proposed a resolution in the Security Council condemning the
Indian action, it could not be moved for lack of support. Pakistan
itself still held back from taking the matter to the Security
Council. India was making no bones about what she was doing.
When, two weeks later, the Security Council did at last take up
the situation, the Indian Permanent Representative, Samar Sen
responded to Agha Shahi's indictment by asserting, 'The Pakistan
representative has declared that we went into East Pakistan after
the twenty-first November. We did. I do not deny it.'

In Belgrade most of the Embassy staff and all diplomatic
officials were Bengalis. When the fighting began the West
Pakistanis left everything else aside and were constantly huddled
around the radio listening to broadcasts from every station they
could catch. They tended to discount the bad news given by the
BBC and other foreign stations as hostile propaganda, and would
come up excitedly to repeat to me stories recounted by Radio

Pakistan of the feats and exploits that were being performed by the Pakistani forces—small units holding out against overwhelming enemy forces, the numbers of enemy tanks and aircraft destroyed, the heavy casualties inflicted on the enemy. The world Press too was reporting pitched battles and fierce fighting by the Pakistani defenders. The nine months of bloodthirstiness and destruction in East Pakistan were beginning to be mitigated by the image of a country fighting alone against heavy odds to defend its territorial integrity. Throughout all this none of the Bengalis budged from their seats. They did not go near the radio and did not look at the news coming over the embassy's ticker, but just sat there, scribbling and scratching away at their files in a pantomime of devotion to duty.

On 3 December Pakistani forces made some tentative moves in the West—air raids against some Indian airfields of secondary importance, a land thrust in the Chhamb sector in Kashmir— and the 'general war' which Yahya had been threatening throughout the year to unleash, was apparently on. The Americans saw all this as phony stuff but it woke them to what was at stake—a threat to the political and military viability of Pakistan—an ally, even though one that had been estranged and kept on short rations militarily for the past several years. If Pakistan were to go down or be reduced to the status of an Indian vassal, it would be a set-back to the United States' strategic position in the region, affect the credibility of its newly restored relationship with China, and give a big boost to Soviet influence in Asia. 'Tilt, tilt to Pakistan!' commanded Nixon, going against the current of American public opinion at the time. But it was too late for any tilt to affect the situation on the ground. Henry Kissinger said in a National Security Council meeting, 'We have done everything too late by two weeks in the present situation.' He rued the fact that when American military aid to Pakistan was cut off in 1965, all the implications of the action had not been carefully considered.[2]

On the fourth the Americans acting on their own, asked for a meeting of the Security Council to consider the situation. Pakistan stood on the sidelines, nervously tugging at their sleeves not to bring up the offending 'P' word, viz., political settlement. The US moved a draft calling for an immediate cease-fire and withdrawal of Indian troops. It was promptly vetoed by the Soviet

Union who moved a draft of their own that passed over the matter of a cease-fire but called for a 'political settlement that would inevitably result in a cessation of hostilities'. It received only two votes. The Soviets spent the next two weeks vetoing every draft resolution that proposed a cease-fire, and in the end, even one that asked for a simple cease-fire in place that would have left Indian troops in occupation of virtually the whole of East Pakistan.

The most virulent exchanges in the Council were not between Pakistan and India, but between the representatives of China and the Soviet Union. China accused the latter of trying to

> ...take advantage of India's inevitable dependence on the Soviet Union in the war to control the Indo-Pakistan subcontinent and the Indian Ocean...and to compete with another superpower for world hegemony...Soviet social imperialists are [engaged in]...aggression, subversion and expansion everywhere...[with the aim] of encircling China.

The Soviet Union's Jacob Malik gave as good as he got, calling his Chinese colleague, the courtly, dignified Huang Hua, 'an imperial court jester', and denouncing 'the Chinese traitors to socialism for their pathological hatred of the Soviet Union'. This went on throughout the session of the Security Council revealing the contest for power and influence that lay behind the regional Indo-Pakistan conflict and that was disguised by the humanitarian issue.

On 8 December I received instructions from Islamabad to proceed to New York to join Bhutto, who had just been sworn in as Deputy Prime Minister and Foreign Minister, and who would be presenting Pakistan's case to the UN Security Council. On the ground the military situation was serious but still open; in East Pakistan the army was resisting with determination and had given up only a few salients; in the West it had advanced in the Chhamb sector on the Kashmir front. Moreover the UN General Assembly had that very morning adopted by an overwhelming majority a resolution calling for an unconditional cease-fire and withdrawal of Indian troops from East Pakistan territory.

There was little sympathy in the world for Pakistan's case. The actions of the military in East Pakistan had aroused universal abhorrence and condemnation. No one thought that Pakistan could be put together again, even if there had been no Indian intervention. India's systematic, well-planned and blatant interference in the situation was no secret but it aroused no sense of outrage. However the vast majority of nations were not prepared to go so far as to give it any kind of sanction or approbation. This was particularly so in the case of African countries divided by artificial boundaries and riven by tribal conflicts, who feared for themselves. The Permanent Representative of Togo speaking in the General Assembly, expressed these fears when he declared, 'Our organization that has 131 members today, might have more than 300 tomorrow.' Hence the 104 votes by which the General Assembly, in the face of the Soviet Union's repeated vetoes in the Security Council, adopted a resolution calling for a cease-fire in East Pakistan and the withdrawal of Indian troops.[3]

Thus when Bhutto arrived at the United Nations, the case had few redeeming features, but he was not entirely without cards to play. When I arrived at New York's John F. Kennedy Airport on the tenth, the Mission official who met me had some unexpected news: a telegram had been received by the UN Secretary General from his man in Dhaka conveying a message from General Farman Ali of Pakistan's Eastern Command. The sum and substance of the message was that the command was ready to give up and wanted the United Nations to arrange the withdrawal of Pakistani troops and officials from the place. The official, Khalid Mahmud, told me that Mr Bhutto who had arrived a short while earlier, was in his hotel and was 'stunned' by this development. I went straight to the hotel, the Pierre on Fifth Avenue, and to Mr Bhutto's suite. I went through the empty sitting-room and knocking at the door, entered the bedroom. One could see at one glance that it was all up for Pakistan this time—distraught faces in a dimly lit room, reflecting the evening gloom falling on the leafless trees of Central Park beyond the windows; a huddle of third secretaries whispering deferentially in the background. Bhutto himself was at the other end of the room, standing over a table and scribbling something on a sheet of green paper. Rafi Raza was by his side, hovering over the same green paper. A tall man, lean and paunchy at the same time, emerged from the shadows and taking me for an inopportune visitor, ushered me back into the sitting-room as Bhutto called after us: 'Yes, yes, do sit down. I shall be with you in a moment.' The lean man offered me a drink and introduced himself as a colonel someone who was accompanying the Deputy Prime Minister in order to keep him briefed on the military developments (more likely, keep an eye on him, I thought!). Someone gave me a copy of Farman Ali's purported telegram and said, 'The Foreign Minister would like you to have a look at this.' Everyone said 'purported' as if to exorcize the looming shades of defeat.

The telegram, referring to the responsibility thrown upon the local authorities by Islamabad to take the 'final and fateful' decision, called upon the elected representatives of East Pakistan to form a government in Dhaka and then came to the point: the UN Secretary General was requested to arrange for (1) an immediate cease-fire; (2) the repatriation with honour of the armed forces to West Pakistan; (3) similar repatriation of all West Pakistan civilian personnel; and (4) the safety of all persons settled in East Pakistan since 1947 and a guarantee against any reprisals. The message asserted that this was a proposal for a peaceful transfer of power and was not to be taken as an offer to surrender. The telegram also proposed that the Consuls of the five permanent members of the Security Council immediately take over control of the city!

When Bhutto joined us, I asked him how he saw the prospect in the Security Council. He answered in a tone of exasperation, 'I don't know! I have just arrived and am confronted with this extraordinary message. Until the meaning of this is cleared up I cannot do a thing.' He had been trying to get through to Yahya Khan on the phone to find out if the message represented government's policy or whether it was a local initiative, as appeared to be the case from the text. But the telephone lines to Islamabad were not working and he was sending Yahya a cable (the green paper) to say that the Dhaka message signified a 'humiliating end to the existence of United Pakistan', and that he refused to be party to such an ignominious surrender.

U Thant had of course immediately informed the President of the Security Council and the five permanent members of the receipt of the message and its text. Chiao Kuan Hua, the Deputy Foreign Minister of China, who was leading the delegation to the

General Assembly, refused to accept the Secretary General's communication and criticized his action in circulating the message as an act of partisanship. On the other hand, the Soviet representative speaking in the Security Council a couple of days later, referred approvingly to the telegram as a sign that 'some important military and political personalities in East Pakistan itself are inclined to approach the situation realistically'. He added, 'If the Pakistan government is prepared now to take into account the realities, then we could come to an agreement on a Security Council decision on the two interlinked questions of calling a halt to the bloodshed and reaching a political settlement in East Pakistan.'

When news spread in the corridors of the UN that Pakistan was ready to give up the fight, it seriously undermined the credibility of Pakistan's diplomatic position. Not that anyone doubted the eventual outcome of the unequal fight in East Pakistan. Cut off from the home base and operating in the midst of a hostile population, lacking air-cover, with units scattered all over the province and the Indians coming at them in superior numbers from every side, it was only a question of time before the Pakistani defenders succumbed to the invader's greater strength. At this terminal stage there could be no winning strategy for Pakistan either on the battlefield or in the UN talk-shop. However at that particular juncture, time was an important factor. Bhutto had come with no specific instructions nor to my knowledge, did he receive any while the drama was played out to its sorry end. My feeling was that he was playing it by ear and hoped that if the line could be held for some time in East Pakistan and the costs of the East Pakistan adventure increased for India, there was still a chance that some sort of 'negotiated' arrangement might be reached to let East Pakistan go its way.

Could the beleaguered and outnumbered garrison have held out long enough to give diplomacy a chance? Western media and military analysts considered that despite the heavy odds and impossible logistics, the Pakistan Army would give the Indians a run for their money. In the US National Security Council, in the first week of the war, the view was that the Pakistanis would be able to hold out for some weeks. David Housego, writing in the *Times* of 13 December, noted that there had been few instances of Pakistani soldiers or units surrendering on their own. Now the message from Pakistan's Eastern Command cast a different light on the situation. But it was still the opinion of some of our friends that Pakistan would gain if it could stand its ground for some more time. The Chinese Deputy Foreign Minister Chiao Kuan Hua called on Bhutto the following morning at the Pakistan Mission. He urged very strongly that the Pakistan Forces make the utmost effort to hold out for another week. Chiao said that if the fighting could be kept up for another week or so, 'there would be great benefits' and added that Beijing was considering what decision it should take in the circumstances. Similarly pressing advice was being received from Washington. On learning of the message from Dhaka, the United States urged Islamabad to keep the fight going for at least two days as it was about to take certain action. This turned out to be the despatch of the USS *Enterprise* into the Bay of Bengal, a gesture that could have little effect on the ground situation but was perhaps meant to send a signal to the Chinese who, under pressure 'to do something', had asked the Americans for assurances as to what they, for their part, intended to do. The Sino-American friendship was still a new-found thing and the Chinese may have been concerned that the United States would drag China into a losing confrontation with the Soviet Union and sit back to watch the fun from the sidelines.

Bhutto strongly urged Yahya Khan to keep the fight going for at least a week more and to launch an effective counter-thrust in the West. Yahya's cable in reply was equivocal. Describing Farman Ali's message as a 'slip' that had been 'nipped in the bud', it went on to say that trying to hold out for another week would be 'fatal to our position' and as for a big push in the western sector, that matter was to be left to the decision of local military commanders. The cable stressed the need for 'the fastest action' to get a cease-fire. In other words, the idea of making compensating gains in the Western theatre for the inevitable setbacks in the East was no longer on and that 'slip' or not, what Farman Ali had more plainly spelt out was just what the regime itself desired.[4]

In a delegation meeting in the minister's hotel room next morning, the question on everyone's mind was, 'Will the Chinese? Won't the Chinese?' Bhutto's chaperon, the Colonel, said that a massive Chinese intervention was needed without a moment to lose. Bhutto asked opinions about what, if anything, China was likely to do. He must have known the answer quite well and was probably testing the diplomatic acumen of the delegates. Each delegate answered the question in his lights or hopes. To me it seemed odd that at that stage of a life-and-death game we should be debating the question. I do not believe that Bhutto had any illusions that the Chinese would, or could, intervene effectively at that stage. However he sent a cable to Yahya Khan urging him to fly to Beijing himself in order to press China for help.

On the evening of 12 December Bhutto presented Pakistan's case to the Security Council. He spoke extempore and concluded his two-hour long statement at midnight. The London *Times* correspondent reported in the next morning's newspaper that Mr Bhutto's instructions could well have comprised just five words 'Sock it to 'em baby!' But also, he distanced himself from the military regime. Admitting that mistakes had been made he declared, 'I spearheaded a struggle against a mighty dictator and my roots are with the people...I speak as the authentic voice of the people of Pakistan.' To this India's Foreign Minister, Swaran Singh (at whom Bhutto had sneered in his statement: 'What is so distinguished about him!') made a somewhat condescending reply,

> I have admiration for his [Mr Bhutto's] abilities and we in India recognize him as the democratically elected leader of the largest single party of West Pakistan...the time is not far off when the military rulers of West Pakistan will also respect the verdict of their people and give Mr Bhutto the opportunity to form a representative government with which it will be possible for us to deal in order to remove the root causes of the tension between our two countries.

In the days that followed there was no time for further niceties. Pakistan's military position in East Pakistan was collapsing hour by hour. Jessore had fallen to Indian troops after a stiff fight by our men. They were reported to be falling back to two assembly points to the north for a last ditch stand. (However, even after foreign correspondents had entered the place with the Indian troops, Pakistan's controlled media was saying that Jessore was still in Pakistani hands!) Now every new move in the Council was a further concession to India, every one of which she rejected.

India had one aim at this point—to seize Dhaka and force the Pakistan Forces to surrender. India needed only a few more days to attain this aim and the time was amply provided by the proceedings of the Security Council. An official of the Pakistan Mission overheard an Indian diplomat asking the Soviets to stall the debates till Tuesday or Wednesday by which time Dhaka was expected to be in Indian hands. The Soviets obliged with endless filibustering—lengthy speeches, points of order, procedural motions. The normally dour Comrade Jacob Malik turned quite gushy, describing the Indo-Soviet friendship as 'the apple of our eyes...Lenin's dream' and so forth. One dilatory move was a Soviet proposal that Mujibur Rahman be invited to address the Security Council. On 14 December, meeting against the background of Indian demands on General Niazi to surrender, the Security Council spent forty minutes debating whether it should meet the next morning at 9.00 or 9.30!

The United Kingdom had been working with France on a draft of their own but were still not ready with it and proposed an adjournment of twenty-four hours 'to allow us to complete our consultations'—and for Dhaka's fall to be accomplished. When this Anglo-French draft (a balanced document that put together in one text three key elements: cease-fire, political settlement and withdrawal of troops) was finally ready to be tabled, it was too late. A British representative told us that in the light of General Niazi's request to the Indian Commander for a cease-fire in place, they would no longer include in their draft the call for withdrawal of Indian troops. He advised that Pakistan should now go for a simple cease-fire. But by now the Soviets indicated that they would veto even such a proposal.

The Indian commander conceded to General Niazi the 'few hours' respite he had requested in order to hold consultations, but made it clear that they would accept nothing less than the unconditional surrender of the Pakistan Forces. They kept up pressure of every kind—military as well as psychological—on the beleaguered and demoralized Pakistani Command. They carried out an air raid on Governor Malik's residence and warned Niazi that 'from all directions the ring is closing around Dhaka'. The fall of the city was now indeed a matter of hours. Governor Malik said his prayers, and with a trembling hand wrote out his resignation from the post of Governor.[5] However the Americans

were still pressing Pakistan to hold out for a little longer. Agha
Shahi said to me that China was about to do 'something'.
Speculation about a Chinese intervention was in fact started by
an Indian Foreign Ministry spokesman when he stated that India
had learnt of certain moves being made by China. India probably
had its own reasons for spreading alarm about Chinese intentions.
What *could* China possibly have done at that stage anyway? We
never found out, for the next day Niazi agreed to surrender and
it was all up.[6]

Around this time the Poles made a move that had little effect
on the situation, but has found a permanent place in Pakistan's
political mythology. They came out with a draft resolution[7] to
which no one in the Security Council paid much attention and
that they themselves did not pursue seriously. In Pakistan, long
after the event, those who were looking for a scapegoat or a *deus
ex machina* have discovered in the Polish resolution a magic
talisman that would have prevented defeat, surrender and
humiliation. The draft called for the transfer of power to the
elected representatives in East Pakistan headed by Mujibur
Rahman, who was to be released immediately; then military
actions were to cease in the region for an initial period of seventy-
two hours; during this period Pakistan troops would withdraw to
pre-set positions for evacuation from East Pakistan; Indian troops
would remain in place and withdraw afterwards 'in consultation'
with the new authorities in Dhaka. There would be no cease-fire
in the West, only negotiations to implement the same principles.
The way out offered by the draft was not particularly honourable
nor a smooth one. It had no such object and was put forward
even as General Niazi was offering to surrender. Its real purpose
was to redress the negative image the Soviets had acquired by
vetoing each and every draft in the previous two weeks. The
Soviets wanted to show that their side too had some constructive
proposals of its own to make. The Polish resolution would have
left Indian forces in place and did not call for their withdrawal.
Pakistani troops were to be assembled and shipped off under the
supervision of Indian forces. Above all, it did not call for a cease-
fire in the West, but for negotiations to bring it about. It thus left
India free to impose its terms for ceasing fire in the West and
these would have undoubtedly included the status of Azad
Kashmir. If the Yahya regime wanted a political settlement, it was

offered many opportunities throughout the ten month operation
in East Pakistan, and even as late as 4 December (before Bhutto
arrived at the UN) when the Soviets introduced a draft calling
for a 'political settlement that would inevitably result in a
cessation of hostilities'.

By 15 December when the Polish draft was tabled, it was too
late. In the Security Council lounge, Charlie Naas of the US
delegation said to me 'The problem now is to save West
Pakistan...'

The surrender was signed in Dhaka on the afternoon of 16
December. It was 9.00 in the morning in New York. As the news
of the surrender was coming over the ticker, a cable arrived for
Bhutto carrying the latest instructions from Yahya Khan. These
were to the effect that he should continue his efforts for
'improvements' in the Anglo-British draft but if these were not
obtainable, then he was to go for a simple cease-fire.

Bhutto had walked out of the Security Council the previous
day, anathematizing it as 'the fashion house where the ugliness
of the world is dressed up in pretty words...' He stormed at the
members, 'You can keep your Security Council. I will not be a
party to the ignominious occupation of a part of my country!' He
then stood up and tearing up a sheaf of papers[8] that he had in
his hands, flung the pieces into the air and stormed out of the
Council chamber, followed by a buzzing swarm of reporters.
Council members stared at his retreating figure in dumbfounded
silence and members of his own delegation sat petrified for a
moment before scrambling after him. Only Agha Shahi claimed
not to have been surprised. 'I am sure he had rehearsed it all in
front of a mirror before coming to the meeting,' he said to me
later.

The surrender ceremony on Dhaka's Paltan Maidan was an
elaborate affair with lunch laid on afterwards. The Indian general
had the refinement to bring his wife along to savour his triumph,
and she stood by his side as Niazi made his submission. Gavin
Young wrote an account of the event in the *Observer* of 19 December,
and spoke compassionately of the 'unfortunate Tiger Niazi' who
that morning had to bear the whole brunt of the humiliation that
was heaped upon Pakistan. His disgrace seemed all the greater
because of his earlier bragging and chest-thumping. But he was
only the instrument of a policy that had led to the disaster. Yahya

Khan had assured him, or so he told Gavin Young, that the Americans and the Chinese were going to intervene.

The concern now was with the fate of the rest of Pakistan. The United States warned the Soviets that the whole range of American-Soviet relations would be affected if they did not prevail upon India to cease and desist. Ambassador Bush put some pointed questions to the Indians in the Security Council: 'Does India intend...to destroy the Pakistan Army in the West?...to annex territory in West Pakistan?... to take parts of Pakistan-controlled Kashmir, contrary to the Security Council resolutions of 1948, '49 and '50? The world has a right to know what India's intentions are.'

The Security Council met at noon on the eighteenth to hear India's answers. Swaran Singh declared:

> We have no intention whatsoever of acquiring any part of West Pakistan or of Bangladesh by conquest or otherwise. Secondly, if Pakistan removes the threat to our security, we shall be glad to consider any proposals for a cease-fire and withdrawals in the wake of a political settlement acceptable to the elected representatives of Bangladesh.

This last stipulation was curious and the declaration was hedged in with ifs and buts; moreover, it omitted to say anything concerning Kashmir.

The Pakistan delegation had stayed away from the Council meeting to avoid the indignity of listening to India's unilateral promulgation of a cease-fire in the Western theatre announced by Indira Gandhi the previous evening. Some of us sat in the Security Council lounge just off the Council chamber in order to keep track of what was going on there. An Indian delegate, then another, walked by on their way to the meeting. Neither could resist the temptation of turning around to stare at the representatives of the now humbled, age-old foe—a gesture human enough, but as inelegant as that of the Indian general in bringing his wife to the surrender ceremony. In the midst of all this, from Islamabad came another surrealistic piece of news: Yahya Khan had promulgated a new constitutional dispensation granting full autonomy to the Provinces, including East Pakistan, and it was to go into effect four days hence!

Bhutto gave a lunch at the Pierre Hotel to thank the fifty or so countries that had given support to Pakistan in the United Nations during the crisis. Before the lunch he called three members of the delegation, Ambassadors Niaz Naik, Akbar Tyabji, and myself, up to his suite and asked us what we thought ought to be done next. My submission was: make a clean break with the past, the military regime and all it stood for, and begin by releasing Mujibur Rahman and sending him home. Among the guests at the lunch were three token East Pakistani members of the delegation. They had played no role through the Council's debates except to be seen as such, but it is doubtful that anyone had noticed them or paid attention to them. They sat at the lunch table, wraith-like and dumb with shock. One of them, lawyer Zulmat Ali, broke down and wept like a child when Bhutto made a speech after lunch. Benazir, who had come down from Harvard, was at the table beside her father. He referred to her presence in his speech, saying that he had asked her to come down for the Security Council's meetings so that when she grew up she would remember these difficult and tragic moments in the country's life and would learn that in the worst of times a nation must hold its head high and in the darkest moments look to the future with hope.

Then a telephone rang in an adjoining room and someone came running in to say that Islamabad was on the line for Mr Bhutto. The line was rather bad and he had to shout into the instrument to make himself heard. He was saying, 'Don't do anything until I come. I am returning directly.' He repeated, 'Don't do anything!' several times. It was Mustafa Khar at the other end, telling him that the situation in the country was extremely tense and liable to spin out of control. Bhutto had already received an urgent summons from Yahya Khan to return without delay. There had been demonstrations all over the country with people calling for Yahya Khan's head. Varying accounts have appeared of what was going on within the army in those critical days but all speak of rage and frustration among the officers and men and of indications that discipline in the army itself had come under tremendous strain.[9] In a meeting at the GHQ, General Abdul Hamid, the Chief of Staff, had been all but manhandled by junior officers. A group of senior officers threatened to take things into their own hands if Yahya and his band did not make way at once for the elected leaders of the country. Some months later when I called on Bhutto at the President's House in Islamabad, he told me that on his return he had found Yahya sitting by himself in the veranda and already in his cups. He was behaving in a hysterical manner, one moment weeping like a child, and then suddenly breaking into spasms of hyena-like laughter. Bhutto said that if he had not taken over the reins that day and there and then, a complete collapse of law and order might have occurred.

In the Security Council debate and dissension continued for some days still. The Soviets even now were threatening to veto anything that did not suit India in any way. The Chinese castigated them as Social-Imperialists and warned India that the millstone of victory would hang heavy around her neck and lead to greater upheavals in the subcontinent. The French Representative then introduced the long-incubating Anglo-French draft and in responding to Bhutto's chiding at their earlier inaction, made a telling point: 'This resolution obviously comes late. We recognize this but after all, the Security Council was seized very late of a difficult situation; whereas some months earlier it would have been possible to prevent what occurred.' True, all too true! The Soviet representative expressing satisfaction that 'reality had prevailed' commended the 'noble intention' of India not to put forward any territorial claims and perhaps by this word of praise also gave her warning not to go any further. The Indian Foreign Minister spoke nevertheless of the necessity to make some 'adjustments' in the Kashmir cease-fire line in order to prevent a repetition of Pakistani attacks and to make the line more rational, stable and viable. 'This,' Sardar Swaran Singh said ominously, 'we propose to discuss and settle with Pakistan.'

I made my way back to Belgrade making a brief stop-over in Brussels. There I found the Ambassador voicing criticisms of the Bhutto government—its policies seemed to be confused and its actions were poorly planned. This was only the third or fourth day since Bhutto had taken over! The Embassy Counsellor kept putting verbal quotation marks around the word 'atrocities' in talking about the army action in East Pakistan and then added a gem of his own: 'Anyway whatever they did was only against the Hindus...' In Belgrade the Embassy Counsellor, a Bengali, had fled leaving behind a note: 'I served the regime of the generals for a year without sincerity. Now everything is clear and Bangladesh is a reality.' There were still quite a few Bengalis among the staff, frightened and uncertain of what to do. The instructions from Islamabad were to take away their passports and not to let them go to Bangladesh. I decided to ignore these instructions and most of the Bengalis drifted away.

The question in Belgrade now was what the Yugoslav government would do about recognizing Bangladesh. The new country was sooner or later bound to receive recognition from the countries of the world. Our policy was not to oppose such action but to ask that recognition be made conditional upon the withdrawal of Indian forces from Bangladesh. It was conveyed to me by the Yugoslav Foreign Ministry that this was precisely the course of action the Yugoslav government intended to follow. But apparently there were differences on the matter within the Yugoslav government. Stana Tomasevic, Chairwoman of the National Assembly's Foreign Affairs Committee, told me that a particularly heated debate had taken place on the subject in the Committee with some members insisting on immediate recognition of the break-away country. The position Yugoslavs leaders, officials and others took on the whole Bangladesh affair depended to some extent on which Yugoslav nationality they came from. The Serbs generally showed a greater understanding for Pakistan's attempt to hold the country together, no matter what the price; Croats and other minority nationalities tended to sympathize with the Bengali urge for autonomy. The Muslim *mufti* held prayers for Pakistan when war broke out on 4 December.

In the end the Foreign Affairs Committee decided to follow the Foreign Ministry's advice: 'Wait and watch.' I got confirmation of this from Foreign Minister Tepavac himself at a dinner given by the Canadian Ambassador, when in the presence of a number of other ambassadors, he said to me: 'Bangladesh is a reality that has to be recognized, but the Foreign Ministry's view is that there has to be a waiting period before formal recognition is considered.'

Two nights later, as I was preparing to turn in after dinner, I received a phone call from the Foreign Ministry's Pakistan desk officer, someone by the name of Serbanovic, saying that he was sorry to be calling at such an hour but could I please go around to see him at the Ministry; something quite urgent had come up that could not wait till the morning. I could guess what it was. The morning papers had reported the return of Tito from his weekend retreat on Brioni island and he must have reversed the Foreign ministry's wait-and-watch policy. The Embassy driver had been let off, and after the Bengali exodus I had no senior officer left whom I could depute to go and receive the unwelcome news. So I got dressed, got the car out, and drove through the deserted, wind-blown streets to the Ministry. The place was in darkness. A bearded young man was waiting at the entrance and led me through long, dimly-lit corridors to Serbanovic's office. There I was given the news. 'We wanted you to be the first to know before the news is released to the Press,' the desk officer said as if a special favour was being conferred, and he added lamely, 'we think it would help Bangladesh from feeling totally dependent on India and the Soviets.' I mentioned the continued presence of Indian troops in Bangladesh, to which he said, 'We never said that the last Indian soldier must be out before recognition can be given.' At this I got up and left saying to the squirming Serbanovic, 'Do let us know when you have news of the first Indian soldier leaving!'

The next morning Radio Pakistan announced that Pakistan was breaking off relations with Yugoslavia although Bhutto had declared earlier that the government did not intend to apply the Hallstein Doctrine[10] with regard to the recognition of Bangladesh. The Yugoslavs were nettled, specially because they felt that Yugoslavia had been singled out among the non-aligned countries for this action. When I announced the news to Serbanovic, it was his turn to be sarcastic, 'We suppose now you will also be breaking off relations with the Soviet Union!' The Soviet Union had recognized Bangladesh that very morning but for obvious reasons, there could be no question of breaking off relations with it.

We got everything packed in twenty-four hours with the help of the embassy staff and in the face of a mini-revolt by its Yugoslav members who, after consulting among themselves, decided that it would be unpatriotic on their part to contribute in any way to a move that was intended to be a snub to their country. However I then received instructions to stay in place till further orders— so we took down the flag and the embassy name-plate, cried off the pending diplomatic invitations, and went into a sort of diplomatic limbo. The Yugoslav government continued to accord to us all diplomatic privileges and immunities and the Pakistan government reciprocated the courtesy to the Yugoslav Ambassador who was in the same situation in Islamabad. Friends, including Yugoslavs, still visited us. Among those who came was Vlado Sestan, who had been Ambassador in Islamabad and was now Tito's Chief of Protocol. I am sure he came with Tito's knowledge and permission in order to show that, despite everything, there were no hard feelings. In another unusual gesture, before leaving for good, I paid a farewell call on Foreign Minister Tepavac who admitted that he had been overruled on the question of Bangladesh's recognition and expressed the hope that the break between our countries would be short-lived. And so indeed it was, but meanwhile the Embassy was redesignated as a Trade Office and a young Foreign Service officer arrived to take charge. I myself was transferred to New York as Permanent Representative to the United Nations and proceeded to Islamabad to receive briefings and instructions.

How did things come to such a pass in Pakistan? Was East Pakistan's breakaway inevitable? And if it had to be, could not the bloodshed and shame have been avoided? On this last matter Bhutto appointed the Supreme Court Chief Justice Hamoodur Rahman (himself a Bengali) to look into what had happened, but his findings and conclusions may never see the light of day. Some piecemeal reports that have appeared in recent years give some idea of what happened and what went wrong.[11] The Commission is said to have recommended the public trial of a number of generals, including Yahya Khan, for a 'criminal conspiracy' to usurp power from Ayub on 25 March 1969 and to maintain Yahya in power by force if necessary, for attempting to influence the results of the 1970 elections and later to incite some of the parties to refuse to join the National Assembly at Dhaka on 3 March. In any case the Hamoodur Rahman Commission's terms were confined to the immediate causes— things done or not done by officials, politicians, generals, etc. In the absence of an authoritative account, in Pakistan the event has been dealt with by the time-honoured method of passing the buck. Bhutto's opponents hold him to be the main culprit. For them it was not the eight-month long reign of terror unleashed

by the Yahya Khan regime, but Bhutto's ambition and hunger
for power that led to the breakup. Bhutto may have had his own
ideas and ambitions but it was hardly likely that Yahya Khan and
his coterie had placed themselves at his disposal to achieve them.
The late Admiral Ahsan, then Governor of East Pakistan, in a
paper he submitted to the Hamoodur Rahman Commission,
spoke of the 'high tide of militarism flowing turbulently' in
Islamabad which he visited in the middle of February, and of
open talk of a 'military solution according to plan'.[12]

Military action against the civil population is a crime against
humanity but it has become commonplace in modern conflict—
witness Lebanon, Bosnia, Chechnya. In Pakistan it did not stop
with East Pakistan, but was resorted to again in Balochistan under
Bhutto, and in Sindh under Ziaul Haq. But in the particular case
of East Pakistan, coming after the Awami League had swept the
polls in the 1970 elections on a platform of autonomy, it was, to
paraphrase Talleyrand, a mistake as well as a crime. Worse still,
the campaign ordered by Yahya Khan against the country's
majority province, seemed to have no specific aim and pursued
no well-defined strategy. Having ordered the troops to sort out
the Bengalis, General Yahya and his advisors simply sat back to
watch events unfold and did not seem to know what to do next
or indeed to care what happened. The regime had Sheikh
Mujibur Rahman locked up and in their hands for nearly nine
months, and yet made no effort to come to terms with him or to
bring him around to a more amenable frame of mind. The
political strategy of the regime seems to have been based on the
puerile belief that a taste of the *danda*—the big stick—would cow
down the Bengali *babu*.

Nor was there a diplomatic strategy to counter India's open
and armed intervention in East Pakistan. In fact the regime had
developed a phobia for the idea of a political settlement and for
that reason did not look for or encourage any third party or
United Nations' involvement in the situation. When Secretary-
General U Thant offered his good offices, his offer was not taken
up. At no stage did the Pakistan government itself request a
meeting of the Security Council out of fear that the Council
would call for a political settlement, that is, a compromise with
the Awami League. In October, in the face of the rapidly
deteriorating situation on the ground, the regime could no

longer avoid recourse to the United Nations, but again did not take the issue there directly. Instead Yahya Khan wrote to Nixon seeking United States' 'help and assistance in this grave hour with a view to facilitating an urgent consideration of the situation by the UN Security Council'. As late as 4 December, Pakistan was objecting to the word 'political' in an American draft resolution that called, among other things, for the creation of 'a political climate conducive to a voluntary return of refugees to East Pakistan'. With Indian troops overrunning large parts of East Pakistan, the Permanent Mission to the United Nations continued to receive instructions to resist any resolution which 'amounts to interference in our internal affairs by suggesting a particular political settlement'.

The absence of a political and diplomatic strategy was accompanied by a misreading of India's objectives and intentions. Pakistan's policy makers proceeded on the assumption that India would be content to seize a piece of territory in East Pakistan and there set up a puppet 'Free Bangladesh' state in order to carry out guerrilla raids and international propaganda against Pakistan. Gavin Young of the *Observer* quotes Farman Ali as telling him at the surrender lunch in Dhaka, 'The President told us that he did not expect a general war with India.' Thus Yahya Khan's reaction to warnings from various quarters about Indian preparations for war was to threaten India with 'general war' if she tried to take any piece of East Pakistan territory. The assumption that India did not want a war may have been valid at an earlier stage of the crisis, but by autumn the Bangladesh movement had gathered such strength in the territory and so much support world-wide, and Pakistan's logistical position had become so difficult, that 'general war' for India was no longer a threat but an opportunity. When the crunch came and Indian troops invaded East Pakistan, Pakistani tactics remained geared to the old strategy and troops were spread thin all over the province trying to prevent any sliver of territory falling into Indian hands.

Bhutto was of course one of the main players in the drama and had his share of responsibility in the tragedy that unfolded. He had opposed the Six Point autonomy demand of Mujibur Rahman and considered that it was tantamount to secession. Aziz Ahmad, his foreign policy advisor, told me that he for his part, had favoured accepting the Six Points if that was the only way of maintaining a link between the two parts of Pakistan. But Bhutto's room for manœuvre was restricted by his West Pakistan constituency which included the army and the Establishment. However it is doubtful that even agreement on the Six Points would have brought about a definitive settlement of Pakistan's fundamental dilemma. As Prime Minister, Mujib would have started to move the headquarters of various institutions such as the State Bank and PIA (and the jobs that go with them) to the eastern province, raising hackles in the West and possibly bringing back martial law. For Bhutto this much must be conceded, that he did make an attempt at compromise and went twice to Dhaka to meet Mujibur Rahman. He believed, rightly or wrongly, that if the Six Point autonomy was conceded to East Pakistan, the smaller Western provinces too would demand greater autonomy and Pakistan could well break up into five units, each with its own currency and external economic policy. Those who hold Bhutto responsible for breaking up Pakistan because he refused to go to the National Assembly in Dhaka, can hardly do so without closing their eyes to India's role and the Indo-Soviet treaty and above all Mujibur Rahman's refusal to give an inch on the Six Point demand.

Mujib too was operating under constraints, partly created by his own excessive rhetoric, and was therefore unable to display any spirit of accommodation or flexibility. He made no attempt to go over the heads of Yahya Khan or Bhutto and appeal to West Pakistan public opinion. Even after he had won the elections, he disdained to pay a visit to the western province of a country of which he was entitled to become the ruler on the basis of the majority he had gained in East Pakistan. Admiral Ahsan who was Governor of East Pakistan and sympathetic to the Bengali grievances and demands, told the Hamoodur Rahman Commission of his vain attempts to persuade Mujib to go to West Pakistan after the election. It was as if Mujib was not interested in ruling over the whole of Pakistan. He is reported to have said to someone who raised the subject with him: 'Baba, do you think the Punjabi generals and civil servants are going to let me rule over West Pakistan?'

The strategic error—if one can ascribe to one particular action what was almost a historic inevitability—perhaps was Yahya Khan's in not having settled the autonomy issue *before* the elections. When he took over power from Ayub Khan, Yahya took a major constitutional step in undoing the West Pakistan One Unit and restoring the four original provinces of the Punjab, Sindh, Balochistan and the Frontier. This bold step removed the most acute cause of contention among the West Pakistan provinces. That was surely the time to have issued a fiat also on East Pakistan's demand for autonomy. If the new Martial Law Chief had straightaway granted four or five out of Mujibur Rahman's Six Points, it might have taken the steam out of the question and not left it to figure as the central issue in the elections. This was the view of some foreign observers. Dr Radovan Uvalic, the head of the Yugoslav Foreign Ministry and formerly ambassador to India, speaking to me in Belgrade before the war broke out, said that Yahya Khan had called elections too soon and without preparing the ground. Now he had painted himself into a corner, said Uvalic, and it was up to India whether his attempts to reach a political settlement would be allowed to succeed.

Still, in reality the problem had deeper, more fundamental roots. They lay in the factor that is common to both Pakistan and India, and indeed to any large multi-cultural, multi-ethnic, multi-lingual society: the conflict between the grass roots attachment people feel for their own kind—in language, race, religion, whatever—and the demands of a larger loyalty. Both in India and Pakistan the whole approach, ethos and thrust of the leadership was, and remains, in favour of a highly centralized State, 'a strong centre'. That is why in the end the British Cabinet Mission's confederal solution for retaining a united India failed. Bangladesh broke away from Pakistan for the same sort of reasons that Pakistan itself had seceded from India. Bengali nationalism was there right from the beginning—hence the use of the plural 'States' in the 1940 Muslim League resolution calling for the separation of Muslim India from the rest. No doubt the nationalism had Hindu and Muslim versions, but it did not follow that Bengali Muslim nationalism was prepared to be absorbed and subsumed in a wider, generalized Islamic nationalism of a North Indian complexion. Bengali nationalism in Pakistan first raised its head when Jinnah was alive and still in charge, over the question of Pakistan's national language. When trouble broke out in Dhaka over the issue he went there and affirmed that

'Urdu and Urdu alone' would be the country's national language. His exhortation silenced the demonstrators but did not settle the issue. The significant fact however is that Bengali particularism did not disappear even after Bengali was officially recognized some years later as Pakistan's other national language. Over the years a number of other concessions were made to Bengali sentiment and grievances—Dhaka was declared to be the country's second capital and the seat of the National Assembly; jobs were reserved for Bengalis in the major civil services; and Bengali units were raised in the armed forces. But what the Bengalis wanted was not simply a fair share of jobs, resources and opportunities; nor, at bottom, was the disaffection caused by the superior airs affected by West Pakistani officialdom in dealing with Bengalis. These were aggravating factors and not the basic cause. What the Bengali was seeking deep down, was the recognition of his separate national identity. Except among the small fraction of the older, Urdu-speaking upper crust, there was not a great deal of mutual fellow-feeling between ordinary Bengalis and West Pakistanis—not even among members of Pakistani communities overseas. The Bengali nationalist feeling was always there; it came to take on an anti-West Pakistan colour because of unfairness in the distribution of jobs and development funds, and the overweening attitude of some West Pakistani officials towards Bengalis.

The 1965 War disproved another cherished axiom of the East Pakistan-West Pakistan link. This was the strategic concept that the defence of East Pakistan lay in the plains of the Punjab. When, in his Assembly speech in Dhaka after the war, Bhutto thanked China for, *inter alia*, preventing an Indian invasion of the province, the obvious questions were immediately raised: why then does East Pakistan pay taxes to maintain an expensive army made up almost entirely of people from West Pakistan; why does the country need such a large army? Why indeed—the question was implicit and would soon be openly asked—does East Pakistan need the nexus with West Pakistan?

The Establishment in Pakistan dismissed the Bengali stirrings as the work of agitators and believed that Bengali Muslims had been led astray by Hindu schoolteachers and intellectuals. The antidote was thought to lie in the 'Pakistan ideology' and the remedy in enforcing it through official means. Pakistan ideology is something that nobody has spelled out or defined in specific terms. It is not, like Marxism or fascism, a precise set of principles or dictums that govern state and society and the lives of citizens. In its more benign form it stands for a sort of Boy Scout patriotism: my country, right or wrong. In the minds—and hands—of militant ideologues, it is a prescription for conformity and regimentation and a rationale for suppressing dissent from the established point of view: a Pakistan, as a French journalist put it to me once, 'that allows only one of everything, one religion, one language, one poet, one culture.' Fortunately, thanks to the idiosyncratic character of the people, that type of ideology has never taken hold in the country, despite years of exhortation and preaching, and notwithstanding eleven years of Ziaul Haq.

The root cause of Pakistan's break up, in a way, was built into the concept of a 'Muslim nation' that had found cohesion mainly in its 'otherness' from the 'Hindu nation'. In Pakistan there was— and this is still the case—a disinclination to recognize the issue for what it is: that Pakistan is not a homogenous nation such as Japan or Sweden, but a state made up of diverse groups with different languages, cultures, ethnic roots and historic memories. It is a State that is striving to become a nation. And let it be added, one that despite appearance and set-backs, has a fairly good chance of succeeding. But nations are built by history and not exhortations, and history takes its time.

But this is not to say that there were no foreign hands brewing the trouble that split Pakistan. There were indeed quite a few cooks stirring the witches' brew of separatism in Pakistan. India had never made any secret of her wishes, hopes and plans in this regard. She was at work from the beginning to subvert the loyalty of not only Bengalis but any disaffected section of Pakistan's population. Pakistan tried to pay her back in the same coin wherever and in whatever way it could. In the case of Bangladesh the Soviet Union also took a hand in the matter because Pakistan's developing relationship with China stood in the way of its plans for the region. For some years the United States too had been fanning East Pakistan's discontent for the same reason— Pakistan's alleged 'flirtation' with China. When the United States realized that things had gone too far and Nixon called for his famous 'tilt', united Pakistan was already *in extremis*; and the USS *Enterprise* sailing into the Bay of Bengal sent a message to China and not to the Indian forces sweeping towards Dhaka. In an interview with David Frost some years after his resignation, Richard Nixon while affirming that he had ordered the move on receiving 'absolutely reliable' information that India was planning also to gobble up West Pakistan, admitted that by moving the *Enterprise* into the Bay of Bengal, he was trying to tell China that the United States was not going to let the Soviets get away with everything.

India asserted that the breakup of Pakistan had disproved the two-nation theory. But if it proved anything it was that the subcontinent was made up of neither one nation nor two, but of many. India's chronic problems in the Punjab and Assam and in the South and Pakistan's simmering regional-ethnic troubles indicate that a lasting solution has not yet been found to the problem of governing the subcontinent. In Pakistan's case, the creation from the start of two separate Muslim states in the north-west and north-east of the subcontinent, perhaps would have been a more rational arrangement than harnessing two distant and disparate regions to one common chariot. The Six Point plan probably was not workable in practice, but an agreed parting of the ways in the spirit of the original Muslim League concept, retaining some sort of symbolic nexus between the two 'wings' was a possibility. Indeed it was not long before the geopolitical algebra asserted itself and the equations changed again, with Bangladesh at odds with India and looking to Pakistan for support. It was also ironical that the Bengalis who had chafed under military rule in Pakistan, found themselves under the rule of another set of generals. Initially the armed forces in Bangladesh were kept firmly under civilian control, but then, as Kaisar Rasheed a Bangladesh businessman and a former Foreign Service colleague put it, 'The ethos imbibed by the Bengali military in the Pakistan Army proved too strong.' Perhaps in a united Pakistan, with an increasing proportion of Bengali troops and officers, it would have been more difficult to use the ethnically mixed Pakistan Army for the purpose of engineering *coups.*

A columnist in the Belgrade weekly *Politika* summed up the ironies, paradoxes and contradictions of the Bangladesh War:

Of the sixty or so wars that have taken place since the end of World War II none have changed the map of the world as the Bangladesh

War has done, and none posed so many dilemmas. In the origin, course and outcome of the conflict, some of the most basic principles upon which the United Nations organization is based, have been directly challenged: the right of people to self-determination; respect for the territorial integrity of states; the satisfaction of the legitimately expressed aspirations of people, and the right of self-defence against the use of force and interference from outside. The old conflicts between ends and means, between justice and war have been renewed in a new situation.[13]

It was not surprising that a Yugoslav should show a special sensitivity to these contradictions for they were reflected in Yugoslavia's own internal tensions and could be sensed in her ambivalent reaction to the Bangladesh crisis.

Yugoslavia—a nation that never was

I close this sad chapter with a digression about Yugoslavia where I was ambassador when the events described in this chapter were unfolding. Though Tito had boasted that the world would not hear any more about the 'Balkan Question', the darkness was even then beginning to gather on the horizon. The monsters had not yet emerged from their lairs, but the echo of their rumbling could be heard again beyond the comforting talk about Yugoslavia's unique system of government and Tito's lasting imprint on its society. Trouble broke out in Croatia very soon after the culmination of Pakistan's troubles in Bangladesh. Spearheaded by university students, it was receiving encouragement and direction from none other than the principal leaders of the Croatian Communist Party. So much for the power of ideology to overcome nationalism! And what were the Croatian grievances and demands? An echo of those over which East Pakistan had broken away from West Pakistan—that the Republic of Croatia should have the use of all the foreign currency it earned and not have to share it with Serbia and the other republics; that the official language of Croatia should be Croatian (which differed from the official Serbo-Croat only in its script); that the Naval Headquarters be located at the Croatian port of Split. There were extremists who demanded the creation of a separate Croatian Army and a separate seat for Croatia at the United Nations.

There also appeared about the same time a very early, rudimentary manifestation of Islamic nationalism in the country. Muslims in Yugoslavia had the status of a 'nationality' and not simply a religious group. Yugoslavia had nearly a million Muslims, most of them in Bosnia. Religious practice was now freely allowed, mosques (the one in Belgrade was reopened thanks to the effort of our former ambassador, General Sher Ali) were filled to capacity at prayer times by young and old alike. But in Sarajevo the official Raisul Ulema came under attack for toeing the official line and not maintaining relations with Islamic institutions abroad. In Croatia the Muslim clergy was energetically opposing a move to annex to Christian-majority Zagreb an area that was 'an Islamic religious community'. A group calling itself 'Anxious Muslims' was distributing pamphlets about Muslim grievances and engaging in other activities of the sort. Yugoslav Communist authorities tried to dismiss it all as the work of 'a small and restless political underground...that is agitating against the system...', and condemned the 'tendentious activities of some religious institutions'. But these were straws in the wind.

The Yugoslav crisis illustrates, in an extreme form, the atavism that lurks not too far below the surface of the human mind and which neither economic progress and prosperity, nor education and civilization, nor political and constitutional devices have been able completely to subdue. Watching the unravelling of Yugoslavia, its descent into barbarity and pure unmotivated hatred, one wonders whether the Yugoslav case is the paradigm for the world of tomorrow?

At the Versailles peace conference after World War I, Woodrow Wilson had helped to constitute Yugoslavia, out of a hotch-potch of Slav minorities and some non-Slav peoples inhabiting the Balkan territories of the Hapsburg and Ottoman empires. He believed that he was thereby promoting self-determination, one of the cardinal principles of his foreign policy. But not all of these people felt the same way towards the new state; what the Serbs welcomed as the fulfillment of an ancient racial dream, might have appeared to the Croat and Slovene people as absorption in another alien dominion—that of greater Serbia. For the history of the Balkans over the centuries has been the history not only of their struggle against the Ottoman and Hapsburg empires which ruled over the region, but also of the resistance of the smaller Balkan nationalities against the Serbian urge for domination and expansion. When the Nazis set up a puppet Croat state during World War II, the Serbs were the victims of gruesome massacres perpetrated by the Croats. After the breakup of Yugoslavia these atrocities were matched and over-shadowed by the more vast and terrible horrors that the victims of yesterday inflicted upon the Muslims of Bosnia.

Like Pakistan, Yugoslavia was often described as an artificial creation—it would be more appropriate to recognize both as complex entities. Yugoslavia was created on the basis of a mystique of race and history as Pakistan was on that of religion and history. Each country contained within itself the seed of growth and development as well as the canker of its own destruction. Geographical situation and the evolution of history destined each to be the crossroads or battleground of contending foreign powers. The struggle for survival, in both cases, called for an exceptional degree of inner cohesiveness and diplomatic skill.

Tito initially used the strong arm to subdue and control nationalistic tendencies in the country, but because he was a man of vision—and perhaps because he himself belonged to the Croat minority—he soon saw that that was not the way to keep this patchwork country together. He tried to trace out for it a new, relatively liberal path which would keep Yugoslavia within the Marxist fold but out of the Soviet strait-jacket: a 'humanist' Communism. This heresy incurred the wrath and personal hatred of Stalin who is said to have boasted, 'When I snap my fingers, Tito will be no more!' Stalin did a lot more than snap his fingers. For years Yugoslavia and Tito personally, had to put up with Soviet threats, attacks and harassment of all kinds—propaganda, economic blockade, even armed forays across the borders. A man possessed merely of political acumen and not political genius, a less imaginative man, might have reacted simply by switching his country's loyalties to the West. Instead Tito stood his ground and seized upon the concept and policy of non-alignment as the way out of danger and isolation for Yugoslavia.

For Yugoslavia, non-alignment was more than a source of diplomatic support and international prestige. It was the fulcrum on which were balanced Yugoslavia's internal dissensions and historic conflicts. Tito and his followers stood on the middle ground while on either side were lined up—and waiting—people with diametrically opposite views on many vital questions and who considered that Tito's concept of a self-managing, decentralized, humane Communist system, either went too far, or did not go far enough. There were those who believed that the salvation and safety of Yugoslavia lay in a highly centralized state and party structures that could prevent the claims of the constituent republics from running away with the interests of the nation as a whole; others saw in such a strong state only a cover for renewed Serbian domination. The 'strong state' protagonists took the Soviet Union as a model while their opponents looked to the West for inspiration and help. Underneath it all ran the visceral, historic and mutual antipathies of the Serbs and the Croats as well as other non-Serb peoples, such as the Slovenes and the Muslims.

The logic of Yugoslavia's situation and the material interests of the Yugoslav people spoke for continued unity. Where else would Croatian manufacturers find ready markets except in the rest of the federation? Would the breakup of the Yugoslav Federation into its constituent republics increase the security and well-being of any of them? The evident answer was that the republics, provided that they enjoyed a sufficient degree of autonomy, stood to gain from maintaining the federation. This was the direction Tito had set for the country from the start and he was beginning to accelerate the move towards further autonomy when trouble began to brew. Logic and analysis have to be qualified by the knowledge that the most momentous events in history have defied both and been triggered by the emotional and irrational.

The Yugoslav malady, one could see even twenty years ago, was not over ensuring fair shares for all, but had its roots in the historic rancours and conflicts among its various republics, ethnic groups and nationalities. One heard, as one hears in Pakistan, the lament that people had forgotten the fundamental values and true doctrine on which Yugoslavia was founded. In Yugoslavia's case it was not religion but Communism. Tito urged the people, particularly the younger generation, to be loyal to Communism and to relearn the True Faith. But if the people had indeed forgotten or outgrown these values and beliefs, then exhortations were not going to bring them back to the straight path. Indeed when exhortation did not work, Tito had recourse to the usual methods. 'People who do not fall in line will not be permitted to go around talking and doing as they please,' he said, 'we shall be very strict with these people.' But Tito faced a real and serious dilemma. Rather too much was made of his personality—indeed one can give too much significance to the factor of personality in politics. As in the case of the Quaid-i-Azam in Pakistan, Tito was able to keep matters under control in his lifetime but was unable to resolve the basic issues.

The role and place of the Yugoslav Army in the country also offer some parallels with Pakistan's case. In Yugoslavia, as in other Communist countries, there was not a clear line of demarcation between the armed forces and the party or the civil authorities. Many of those who held important positions in the government and the party were former partisan fighters and comrades-in-arms of serving generals. The top generals were members of the League of Communists, which moreover had a political cell in each unit of the forces. Under Tito, the recruitment to the officer corps had been diversified and it was now representative of all the republics. But seventy per cent of the men still came from Serbia. The other republics, Croatia in particular, expressed a lack of confidence in an army that in its view, was ethnically imbalanced. The army's own view of its role was neither as an arbitrator in society nor as a neutral party, but as a factor for the uncompromising defence of the country 'precisely as it is constituted—as a socialist, non-aligned, united community of free nations.' There was an echo here of the vocation the Pakistan Army was to be given during the Zia years, of defending the so-called 'ideological frontiers' of the country.

NOTES

[1] Keesings Contemporary Archives, 15-21 May 1971; p. 24600.

[2] Meeting of the US National Security Council's Special Action Group on India and Pakistan; 8 December 1971; cited in the Anderson Papers.

[3] Resolution No. 2793 (26) of 7 December 1971.

[4] According to excerpts published in *The News*, Lahore, 16 December 1990, the circumstances in which the Eastern command sent such a message directly to

the UN Secretary General, was among the matters that the Hamoodur Rahman Commission recommended for investigation.

[5] Gavin Young in the *Observer*, London of 18 December 1971.

[6] Paul Marc Henry, who was the UN Secretary General's Special Representative in Dhaka at the time, told me many years later when he was French Ambassador to Lebanon, that the Pakistani surrender had been pre-arranged between Niazi and the Indian commanders in the fashion of the war-lords in medieval China, who would settle the fate of a battle on paper by calculating the odds in terms of each side's strength and position, instead of getting a lot of people killed in order to find out. Henry said that Niazi wrote to him denying this charge, but claimed that he had saved countless lives in deciding not to take a stand and fight it out.

[7] Draft resolution no. S/ 10453 Rev. 1; 15 December 1971.

[8] This was not the Polish resolution, but the text of the closing speech prepared by his speech-writer Yusuf Buch, in which Pakistan's indignation at the Security Council's inaction was expressed in more measured words.

[9] *See*, for example, article by Brigadier F. B. Ali in *The News* of Lahore dated 18 September 1993, and Lt. Gen. Gul Hassan, op. cit.

[10] This was the West German policy of not maintaining diplomatic relations with any non-Communist state that recognized East Germany.

[11] *Nation*, Lahore, 16 December 1989.

[12] *Dawn*, Karachi, 16 and 17 December 1992.

[13] Dusan Simic; *Politika*, Belgrade, 18 December 1971.

CHAPTER 11

THE NEW PAKISTAN

As Indian troops advanced on Dhaka and the Security Council sat immobilized by Soviet vetoes, Bhutto flung defiance at the world: 'So what if Dhaka falls? So what if the whole of East Pakistan falls? We shall build a new Pakistan. We shall build a better Pakistan, a greater Pakistan!'[1]

As soon as he returned to Pakistan and took over the government from Yahya Khan, he set about this task briskly and authoritatively—and inauspiciously—under the umbrella of martial law. He declared that martial law was needed in order to carry out without any obstruction and impediment, the fundamental reforms he wished to introduce. He had a precedent in Britain's post-war Labour government which also had retained the government's war-time emergency powers with the same end in view. But Pakistan, with its history of military *coups*, was not Britain, and Bhutto's majority was large enough to allow him to do whatever he wished in the way of reforms, without the aid of emergency powers. The army had handed over power only under the compulsion of defeat, and in assuming the mantle of Chief Martial Law Administrator, Bhutto decidedly struck the wrong note. It wasn't a good augury but to some minds it was an act entirely in character for Bhutto. Misgivings about his style of government were strengthened when he used the emergency powers to settle personal scores. The sight on Pakistan Television of someone like the retired General Habibullah being led away in handcuffs to detention under the Defence of Pakistan Law, was not reassuring as to the way Bhutto meant to run the country, nor indeed for his own future, if the wheel turned again.

In extenuation one has to concede that he had assumed power in a situation of extreme crisis. The Establishment and conservative circles who had feared and hated him from the beginning, bitterly resented his accession to power and questioned its democratic legitimacy (the same people who had happily collaborated with Ayub's and Yahya Khan's dictatorships). They were not disposed to make things easy for him and Bhutto fully expected them to put all kinds of difficulties in his way. 'The first thing I know, someone is going to start trouble over the language issue!' he said to me before leaving New York to take over as President. Indeed trouble broke out in Karachi almost at once, when the PPP moved a bill in the Sindh Assembly the main feature of which was that Sindhi would have to be taught in schools in the province upto a certain level. The move was not unreasonable in itself, and moreover was a reaction to the Ayub era policy of making Urdu compulsory at all stages in West Pakistan schools, and virtually excluding the teaching of provincial languages. However the Urdu speaking community in Sindh viewed the move as an attack on Urdu, and riots broke out in Karachi.

The new Pakistan was much reduced in population but not in size and resources. What Pakistan had lost in numbers, it made up by the relatively homogenous character of the West Pakistani population—or so it seemed. 'The Aryan Pakistan' an American newspaper called it. A Yugoslav political commentator described it as 'more compact and economically better developed, with a rational geography and a more reasonable place and perhaps, more reasonable ambitions, in the subcontinent.'[2] The smaller Pakistan was without doubt a coherent geographical and economic entity, linked by the Indus River and its irrigation network, the railway and road systems, an electric grid, and so forth. When the shock of the secession subsided, most people realized, perhaps only subconsciously, that the operation had been not an amputation, but rather a separation of Siamese twins. Of course the new Pakistan could no longer claim to be the homeland of Indian Muslims, and aware of this deficiency, Bhutto tried to find territorial moorings for the residual Pakistan. In one flight of eloquence he traced its origins back to Ashoka's empire!

Before Mujibur Rahman returned to Dhaka when Bhutto ordered his release,[3] they met in Islamabad. The meeting took place in a friendly atmosphere and Bhutto made an effort to persuade the Bangladesh leader of the merits of maintaining

some kind of a link between the two countries. I learnt from
Foreign Minister Aziz Ahmad, who was at the meeting, that
Mujibur Rahman had been quite responsive but had said that he
would need time to work things out. In Belgrade the Indian
Ambassador was saying to his diplomatic colleagues that India
would have no objection to the two former wings of Pakistan
restoring some of their old links provided India too could join
the arrangement. I myself was sceptical about the prospect.

I was transferred at this time from Belgrade to New York to
head the Pakistan Mission to the United Nations. Bhutto's brief
to me, when I was leaving to take up my post, was to keep a low
profile—very sensible advice and indeed the only thing to do at
the time, seeing how low had sunk Pakistan's image in the world.
The President also told me that we were not to take a stiff line
towards Bangladesh, for he looked to the day when, in the nature
of things, the two countries would find themselves taking a
common view of things in the subcontinent. In the spirit of those
instructions, and also from personal belief, when an occasion
arose to speak on the subject in the UN's Economic and Social
Council, I said, 'We look back beyond past errors and lost
opportunities to the years of common struggle for freedom, and
we look beyond the turmoil of today to a future of reconciliation.'

Pakistan's immediate priority was to obtain the release of the
93,000 men who had been surrendered to India in Dhaka.
Mujibur Rahman was talking about holding war crimes trials. He
may actually have meant to do this, or possibly was using the
threat in order to obtain Pakistan's recognition of the breakaway
province. Dhaka had also been throwing out hints that the release
of POWs was to be linked to the subject of the division of assets
between the two former wings of Pakistan. The focus of
diplomatic activity on these issues was at the United Nations. On
the POW issue Pakistan was in the right, for it was plainly against
the letter and spirit of the Geneva Convention on the treatment
of POWs, to use them for the purpose of political bargaining.
India demurred that she could not act in the matter on her own
since the Pakistanis had surrendered to a 'Joint Bangladesh-India
Command'—a transparent fiction that no one believed.

Nevertheless, the cards were stacked against Pakistan because
India was impervious to international pressures on the matter
and our capacity to generate pressure was still limited by the

antagonism and opprobrium that Pakistan's actions in East Pakistan had attracted. In my initial discussions with him on the subject, the newly-elected UN Secretary-General, Kurt Waldheim, was inclined to assume an aloof and reproving demeanor, as if anything I said was liable to be used in evidence against Pakistan! Also, as one Arab supporter told me, 'Frankly, some of our brothers feel embarrassed to come out for Pakistan because nobody wants to be with the loser!'[4]

Caustic letters were exchanged between the Pakistani and Indian Foreign Ministers. They held meetings in New York; so did Aziz Ahmad and the Bangladesh Foreign Minister, Kamal Hossain (who being my brother-in-law, an Indian newspaper warned darkly, 'Blood is thicker than water'!). The meetings took place in a reasonably amicable atmosphere but led nowhere. All that could be accomplished at this stage, thanks to a personal initiative by Kurt Waldheim, was a partial exchange of some Pakistani POWs against a number of Bengalis, including government officials and troops detained in Pakistan. But the bulk of POWs remained captive in India's hands.

The log-jam broke when moves were initiated to seek the admission of Bangladesh into the United Nations. It was assumed that Bangladesh would be able to walk into the organization without too much trouble; China, having done its bit for Pakistan, would not now, it was supposed, wish to hand the Soviet Union propaganda points by using its veto. In political logic this made sense, for after all, the admission of Bangladesh into the United Nations was inevitable sooner or later. However I got the first hint that the Chinese might be prepared to use the veto when the Chinese Permanent Representative, Ambassador Huang Hua told me that China would *prefer* it if the matter could be resolved without recourse to the veto. In the event, the supporters of Bangladesh, rejecting our pleas to hold their hand for a while, pressed the matter in the Security Council and China vetoed the application.

The issue was then taken to the General Assembly by Yugoslavia, acting for Bangladesh and India—and trying also to curry favour with the Soviet Union. The Bangladesh bandwagon had not stopped rolling yet and the Yugoslavs expected to get a thumping majority in the Assembly endorsing the Bangladesh application and putting China under pressure to revise its position. The Yugoslav move had also another aspect. In December, after the Soviets had vetoed a resolution in the Security Council calling for a cease-fire and withdrawal of Indian troops from East Pakistan, the General Assembly by a majority of 104 votes, including those of virtually the entire non-aligned group, reiterated these demands. This was a stinging diplomatic rebuff to the Soviet Union and India and it rankled still. The Yugoslav move· was a chance to even the score.

China had just been admitted to the United Nations. The Bangladesh crisis was, as it were, her maiden venture in the organization and almost straight away, she had found herself being compelled to do what the Soviet Union was often criticized for doing—veto a membership application. The decision was not an easy one for China—politically and otherwise. At that session of the Assembly, China was represented by the Deputy Foreign Minister, Chiao Kuan Hua,[5] a tall, good-looking man with an urbane and soft-spoken manner and an easy laugh. We were in constant contact with him throughout these discussions and I never detected the least sign of embarrassment or hesitation or any looking about on China's part for some way to get off the horns of the dilemma. China acted with confidence and felt sure of her ground, which was that before ·Bangladesh could be admitted to the international organization, it must demonstrate respect for its principles and decisions, by facilitating the release of Pakistani POWs. As a matter of fact, contrary to Soviet expectations, China's veto did not bring any odium on China; on the contrary, it was seen as evidence that China remained loyal to her friends, even at the cost of temporary political embarrassment. It was not difficult to see that the Soviets were more interested in embarrassing China than in getting Bangladesh into the UN, and the great majority of UN members were not willing to lend themselves to this game. Nor did they take well to Bangladesh and India trying to use Pakistani POWs as pawns for attaining political objectives.

On the other hand, members were not comfortable with the idea of membership being denied by a veto or being made subject to a condition (that the Security Council resolution asking for the repatriation of Pakistani POWs should be implemented). The issue was resolved by a typical UN compromise, the adoption of two resolutions—one endorsing Bangladesh's right to be admitted to the United Nations, and the other asking for the repatriation of POWs—each resolution nominally independent of the other and adopted separately, but linked by an agreed statement read out by the Assembly President to the effect that both things ought to be done. The twin-resolution device was thought up by the influential Permanent Representative, of Iran, Fereydoun Hoveida, who persuaded Yugoslavia and the other friends of Bangladesh that this was the only way out. The principle accepted, it still took a long and tedious negotiating session between the Yugoslav Ambassador, Lazar Mojsov, and myself before agreement was reached on the final text. Mojsov then had to work hard to convince the Bangladeshis of the merits of the proposed arrangement. Even so, things did not pass without a last minute hitch. The Bangladesh delegation had been more or less dragooned by Yugoslavia into accepting the agreement and felt they were being cheated out of a triumphal entry into the organization. Just as the General Assembly was being summoned to dispose off the matter, they withdrew their consent to it. For a couple of hours delegates milled around in the narrow vestibules of the Assembly hall, while the Yugoslavs publicly remonstrated with the glum-looking Bangladeshis, and the Indians and Russians went hither and thither, not sure whether the Bengali move was a good thing or bad. In the end the Yugoslavs managed to bring Bangladesh around again, this time, so I was given to understand, with help from the Indians who realized that the whole exercise was becoming counter-productive.

Another problem that raised its head straightaway was the status and fate in mono-ethnic Bangladesh of the Biharis, Urdu-speaking immigrants of the 1947 Partition. Not only did the Biharis feel no link of any kind with the Bengali state, but many of them had joined para-military units set up by the army and had assisted it in actions against the Bengalis. The latter did not want them in Bangladesh. Some Bihari collaborators had been the victims of spectacular and well-publicized counter-atrocities after the army's surrender. The Urdu-speaking Biharis themselves wanted no part of Bangladesh. On the other hand, Pakistan was far from keen on receiving another flood of refugees (the figure of two and a half million was mentioned at the time) that would threaten the already uneasy ethnic equilibrium in Sindh, where they were most likely to settle. Their coming was therefore strongly resisted in that province.

A couple of organizations were set up in New York to lobby the Bihari cause, and one morning I found a demo being held in front of the Ambassador's residence. I invited the leaders in, and over a cup of tea explained to them the basis of the government's policy on the matter. This was that Pakistan could not accept as citizens all or anyone whom Bangladesh government wanted to throw out of the country; it was the legal and moral responsibility of that government to look after the welfare of Biharis who had made East Bengal their home and where many of them had been born. A large and sudden influx of refugees into Pakistan would cause social and economic problems and exacerbate ethnic tensions in Sindh. The group as a whole was receptive to these points but some— Biharis themselves with relatives in Bangladesh—tended to be emotional and extreme in their views. One of them proclaimed that if they were not allowed into Pakistan the Biharis would, like the Palestinians, unleash a terrorist campaign not only in Pakistan but right there in New York. A not very subtle threat! Another asserted that the government's policy was guided by the fact that it was headed by a Sindhi.

In fact, under an agreement with the Bangladesh government, the Bhutto government did take in some 200,000 Biharis in 1973. Since then no more have been admitted through the official channel. A British mission headed by David Ennals that went to Dhaka in May 1972, received an assurance from Mujibur Rahman that he would personally ensure the safety and well-being of the Bihari minority.[6] The mission, commending his words, counselled the Biharis that the answer to their problem was integration in Bangladesh and not a further displacement to Pakistan. The irony of the whole situation, as the Secretary-General's representative in Dhaka told me, was demonstrated by the fact that many skilled Bihari workers were sitting jobless in camps from where they could look across at the mills and factories where they used to work and that were now closed or working at half capacity for lack of skilled labour! But after more than twenty years the 'Bihari Question' remains on the Pakistan-Bangladesh agenda and figures in their joint communiqués in deliberately ambiguous language. It figures from time to time also in the polemics of Pakistan's domestic politics. No formal solution is in sight, but in reality large numbers of Biharis (and Bengalis too) have found their way into Karachi by clandestine means in search of jobs.

18. PLO's Foreign Relations Advisor Farook Kadoumy, 1976.
'The PLO needs an occasional American veto...'

19. Debate on nuclear proliferation, May 1976. A serious disagreement.

20. After the debate, a lighter moment.

21. President Anwar al Sadat and the author, Cairo, 1970.

22. Security Council takes a vote, 1977.

Bangladesh had been described as one of the world's basket cases[7] and so it seemed at that time, but in retrospect this proved to be an unduly pessimistic assessment. Bangladesh, despite natural calamities and inherent deficiencies, has managed to keep its end up, and done rather better than Pakistan in some respects such as in curbing population growth and promoting exports. However in the immediate aftermath of victory, and when the euphoria of freedom abated, the reckoning for Bangladesh was disillusioning. Ambassador Lacoste of France, who was the Secretary-General's representative in Dhaka at the time, called on me during his visits to New York and briefed me on the prevailing situation in Bangladesh. Mujib, he said, was the 'Banglabandhu', the unquestioned leader, above criticism and cavil, the only man who mattered and held things together. But Mujib had no time or inclination for the tedium of administration which was poorly run despite all the bright, well-trained men in the Civil Services. Many of them had been promoted to high posts out of turn, and looked forward with very mixed feelings to the return of their senior Bengali colleagues from Pakistan. Bengalis had suffered cruelly at the Pakistan Army's hands and the wounds were still fresh. But as a result, Ambassador Lacoste said, they seemed to be living in a closed world, hearing only their own voices, reading only their own words. Even so, he found that anti-Indian feeling in Bangladesh was on the rise and growing. On the other hand, some among the intelligentsia were already beginning to speak of the need to restore economic relations with Pakistan.

As for Pakistan, very soon—much sooner than any one had thought possible—it was coming out of the woods. The advent of Zulfikar Bhutto represented the return of democracy, however flawed it was in practice by the continuance of the state of emergency. The crowning achievement of Bhutto's rule was the unanimous adoption in 1973 of a new Constitution, a Constitution that more than twenty years later remains the sheer anchor of democracy in the country, despite the vicissitudes it has suffered over the years—its suspension under martial law, Zia's denaturing amendments, Bhutto's own tampering with its spirit. I was privileged to witness the initial stage of the process when I attended a session of the National Assembly held in Islamabad on 14 April 1972. The meeting took place in a very tense atmosphere because of the breakdown of the Government-Opposition accord under which, *inter alia,* Bhutto was allowed to rule under martial law for a period of three months. There was a great deal of undergraduate commotion in the hall raised by members unaware of parliamentary procedures and frustrated at one thing and another. Most of the hullabaloo was being caused in fact by a PPP back-bencher who was constantly raising 'points of order' to rail against the continuation of Martial Law by his party chief, Bhutto. PPP 'loyalists' raised a countervailing din in support of Bhutto, making it impossible even for the PPP leaders to make themselves heard. In this atmosphere, old timers like Sardar Shaukat Hayat, citing rules of procedure from 'May's Parliamentary Practice', seemed completely out of place. But in the evening session when Bhutto came to take his oath, he had a surprise up his sleeve, and announced it in his characteristic way: '...and now I come to the most momentous part of my statement', and this was that martial law, which the Opposition had allowed him to maintain till 15 June, would be lifted the very next week! Not everyone seized at once the import of the announcement and the applause began in a tentative way—Opposition members now clapping, now stopping, looking at each other for cues—but soon the entire house was on its feet for a standing ovation that went on and on. The vote of confidence in Bhutto that followed was unanimous, and Opposition leader Wali Khan—Bhutto's once and future political foe—took the floor to pay him a handsome, even fulsome tribute. It was a moving moment and in retrospect, it appears poignant for the promise it held.

Not all of Bhutto's reforms were well thought out, but his energy, style and panache transformed Pakistan's image in the world. Barely two years after the war he brought the Islamic Heads of State to Lahore for a summit that reconciled Mujib with him, and Pakistan with Bangladesh. Pakistan's ship of state, as one columnist wrote, was in the mainstream again. In an editorial, the *New York Times* wrote of Pakistan as a 'strange phoenix-like country' that always seems to arise from its ashes. The consecration of Pakistan's reinstatement in the world community came with its election to the Security Council in 1976, in a closely fought contest with India. Pakistan also took the chairmanship of Economic and Social Council and of the G77, as the group of (now) more than a hundred developing countries was called. A hat trick!

After putting his house in order Bhutto came on a state visit to the United States in the autumn of 1973 in the course of which he also visited New York and addressed the UN General Assembly's annual session. The two principal aims of the visit were to obtain the lifting of the US embargo on arms deliveries to Pakistan and to refurbish Pakistan's badly tarnished image in the world. Nixon's election and his so-called 'tilt' to Pakistan during the Bangladesh War had raised hopes that the new administration would be sympathetic to Pakistan's security concern. Indeed the joint communiqué issued at the end of Bhutto's visit to Washington declared that Pakistan's security and independence were a corner-stone of US policy. However, the hoped-for lifting of the arms embargo did not materialize. In the public mind Pakistan had not yet emerged from the shadows of the military action against East Pakistan. Moreover, the general public mood in America at that time—one might call it almost a re-discovered conviction—was in favour of disengaging from excessive involvement in the affairs of other countries. There were the first murmurings against the security commitments given to Europe and the permanent stationing of American troops across the Atlantic. The Senate passed a resolution calling for cutting down the number of US troops in Europe.

With regard to the subcontinent the mood was one of disinterest verging on indifference. The days were over when Ayub Khan could bring the Congress to its feet by pledging Pakistan's friendship and loyalty to the United States. India, that once had figured as a Third World paradigm of development with democracy, an alternative model to Communist China's totalitarianism, had disappointed hopes in both respects. As fervent an admirer of India as Senator Patrick Moynihan, former ambassador at Delhi, described Mrs Gandhi's emergency rule as a disaster for democracy 'in which half the people in the world with democratic rights had lost those rights'. He warned, 'It is too soon to write off India but hardly too soon to take note of what is happening there.'[8]

The Nixon administration was well-inclined towards Pakistan but constrained by the public mood. Nixon had invited Bhutto to see him in Washington before he flew back to assume the Presidency in 1972. It was a clear signal of Nixon's personal sympathy for Bhutto and support in the task he was about to undertake. Nonetheless, there remained among American officials a residue of wariness with regard to his leftist leanings, his past anti-American rhetoric, and generally about Bhutto's personality. Against this background, though Pakistan's case for a credible deterrent against India's growing and Soviet-supplied military machine was not disputed at the official level, it failed in the prevailing atmosphere to evoke an immediate response.

However Bhutto's speech at the UN's thirtieth session, and Bhutto himself—a familiar figure in the UN—were both well-received. *New York Times* gave it prominent coverage, next in importance only to Secretary of State Kissinger's speech. India reacted sharply to what Bhutto had to say about India's role in Bangladesh's secession and on Kashmir but not as sharply as expected. Foreign Minister Swaran Singh was content to call it a 'crude attempt to nibble away at the Simla Agreement'. Later when he came to lunch at my place with Minister of State Aziz Ahmad, he said that he had overruled advisers who wanted him to make a strong riposte to Bhutto's speech straightaway.

Swaran Singh also asserted that the war as such was started by the Pakistani air attacks on India from the west. He felt that in fairness, Mrs Gandhi should be given credit for the initiative that led to the Simla Agreement. He pointed out that never before in history had war and its aftermath—cease-fire, withdrawal of troops, exchange of territory, exchange of prisoners and stranded civilians—been wound up in so short a space of time.

Bhutto was invited to lunches by the editorial boards of the *New York Times* and *Time* magazine—both publications had been very critical of Pakistan in recent years and particularly of the East Pakistan operation. They were keen to know the views of Pakistan's new ruler, himself known for his sharp criticisms of US policies, and who had now come in order to befriend their country. Bhutto's candor and good humour in tackling their pointed questions created a good impression; and even if everything he said was not accepted at face value, the meetings served to restore some of the old ease of communication between Pakistan and the American Press. However no change in the general attitude of the Press was apparent. All had approved of the administration's decision not to lift the arms embargo even while noting that India was building up its military strength with massive Soviet aid. The attitude of *New York Times* was that the

United States need not follow the Soviet Union's bad example. There was trouble in Balochistan and it was possible that the Soviet Union was fishing in those waters. But this was seen as Pakistan's headache and Russia's involvement in it was too shadowy to provoke Washington's concern. At that stage the United States saw Israel's dominating position in the Middle East and Iran's military buildup, as sufficient protection against Soviet mischief in the region. US policy in the Middle East seemed to be wholly taken up with matters like the Soviet ban on Jewish emigration.

In 1973 Pakistan was elected to the Economic and Social Council of the UN and in 1975 to the Security Council, in both cases in a contest with India. For the first time Pakistan was a member of the two top UN organs and India of neither—an anomaly that caused a certain amount of head-shaking among old UN hands. India's poor showing at the UN was indeed puzzling. It was not due to her internal difficulties, and certainly not, as some idealists in the West would have liked to believe, due to 'moral revulsion' at her 1974 nuclear explosion! One New York newspaper, reporting Pakistan's win in the Security Council election, under the headline 'Pakistan Bombs Out India', suggested that people had just grown tired of India and her pretensions.

I don't know if this was so, but it was a fact that two years after the euphoria of the Bangladesh victory, India seemed dispirited and in disarray, whereas Pakistan had emerged from defeat to play a more active and prominent role on the world stage. At home too Bhutto's vigorous leadership and reforms had created an image of a dynamic country that had turned its back on the past and was trying to return to democracy. The Indians themselves were conscious of the relative decline in India's position. On one occasion when India's Defence Minister Chavan came to lunch at my residence and I escorted him down to his car afterwards, the car would not start and we found that its battery was flat. It took only a few moments to jump start it from the battery of the Pakistan Mission's car. I said, 'Mr Minister here is a practical demonstration of what we can do through peaceful co-existence!' He replied with a grin, 'I know, but Pakistan likes to co-exist only when India's battery is down.'

However we had to fight hard for the seat on the Security Council. For some reason the Foreign Ministry had delayed its decision to run for the seat until after India had announced its candidature. India had meanwhile obtained the formal endorsement of its candidature from the Arab League and increased the odds against Pakistan's candidature. India had come off the Council only two years earlier and was clearly making a bid to establish its status as a semi-permanent member. For some years, with the same aim, Japan had been following the same technique of standing for Security Council membership every alternate term. Members in general did not care for the idea that the limited number of non-permanent seats should be nibbled away in this way by the larger countries.

The non-aligned group held its summit meeting in August that year in Lima, the capital city of Peru. India was likely to make a try for the group's endorsement of its candidature in some form or another at that meeting. I was instructed to go to Lima at the head of a fairly high-powered delegation in order to spoil India's game. Pakistan was not yet a member of the non-aligned group but we made a request to be allowed to attend the Peru meeting as an observer or a guest delegation in the same way as Austria, Portugal, Philippines, and Romania. As on previous occasions, the Indians successfully blocked our bid on various grounds—more or less specious, but actually by threatening to walk out if Pakistan was admitted in any capacity whatsoever. India's unreasonableness in this matter gained Pakistan some sympathy and helped our other and real object at that meeting which was to prevent India from getting a non-aligned endorsement of its candidature. In this we were successful though we failed to get into the meeting. While the Indian delegation was kept busy fending off our attempt to get into the conference, the Pakistan delegation, waiting in the lobbies, used the time to lobby Pakistan's candidature to the Security Council.

The election in the General Assembly was a difficult one and there was intensive lobbying by both sides. It took several ballots, with India in the lead in the first, and Pakistan in the several that followed, but neither gaining the two-thirds majority needed to win. The deadlock was complete but with Pakistan in the lead. It was suggested that the two countries might split the two-year term. There was a precedent and India seemed inclined to accept, but Pakistan refused and in the end India was persuaded to withdraw in exchange for a promise that her candidature the following year would not be opposed. Both countries made nice little speeches in praise of each other's spirit of compromise and sportsmanship. As I was walking out of the Assembly hall, I ran into the Indian permanent representative who shook his head ruefully and said, 'Will you believe it that we had *written* pledges of support from at least twenty more countries than the number of votes we received.' The discreet charm of the secret ballot!

The UN to which I returned in 1972 after a lapse of eight years, was in many ways a different place. There were many more members; some of the new countries were of microscopic size and not easily found on the map. But what had changed the character of the organization in a fundamental way was the entry of the People's Republic of China. In the first place, it enhanced the organization's credibility by giving representation to the hitherto excluded one fifth of mankind; it caused greater weight to be given to the concerns of the Third World and above all, it shifted the focus of contention from the cold war to Sino-Soviet differences. The Americans and the Soviets went on having their duets as before, but there was a change of key and the big kettle drum was that of China denouncing both superpowers. But while she attacked both, there was always a coda castigating the Soviet Union as the worst of the two. The United States which had feared and opposed the entry of China in the UN, found itself in the relatively happy position of watching from the sidelines her two most feared and abhorred adversaries slugging it out between themselves. The Soviet Permanent Representative, Yacov Malik, a big burly, red-faced Ukrainian, would go even redder in the face when the quiet, scholarly Huang Hua launched his well-aimed barbs at him. Malik sometimes seemed to fumble for words of sufficient weight with which to crush his Chinese opponent's arguments. He asked me once, 'Why is China constantly attacking the Soviet Union? What does Pakistan know about China's intentions—Pakistan which knows China better than many other countries?' Then he added wryly, 'Except, perhaps, Washington now!' Malik asserted that the Vietnam War would have ended long ago if China had stood with the Soviet Union in helping the Viet Minh. When the Americans had bombed Haiphong Harbour the previous year, he said, China had refused to allow Soviet arms for Vietnam to be transhipped through her ports.

Yacov Malik's quip about Washington was not misplaced. Behind China's even-handed damning of both their houses, she was slowly but surely developing a new relationship with the United States in a variety of spheres. A school of thought in the US academic establishment favoured close collaboration with China in the defence field—an example was an article in the magazine *Foreign Policy* of October 1975 by Michael Pillsbury, a Rand institute analyst. Lacking adequate air cover and dependable nuclear missiles, China, he wrote, was vulnerable to a Soviet armoured drive across flat Mongolian territory that could take Beijing in a surprise attack.[9] In the circumstances some Chinese military men were inclined to come to terms with the Soviets. To prevent this from happening and to reduce the 'crisis instability' of the Sino-Soviet nuclear balance, Pillsbury suggested that the US should provide China with advanced defensive equipment such as a phased array radar system and hot-line capability to enable Beijing to receive US warning of Soviet attack in time to begin refueling its liquid fuel missiles. (Talking to me on the subject of his proposal, Pillsbury said that logically it would need Pakistan's co-operation. Logical it would be, but a very risky venture for Pakistan.) A year before Brezhinski had made a suggestion to the same effect for improving China's C3 (command, control and communications) capacity and providing her with electronic locking devices, etc., for her nuclear weapons.

In the United Nations, China maintained a low profile, supported the Third World in general terms, but took no major initiatives, and more often than not, 'declined to participate' in the voting on issues which were not of concern to her. This Chinese variant of a mere abstention, was a procedural innovation that implied not merely a refusal to take sides, but an attitude of 'a plague on both your houses'. The practice soon caught on as more valiant than running away at the time of voting! The Chinese delegation were not shy about asking advice on procedural points and often consulted members of our delegation on such questions, as undoubtedly also other delegations. At the UN we helped the Chinese delegation in whatever small ways they wished us to. Deputy Foreign Minister Chiao Kuan Hua wanted to meet 'ordinary Americans' viz., corporate chairmen and the like. We organized a reception in his honour at the ambassador's residence and Chiao hit it off

very well with the American capitalists.[10] Later, Permanent
Representative Huang Hua asked me to arrange a meeting for
him with the powerful Senator from New York State, Jacob Javits.
I arranged a dinner at home with the Javits, Huang Hua and his
wife, my wife and I. Brezhnev had just been visiting Washington
and signed an upbeat joint communiqué with Nixon. Huang
Hua was keen to know what it all meant. Javits played down the
importance of the visit and said that, for instance, the expansion
of US-Soviet trade would depend very much on Soviet Jews being
allowed to emigrate freely. He said that in order to carry
conviction regarding its intentions, the Soviet Union would have
to give proof of a whole new approach in its foreign relations,
including its policy in the Middle East. Speaking of relations
among NATO countries, Javits said that western European
countries seemed to have an ambivalent attitude towards the
United States, in particular in France, where 'they wanted the
Americans at the same time to stay and to get out of Europe'.
Huang Hua expressed the opinion that in this matter France's
position was 'against her own interests'. Speaking quite like a
conservative Republican, he said that some European statesmen
had given a false sense of security to their people about the
Soviet Union's intentions.

Africans now constituted the largest regional group in the
United Nations and 'African issues'—apartheid and racial
discrimination, the wars in Angola and Mozambique—were still
near the top of the UN agenda. One still heard fine pieces of
eloquence as when President Dos Santos of Mozambique
speaking in the General Assembly, declared: 'Liberty is not a gift,
nor a concession; it is a conquest, won by the blood of martyrs
and by sacrifice.' Nonetheless the focus of attention was gradually
shifting to more mundane economic and social issues, to the
issues of North-South economic disparity and the widening gulf
between the rich and poor countries. As on the colonial issue,
the West again found itself ranged against the Third World with
the Soviet bloc in a supporting role. But the Soviets did not feel
comfortable with economic and social issues. They did not like
to be lumped with the Western countries in the same category as
the industrialized North. Moreover, Soviet contribution to foreign
aid, except to the East European countries or special allies such
as Cuba and India, was negligible. A more basic problem was

that the North-South debate was about making the free market
system more equitable rather than replacing it and thus there
was an implicit rejection of the Marxist alternative.

Discussing the subject with me, Soviet Ambassador Yacov Malik
regretted that the Third World's preoccupation with social and
economic issues was downgrading the political function of the
UN at a time when already the trend was that more and more of
the major political problems were being tackled and settled
outside the framework of the United Nations.

One of the most remarkable initiatives in diplomatic history
was the Marshall Plan under which the United States helped
West European countries, allies as well as former enemies, to
rebuild their shattered economies after World War II. It was a
complete reversal of the vindictive peace of Versailles, which
sowed the seeds of the war. On the foundations laid by the
Marshall Plan was built the triumph of the West's free enterprise
system over communism.

However there was no equivalent of the Marshall Plan vision
for the world as a whole and for bridging the gulf between rich
and poor countries. The UN Charter was drawn up by the
principal victorious powers of World War II. The handful of
developing countries that were then independent tried to get
adequate attention for the economic and social problems of the
poor countries but failed to carry conviction. The UN Charter
called on the organization to 'promote social progress and better
standards of living in larger freedom' for all, but nothing was
mentioned in it about the problems of mass poverty and of the
gap between the rich and poor countries. The idea of economic
equity and any suggestion that the rich countries should
contribute to the development of the poorer ones did not figure
in the thinking of the times. The Bretton Woods system and
GATT were concerned mainly with promoting the trade and
economic stability of the Western developed countries.

But in due course the cold war competition for 'hearts and
minds' as well as the links between former colonial powers and
their newly independent colonies, brought into being the
institution of 'foreign aid'—and foreign aid became one of the
principal elements of the developed countries' policy towards
the Third World. Undeniably it helped in the economic

development of many countries but it did not open the way to a breakthrough or close the gap between rich and poor countries.

In comparing the success of the Marshall Plan with the relative failure of foreign aid, one obvious difference was that the Marshall Plan funds were massive (in terms of the prevailing money values) and were tailored to the tasks to be performed. The other difference was in the nature of the tasks to be performed. In Europe it was a matter of providing seed money and it fell on the fertile ground of well-developed social, economic and political institutions and among educated, disciplined and healthy populations. Moreover the Marshall Plan programme was motivated by the common political and economic interests of all the parties, and the ethnic, cultural, racial, and historical affinities among them. This had a great deal to do with the vigour and interest with which the enterprise was pursued to its completion.

In the case of the developing countries the story was different in every way. They were not partners, but former colonies and dependencies of the aid-giving countries. Political independence had not done much to change their peripheral position in economic and other spheres *vis-à-vis* the former metropolitan powers or the industrialized West as a whole. The job in their case was not simply to reconstruct and rehabilitate, but to create and put in place new structures, transform social and political systems, and make room for them in the existing economic order. The three-fold transformation—political, economic and social— that had occurred in Europe and America over centuries, had to be compressed into a few decades in the case of the developing countries. India and Pakistan which (along with Bangladesh) account for much of the world's mass poverty are further handicapped by the fact that their already huge populations are growing rapidly while they spend a good bit of their resources on fighting, or preparing to fight each other with the most modern and costly weapons. Thus on the one hand foreign aid wasn't enough for the enormous tasks at hand and on the other, many of the problems faced by the developing countries were not such that they could be solved by outside intervention. The recipients resented—disingenuously—the strings attached to aid. The donors resented the idea that they should give aid to the newly independent countries—as some of them claimed—by way of reparations for past colonial exploitation.

In time foreign aid became unpopular all round—among the recipients because it wasn't enough, and made them feel like supplicants (*vide* the title of President Ayub Khan's biography *Friends Not Masters*) and among the donors because they felt that they were getting no thanks. The State Department took to making up lists of how members voted at the UN, and found that among those who voted the most often against or differently from the US, were many who got the most American aid. The voters in the donor countries turned against foreign aid and it came to be seen there as a tedious duty of little efficacy and, seeing the way the rulers and the elite lived it up in some aid-receiving countries, a policy of dubious moral value. A half-truth, gained currency and was aired by Jimmy Carter when he was running for President: 'Why should the poor in the rich countries pay for the rich in the poor countries!'

The oil embargo and oil price crisis of 1975 gave a severe jolt to existing assumptions and conceptions. It suddenly made the industrialized countries aware of the interdependence of the world's economy, or better said, that inter-dependence was not a one-way street. The initial reaction was of shock and a kind of psychosis developed in the public mind. The Third World was no longer seen as a marginal region to be saved from Communism or from hunger, but as an unfriendly entity that had the potential to hold the rich countries to ransom. In the case of oil, in the United States there was the inevitable political angle connected with Israel. Thus even before there was an oil embargo and oil prices rose, the *Wall Street Journal* was writing about the oil-producers' new wealth[11] and worrying that on account of it 'Washington may have to pay more attention to Arab wishes and sensitivities...' Hubert Humphrey declared anxiously, 'The Sheikhs of Arabia will control the dollar!'

In fact there was no actual oil shortage in the United States though for a while there were lines at petrol stations in New York and other cities.[12] Saudi production was undiminished. The immediate beneficiaries of the oil price rise were the major oil companies whose average net profits rose fifty to sixty per cent. Then there followed a scramble among industrial countries to sell the new-rich oil countries whatever they desired—industrial equipment, fighter planes, luxury yachts, the Dorchester Hotel, eight-lane highways through the desert, and even Antarctic icebergs.[13]

The non-oil producing developing countries (sometimes called the NOPEC countries) were caught in a double squeeze having to pay more for oil as well as for other imports which had gone up with the price of oil.[14] Their hopes of getting a special deal from the oil producers on the basis of Third World solidarity were quickly dashed. The idea of a two-tier oil price system did not find favour because it could lead to an underground market based on the cheaper oil sold to developing countries; moreover OPEC objected that such schemes would amount to concealed foreign aid from one set of developing countries to another.

Under the impetus of the oil price crisis, an idea took form that had been simmering for years in the debate between the rich and poor countries as to their respective rights and responsibilities and their shares in the world's resources. The developing countries felt that they would never break through the circle of poverty and dependence unless the existing economic system was radically reformed. Their specific demands in this regard included not only enhanced foreign aid and some mechanism for the automatic annual transfer of resources to the poor countries, but also a number of other measures such as commodity price stabilization, tariff concessions, trade preferences and industrial adjustment. In two special sessions of the UN General Assembly held in 1975 and the following year, these and other similar demands were adopted as the Declaration of the New International Economic Order (NIEO). In preparatory meetings there were very heated debates between the two sides and much hair-splitting on whether one was talking about 'a' new international economic order or 'the' new international economic order. The fact of the matter was that the UN General Assembly was mainly a sounding-board and had little power of decision in these matters. Effective international economic decisions are taken in the IMF and the World Bank where the money is, and which are controlled by those who put up the money. But the momentum generated by the special sessions and the anxiety of the West with regard to oil supplies, led to agreement to discuss a specified agreed list of priority issues at a conference among a limited number of countries. Pakistan was one of the countries chosen to represent the Asian group at this Conference on International Economic Co-operation (CIEC) which was held in Paris. This was the nearest thing to a serious North-South negotiation in the proper sense at the time but the results were meagre.

Pakistan had always played a very active role in the UN's economic diplomacy and under permanent representatives like Mir Khan and Syed Amjad Ali, the Pakistan mission had earned a reputation for its serious and moderate approach. I was Chairman of the Group of 77 as well as President of ECOSOC (United Nations Economic and Social Council) in 1976, and this put Pakistan on the inside track in the proceedings of the special sessions. Nothing much came however, of these conferences. The industrialized countries were not prepared to make any fundamental changes in existing institutions and structures or impose sacrifices on their own people.

Opposition to the NIEO came not only from governments and multinational corporations in the West, but also from organized labour. At a meeting with representatives of the Group of 77, Lane Kirkland, Secretary-General of AFL-CIO accused Third World countries of repressing their trade union movements and labour in order to attract investment by multinational corporations. He pointed out that the NIEO contained no provisions relating to the working classes. What was at work here was not simply working class solidarity but concern at the transfer of American jobs to foreign countries with low wages. (As to the opinions of capitalists, I heard a story from one of them which was meant to be funny, but which could have been true: At a businessmen's lunch at the exclusive River Club in New York an African ambassador told the chairman of a great American corporation about all the facilities and concessions his country had offered to foreign investors, but it had not succeeded in getting any foreign investment. 'What more would you like us to do?' he asked. The chairman replied, 'Install a right wing military dictatorship!')

Western countries countered the Third World's reforming fervour with proposals aimed at turning the dialogue in a pragmatic direction—a programme to cope with the basic human needs in the developing countries, facilitate investment by transnational corporations, promote some stabilization of commodity prices and some preferential tariffs to provide access to industrialized markets for these countries. Henry Kissinger came himself to one of the special sessions of the General

Assembly, and while he lectured to the Third World on what *they* themselves should be doing, he also made some proposals of a practical nature for promoting food production and investment in the Third World. The fact that the United States sent its super star Secretary of State to participate in the session showed that it was beginning to focus attention on the North-South issue. At a working lunch at Pakistan House, World Bank's President McNamara who was sympathetic to Third World problems, advised the representatives to put an end to the climate of contentious debate and instead formulate proposals on items on which global agreement was 'both essential and possible'.

The points were well taken, but there was a touch of paternalism about the advice, and the underlying assumption was that no basic change in the prevailing North-South relationship was necessary. Responding to the United States' statement in the General Assembly's Special Session of 1976, I said, 'This approach seems to postulate that the development of the Third World can only be a by-product of the growing affluence of the industrialized countries,' and that they must tailor their needs to what can be made popular in the developed countries according to the shifting mood of popular opinion.

But, the Third World was not in a pragmatic mood and the trend was to take a doctrinaire, all-or-nothing position on the NIEO. The fact is that there was no unified Third World position. It had proved difficult to work out a unified position among more than a hundred countries representing the most diverse conditions and interests. The Special Session's declaration on the subject was drawn up largely by the Latin American group's experts and laid emphasis on Latin American concerns—debt relief, special preferences, commodity prices.

On the other hand as the Western world absorbed the oil shock and then began to take in and recycle the huge surpluses of the newly-rich oil producers, the steam gradually went out of the whole enterprise of creating a brave new world in which the good things of life would be equitably shared between rich and poor. Jimmy Carter who had come to power on a liberal platform, said not a word about the North-South issue when he made his maiden speech at the UN. Even before his election, I had been cautioned by people close to him not to pitch our expectations too high on Carter in this respect.

In Third World forums, there was much bitterness behind closed doors. The poorer countries who were in a double bind and had supported the oil producing countries, felt that they were entitled in return, to receive special treatment from their rich OPEC cousins. With that end in view, countries like Bangladesh and India kept coming up with proposals and devices—special oil supply contracts, South-South co-operation, mutual co-operation funds. (Pakistan too hoped for a share in the OPEC winnings but maintained a discreet silence, putting its hopes—with not much more success—on Islamic brotherhood.) But the oil producers weren't biting and were busy taking care of their own interests. After a particularly acrimonious session at the Havana non-aligned summit, Idriss Jezairy of the Algerian delegation said to me that some countries were always reminding the oil-producers of the political support they gave to them. 'What does it all amount to—clapping hands at our statements!' he said. 'We can reach an agreement with the industrialized countries any day we wish, and can very well do without the Third World's applause!' Jezairy pointed out that the power of OPEC lay in the nature of the commodity it controlled and not in the political support of international forums.

He was quite right as to that, but the oil producers were oversimplifying the situation and misread the extent of their economic and diplomatic clout. The oil embargo was imposed for a political purpose—a settlement of the Palestine problem—and in the nature of things its impact was of a temporary nature. But OPEC's economic leverage was also a passing phenomenon. Discussing the subject with me at the height of the oil crisis, C.S. Sulzberger of *The New York Times* put the matter very succinctly, 'If the Third World gets its act together now they can bring about a change in America's Middle East policy. In a few years there will be plenty of oil, from Alaskan fields and elsewhere, and the OPEC's leverage will be gone.'

And that is how things turned out on both political and economic planes. The enormous new wealth of the oil producers gave them a sense of power but the fact that the bulk of it was invested in Western countries, also made them very cautious now about rocking the boat of the Western economy. The Iran-Iraq War, followed by the Gulf War sapped the economic and diplomatic power of the Middle East oil producers and gradually things went back more or less to square one as far as they were concerned.

But to return to the debates in the UN, the developing countries, having no other choice, continued to clap their hands at OPEC speeches but it soon became clear that outside the domain of political rhetoric, the Third World's oil producing and oil consuming countries did not share many common economic interests. It was clear in any case that the NIEO wasn't getting very far beyond the UN's debating halls and was too broad-based to serve the specific interests of countries like Pakistan. The interests of the latter would be better served by measures to meet basic human needs, promote foreign investment and transfer of technology, facilitate trade—the sort of pragmatic proposals that were being suggested by the more sympathetic industrialized countries like those of the Nordic group, the Netherlands, and Canada. There was clearly a need for an effort to break the rhetorical log-jam on the issue.

I wrote a letter to Prime Minister Bhutto putting forward these views and suggesting that, with his impeccable 'Third Worldist' image and credentials, he might personally take the lead in organizing a bridge group of like-minded countries from both the North and the South; a group that would act as a catalyst for new ideas and approaches, and as a mediator between extreme positions, could help to break the existing impasse. Such an initiative would at the same time consolidate the position of leadership Pakistan had come to acquire in these matters in the UN and the world at large.

I got a positive reaction to these ideas but was taken aback when I read in the papers shortly afterwards a summary of Bhutto's declaration in Pyongyang, proposing to summon a Third World summit conference to discuss the stalled agenda for international economic co-operation. Elaboration of the proposal came in the form of an 'article' over Bhutto's signature. It declared, 'We, the Third World countries, are called upon to squeeze centuries into decades. Not for us is the relaxed stance of countries that built their economies in an earlier and more tranquil age, who had to dismantle no institutions and who could be content with gradual reform and the steady work of social change.'

It rejected the thesis that the development of the poor must depend on the continued rapid growth of the rich. The burden

of oil price rise had been shifted by the rich countries to the
shoulders of the poor; prices of primary products exported by
the poor were set by the rich; goods manufactured by the former
were subjected to tariffs and other restrictions. The debt burden
was becoming unbearable day by day. However, the article went
on to say, the proposal for a Third World summit was not a call
for a global class war but a 'call for that redistribution of
economic power which alone can prevent unceasing strife and
recurrent upheavals.'

To justify the necessity for a Third World summit, the article
took the line that existing forums were inadequate or unsuitable,
being confined to a certain continent, region or faith, while the
non-aligned group still excluded a large number of developing
countries. The article brushed aside differences of interest among
developing countries as unimportant, and said that what mattered
was their common urge for 'the achievement of a position of
equality in the world economic order' and that they were 'united
by common suffering and the common struggle against
exploitation'. Starting off with an appeal for a 'creative dialogue'
between the rich and poor countries, the article concluded with
a clarion call: 'The impoverished masses of the Third World are
yearning for a new focal point of their collective will. They are
seeking a new bastion of power to wage the crusade for man's
final victory against inhumanity. This is the need of the hour, the
priority of the poor.'

Now much of this was very true and it was well put. But the
industrialized countries did not take kindly to the various
strictures and prescriptions directed at them, and liked it even
less that these were being issued from the capital of North Korea,
one of the West's bad boys. They saw the summit proposal as yet
another move to set up the West as a whipping boy. But the
proposal also stirred up suspicion about Pakistan's intentions
within the ranks of the developing countries, in particular among
the leading members of the non-aligned group. The latter felt
that this was an attempt to sideline the non-aligned movement
and to provide China with a platform against the other great
powers.

Thus it was not going to be easy to get the summit together.
The proposal was nevertheless making some headway when
Bhutto became involved in trouble at home. After his overthrow

the Zia regime quietly dropped the proposal and included it in its charge sheet of denunciations, as yet another manifestation of Bhutto's 'megalomania' and his 'vaulting ambition' to play a role on the world stage. Bhutto had an impulse for the dramatic gesture and seemed to model his public style on the verbal dash and flourish of leaders like Nasser and Sukarno whom he admired. But he also had an analytical mind and a sense of realities that kept a rein on his impulses. When he visited the United Nations again in 1976, talking about the subject to Secretary General Kurt Waldheim, he said,

> We are not unrealistic. We are not seeking retribution nor atonement. But we are politicians and speech is our only weapon. The Third World rhetoric may sound harshly in Western ears, but at the negotiating table we are prepared to take a rational and pragmatic approach. We must move from slogans and semantics to substance...the world stands at the threshold of new opportunities.[15]

As mentioned, the State Department had started keeping tabs on how UN members—specially those receiving US aid—were voting on issues that interested the United States, and they did not like what they saw. Western countries in general continued to be reviled and assailed by Third World countries on a variety of issues. In voting in the General Assembly and other forums almost invariably a Western minority of twenty-odd members found itself facing the huge Third World mass with the Soviet bloc often alongside. The West accused the Third World of practising double standards between the West and the Soviet Union and of using its 'automatic majority' to bulldoze the UN. When Yasser Arafat was received in the General Assembly like a head of state and addressed it wearing the holster of his revolver (the gun itself having been deposited in the Assembly President's chamber behind the podium), it must have seemed to the glum Western visages like a materialization of Spengler's dire predictions in his *Decline of the West*.

But the limit of the West's outrage was attained when the General Assembly adopted a resolution declaring that Zionism is racism. The furore in the West and in particular, in the United States was unprecedented. *'Kristallnacht'*,[16] cried the Israeli ambassador. 'This evil deed...an obscenity...a day of infamy',

echoed other Western representatives. Indeed it was an exercise
in baiting the West, with no other evident aim. I cabled to the
Prime Minister that the uproar, fueled by Jewish fears and
Christian guilt, would take a long time to die down. Indeed it did
so eighteen years later, when the resolution was rescinded by the
General Assembly on a motion by the United States in 1993. In
the meantime Israeli propaganda used the passing of this
allegedly 'anti-Semitic' document to distract attention from the
real issues in the Middle East and to demonstrate that the Arabs
hated Jews and would never make peace.

It was characteristic that the resolution was moved by the PLO
not as the result of any strategic objective or forethought, but for
lack of anything else to do. For several years the PLO had tried
to make Western flesh creep by talking about expelling Israel
from the UN. That year there wasn't enough support in the
Third World for a credible attempt in that regard. The PLO
then tried to include a reference to Zionism in an African
resolution condemning racism and apartheid, but the Africans
did not want any distractions from the subjects of interest to
them. So someone thought up a draft on Zionism though only a
few among the Arabs themselves were keen on the idea. Egypt
tried to soften the impact of the draft by trying, unsuccessfully,
to include in it a condemnation also of anti-Semitism. At a
discreet hint from the Jordan ambassador, the ambassador of
Iran and I tried to persuade the representatives of the PLO, Syria
and Libya to add some nuance to the language of the resolution.
But they were not receptive to any suggestions. The high-decibel
Israeli-US attack on the draft and its sponsors had the opposite
effect and stiffened attitudes all round. In the end the PLO draft
was tabled as it stood and went through with a large majority.
Pakistan voted for the resolution, of course, though we did not
see what good would come of it for the Palestinians. In explaining
the vote our delegate made the following points: the resolution
was not an attack on Judaism as a religion, or the Jews as a
people; the Muslims shared with the Jewish people many spiritual
and cultural links; and Muslim hands were not guilty of the
holocaust which the Jewish people had suffered during the
present century or their age-old sufferings on account of
prejudice and racist arrogance. However, it was a fact that the
Zionist movement in the Middle East had, on racist grounds,

caused the expulsion of the Palestinian people from their homes and the extinction of their homeland.

When the resolution was adopted to applause from its supporters, the US Ambassador Patrick Moynihan made a great show of going up to the Israeli ambassador to embrace him. He called the resolution an 'act of abomination' that his own country would never forget. He himself launched a campaign of abuse and invective against the resolution that went too far in the eyes of some members of the Western group but did the ambassador no harm when he ran for the Senate from New York the following year and won the seat. The US Congress adopted a resolution calling on the US government to review its participation in the United Nations. A year earlier the US and the West had boycotted UNESCO over its treatment of Israel and put the ILO on notice in the same connection. Secretary-General Waldheim told me that the US had started deliberately to go slow in its contribution to the UN's working capital fund so that the organization at times did not have enough in the kitty to pay all its bills.

The resolution on Zionism had brought to a head a wider and long-simmering American dissatisfaction with the international organization. In the beginning the United States had looked upon it with the fatherly pride inspired by a well-behaved and promising youngster who is expected to help with minding the family business. Later when India and Pakistan—precursors of the Third World flood—began to voice their claims and complaints, it created some unease among the founding fathers. But it was attenuated by the fact that it was all done in Queen's English and parliamentary style. Then for a while the Americans just lost interest in the United Nations. *New Yorker* magazine summed up the attitude in its laconic way by putting the UN under the rubric '*inter alia*' in the entertainment column alongside book signings, stamp collections and the Bronx zoo. This benign neglect was unflattering, but it did not last. By the mid-seventies the UN was news again, mostly bad news, and the object of disapproval and reproach in conversations at cocktail parties and with New York cab drivers. When Patrick Moynihan, a combative Irishman, took over as US Permanent Representative, he decided to take on the Third World and to answer their attacks tit for tat. He called the 1975 General Assembly 'a profound, even alarming disappointment'. He went on to theorize that the United Nations was the way it was because the governments represented in it, barring some twenty-eight or twenty-nine, did not themselves govern by consent but by decree, and had majorities that were summoned only to rubber stamp government decisions. The General Assembly should, he suggested, establish some minimal standards by which governments treat their own citizens. He moved a resolution asking for a world-wide amnesty for political prisoners (it failed to pass) When Idi Amin of Uganda addressed the Assembly in his capacity as the head of the Organization of African Unity and called *inter alia* for the 'extinction' of Israel, Patrick Moynihan went quite overboard in saying, 'It is no accident that a racist murderer is head of the OAU', most of whose member countries were ruled by despots and dictators. Not all Western delegations shared such views or approved of Moynihan's contentious manner.

Gaston Thorn, the Foreign Minister of Luxemburg who was the General Assembly's President, made a criticism that was measured and more to the point: many resolutions remained a dead letter because they did not represent negotiated compromises, and an unfortunate development had been the adoption on some topics of two resolutions representing diametrically opposite points of view.

There was indeed lack of order and restraint in the procedures of the General Assembly and other UN organs. Moynihan's own agitational style and invective were meant to be a mirror image of the conduct of many Third World delegations. But the idea that the Third World was a well-knit and disciplined political machine, a monolith riding roughshod over the interests of the Western countries in league with the Soviet Union, was simply not correct. If anything, the General Assembly sessions increasingly revealed fissures in the seeming solidarity of the non-aligned group. On economic issues, the Group of 77 continued to maintain a front but only because in the UN economic issues were dealt with in terms of generalities and abstractions; in reality, the difference between oil-producing and consuming countries was all too evident as was the conflict between exporters of raw materials and countries which were net importers.

The Palestine issue was among those that were at the top of the General Assembly's agenda and it got a thorough airing every year. In January 1976 the Security Council took up the issue and for the first time since the debates of 1948, it occupied the centre of the stage in the Security Council and PLO representatives participated in the meetings in their own right. The remarkable new development was that the US had declined to use the threat of its veto to block the debate.

There had been other straws in the wind. An article by Joseph Alsop in *The New York Times* magazine,[17] took Israel severely to task for stalling the peace process and interfering in American politics. 'Most Americans,' he wrote, 'are prepared to take great risks to preserve the state of Israel but not to preserve Israel's conquests. American opinions are life and death for Israel whose survival cannot be ensured if the American majority becomes alienated.' Going even further, Harold Saunders, Deputy Assistant Secretary in the State Department, had indicated a substantive change in the US position in declaring that a just and permanent status for the Palestinian people needed to be defined. He also expressed satisfaction that the PLO had indicated a willingness to consider co-existence between separate Palestinian and Israeli states.

But as so many times before and since, all this turned out to be a mirage. Pakistan had just taken its seat on the Security Council and charged by the PLO and Third World members of the Council, we drafted, negotiated and tabled a resolution on the subject. It was vetoed by the United States, their apologetic explanation being that they did not oppose Palestinian aspirations but desired to preserve the 'established framework for negotiation', meaning resolutions 242 and 338. The British who had promised us their vote, got out of it by proposing a last minute amendment which would reaffirm these earlier resolutions and state that the new resolution did not supersede them. The amendment received only the votes of France, UK, Sweden and Italy (the automatic minority!) and was not carried but gave them the pretext to abstain. Waldheim told me that Premier Wilson had personally instructed the delegation to do so because of a soft corner he had developed for Israel while working on a kibbutz when he was a young man. The real reasons for the abstentions on a resolution that was noted all round for its moderation and balance, was that the US had been compelled by the Israeli lobby to veto it regardless, and its Western partners did not want to leave it so flagrantly isolated. I sounded out the Arabs on calling the UK bluff by accepting its amendment, which was only stating the self-evident, but here inter-Arab differences came in the way. PLO's 'Foreign Minister' Kadoumy said to me, half-jokingly that the PLO leaders for their part, needed an occasional American veto to prove their mettle to the rank and file who judge the leadership by its capacity to stand up to the Americans!

In 1978, after six years as permanent representative at the United Nations, I was transferred to the embassy in Paris where my stay was relatively brief and concerned almost entirely with one issue—Pakistan's nuclear programme and the plutonium reprocessing plant that was a key element of it and that the Bhutto government had contracted to buy from France. Issues relating to nuclear disarmament and non-proliferation were among the most important on the agenda of the United Nations, and in the years since the Indian nuclear explosion of 1974 had acquired, in the eyes of the Western powers and specially the United States, an importance and priority, above all others. These developments are the subject matter of the following chapter.

NOTES

[1] *Dawn*, 19 December 1971; at a press conference in New York.

[2] Dusan Simic in the weekly *NIN* of Belgrade in December 1971.

[3] In 1977 Bhutto said to the Soviet ambassador that he had done this at Premier Kosygin's request, but he was thinking of it already in New York during the Security Council debate on the Bangladesh War.

[4] However, a number of countries stood loyally by Pakistan, and their representatives—including Huang Hua of China, Abby Farrah of Somalia, Rashid Driss of Tunisia, Fereydoun Hoveyda of Iran—used to meet as needed at the Mission or my house to plan moves and tactics.

[5] Later he fell out of favour for his involvement with Mao's widow and the so-called 'Gang of Four', and disappeared from view.

[6] *Times*, London, 4 May 1972.

[7] Anderson papers, NSC's Special Action Group meeting, 6 December 1971.

[8] UN General Assembly, October 1975.

[9] When I mentioned Pillsbury's thesis to the UN Under Secretary General Tang of China, he said, 'It may or may not be easy for Soviet tanks to push into China, but they will find it not so easy to stay there or to get out.'

[10] The Pakistani servants were all togged up for the occasion in white *achkans*, starched turbans, etc. Bending over to pick up a tray in the kitchen, one of them

set his turban on fire and immediately the US security men guarding China's Deputy Foreign Minister, pulled their guns, and there was quite a commotion downstairs. Upstairs the party went on unawares, but the embassy's Social Secretary, Dorothy Stewart, came panting up to tell me in a whisper, 'Khawaja is on fire downstairs, but I saved the caviar!'

[11] 23 January 1973.

[12] The energy crisis was to some extent a state of mind brought about by the Arab oil embargo. Years later on the day the Gulf War broke out, I was in Paris and watched on television Parisian housewives stocking up on cases of Evian and Vichy water, against the peril of Saddam Hussain interrupting supplies!

[13] This last item was proposed by a Belgian skin-diver who offered to fasten a net around a large iceberg (some of which could be almost the size of some of the new UN members states!), tow it to a place off the Saudi coast, and pipe in the melted water. An iceberg shuttle was to be arranged to ensure a regular supply.

[14] Developing countries in general bought their oil not from the producers but from oil companies, which in many cases had been charging them higher prices than the market for many years.

[15] Author's notes.

[16] The night on which began the persecution of German Jews with the breaking of Jewish shop windows by Nazis.

[17] 15 December 1991.

CHAPTER 12

PROMETHEUS UNBOUND
The nuclear question

During Jimmy Carter's campaign for the presidency in 1976, a seminar was organized at the United Nations on the subject of nuclear energy and nuclear proliferation in order to provide him with an international forum for expounding his views. The Carter campaign was under criticism for ignoring issues and in particular for its neglect of foreign policy. Perhaps to meet this criticism, Carter had made nuclear proliferation his main foreign policy plank. In his statement at the seminar, he supported the development of nuclear energy but called for an 'absolute halt' to the sale of reprocessing and enrichment equipment, through a voluntary moratorium by supplier countries. He proposed that in order to set an example, the United States should put its own peaceful nuclear facilities under safeguards (but he did not do it when he became President). He referred to the Indian explosion as a warning that weapons technology could be developed in the process of developing nuclear energy for peaceful purposes, but he refrained from saying what might be done about the Indian case as such. In fact the United States did little with regard to India and in due course India received supplies of enriched uranium from America for the Tarapur reactor without having to give any commitments with regard to her nuclear programme; on the other hand the US cold shouldered a Pakistani proposal for a nuclear weapon free zone in South Asia. As for Israel even a mention of its nuclear programme was taboo in the US at the time. The Carter administration focused its attention mainly on Pakistan's nuclear programme.

The development of nuclear energy, and the history of efforts to prevent its diversion for military purposes, is full of such inconsistencies and contradictions, double-talk and double standards. Jacques Cousteau, French explorer and naturalist, who was one of the participants in the debate mentioned above, pointed to the intrinsic nuclear dilemma by recalling the legend of Prometheus whom the gods had punished because he stole the divine fire and put it into the reckless hands of man. The paradox is that though Prometheus was punished, the gods never took back his gift to mankind. And in time he was unchained.

The effort to stop the spread of nuclear weapons started as soon as the first bomb fell on Hiroshima. The Baruch Plan, proposed by the United States, would have placed the development of nuclear energy under international control. It was a good idea as such, but was rejected by the Soviet Union because it would prevent it from acquiring an independent nuclear capability. In its turn, the Soviet Union refused to help China to develop nuclear weapons capability. When the Non-Proliferation Treaty (NPT) was concluded in 1968, the number of recognized nuclear powers was five—all of them being, as it happened, also permanent members of the Security Council who bear, in theory, a special responsibility for the world's peace and security. The express purpose of the treaty was to prevent any increase in the number of nuclear weapons powers beyond these five. The bedrock on which the NPT was built was the fact that a number of countries which had the ability to go nuclear, had expressly refrained from doing so: countries like Canada and Sweden on idealistic grounds; others such as West Germany and Japan for political and strategic reasons.[1] The great majority of countries in any case, did not have the ability to go nuclear in the foreseeable future. When the Non-proliferation Treaty was concluded, Charles de Gaulle is said to have remarked sarcastically that the Treaty would prevent proliferation only by countries that did not want to go nuclear and those that were not able to. In fact the NPT was aimed essentially at the handful of countries that had the means or potential to develop nuclear weapons and were suspected of having the motive to do so. The argument was that if this group of countries could be restrained, then the NPT's five-power equilibrium would be a stable one—at least for a reasonably long period.

Most of these countries did not sign the treaty. Moreover, reality had already overtaken the assumptions of the NPT. Even as the treaty was being finalized, a sixth nuclear power, Israel, had emerged on the scene, albeit clandestinely and with a fog of ambiguity around its capability. The cloak and dagger means by which this had happened—piracy on the high seas, disappearance of barrels of uranium from an American enrichment plant—are now public knowledge. There can be little doubt that the Americans knew what was going on, and circumstances point to a degree of US complicity (at a crypto-official level) in the enterprise. The curious thing was the muted Arab reaction to a development that radically changed the power relationship between the Arabs and Israel. As mentioned in Chapter 10, in Egypt the Press was officially directed to play down the subject. Nor did one observe any special effort to gear up Egypt's own nuclear programme; on the contrary Egypt went ahead to sign the non-proliferation treaty, as did most other Arab countries. Iraq's alleged nuclear effort came much later. The low-key Arab reaction may have encouraged the United States to believe that despite the Israeli development, the fiction of a five-power nuclear scenario could be maintained. In particular, they seem to have assumed that in South Asia where India was clearly heading towards nuclear weapons capability, Pakistan would simply have to lump it.

India opposed the NPT on two main grounds that were not in themselves unjustified. The first was that the Treaty was discriminatory. The other concerned the trade-off between vertical and horizontal proliferation—in other words, if non-nuclear weapons states were to surrender the option to develop nuclear weapons, then the nuclear weapons states must begin to reduce and eliminate *their* nuclear arsenals. This principle of equity was indeed embodied in the Treaty as a declared and reciprocal commitment between the non-nuclear weapons states and the nuclear weapons states. But the nuclear powers had failed to carry out and in fact flagrantly violated this commitment. The major nuclear powers wanted non-proliferation without surrendering in the slightest degree their own freedom of action or dominance in the field.

All of this was very true, but the fallacy in India's argument was that by definition, a non-proliferation regime involves discrimination between nuclear weapons powers and those that agree to eschew these weapons. However Pakistan's problem with

India's position was not its logic but its purpose. It was plain for all to see that the purpose was to retain India's nuclear option and provide a rationale for the development of her own nuclear weapons capability. From Pakistan's point of view there was another problem: even if India signed the NPT, the Treaty could not take away from her the option that she had already acquired. On the other hand, it would bar the road to Pakistan, which was still on the way there. Nor, as far as Pakistan was concerned, would NPT be the end of the matter; other means and methods were sure to be devised to prevent Pakistan from acquiring nuclear capability even if it was under IAEA safeguards.

In the beginning of 1968, soon after the NPT was signed, a team of US officials came to Islamabad to press Pakistan to join the Treaty, and in response to our question about India, said that Pakistan's signature of the Treaty would set a moral example for India. In fact far from being an example, Pakistan's unilateral signature would relieve India of the only incentive she might have to sign herself—the fear that Pakistan would follow India in developing nuclear capability. The Americans were followed by the Soviets who also had no answer regarding India's intentions, but like the Americans they too asked us to sign up and set a good example.[2] However we were not put under undue pressure since at that time the possibility of Pakistan acquiring nuclear capability was considered to be fairly remote.

Nehru had set up the Indian Atomic Energy Commission soon after Independence and the Indian nuclear programme got a head start under his political direction and the top class professional team that was put in charge. Those were early years of euphoria about the promise of nuclear energy, reflected in Eisenhower's 'Atoms for Peace' policy. No one thought it possible that developing countries had the capacity to go beyond using nuclear isotopes for research in agriculture and things of that sort. Nehru himself had declared that India would not produce nuclear weapons under any circumstances whatsoever. Evidently this did not exclude acquiring and developing the technology to do so, which being the same as the technology for peaceful uses, India had a ready answer to any questions that were raised about her intentions in the matter. At all events India had little trouble in obtaining external assistance for its nuclear programme with minimal safeguards. Thus a 40 MW research reactor supplied by

Canada was safeguarded by nothing stronger than a unilateral Indian declaration to use it only for peaceful purposes. (It seems that Pakistan passed up a similar Canadian offer at the time.) The fuel produced by the Canadian reactor was in fact the one used in India's nuclear test.

However, it was not long before the military side of India's nuclear programme could no longer be overlooked. A book by an English writer, Leonard Beaton, published in the sixties,[3] described the Indian programme in considerable detail, and concluded that India's programme had an 'inescapable shape' which showed that India was moving towards acquiring a nuclear weapons option; at the centre of the programme was a plutonium separation plant that could have no other purpose. (Director General Eklund of the IAEA pointed out at a meeting in 1976 that it was the only plant in the world producing plutonium for—ostensibly—peaceful uses only.)[4] Indian leaders, obliged to play at the same time to the hawks at home and to critics abroad, were now far less unequivocal in renouncing nuclear ambitions. Defence Minister Chavan, answering a question in the Lok Sabha, said on 3 March 1966, 'There is no *brahmacharya* [continence] as far as science is concerned.' Mrs Indira Gandhi, when she was Prime Minister, struck a different note from Nehru's pledge against nuclear weapons, in declaring that India's security needs would be the paramount consideration in the matter.[5] Dr Homi Bhabha, head of the Atomic Energy Commission, was more specific: given the go-ahead, he declared in a broadcast over All India Radio, his people could produce a nuclear weapon within eighteen months.

The United States and other Western powers chose to turn a blind eye to all this. It was not that they believed India's professions of peace and non-violence or were unaware of her plans. Cold war calculations were among the reasons for the absence of firm Western action in India's case. Thus India succeeded in obtaining American aid and fuel for the Tarapur power reactor without having to accept full-scope safeguards in return; the Kennedy administration justified its leniency in this case on the ground that India might otherwise go to the Soviet Union to get what it needed. In 1977 Yugoslavia's Deputy Foreign Minister Lazar Mojsov told me that according to Foreign Minister Vajpayee, India was under intense pressure from both the US and USSR to accept full-scope safeguards. Vajpayee had added moreover that if the Tarapur reactor were closed down for lack of fuel, there would be a twenty per cent cut in the electricity supply to two Indian provinces. This indicates the extent of the leverage the United States did have on India if it wished to exercise it. But in the United States there was an unspoken assumption that it was inevitable for a country of India's size to go nuclear sooner or later. In the Camelot visions of the Kennedy years, India had cut an important and shining figure, as a potential great power and was viewed as a democratic counterfoil to totalitarian China. A corollary of this view seemed to be that there was nothing wrong if India did go nuclear.

It is an axiom of the South Asian strategic equation that where India goes in the matter of armament, Pakistan cannot be far behind. But when India set off its nuclear explosion in 1974, a Western colleague at the UN said to me 'One would have expected that in *this* particular field Pakistan would have been the first.' His argument was that in military logic, Pakistan, as the smaller and weaker country, had the greater strategic motive to rely on nuclear weapons to neutralize its disadvantage in size and numbers. The Pakistan Atomic Energy Commission (PAEC) was set up in the fifties not long after India's, and under the dynamic leadership of the late Dr Ishrat Usmani, a good deal of training and research got underway at a fairly early stage. It was apparent that in the course of things Pakistan too could acquire nuclear capability and in time, reach a rough parity with India in nuclear technology. The crucial question was that of the time gap between the achievement of nuclear-weapons capability by the two countries. This factor was crucial for Pakistan on two grounds: firstly, Pakistan's military and diplomatic disadvantage could become virtually absolute *vis-à-vis* an India armed with nuclear weapons; and secondly, as soon as India went nuclear, Pakistan would become the main target of the non-proliferation diplomacy that was being spearheaded by the United States. Unfortunately, Pakistan's nuclear effort at that stage did not have the kind of political and financial support that Nehru had ensured for the Indian programme. Far from being gung-ho about the matter, the Pakistani leadership was sceptical and the attitude of decision-makers in the early stage was marked by diffidence and self-deprecation. What, *Pakistan* go nuclear! The very idea seemed extravagant and wacky to many of them. In a discussion on the subject one senior official laughed at my arguments, 'Let us first learn to manufacture a proper bicycle!'

Moreover, Pakistan's diplomatic policy on the subject suffered from contradictory, almost mutually-incompatible aims: should Pakistan focus on developing its own programme or on hindering India's? As to the first, Pakistan did make an early enough start, but the initial efforts were not very purposeful. On the second, Pakistan's policy was two-fold: support stronger safeguards, the NPT and other such measures in order to foil India's nuclear intentions, and expose India's real intentions through her opposition to such measures.

Essentially Pakistan's primary aim at that stage, was to prevent India from going nuclear, rather than to go for nuclear weapons itself. Thus Pakistan was always in the forefront in efforts to extend and strengthen nuclear safeguards of all kinds and gave strong backing to the proposal for a non-proliferation treaty. This continued to be the thrust of Pakistan's nuclear diplomacy even after India's programme had gone past the stage where it could be hindered by international safeguards or other external pressures, and where these were liable to interfere with Pakistan's efforts far more than with India's.

Zulfikar Bhutto was among the few who saw things clearly from the start. In 1966, in his last days as Foreign Minister, he directed the Foreign Office to convene a meeting of all concerned, in order to consider the nuclear question and put up recommendations for action to the government. A working group was constituted with senior army and intelligence officers, some Foreign Office officials (with myself as point man), and the Chairman PAEC, Ishrat Usmani. The group held a number of meetings and in its report unanimously recommended the setting up of a plutonium separation plant as a first step towards keeping up with India's nuclear capability. Dr Usmani had been in touch with the French Atomic Energy Commission and they had offered to set one up at a cost of about $25 million and to provide financing on favourable terms. The plant would have to be placed under IAEA safeguards but at the time these were not very stringent and what was important, there was to be no provision forbidding the recipient country from developing its own reprocessing technology. The conclusions and recommendations of the group were to be submitted to Bhutto, but a meeting called for the purpose was called off at the last minute, on orders from the President's House. Not long afterwards, Bhutto was made to leave the government and no formal action was taken on the recommendations of the working group.

The working group was disbanded and its report was put away in some file. The recommendation concerning the plutonium plant ran into a wall of scepticism, reticence and obduracy on one ground or another from almost all the top policy makers. Finance Secretary Ghulam Ishaq Khan objected that the $25 million project was likely to be the thin end of the wedge, and that the country would inevitably find itself in a spiral of expenditure on research, then bombs, then missiles. All this, according to him, Pakistan could not afford, and it was no use entering into a race in which it could not keep up with India. The Foreign Secretary S. M. Yusuf also raised financial objections, and even the Defence Secretary—ordinarily the last person to be stricken with financial qualms—said that Pakistan could not afford the resources to develop nuclear capability. Moreover, he said, we did not even need it because India would not 'dare' to use nuclear weapons against Pakistan for fear of world opinion. On the eve of President Ayub Khan's visit to France, the Defence Secretary's brief for the President expressly recommended that he should *not* ask General de Gaulle for a reprocessing plant.

The financial argument was valid up to a point, but on the other hand the fact was that over the long run it would be far more costly for Pakistan to keep pace with India in conventional arms. For every gun, tank or plane that Pakistan purchased or acquired, India could buy or make as many and more. Pakistan could not afford a weapon-for-weapon competition with India or win the race for numbers. All we could do, at increasing expense and opportunity cost, was to maintain some sort of deterrent ratio with India's military strength. However in the nuclear field the arithmetic is fundamentally different. The numbers need not match; what matters is the ability of each to inflict unacceptable damage on the other.

As to the question of delivery vehicles and missiles, the assumptions that applied in the case of the United States and the Soviet Union, separated by 5,000 miles of land and ocean, did not hold good in the case of countries that have a common border. But the basic fallacy in the Defence Secretary's line of thinking was that a nuclear weapon does not have to be *used*; it is a weapon in diplomacy, designed to reduce the adversary to silence or paralysis. Moreover, we were not talking about the production of nuclear weapons, but the development of nuclear capability.

It was very difficult to understand the reasons for the negative consensus among the top policy-makers of the country on a matter of such vital importance for the country's security. Was it caused by an innate diffidence, by incomprehension, or by anti-nuclear brainwashing? It is hard to tell. The result was an irretrievable delay in Pakistan's programme. Irretrievable, not merely in giving India a lead over Pakistan, but also because perhaps everything might have been different—the story of non-proliferation in South Asia, the power equations in the region, Pakistan's relations with India—had Pakistan been in a position to match India's action in the seventies. Prime Minister Indira Gandhi is reported to have put forward the likely Pakistani reaction as one reason for not going forward after the Pokhara test, to develop a full-fledged nuclear arsenal. If so, this indicates that the Pakistan factor was very much in the minds of India's nuclear policy makers.

I spoke on the subject to President Ayub when I paid a farewell call on him before leaving to go as ambassador to Cairo in 1968, and tried to persuade him of the importance and urgency of taking up the French offer of a plutonium reprocessing plant. He listened intently and spoke of his excitement at a reported uranium find in the north. I submitted that meanwhile we could import 'yellow cake' (unprocessed uranium) that was available in the market. But nothing further seems to have been done in the matter until Bhutto returned to the scene in 1972. In 1973 negotiations began with France for a plutonium recycling plant and they were completed in January 1976. Meanwhile India had entered the nuclear ranks with its 'peaceful' nuclear explosion.

When India carried out an underground nuclear test in Rajasthan, and described it as an experiment in the use of nuclear energy for peaceful purposes, it followed to the letter the scenario that Pakistan had anticipated and tried to bring to the attention of the United Nations in the late sixties. The Disarmament Commission had then declined to accept for circulation a

Pakistan letter on the subject, on account of procedural objections raised by India. In the world at large the reactions were mixed. They ranged from the Soviet Union's embarrassed silence to an ineffectual wringing of hands in Western countries. Countries that had known all along what the Indians were up to—since they had provided her the wherewithal to do it—spoke sorrowfully that India, the apostle of non-violence and devotee of peace, could do such a thing. On the other hand, the French Atomic Energy Commission thought it an occasion to offer congratulations to Indian scientists on their achievement.

The one immediate and predictable reaction to the Indian nuclear test was to turn the world's attention to Pakistan. It was assumed, not unreasonably, that Pakistan would want to follow suit. A paper on the subject by an influential US think-tank, admitting that 'it would be unfair in the highest degree', urged that Pakistan had to be stopped, come what may, from doing so.[6]

For India, leaving aside the brief tut-tutting by the West, the gains from the nuclear test, immediate and potential, were important: (1) India's strategic superiority over Pakistan was now unchallengeable, at least until Pakistan caught up; (2) the timing of the blast would help India to keep ahead because tightened future restrictions would mainly affect Pakistan; (3) India's new nuclear status would also strengthen her diplomatic position by facilitating a settlement with China, increasing her leverage with the US and the USSR, and would bolster India's claim for a permanent seat on the Security Council. Pakistan, on the other hand, faced a radically altered strategic threat. It found itself in a weaker bargaining position, and would have to reckon with Draconian restrictions on its nuclear programme.

Indira Gandhi wrote to Bhutto on 22 May asserting that India's nuclear test had no 'political or military implications', and reaffirmed the pledge that India would not develop nuclear weapons, and described the peaceful uses of nuclear energy as 'a ray of hope' for mankind. In his reply dated 5 June, Bhutto drew a distinction between intentions and capabilities, and recalled how India's solemn pledges on Kashmir had remained unhonoured. He also referred to India's rapidly developing programme to build medium-range missiles. 'One can have access to nuclear technology and energy without having to conduct nuclear explosions,' Bhutto pointed out. He declared, 'Your nuclear explosion has introduced an unbalancing factor at a time when progress was being made towards normalizing relations [between the two countries].'

Writing to the UN Secretary General on the subject on 25 May, he spoke of the 'unique kind of anxiety' felt by Pakistan at the nuclear demonstration staged by India, and recalled that the international community had refused to heed Pakistan's repeated warnings about the nature of India's nuclear programme. He said that the Indian nuclear explosion had shattered the restraints existing hitherto on nuclear threshold states, and that Pakistan would face increasing pressures to move towards a nuclear option if it received no credible political insurance against nuclear blackmail. He called for 'binding guarantees of immediate assistance from the five permanent members of the Security Council acting collectively or individually, to counter any nuclear threat against a non-nuclear weapons state.'

Pakistan had floated this idea some years earlier at a conference of Non-Nuclear Weapons held in 1968 in Geneva. The conference was convened at Pakistan's initiative and its rationale was that the non-nuclear weapons states may be able to find common ground on non-proliferation, peaceful uses and other nuclear issues if they met on their own and free of the pulls and tugs of the strategic considerations that govern the policies of the nuclear states. An unstated objective of Pakistan's move was to focus attention on and mobilize moral pressure against India's bid for nuclear weapons capability. India, as expected, strongly opposed the move and cast the only negative vote against the proposal when the UN General Assembly approved it.

Pakistan's proposal on security guarantees called for a joint, binding commitment by the US, the USSR and the UK, the three signatories of the NPT, that in the event of a nuclear attack or threat against a non-nuclear weapons state they would collectively or severally come to its aid. This was scarcely practical politics and even less so in the context of a conflict involving India and Pakistan. In the wider perspective, the idea ran counter to NATO's basic strategic doctrine that its nuclear threat against East Europe was essential to neutralize the Warsaw Pact's advantage in conventional weapons. In fact neither the United States nor the Soviet Union was prepared to go beyond the guarantee provided in the NPT which, envisaging action through the UN Security Council and therefore subject to the veto, did not amount to much.

In strict logic, a guarantee against nuclear use or threat is inherently meaningless. In the case of actual use, there would not be much left to guarantee; as for deterrence against the threat of use, the threat is implicit and immanent, and need not be extended by specific word or deed. From Pakistan's own point of view, there were other difficulties with the idea. Assuming that one or the other nuclear power was willing to give Pakistan such a guarantee, it would demand in the first place that Pakistan should renounce the nuclear option, and not resort to it even in the case that India went nuclear; and then the guarantor power would surely expect a degree of control or supervision over Pakistan's defence and foreign policies, to guard against being dragged into a nuclear war by Pakistani actions.

An alternative to a binding security guarantee was the negative guarantee—a promise by nuclear weapons powers not to use nuclear weapons or threats against a non-nuclear weapon state. In this case too there was a problem of credibility. A negative guarantee is only an act of self-denial, a unilateral and revocable declaration of intent. At best the credibility of the guarantee would depend on the specific circumstances of each case. Who could be sure that in an emergency, where all is at risk, a nuclear power would in all circumstances stand by its pledge not to use nuclear weapons? From Pakistan's point of view there was a catch-22 aspect to the idea: as long as India was treated as a non-nuclear country, she need not give any such pledge to Pakistan whereas she herself would be entitled to receive one from China; if eventually she came to be treated as a nuclear power, Pakistan would have surrendered its nuclear option in exchange for a non-attack pledge by India.

Pakistan had experienced during the 1965 War, and again in 1971, the limits of security guarantees and alliances that are not founded on common political and strategic objectives. In the nature of things the relationship of smaller powers with the great powers tends to be of an expedient nature since they pursue global ends which may or may not coincide with the former's more limited and specific objectives. The fact was that India could no longer be stopped, and would go nuclear despite safeguards or treaties. Security guarantees, even if they could be obtained, would not redress the consequent military and diplomatic imbalance for Pakistan.

We looked at a number of other diplomatic options. One of these was suggested by the US officials' team that came to Islamabad in 1968: sign the NPT with the caveat that if India went nuclear, Pakistan would quit under the relevant treaty provision. Moreover, according to one view, the NPT did not restrict the freedom of signatories to take all steps towards the manufacture of nuclear weapons (these being the same as for producing power) short of assembling warheads. NPT members, having the right to receive full co-operation in developing nuclear energy for peaceful uses, in theory at least, would be entitled to develop the full fuel cycle. However, this provision of the NPT has been honoured almost wholly in the breech on account of various new restrictions and controls such as those imposed by the so-called London Club of nuclear suppliers.[7]

Another possibility was that Pakistan could also take the PNE route and thereby turn the tables on India. However, this would mean reversing for obviously expedient reasons, our long-standing policy that there was no difference between PNEs and nuclear weapons and giving legitimacy to the Indian position.

In truth the proposal for security guarantees was something of a red herring across the trail through at times it tended to look like a wild-goose chase. But it served the purpose of focusing attention on the security problem that had been created for Pakistan by India' nuclear test. Moreover the refusal of the nuclear powers, in particular the United States, to take into account Pakistan's genuine security concern strengthened the moral and political grounds for the direction that Pakistan's own nuclear programme might be obliged to take if there was no way of halting India in its tracks.

In the UN General Assembly we proposed the establishment of a nuclear weapons free zone (NWFZ) in South Asia. The concept of NWFZ was universally accepted (including by India); the US and the Soviet Union had commended it, and it had been applied in two specific regions: Latin America and the Antarctic. Our resolution on the subject was presented to the 1974 session of the UN General Assembly, and was carried by an overwhelming majority—with only one vote against, that of India.

But the United States, the USSR as well as the majority of Western states abstained on the draft though it went no further than asking the regional countries to consult among themselves on the subject in a meeting to be convened by the UN Secretary-General. Thereafter we proposed a similar resolution at every session of the General Assembly, with always the same results.

The United States' abstention could be explained on a number of grounds, though none were clearly spelled out. One of these was the reluctance to annoy India. But no doubt the abstention had something to do also with the United States' own nuclear deployments and intentions in the Indian Ocean region. Possibly, for the United States the most important consideration was that Pakistan was a case *sui generis* which had to be stopped regardless of what happened elsewhere, of regional factors, Pakistan's own security concerns and all other considerations. Therefore no notice, direct or indirect, was to be taken of Pakistan's case for linking its nuclear programme with India's. One of our diplomats abroad reported a remark made to him by an American colleague: 'President Carter would sooner have Pakistan overrun by the Soviet Union than see it trigger a nuclear holocaust.' The remark reflected the mind-set at the time, of the US administration and many influential Americans.

Under Carter, United States nuclear policy had came full circle from the Eisenhower period 'Atoms for Peace', to a policy of restriction and restraint that took into account neither the security concerns nor the economic needs of non-nuclear states. To the discrimination of the NPT, it added new distinctions— between supplier and consumer countries, between countries that already had certain kinds of technology and those that did not, between industrialized countries and the Third World. The new curbs were designed not to promote non-proliferation, but to maintain the *status quo*, to preserve a given power balance, and to protect the security of some states at the expense of others.

There was more than one reason why Pakistan was singled out for attention and considered a test case for the Carter administration's pledge to stop all further proliferation. The obvious reason was the chronic Indo-Pakistan conflict and arms race which gave Pakistan the strongest motive to follow India's example. Then, while India as a potential world power was seen as a special case, it was thought that if a country of Pakistan's size and situation were to go nuclear, it would create a very bad example and open the floodgates through which many others would come—the Koreas, Iran, Argentina and Brazil, Italy, perhaps even Germany and Japan.[8] The President of the Aspen Institute, a well-known American think-tank, told me that when he visited Iran soon after the Indian test, the Shah said to him, 'If one other country goes nuclear, be it Pakistan, Iran will do the same.'

Of all the various factors that determined US policy on the subject, no doubt the decisive one was the 'Israel factor', the fear that Pakistan—for love or money—could be the conduit for supplying nuclear know-how to Israel's enemies in the Middle East. The fear was given further point when Bhutto talked about the need for the Islamic civilization to match the nuclear capability acquired by the Christian, Jewish and Hindu civilizations. Western media were quick to coin the term 'Islamic bomb' to haunt the nightmares of their readers. Finally, as a major recipient of Western economic and military aid, Pakistan was considered to be more easily susceptible to external pressures, and its incipient nuclear programme elementary enough to be nipped in the bud.

The specific target was Pakistan's contract with France to build a plutonium reprocessing plant near Chashma in the north of the country. The plant was to be placed under specially stringent safeguards that went beyond the standard IAEA safeguards and applied not just to the plant itself but to the technology on which it was based. These provisions put the plutonium process in a strait-jacket and could have given France or the IAEA access to Pakistan's overall nuclear problem under the guise of verifying if the French-supplied technology was not being applied in other nuclear projects. The contract was examined and approved by the IAEA. Nevertheless, the United States remained unsatisfied, and put Pakistan under heavy and unrelenting pressure to give up the project, and France under equally heavy pressure to renege on the contract.

For the Carter administration the matter of safeguards was irrelevant in this case. As Fred Iklé, the Democrats' arms expert put it, 'Safeguards are a burglar alarm, not a lock.' Jimmy Carter himself took the position that, '...even if such facilities [like plutonium reprocessing] are subject to international inspection and safeguards, and even if the countries concerned are parties to the NPT, plutonium stockpiles can be converted to atomic weapons at a time of crisis without fear of sanctions by the international community.'[9]

Though the Indian nuclear explosion had been received with comparative equanimity by Western countries, it was a demonstration that some Third World country had the capability to develop nuclear weapons and to do so under the umbrella of peaceful uses. According to some estimates, in twenty years there would be fifty to seventy-five countries with nuclear capability, if not actual nuclear weapons. This aroused the spectre of nuclear power falling into 'irresponsible' hands such as Libya's Gaddafi or Uganda's Idi Amin, and revived atavistic fears of Western civilization being held to ransom by the barbarians at the gate.

All sorts of apocalyptic dangers were seen to be looming. Nuclear weapons might be used anonymously by an ill-intentioned third country to provoke a nuclear exchange between the superpowers. They could be introduced clandestinely into the US for actual use or blackmail, by a terrorist organization, an aggrieved government or a fanatical cabal of officers.[10] Local tussles and civil wars in unstable nuclear countries could spill over their borders and threaten world peace. In liberal democracies, civil liberties might have to be drastically curbed in order to meet the threat from proliferation and a siege mentality could take hold of them.

This was a time when the West was suffering from a crisis of confidence as a result of a number of developments. The first was the Arab oil embargo of 1974 and the jump in oil prices imposed by OPEC. Then in Iran the US Embassy had been taken over and captive American diplomats were pilloried and humiliated. The halls of the UN echoed with ceaseless denunciations of the West and demands for a new international economic order. Secretary of Commerce Elliot Richardson, when asked at a meeting of the Council on Foreign Relations as to what the Third World would do if its economic demands were not met, revealed the American state of mind in replying, 'Well, Third World countries are now beginning to acquire nuclear weapons.'[11] As if nuclear bombs could be used to raise a country's textile quotas or stabilize the price of cocoa!

These nightmare scenarios ignored the specific, real issues at hand and disguised the fact that a major purpose of non-proliferation was to preserve a given power balance in the world. India fitted into that pattern; Pakistan did not. That was the basic reason why the West reacted differently to India and Pakistan in the nuclear matter. It was therefore no surprise that after India's nuclear test in 1974 the United States, far from making efforts to get India to join the NPT or a NWFZ, concentrated instead on inducing her to become, like France and China, a silent partner in preventing further proliferation. This was something that suited India's book in every way—it would be a step towards recognition of India as a full member of the nuclear club and meanwhile make her the West's partner in stopping any Pakistani attempt to catch up. At a seminar on Disarmament held in Mexico in 1977, an Indian representative declared that though India still did not care for the NPT, she would voluntarily observe the Treaty provisions relating to proliferation. He called for another treaty or agreement that would provide for stronger controls on plutonium production and ensure against the transfer of nuclear technology to third countries. At the same time India began to go slow on implementing her nuclear co-operation agreements with other non-nuclear states, such as Argentine and Yugoslavia. All this greatly delighted the Americans and they talked excitedly about the 'positive signals' coming out of Delhi. One State Department official said to me, 'Unlike Mrs Gandhi, this guy Morarji is really sincere. We can do business with him.'

Around this time the first signs began to appear also of a shift in the position of France. She had declined to join the NPT and criticized the treaty as 'discriminatory, misleading, illusory, fallacious, and in the end, ineffective'.[12] However at the same meeting in Mexico, the French ambassador to the UN, Jacques Leprette, while reiterating his country's reservations on the NPT, declared that France would act in the future in this field exactly as the states adhering to this treaty. Moreover, he went on with a side-long glance in my direction, 'Not only will France comply with such criteria, but she is ready to implement the stricter measures coming out of the London group.' This position was stated also in a Franco-Soviet joint communiqué issued in July 1977 at the conclusion of Brezhnev's state visit to Paris.

France, however, continued to affirm in private as well as public, that the contract signed with Pakistan for a reprocessing plant was not affected by the shift in France's nuclear policy and that it would go through. The French permanent representative's statement too was qualified in the same way. On the other hand, the fact was that the supply of certain essential pieces of equipment had been held up, and France was now proposing some changes in the design of the plant.[13] A special emissary had been sent to Islamabad to discuss this proposal with the Pakistan authorities. In June 1977, together with Foreign Secretary Agha Shahi, I met Foreign Minister de Guiringaud of France in New York to tell him that the French proposal for modifying the plant was not acceptable. De Guiringaud expressed his disappointment at this and questioned whether Pakistan's nuclear programme did indeed require a plutonium plant at that stage. Nonetheless, he repeated once again the assurance that France would go through with the contract. But not much progress having been made in the months that followed with regard to the supply of all the needed equipment and training programmes. I met Guiringaud again in October when he came to New York for the UN General Assembly's annual session. He reiterated that France stood by the nuclear contract but he was evasive on specifics and in particular about the delays that were occurring in supplies of certain pieces of equipment and training schedules. Henry Kissinger had said to our ambassador in Washington: 'The French are playing games with you and will never deliver the real stuff.' This appeared to be what was happening.

When I arrived in Paris in May 1978 to take over as ambassador to France, at the airport itself I was informed by the embassy officials concerned that the suppliers of machinery and equipment for the plant had just received orders to suspend work on it.

I presented my credentials to President Giscard d'Estaing on 31 July, and after the exchange of formalities he himself referred to the 'very delicate problem' that had arisen between France and Pakistan. He said he wanted to make one thing clear at once, that there was no American pressure whatsoever in the matter, and nor would France give in to such pressure. France itself had come to the conclusion, he affirmed, that Pakistan did not need plutonium at the present stage. France was against nuclear proliferation and considered nuclear weapons to be dangerous and useless. I said in reply that all these factors had indeed been taken into account before the contract was signed, and they were provided for in the safeguards to be applied to the plant. These safeguards were much stricter than those of the IAEA and had been approved by the international body. In view of the signed contract and the statements repeatedly made by French officials until only the other day, nothing had prepared us to expect this development, which seemed to be based on an unspoken distrust of Pakistan's motives.

There was some discussion back and forth on these lines. Giscard looked embarrassed and uncomfortable and was obviously not eager to prolong the discussion. He said he did not feel qualified to enter into 'technical' questions and I would undoubtedly have the occasion to discuss them with the Foreign Minister and other concerned officials.

The following afternoon I called on Foreign Minister de Guiringaud at the Quai d'Orsay. De Guiringaud was a former cavalry officer with a gallant World War II record. He had been taken prisoner and tortured by the Gestapo. He had been my colleague at the UN as French Permanent Representative and we were on friendly terms. The discussion with him was less oblique. The first thing he said when I sat down was, 'I should like to tell you that the decision of the French government is irrevocable.' It had been taken, he explained, as far back as the departure of Jacques Chirac from the Prime Ministership in September 1976, but 'its implications had evolved gradually'. It was France's assessment that Pakistan did not need plutonium at that stage for peaceful purposes, and therefore France would not transfer technology that might enable Pakistan to produce weapons-grade plutonium.

Then why the devil was this not said to Pakistan there and then, I said (using more polite language), instead of the protracted shilly-shallying, procrastination, ambiguity, false affirmations, misleading re-assurances and repeated and categorical declarations that 'France will honour the contract'. I reminded him of what he himself had said to me in New York only a few weeks before. In reply de Guiringaud said shiftily, 'Oh, but I was referring only to a contract to produce nuclear fuel, not pure plutonium.' He knew that he was playing with words, that in truth France was going back on a solemn agreement under US pressure, or in return for a deal of some kind. Meanwhile in consequence, in Pakistan everything had been turned upside down; the door opened to Martial Law and as Kissinger had warned Bhutto, the country was being made into 'a horrible example'.

All de Guiringaud offered was help in window-dressing the affair *(habillage)* to minimize the Pakistan government's political problems. To some extent the *habillage* would also alleviate the French government's own embarrassment, for its bad faith was patent and flagrant. Echoing the Americans, the French Foreign Minister suggested to me, 'Let us not say that the project has been cancelled, or even suspended. You can even go on for a while with the civil works; your scientists can continue to come to France and work jointly with ours on non-proliferating technologies.' France was prepared also, he said, to supply nuclear reactors to Pakistan. The Foreign Minister of France was asking us to join in staging an elaborate farce in order to fool the people of Pakistan! I said to him that sooner or later the truth would become known and it was little use trying to dress it up as he was suggesting. I also told him that the world would not believe that American pressure had nothing to do with France's decision to break the contract with Pakistan. Carter had declared that he would make France go back on the contract, and that is exactly what was happening.

There was little doubt that American pressure and blandishments were the major reasons for the French decision. But there were other factors also: the prevailing anti-nuclear sentiment all over Europe; the opposition of India, Israel and Iran to Pakistan's nuclear plans; and also, to some degree, the relatively modest size, in financial and economic terms, of the Pakistan deal. The decision was not without some political embarrassment for the Giscard government. The Gaullists were not pleased at its giving in to an American diktat. The nuclear industry was unhappy at losing business in a bearish market for nuclear equipment. Michel Debré, Gaullist ex-Prime Minister put down a question in the National Assembly on US interference in the matter of the reprocessing plant, and when I paid a call on him, expressed his unhappiness at the decision.

Secretary-General Soutou of the Foreign Ministry on whom I called in due course, spoke on the subject with a disarming candour. He said that France had indeed broken its contract with Pakistan. There were no two ways about it, he said, and

France was clearly to blame. The decision was a difficult one for France in terms of its relations with Pakistan, her image in the world, and also in economic terms. Pakistan could very well accuse France of hypocrisy. But France was under intense pressure from the US-Canada-Australia uranium combine which was a powerful entity and was in a position to make its pressure felt. 'One resists to the extent one can,' the Secretary-General said, 'but diplomats and government leaders are not Don Quixotes and have to look at the practical consequences of their decisions.'

The decision, he said, was taken by France's Nuclear Policy Council which had also decided, in light of the political developments in Pakistan, not to cancel the contract outright, but to suggest modifying it in such a manner that the plant would not be able to produce weapon-grade plutonium. France did not want its decision to provide fuel for political controversy in Pakistan. Soutou tried to soften the blow by mentioning that France had also stopped the supply of sensitive technology to India and Iraq. The fact was that India was not buying sensitive technology from France at that point, and as for Iraq, matters were resolved in another way.

A nuclear agreement between France and Iraq had been negotiated by Jacques Chirac when he was Premier and was very wide-ranging. Under its terms, France was to train Iraqi scientists and technicians; raise capital in Germany and Belgium for Iraq's nuclear research centre; ship U-235 to fuel the reactor, and also to prospect for uranium in Iraq itself.

During the night of 5 and 6 April 1979, saboteurs entered a warehouse at the port of Toulon, and using explosives, blew up components for the core of a research reactor in Iraq that had been brought to a dockyard warehouse a few days earlier for shipment to Iraq. The warehouse had been put under heavy guard, with coded electronic locks and police watch-dogs, and the sea entrance was guarded by coastguard patrols. The shipment was to take place on 9 April. Was all this a screen for the French security services doing the job themselves? The French had been shilly-shallying over the shipment which had been delayed repeatedly. A firm date was set only after a visit to Paris by the Iraqi Commerce Minister in the course of which the French negotiated the purchase of an additional five million tons of oil from Iraq.

An anonymous group of 'ecologists' claimed responsibility for 'neutralizing machines dangerous to human lives'. It was evident that (1) the job was done by experts in handling military explosives; (2) they must have had inside accomplices since the internal alarm system, operated by a code known only to security personnel, had been switched off. The finger of suspicion pointed at the Israeli intelligence agency, Mossad, possibly with help from sympathizers within the French government. Flora Lewis, the well-informed correspondent of the *Herald Tribune* wrote that 'someone very high in the French government' had secretly ordered the sabotage.[14] The Paris weekly *Le Nouvel Observateur* wrote that, whoever was responsible for the act, the sabotage had 'removed a sharp pebble from President Giscard d'Estaing's shoe.'[15]

The authorities were tight-lipped and to this day the culprits have remained undetected. Iraq itself maintained the utmost discretion on the incident and apparently fell in with the subsequent French offer to modify the plant for use only with the so-called 'caramel' fuel.[16]

When I paid a courtesy call on Jacques Chirac who was then the Mayor of Paris, he reminded me that the reprocessing contract with Pakistan was signed when he was Prime Minister, and with the full knowledge and approval of President Giscard. He said that the decision to break the contract was 'improper and absurd' and not justified by any overriding French interests. The absurdity of the decision he said, lay in the fact that all plans and drawings of the plant had already been delivered to Pakistan and it could go ahead and complete it on its own or with China's help. China would be only too pleased to obtain, in this way, knowledge of advanced French technology. However Chirac said that though the Americans had much to do with Giscard's decision, it was in fact, the President's own decision; the Cabinet had been divided and Premier Raymond Barre was unhappy with it. Chirac said that Giscard fancied himself as a man of peace and had come to adopt leftist ideas on non-proliferation. What sort of non-proliferation was it, Chirac asked, when India had the bomb and only Pakistan was being put under pressure? It would be a more stable situation, in his view, if a solution was sought on a regional basis. He said that he had opposed the decision and would speak to all concerned, but he could not take issue publicly with a decision taken by a government of which his party was a coalition partner.

Ziaul Haq returned a soft answer to the French rebuff, and generally Pakistan reacted in a moderate and low-key manner. This created a good impression—and relief—in France, for Pakistan could have pilloried France in the world at large or taken the matter to court in France itself or used the Gaullist Opposition and the nuclear industry's lobby to make things awkward. Not only did the Pakistan government abstain from any of these actions, but on the contrary, we maintained all the other major contracts with France—relating to the television system, truck manufacture and defence purchases. On the nuclear issue we decided to enter into the spirit of the French game. Thus to counter the French proposal to modify the design of the plant, Agha Shahi came to Paris a couple of months later bringing a new proposal relating to safeguards. This was to associate France with the management of any separated plutonium that was in excess of Pakistan's reactor requirements. That, we said, ought to reassure the West against diversion of plutonium to third countries. President Giscard, taken by surprise, seemed to concur with the proposal when he said that the general approach outlined by Mr Shahi was acceptable to him, and that France would be willing to hold a meeting of experts of the two sides to discuss the proposal.

We also held out a carrot: the prospect of a long-term relationship in the defence field with France to replace the long-standing past arrangement with the US. Pakistan would purchase from France a number of aircraft for the Air Force straight away, a larger number five years later, and thereafter there could be local assembly and gradual manufacture of the Mirage 2000 Fighter in Pakistan. Giscard sat up and took notice and said he fully appreciated the 'political implications of a long-term arrangement between the two countries'.

But what exactly did Giscard mean by accepting the 'general approach' of Pakistan's proposal on plutonium management? Did he see it as a more elaborate form of window-dressing for dropping the reprocessing plant? This was my own impression, and we got a hint the next day at de Guiringaud's lunch, that in fact this was the case. Agha Shahi pleaded that if the nuclear contract was not fulfilled, there would be great political difficulties in Pakistan where the question had been linked with the fall of Bhutto and the Opposition was alleging that the present government had made some sort of deal with France. The mood at the lunch, helped by coffee, cigars and mutual ambiguity over the question at issue, was expansive and cordial. De Guiringaud himself repeated that France was ready for expert level discussions on the new Pakistan proposal, but added that a final decision on it could not be taken until the conclusion of the international study on the nuclear fuel cycle (INFCE) that had been undertaken at the initiative of the US and was going on in Washington.[17] However, the French nuclear policy adviser, Jacomet, who was a bit less under the influence of the post-prandial *bonhomie*, muttered that the 'plutonium problem' would remain. The weakness in Pakistan's case, he said, was that Pakistan did not have enough irradiated fuel to reprocess nor a major programme to set up reactors.

I called on Jacomet a few days later in order to pursue the proposal. He said that President Giscard had gone a little too far and too fast in accepting even the principle of the new Pakistan proposal, since it implied that the reprocessing plant would be built as planned, whereas the French position now was that the plant was *not* to be built as planned. He said he did not know exactly what the President had agreed to and that he himself had received no instructions. This was a line that would be repeated by French officials throughout the discussions on the subject.

A Gaullist journalist told me that there had been no change in the French position as a result of the Pakistan proposal, and that they were just playing along at having a dialogue. Giscard had met Carter at Guadaloupe recently and given him an assurance that the French stood firm on their repudiation of the Pakistan contract. One result was that the US eased its stand against France's own breeder reactor programme which was based on reprocessed plutonium.

Expert-level talks did take place just the same, and went on for several days, but nothing came of them. Our side talked about meeting France's proliferation concerns within the 'integrity of the contract'; the French side agreed on the international management of plutonium, but said they could not talk about it in connection with a plant that France had decided *not* to build. The French then proposed that Pakistan write a letter to France formally proposing joint management of plutonium. I pointed out that Pakistan was making a major concession and it could only be done through an exchange of agreed letters in which France would resume its assistance for building the plant. This was, of course, not acceptable to the French. However when I paid my farewell call on the new Foreign Minister François Poncet in September 1979, before leaving to take up a new job as the UN representative in Beirut, we agreed to go on with talks on the proposals and counter-proposals made by the two countries, though both of us knew that the whole thing was a charade. The useful thing about diplomacy is that matters need not always be brought to a conclusion.

So it went, until the whole thing was overtaken by news that Pakistan had managed to develop the technology to enrich uranium. A French newspaper wrote that one could now understand the relative serenity of Pakistan's reaction to the cancellation of the French contract.

Meanwhile, one morning I was summoned to the Quai d'Orsay by Secretary-General de Leusse to be told of the French government's 'surprise, astonishment and shock' at an attack by unknown assailants on their ambassador and his counsellor in Islamabad. He said the attack appeared to have been pre-meditated and was not a robbery, since nothing was taken from either man. But the Secretary-General's protest was delivered in a pro forma manner, for he knew no doubt that the two gentle-men had been roughed up while going on a highly improbable 'picnic' in the scalding afternoon heat of midsummer near Kahuta, the controversial nuclear establishment. Ziaul Haq had already phoned His Excellency to express his shock and sorrow, and I too said how sorry I was.

De Leusse took the occasion to deny a statement by Indian Foreign Minister Vajpayee to the effect that France had assured India that it would give no assistance to Pakistan to make a nuclear bomb. Not that France intended to give Pakistan such assistance but, said he, France was not Pakistan's 'governess'; if Pakistan wanted to make nuclear bombs it was not for France to intervene.

In actual fact, France had begun to co-operate quite closely with the US in the field of non-proliferation. After the cancellation of the reprocessing contract the US nuclear policy expert Joseph Nye came to Paris to complain that French suppliers were still trying to get some equipment to Pakistan through Italy, Belgium and other countries. French Customs were then given instructions to watch out for any and every shipment to Pakistan, and warn the government in case of anything suspicious. This was with a view to cover items not already included in the sensitive equipment list.

Around this time a ground swell of anti-nuclear sentiment was beginning to develop in various parts of the world. Nuclear energy, hitherto considered the gateway to universal prosperity and progress, was now seen as dangerous and immoral; instead solar, wind and tidal power were extolled as clean, safe, and inexhaustible substitutes. Some of this public agitation was genuine, but it is safe to assume that some was instigated and orchestrated by the interested intelligence agencies. Pakistan's nuclear plans and the 'Islamic Bomb' figured a good deal in all of this, and the Western Press kept up a drumfire of speculation and rumour and disinformation on the subject. There was talk of an alleged Pakistan-Libya nuclear deal; TV stations never seemed to tire of showing a film entitled the 'Islamic Bomb'; China was warned that any nuclear help to Pakistan could jeopardize the supply of French reactors to China.

In fairness it must be said that the French Press was not of one mind on the subject. At a lunch I gave for a group of French pressmen concerned with the issue, they argued with me and also with each other: why doesn't Pakistan accept co-processing? Where is the plutonium you want to reprocess? One mentioned the West's double standards and recalled that when India carried out her nuclear test, the Head of the French Atomic Energy Commission sent his counterpart a telegram of congratulations. Another said, 'Why shouldn't Pakistan as a sovereign country have a nuclear bomb if India has one?'

At the academic level and on the seminar circuit, a lot of carrot and stick ideas and proposals were tossed around for dealing with the situation. A Soviet expert proposed that Security Council sanctions under Art. 41 of the Charter be jointly applied by US and USSR against any state, even if it was not a Treaty adherent, which violated the NPT regime. US experts did not go along with this idea but proposed that proliferation should be treated as an 'international tort' with a system of rewards and deterrents.

These would range from incentives in the form of conventional arms supplies and security guarantees to active dissuasion by precision bombing or sabotage of the nuclear facilities of threshold states. A variant of the security guarantee idea was that a state which insisted on going nuclear (such as India), might be dissuaded by a threat to sell, give, or make available nuclear weapons to its potential target country (such as Pakistan). A sinister—and more practicable—proposal was that the US should on the contrary give massive technical assistance to India in order to increase her lead and make it futile for Pakistan even to try to catch up.

On the other hand, voices were also raised advocating a more measured view of the problem and what needed to be done about it. The influential Trilateral Commission (made up of leading personalities from the US, Europe and Japan) in its draft Report for 1977, made a dispassionate analysis of the nuclear question and reached the following conclusions:

(1) Every country has the sovereign right to utilize nuclear energy.

(2) Ensuring the security of supply is a valid reason for uranium enrichment. Third World countries reject monopoly control of this material by the industrialized countries for the same reasons that the latter seek to diversify their sources of energy supply.

(3) Enrichment technology, however, provides opportunities of misuse even under IAEA safeguards, specially in strife-ridden regions and 'soft states' that may be unable to prevent accidents or theft.

(4) Reprocessing raises similar problems, but there is an economic and ecological case for reprocessing (as it burns up toxic plutonium that would have to be stored it at great cost and risk), provided it is justified by the existence of a large number of reactors.

The Trilateral Commission recognized that a solution could not be imposed by the supplier countries alone. Sensitive technologies may have to be transferred under workable safeguards; otherwise a number of developing countries would develop their own unsafeguarded nuclear capacity in an atmosphere of resentment and confrontation.

A sign of America's irrepressible pragmatism was that some thinking was already beginning to be done on the unthinkable.

In a seminar at the Aspen Institute held in August 1976, one of the themes was 'How to Cope in a Proliferated World?' Taking the worst case scenario in which there might be as many as forty nuclear weapons powers, it was suggested that a feasible policy aim should be to try to limit the number to fifteen or so and to persuade most of these to be satisfied with making one or two demonstration explosions for prestige reasons. But it was feared that the early generation weapons of most of these neo-nuclear powers would lack safety features and be liable to accidental detonation; special controls would therefore be needed to prevent their unauthorized seizure or use, specially in *coup*-prone countries (such as Pakistan). Lacking PAL (permissive action link), the coded electronic locking device, these countries would be obliged to keep the weapons in disassembled condition, thereby reducing their operational readiness and making them more vulnerable to surprise attack. This was seen as a problem for Pakistan *vis-à-vis* India. Deficient C3 (command, control and communications) systems would also increase the risk of pre-emptive strikes. In the early stage when both India and Pakistan would have small nuclear forces, rely on aircraft for delivery, possess low-reliability C3, with limited warning and long scramble time, there would be reciprocal vulnerability, but gradually India could move ahead of Pakistan in these respects and attain unilateral capacity to launch a successful pre-emptive attack on Pakistan. Pakistan could use nuclear ground bursts on its own territory to stop an Indian Army advance. It was estimated that a limited nuclear exchange between India and Pakistan would cause ten million deaths on each side.

As a remedy for this unstable situation, it was proposed that the new nuclear powers should be helped to develop safer weapons, a reliable C3 system, and a special PAL device; in an extreme case a surrogate second strike capability could be provided to the weaker or to non-nuclear states, for example, by the transfer of weapons under a two-key system.

Despite Carter's fervour on the subject, opinion was growing even in administration circles that some further proliferation may be unavoidable and the world would have to learn to live with it. US non-proliferation policy was now aimed at stabilizing the *status quo* which meant the acceptance, tacit or otherwise, of India as a nuclear weapons power, and leaving Israeli and South

African nuclear capabilities in the fog of ambiguity in which they had been carefully shrouded. The remaining threshold powers had to be delayed if they could not be stopped.

But Pakistan did not figure in any of this rethinking and was considered a case apart, whose nuclear venture *must* and could be stopped. The reasons for this step-motherly treatment of Pakistan, were the 'Israel factor', Pakistan's vulnerability (as a country dependent on foreign aid) to external pressure, and the feeling that stopping Pakistan might stop the rot or delay the inevitable. Existing US legislation provided for a variety of sanctions against countries that went for plutonium reprocessing, but the President could waive these if that would promote US policy interests. Thus, further nuclear ventures by India, even PNEs, could go unpunished if India promised not to export nuclear technology to other countries. Pakistan could not expect such indulgence, and the Americans were prepared only to allow Pakistan some kind of face-saving device for giving up the project.

The official US effort to halt Pakistan's nuclear programme was therefore unrelenting, and took the form of coercion and duress as well as advice and inducements. Within days of Ziaul Haq's *coup*, US Ambassador Arthur Hummel called on him with a warning that aid would be cut off if the reprocessing plant problem was not resolved. The US wanted the project to be 'put on ice' immediately in order not to prejudice a final decision that the forthcoming elected government might wish to take! In a chat over lunch two years earlier, Fred Iklé, who was then candidate Jimmy Carter's nuclear policy adviser, suggested the same idea to me: 'Why doesn't Pakistan just stretch out the period of completion of the reprocessing plant? It will give you people time to think things over, and perhaps even to drop the project altogether.' The US hope was that if the Left came to power in the following year's elections in France, the contract would be cancelled as the Socialists had not approved the project and were not sympathetic to Pakistan.

After seizing power, Ziaul Haq declared that the Martial Law regime 'would honour all agreements, commitments and contracts signed by the outgoing government'. This was read by all concerned as referring to the French contract, but scepticism about the matter persisted in Pakistan where it was assumed that the Americans had engineered the *coup* in order to stop Pakistan's reprocessing project, and that the Martial Law regime would be induced to give it up in some guise or the other.

The French Foreign Ministry were apparently inclined to see Pakistan's proposal for joint management of plutonium as a cover for giving up the reprocessing project. But whatever he may have had in mind, Ziaul Haq gave no indication that he intended to give up or modify the nuclear programme. On the contrary, when the news about uranium enrichment by Pakistan broke in the media, Zia took credit for it and claimed that he had gone one better than Bhutto.

As part of his campaign to vilify and malign Bhutto, Zia tried to establish that Bhutto was prepared to give up the reprocessing plant in order to mollify the Americans. In an Envoys' Conference he summoned in July 1979, Zia claimed that within his own hearing Bhutto had said, 'To hell with the reprocessing plant, as long as the onus can be put on France!' This was quite the opposite of whatever I knew about the matter. Bhutto was keen to set at rest US fears about Pakistan's and his own intentions in the nuclear matter. He would very much have liked to do so in a face to face meeting with Jimmy Carter and asked Ambassador Yaqub and me to see if such a meeting could be arranged. But he told me to make it clear that there could be no compromise on principles. On another occasion in order to clarify an ambiguity on the subject in a telegram sent by State Minister Aziz Ahmad, I telephoned Bhutto from New York in order to seek a personal clarification from him. He told me that Pakistan stood firm and would resist any French attempt to wriggle out of the contract. After Kissinger's famous 'horrible example' talk with him in Lahore, Bhutto phoned me in New York to say that Kissinger had tried to sell him the idea that Pakistan could get off the hook if France, acting on its own, backed out of the contract. Bhutto said that he had rejected the idea, and had taken the precaution of conveying to Paris that Pakistan stood firmly by the nuclear contract and did not want it annulled, and that they should not believe anything to the contrary that Kissinger might say to them on the subject.

In the Envoys' Conference we were told about the still hush-hush uranium enrichment project, the Foreign Secretary making a Freudian slip when he explained that it was a process based on 'experimental subterfuges'. There was much discussion on how

to square the circle of maintaining the nuclear programme and
retaining US friendship and assistance. Ambassador Sultan Khan
said that Israeli intelligence had told Washington that they had a
tape recording of a meeting of the Libyan Cabinet in the course
of which Gaddafi spoke about obtaining Pakistan's help to make
a nuclear bomb for the Arabs. Ambassador Sultan said that things
had become very chilly for Pakistan in Washington; embassy
officials were tailed when they went calling on congressmen.

In June, at a conference in Helsinki, I had a long chat on the
subject with Bill Maynes, Assistant Secretary of State for
International Organization Affairs and member of a non-
proliferation group headed by the US arms negotiator,
Ambassador Gerard Smith. He said that the US had reliable and
incontrovertible information that Pakistan's nuclear programme
was headed all the way towards the production of weapons. The
United States considered this development as the gravest threat
to world security since the end of World War II. He dismissed
talk about an 'Islamic Bomb' and a Libyan connection as 'media
stuff' to which the US did not necessarily give full credence.
What was causing real and deep concern was the certainty that if
Pakistan went nuclear, then it would only be a matter of time
before Germany and Japan, forced by their public opinion, also
decided to go nuclear. Then the whole central strategic balance
and the system of security based on NATO and the Warsaw Pact
would collapse. A new situation with unpredictable but far-
reaching implications would be brought into being. That was the
reason why Pakistan's nuclear programme was given number one
priority in Washington and why Pakistan *must* give it up.

The US, he said, was not singling out Pakistan in the matter: it
was simply that existing legislation left the administration with
little choice except to cut off aid to any country that was
developing plutonium reprocessing. The US was also putting
pressure on India which might have to close down electric supply
to half of Bombay if American fuel supply for Tarapur was
stopped. (But it wasn't, and Tarapur continued to receive
American fuel as before.)

All this was specious reasoning and Maynes must have known
that it was. Public opinion in both Germany and Japan was
strongly opposed to going nuclear. Both countries were part of a
security system which guaranteed their security far more

effectively than their own nuclear bombs could do. There was no reason why they should scuttle that arrangement because Pakistan was putting up a plutonium plant, when they had not reacted in any way to an actual nuclear explosion by India. The real reason for US panic over the Pakistan project was precisely the 'media stuff' that Maynes professed to deride. This became clear when in response to my disclaimer he said, 'Oh if somebody gave you enough money, you could quickly turn capability into option!'

The security and interests of Israel have been the primordial and overriding concern of United States policy in the Middle East. It is to the credit of Israeli diplomacy and statecraft that a tiny state, vulnerable in the extreme, with no resources and nothing to offer in return, has managed to harness the power of the most powerful country in the world to its own ends and purposes. One of these, since Israel developed nuclear capability, was to prevent its strategic advantage being eroded or challenged in any manner. In this context a Pakistani nuclear capability, even if primarily a response to India's nuclear development, was seen as a potential threat to Israel. In point of fact, Pakistan's support of the Palestinian cause was in substance not much different from that of a hundred other countries who backed a settlement under Security Council resolution 242 calling for a return by Israel of conquered territories and Arab recognition of Israel's right to exist within recognized borders. But Pakistan's stand on the issue was voiced with a fervour and rhetorical vehemence that made out Pakistan as a particularly implacable enemy of Israel. Against this background, it was not difficult for Israelis and Americans to fear that Pakistan might pass on its nuclear know-how to Israel's enemies. So it was that India's bomb was accepted with a little bit of grumbling, South Africa's with embarrassment, but Pakistan's reprocessing plant, to be set up under the most stringent safeguards ever devised, was depicted as capable of destroying NATO, the Warsaw Pact and the whole strategic balance on which rested the security and peace of the world!

Another fear was less specific, but more widely shared in the West as well as the Soviet Bloc; this was the fear of the so-called Third World, seen as an amorphous, unpredictable, menacing, vindictive mass, and personified at the time by the likes of Idi Amin, Muammar Gaddafi and the masked Palestinian terrorist.

Pakistan was not quite counted among such bogeymen but had to be stopped from setting a bad example.

Maynes asked me what could be done, or offered, to induce Pakistan to give up its nuclear course. I pointed out that Pakistan had initiated its nuclear programme many years ago which, while peaceful in intent, must in the nature of things, give Pakistan the nuclear option. However nuclear weapons capability was a different matter and we were prepared to accept restrictions on it in tandem with India. Pakistan's policy was aimed not at acquiring nuclear weapons, but preventing India from introducing the nuclear race in the region. Hence our proposals for a NWFZ. If the US government wanted to stop nuclear proliferation in South Asia, then it must first of all, recognize that the problem was regional in character and concerned the security of countries like Pakistan.

The discussion with Assistant Secretary Maynes ended inconclusively, except for his warning that Pakistan should in no way underestimate the concern at its nuclear plans and intentions felt in Washington, where they were seen as an issue of the greatest urgency and importance.

In Paris US Ambassador Hartman spoke to me in similar terms at a lunch at his place. He too said to me that United States policy on this matter was not based on an attitude of generalized 'do-gooding', but was dictated by concern for United States' own security. This he said, should be a matter of consequence also to other countries because on the existing nuclear equilibrium depended the security of the world. 'Why do you need a reprocessing plant? Where are your reactors? Where is the plutonium you want to reprocess?' he asked me, the same questions that had been echoed by Foreign Minister de Guiringaud.

My view, which I expressed at the Envoys' meeting in Islamabad, was that existing US threats and actions notwithstanding, it might be easier to come to terms with the United States once the country's nuclear capability had advanced to the stage where the Americans considered it invulnerable to pressure or to sabotage. A straw in the wind was a new US offer to discuss Pakistan's security against a nuclear attack or threat. This was a new departure in that for the first time mention was made of a threat from within the region. *Herald Tribune* reported that fighter aircraft would be offered if Pakistan accepted full-scope safeguards, implying that Pakistan could retain 'sensitive' nuclear technology provided it was placed under safeguards. A year earlier when Joseph Nye, the State Department's man on nuclear proliferation came to New York to discuss with the Pakistan delegation a Pakistan-Yugoslav draft resolution on the transfer of technology, he had taken the position that reprocessing plants should not merely be safeguarded, but should be safeguardable, that is, incapable of producing weapons grade material, or that it should be designed so as to give timely warning of intended misuse so that counter-measures could be taken.

The Americans had another grievance and this concerned Pakistan's alleged double-talk on the subject. In my conversation with Bill Maynes, he had complained that what made the administration especially nervous was not knowing exactly what Pakistan was up to, and what were its intentions. He said it might be better if Pakistan could declare frankly that it *was* going for the nuclear option instead of all the fudging around regarding its peaceful intentions. One could see the point of this, and it seemed to me that we could be more forthright about the fact that our nuclear programme would give Pakistan the nuclear option. A degree of transparency about the programme would make it easier to defend it diplomatically, and might be helpful in disarming the US. This came some years later in Dr A.Q. Khan's interview with Kuldip Nayyar, an Indian journalist,[18] and Ziaul Haq's own statements on the subject.

Not all American allies took as dire a view of the dangers of proliferation as did the Carter administration, or agreed with it on how to deal with the problem. A Japanese view was that the compact embodied in NPT had not been carried out, and that Carter's policy on plutonium reprocessing was detrimental to interests of countries like Japan. In Germany too there was doubt about Carter's carrot and stick policy, and the view was that all countries had the right to nuclear energy and if there was to be sacrifice of national sovereignty to prevent non-proliferation, *all* countries must make it. A Swiss paper circulated at the Special UN Session on Disarmament held in 1978, while noting the danger of proliferation, made the point that there could be no question of prohibiting certain technologies or restricting their use to a small circle of selected states.

Summing up his views for the benefit of the Envoys' Conference, Ziaul Haq said that Pakistan could not give up its nuclear programme. The United States, Zia said, were jittery and would go to any lengths to stop Pakistan's nuclear programme. But they could do 'damn all' to knock out our installations from the air. Sabotage was another matter, he said, and we had to fear and guard against it.

Bill Maynes had asked me whether we did not fear that India might use pre-emptive methods to 'take out' Pakistan's nuclear option before it developed much further. I said we had to reckon with this possibility—not only India, but others including the US itself, had been mentioned as having the motive to do so, but whoever attempted such action should carefully weigh its consequences.

In Pakistan the US Ambassador had given a categorical assurance that US did not intend to use military force or any illegal means against Pakistan's nuclear projects. But what if someone else, India or Israel or masked gunmen, were put up to do the job? This was a distinct possibility, but in due course fate took a hand and with Carter's defeat and the Soviet invasion of Afghanistan, there was a different situation and new American priorities. Ziaul Haq had been lucky again, but it has to be conceded also that he had not blinked in the face of pressure.

My last major official act at the United Nations before leaving on transfer to Paris, was to participate in the UN's first Special Session on disarmament held in June 1978. One notable feature of the situation was that even while the General Assembly was setting disarmament goals for the future, in Washington DC a meeting of NATO powers was taking decisions, under US inspiration, on a greatly increased rearmament programme for the Alliance over the coming fifteen years, that would nullify these goals.

The session adopted without dissent a declaration with the grand title of the International Disarmament Strategy, but agreement on the text was reached only during a sleepless forty-eight hour extension. A US delegate called the agreement a 'small miracle', but the miracle was accomplished not by genuine compromise, but thanks to verbal ambiguity which postponed debate to other occasions or shifted it to other forums. Disagreements were moved down to footnotes in the form of reservations by various countries to a variety of enunciations that appeared in the agreed text. Among these was the so-called 'nuclear complex' of issues which was the subject of special interest to Pakistan.

On the other hand, a curious phenomenon observed at the Special Session was that while the two superpowers were engaged in intense military competition with each other, and clashed sharply on Africa, the Middle East and human rights, they seemed to move along parallel lines on many disarmament issues. Private meetings were held between them to exchange assurances that their bilateral talks would remain on track regardless. For them the decisions on disarmament were a matter of rationalizing their arms race. The Third World played the role of a Greek Chorus, standing on the sidelines and uttering lamentations, dire prophecies and exhortations.

Speaking for Pakistan in the Special Session I said:

> Developing countries who are being dissuaded from producing nuclear fuel, even under safeguards, cannot ignore the fact that the price of nuclear fuel, which is under the control of a handful of advanced states, has risen eight-fold in the previous five years—that is, more than the rise in the price of oil that caused so much concern and anxiety in the industrialized countries. Moreover, the supplier countries reserve the right to supply fuel or deny it, to whom they please and set conditions or waive them as they wish. States are sovereign, independent and equal only in name; the assumption by any state of the right to compel 'responsible' behaviour on the part of other states, will lead to the re-emergence of the system of domination and exploitation from which the Third World is still struggling to free itself.

> Fears are expressed that sensitive nuclear technologies may fall into the hands of 'irresponsible' governments. Who is to determine whether a government is responsible or not? At various moments in history, the government of one country or another, has done things that history has judged as irresponsible or criminal. No individual state or group of states, however powerful, has the right to set itself up as judge of the credentials of another sovereign and independent state.

But in the real world, powerful states do not always need the legal right to do what they want, it is enough that they have the means to do it. Development of technology was producing new weapons—'smart bombs' (PGMs), remote sensing techniques, spy satellites and lasers that were going to change the art and mode of warfare. These weapons would be far more effective instruments for applying military power than nuclear bombs, and permit the selective use of force for attaining specific objectives such as destroying the nuclear installations of an 'irresponsible' state. As India and Pakistan raced each other to attain nuclear capability, the age of the atom bomb was perhaps already reaching its end.

NOTES

[1] In an Aspen Institute meeting in 1976, a German representative said that NATO's protective shield had kept Germany from going nuclear; if it was removed or weakened, her position on non-proliferation may have to be reconsidered.

[2] The world's two main nuclear rivals and adversaries had a common nuclear policy vis-à-vis the rest of the world. Parallel studies carried out by the UN associations of the US and the Soviet Union in 1972 showed agreement on most issues: the NPT; stronger IAEA safeguards; security guarantees for non-nuclear states.

[3] Leonard Beaton, *The Spread of Nuclear Weapons*, Praeger, New York, 1962.

[4] Author's notes.

[5] Rajya Sabha, 10 May 1966.

[6] 'What is New on Nuclear Proliferation?' Aspen Institute, Colorado, 1975.

[7] This informal group of fourteen supplier countries (minus France) had existed for some years to enforce an agreed set of standard controls on export of nuclear equipment and fuel.

[8] Though they were inhibited by their history and own public opinion, neither Germany nor Japan had adhered to NPT at that stage. Italy had ambitions of its own and would have liked, in return for renouncing nuclear weapons, to get some reward in terms of prestige and influence (such as a permanent seat on the UN Security Council).

[9] Author's notes of a meeting of the Institute of Science and Man, Rensslaerville, New York, May 1976.

[10] An example near at hand was the 1961 'Revolt of the Generals' in Algeria, when de Gaulle ordered a nuclear bomb at an Algerian base to be de-activated immediately, for fear that it might fall into the hands of the rebels.

[11] Philadelphia, June 1976.

[12] In the First Committee of the UN General Assembly's 29th session, 1974.

[13] The modified plant would produce not plutonium but 'caramel', a non-fissile admixture of some other element with plutonium; but whether 'caramel' could be used as nuclear fuel, was far from proven.

[14] 11 May 1979.

[15] Mid-April 1979.

[16] Apropos Israel's subsequent destruction of Iraq's research reactor, Lebanese President Amine Jemayel, told me that according to his information, Israel had infiltrated the team of French technicians working on the project, one of whom had installed some sort of electronic signalling device near the core of the Osirak reactor to help the Israeli bombs home in on the target.

[17] The subject of the study was to consider ways of producing nuclear fuel that could not be used for making bombs—the nuclear age equivalent of the medieval quest for the 'philosopher's stone'.

[18] *Observer*, London; 1 March 1987.

CHAPTER 13

THIRD WORLD CAESAR
Zulfikar Ali Bhutto

A senior army officer once said to me, 'A combination of political acumen and military power leads to Caesarism.' We had been talking about Zulfikar Bhutto. Bhutto never directly wielded military power but it was not too fanciful to see points of analogy between Caesar and Bhutto. He was not a military conqueror but a leader who after a defeat without honour, had recovered what had been lost on the battlefield and redeemed the country's self-respect. Like Julius Caesar, Bhutto was a man caught between his radical ideas and the interests of his own land-owner class; his reforms and diplomatic triumphs re-unified a country emerging from civil war and dictatorship. His ambition was in conflict with his professed ideals. His rise was meteoric and the fall, at the hands of people who were closest to him, sudden and tragic.

In the early thirties my father was District and Sessions Judge in Larkana, and we lived a short way up a tree-lined street from the Bhutto family's house. Sir Shahnawaz Bhutto, Knight of the British Empire and member of the Bombay Governor's Executive Council, was active in politics. He played an important role in the separation of Sindh from Bombay Presidency. My first vague memory of Zulfikar is as one among a turbulent group of Bhutto children who used to come to play when they came down for the winter vacations from their school in Bombay. Then I met him again nearly a quarter of a century later, at a party in Karachi in 1958. He had recently returned from Berkeley and Oxford, and I too was just back from postings abroad for a stint in the Foreign Office. He was a barrister and man-about-town who wore natty Italian suits, was seen at all the parties, went to the races, chased skirts. He was a bright young man for whom it was easy to predict

a brilliant future, and indeed he entered politics effortlessly, as
one might come into a heritage, as a member of General Ayub
Khan's Martial Law Cabinet, and in a few years as his Foreign
Minister. There was nothing in his life till then that foreshadowed
the triumphs and tragedy that destiny had in store for him—the
summit of political power in Pakistan and world-wide renown,
and from those heights a sudden fall to the depths, and his life
taken in its prime. The life of such a man is both history and
metaphor. The Press described it as meteoric in its rapid rise and
abrupt fall. But a meteor brightens the sky for a while and then
vanishes, leaving no trace behind. Bhutto's works, for good or ill,
are still with us. Even in death he remains a potent force in the
country's politics, a focus of controversy, stirring in equal degree,
intense devotion and bitter animosity.

He became Foreign Minister at a time when the border fighting
between China and India in 1962 had abruptly changed the strategic
picture in South Asia. Non-aligned India was getting military
assistance from the United States, and pro-West Pakistan, feeling let
down by its Western allies, was mending fences with China. The
change led to much heart-burning in Pakistan and bitterness with
the US, but ultimately it proved useful in provoking an overdue
rethinking of Pakistan's foreign policy assumptions. Bhutto was of
course, just the man to do this. The country's foreign policy had
until that time been set in a well-marked groove. Pakistan had
thrown in its lot with the West in the hope of redressing the strategic
imbalance with India and obtaining some diplomatic leverage in
the dispute over Kashmir. But gradually the quest for security had
become simply a search for weapons. In seeking to protect the
country's independence, Pakistan had entered into alliances and
arrangements that restricted its freedom of choice.

Bhutto was not against the American connection—far from it.
An unstated object of Pakistan's *rapprochement* with China at that
stage was to put the United States on notice not to ignore
Pakistan's security interests. But he did not think that it made
sense for Pakistan to put all its eggs in one basket. It was a
mistake, he wrote, for Pakistan to have ignored 'the powerful
reality that was the Soviet Union protruding over its head' and
adopt a belligerent attitude towards it, permitting dangerous
provocations such as the CIA's U2 spy flights. He considered it
absurd that Pakistan had abstained even from cultural and

commercial contacts with the Soviet Union, and even banned
the dissemination of Soviet technical literature.

For him, the position taken by each of the three great
powers—the United States, the Soviet Union and China—towards
India and Pakistan, was influenced by the cold calculations of
their own global interests and their relations among themselves.
The United States had developed a relationship with Pakistan
only after failing to bring Nehru's India under its wings, and
partly no doubt as a means of putting pressure on India. But
Nehru's indignation and wrath Bhutto noted, had not stopped
the United States from giving military aid to Pakistan when it was
in the American interest to do so; Pakistan's reproaches and
protests were no more likely to hinder US aid to India in the
aftermath of Sino-Indian border war. He pointed out that on the
other hand, Soviet policy towards Pakistan too had undergone
some change for the better in the sixties, but again this had
occurred in response to shifts in the global situation and not
because Pakistan had done anything to placate the Soviets.
However, he noted that the Soviet move in Pakistan's direction
was less pronounced than the US' shift in favour of India. Thus
on the Kashmir issue, after initially supporting Pakistan's basic
position, the United States had gradually moved to a neutral
position, which meant, in effect, that it favoured the *status quo* in
Kashmir; whereas the Soviets while they no longer spoke of the
Kashmir question as a settled matter in which Pakistan had no
legitimate interest, continued to support India on substance.

Even before he received the Foreign Affairs portfolio, Bhutto
had such considerations in mind. As Minister of Industry and
Natural Resources, he decided to turn to the Soviet Union for
help in oil exploration. This alarmed the conservative Pakistan
Establishment of the time, who felt that hob-nobbing with
'godless Communism' was a bad thing in itself and would put
ideas in the heads of the lower classes. Bhutto had to fight an
uphill battle to overcome the obstructionism within his own
ministry of natural resources, and resistance from the
Establishment in general, in order to bring these negotiations to
a successful conclusion. The oil agreement did not usher in the
feared social revolution (nor did it help in finding much oil) but
it gave a small turn to the wheel that could begin to change the
direction of Pakistan's foreign policy.

Pakistan's new foreign policy gradually took shape when Bhutto took charge of the Foreign Ministry; a policy of balance in our relations with the three major world powers that mattered most to Pakistan. It was not that Pakistan's foreign policy was turned around completely, but Bhutto gave it a new orientation and a new style, and he gave it relevance in the light of the changing world situation.

He spelled out his ideas in a series of papers on various aspects of foreign policy-making.[1] In the post-war world, he pointed out, the concept of regional balances of power had been replaced by a stand-off between powers with a world-wide reach and global designs. Classical imperialism had made way, he held, for a new type of domination in which the instrument of expansion was not the gunboat but ideology, and where the physical occupation of the colonized territory was no longer necessary.

'The small nation that does not understand the new rules is doomed to frustration, a sense of helplessness and isolation...', he cautioned. 'A small country,' he said, 'should not completely identify itself with the interest of one great power to the exclusion of others...it must avoid controversy and confrontation and seek a workable equilibrium.' But he warned, 'It is the quintessence of folly to pursue a policy of provocation.' He saw the tensions among the great powers as a boon as well as a danger for smaller countries, and counselled prudence. 'When differences develop, a small country should not take on a great power head-on, it is wiser for it to duck, detour, side-step and try to enter from the back-door.' On the other hand, he advised, neither cringing, nor sycophancy, neither sentiment nor nostalgia should find any room in a small country's dealings with the great powers.

Bhutto did not have any illusions about the Soviet position. He realized that there were limits to a *rapprochement* with the Soviet Union set by its relations with India. He was aware that there was little prospect of a change in the Soviet Union's stand on Kashmir. Indeed in this regard, Bhutto noted Pakistan's own double standards as between the United States and the USSR. From the former, Pakistan expected full support, and nothing short of it, on the Kashmir dispute and in general with regard to India; as against this, eager to improve relations with the USSR, Pakistan was thankful for any favourable Soviet word or gesture, even while the Soviets continued to accept India's claim that

Kashmir was an integral part of India and to support India in
almost all things. But *realpolitik* is not worried by inconsistency,
and Bhutto wanted to improve relations with USSR because it
would improve Pakistan's leverage in dealing with the other great
powers, and also to neutralize Soviet hostility.

As for China, Bhutto noted that even in the time of 'Hindi-
Chini bhai bhai! [Indian and Chinese are brothers!]' when
China's relations with India were very close, and certainly far
better than with Pakistan, China had refrained from recognizing
India's claim to Kashmir and Premier Zhou Enlai had declined
an invitation to visit Srinagar. It had to be assumed therefore
that the seeds of Sino-Indian differences and rivalry already
existed even then, and Pakistan could find the counter-weight it
was seeking against India in a relationship with China. Bhutto
was thus a strong advocate of Pakistan's *rapprochement* with China
and was able to persuade President Ayub of the merits of the
policy. But he advised, 'We should be cautious in making new
friends and rejecting existing ones.' In improving relations with
China, Bhutto moved carefully and in a measured way. Initially it
was a matter of 'my enemy's enemy is my friend'. The underlying
objective at that stage was to put a brake on the United States'
rapidly developing military relationship with India. The
relationship gained substance and momentum as events
unfolded, and it acquired a degree of reciprocity when Pakistan
was able to help alleviate China's diplomatic isolation in the
world. The fruits of the policy came only when the United States
changed its own attitude towards China, but this was later under
Yahya Khan's rule.

The immediate consequence of the adjustment in Pakistan's
foreign policy was Pakistan's estrangement from the United States
and Bhutto's own exit from Ayub's government. When he went
to Washington in 1963 to represent Pakistan at John F. Kennedy's
funeral, President Johnson made no secret of his displeasure at
the new turn in Pakistan's foreign policy and took Bhutto
personally to task for Pakistan's growing closeness to China and
his personal contacts with Sukarno.[2] In 1977 when he was facing
country-wide political turmoil and when relations with the United
States were beginning to sour again, Bhutto spoke to the
American chargé d'affaires about these past misunderstandings
and pointed out that subsequently, the United States itself had

mended relations with the People's Republic of China and done so through the intermediary of Pakistan. He said to the American official that he had welcomed this as a positive development of the world power balance and it was something that he had been strongly commending in his discussions with Chairman Mao and Premier Zhou Enlai. Bhutto was evidently trying to make the point that in time the United States' perceptions on the nuclear issue too may change, and that the existing differences between the two countries would be resolved.

He gave his approach the name of 'bilateralism', but it was not really a theory or a philosophy or even a new strategy, but rather a manual of practical diplomacy. Diplomacy is both an art and an instinct. Some have one but not the other. Bhutto had both. He had a feel for when to press an issue head-on and when to seek the desired objective by a movement from the flanks. He was an accomplished practitioner of diplomacy, adept in the techniques of the art—a skilful and persuasive negotiator.

In a note he wrote on relations with Nepal, one sees a specific illustration of his approach: Nepal, he wrote, was a Hindu kingdom, fearful of the weight of its huge fellow-Hindu neighbour, and was to Pakistan what Afghanistan was to India. Support to Nepal must be given

> ...quietly and with dignity without arousing any suspicions or giving the impression that we are happily fishing in troubled waters. Rashness and over-exuberance may frighten Nepal away from our hold. Our influence should grow materially and tangibly rather than superficially. It should be gradual and cautious. We must not over-do things...A right balance is what we need.

However his approach wasn't always based on Cartesian logic and cold calculation. He had described foreign relations as an area of 'romance' in his speech at the Foreign Office's farewell for him. He shared to some extent the popular wishfulness on Pakistan's supposedly 'historic' links with Islamic countries, near and far, and this led occasionally to contradictions between his analysis and articulation, between what he did and how he talked about it. This was apparent, for instance, in a speech he made in Karachi in June 1965, at the Islamic Council of International Affairs, on Pakistan's relations with Muslim countries, and its

place and role in the Islamic world. It contained a good deal of
invective and censure against Imperialism and the West in
general. Foreign diplomats were present in strength, among them
most Western ambassadors. The latter listened in stony silence
and raised eyebrows and exchanged glances at Bhutto's
unrelenting strictures against the West and against some of their
countries. However his purpose was not so much to hector the
West as to chide the envoys of the Muslim countries whose
reciprocity in the matter often left something to be desired.
Bhutto recounted all that Pakistan had done for its Muslim
brothers in the Maghreb, Somalia, and during the Suez Crisis,
for Egypt (whose ambassador too may have raised an eyebrow at
Bhutto's revisionist account of the event). And he asked
plaintively, 'The Muslims of India have given much and sacrificed
greatly for the cause of Muslims beyond their own frontiers. Is it
too much to hope that they in their turn, will not be abandoned
by the Muslim world in their hour of peril?'

He spoke of the problems facing Muslim countries and peoples:
thus Ethiopia was unjust to its Muslim citizens and had a dispute
with Somalia, and therefore it was all the more necessary for
Pakistan to have contacts with Ethiopia. From the *realpolitik*
perspective of his theory of 'bilateralism', one could ask why? How
was this concern with Ethiopian and Somalian Muslims compatible
with his caveat against nostalgia and sentiment in foreign relations?

His pan-Islamist approach was anathema to many of the
Muslim countries whose representatives he was addressing and
he himself was aware of the shortcomings in the concept. He
went on to ask, 'The questions then arise: can the consciousness
of the universal polity of Islam be given concrete political
expression in our times? Is the Koranic concept of the universal
community of Islam transcending national barriers, still valid?'
He gave a qualified answer: 'It is true that a lasting association
cannot be based on doctrine alone, as this would inevitably lead
to dissension and strife on account of differing interpretations.
Nor can we hope to build on sentiment and nostalgia because
with the passage of time, the world and its events have left these
memories behind.' But he went on bravely, 'The future of Islam
is beginning to take shape', and professed to see it in the periodic
summits of the Arabs, the Maghreb states, RCD and IPECC.[3] He
affirmed that the next phase of co-operation would 'inevitably'

include the development of intra-institutional relations between these various regional organizations.

He saw for Pakistan a 'role of the utmost importance' in this process but described it in ecumenical terms:

> The Muslims of Pakistan have inherited, along with their Islamic fervour, an admixture of all the other great civilizations that have helped to shape human destiny. From the Buddhists and Hindus among whom they have lived for almost a thousand years, their extensive contacts through Central Asia with the ancient civilization of China and their association with the West which has left its own legacy, the followers of Islam in Pakistan have developed a rich and uniquely cosmopolitan outlook.

He spoke too of the 'Pakistan ideology', but in quite different terms from its orthodox exponents:

> The ideology of Pakistan was not only confined to the need for the emancipation of the Muslims of the subcontinent. It is vitally concerned with the manifestation in the twentieth century of the Islamic values of social justice and universal brotherhood...and is dedicated to the emancipation, solidarity and progress of Islam in the twentieth century.

I referred to the 'style' of Bhutto's foreign policy—that is to say the distinctive stamp he put on the conduct of foreign relations. In its reliance on rhetoric, Bhutto's style could be called 'Third Worldist'. He had great admiration for leaders like Nasser and Sukarno—for the way they stood up for their countries' rights and honour and were not afraid to confront the great powers, and for their ability to sway crowds with the power of the word. As an orator, he himself could arouse and inspire crowds but was sometimes carried away by the flow of words into disregarding the dictates of discretion. Oriana Fallaci, the provocative Italian journalist whom I met in Beirut, told me about the free-wheeling interview Bhutto had given her in Islamabad after taking over as President. But afterwards, realizing that he had spoken a little too harshly about Mrs Gandhi—whom he was shortly to meet in Simla—he phoned Oriana to plead with her to take out some of the expressions he had used. 'You have the destiny of 600 million people in your hands!' he said to her.

There was something a little 'raw' in Bhutto's style—an admixture of impulsiveness (but sometimes a calculated impulsiveness), and of emotionalism—as in the matter of Islamic solidarity—and a degree of touchiness. The touchiness often came out in his attitude to the West. There he was seen as 'anti-Western' and undoubtedly there was something of a 'chip on the shoulder' in his attitude towards the former colonial powers. There was much he admired in European culture and he did not suffer from xenophobia. But a proud man himself and a fervent nationalist, he reacted sharply to any sign of arrogance, real or imagined, in foreigners towards himself or his country. When he was Minister of Commerce and Natural Resources in 1958, the Chief of a British oil company in Pakistan, a socialite on close terms with the highest in the land and himself considered a power in the land, was given twenty-four hours to leave the country when at a meeting he showed 'impertinence' to Bhutto (or it may be that he used the incident to get rid of someone who, behind the scenes, was opposing the proposed oil agreement with the Soviets).

Another illustration of Bhutto's sensitivity and emotionalism was his decision to take Pakistan out of the Commonwealth in 1972 when Britain moved too quickly to recognize Bangladesh, and on account of its generally hostile attitude towards Pakistan during that period. It may not have been a purely emotional reaction, and possibly he saw in such actions some sort of catharsis for the nation's hurt ego. Britain and some other Commonwealth countries made efforts to dissuade Bhutto from doing so and the Commonwealth Secretary General, Arnold Smith, went to Islamabad to make a last ditch personal effort with Bhutto. Bryce Harlan, the New Zealand permanent representative to the UN, told me a story about this visit that illustrates an aspect of Bhutto's style: arriving by road from Delhi, Arnold Smith telephoned Bhutto directly to explain the purpose of his visit and ask for a meeting. Bhutto gave him a time late in the evening and said he could not make it earlier as he was to speak on television. Switching on the TV in his hotel room to listen to the Prime Minister's speech while waiting for the meeting, Arnold Smith heard Bhutto announce Pakistan's exit from the Commonwealth.

The strain in US-Pakistan relations was related to a basic change in South Asian geopolitics as a result of the Sino-Indian

War, but these elements in Bhutto's style were perhaps responsible for the fact that in US eyes he was seen as personally responsible for Pakistan's pro-China shift. (In Tashkent the Soviets too displayed a wariness towards Bhutto because they considered him to be the leader of Pakistan's war party and the architect of its China policy.)

When Ayub dismissed Bhutto in 1966 it was popularly believed that he had done so at Johnson's behest. That Bhutto was the American *bête noire,* of that they made no secret, but the truth is that Ayub did not need much prodding to get rid of a man who was developing a dangerously popular base and whose ambitions were all too evident. Their policy differences may have originated even earlier if the following passage from a note on Nepal that Bhutto wrote in 1963 was intended as a homily for Ayub: 'The silent King demonstrated the quality of leadership and that quality was that he had the guts and nerve to call the [Indian] bluff.'

In his farewell encomium, Foreign Secretary Aziz Ahmad summed up the contribution Bhutto had made to Pakistan's foreign policy:

> We look at the world today from a different perspective and the world itself sees Pakistan in a new light. If a new equilibrium has come to be established in our relations with the world, if today this nation is aware of its rightful place in it, it is due in large measure to the youthful outlook, the energy and vision that you brought to your stewardship of the Foreign Ministry.

I was among the small group who saw Bhutto off at the Rawalpindi railway station when he left for Karachi. Intelligence Bureau Chief Awan was also there both as a friend and also to check on Ayub's behalf, who else was seeing him off. Bhutto was out of office for a couple of years but they were not years in the wilderness.

In 1968 when the tide turned and Bhutto was leading the crowds against Ayub, I recalled President Nasser's words, 'Such men are best kept within the fold and under one eyes.' Ayub had him locked up for a while, believing that a spell in the jug would quickly put to rights the ease-loving Sindhi *wadera* born with a silver spoon in his mouth. So said Ayub's daughter, Naseem

Aurangzeb, when she and her husband came visiting us in Cairo. But a spell in jail was just what Bhutto needed at that time to counter his reputation as a playboy politician weaned into politics under Ayub's Martial Law.

By that time he had established the Pakistan People's Party with the help of people like former ambassador J. A. Rahim, Dr Mubashir Hassan and Shaikh Rasheed. I met some of them when I called on him in Rawalpindi after an envoys' meeting summoned by the new Martial Law Administrator, General Yahya Khan, in May 1969. There was Mubashir with the piercing look of the single-minded man, and Rahim whom facial paralysis had left with a permanently caustic expression that seemed to reflect his view of the political situation. They indulged in ideological talk about Fabian socialism, non-alignment, and imperialism. It all sounded like an academic seminar and there was an air of irrelevance and passivity about it. Men like Rahim and Mubashir were ideologues and men of goodwill who brought to the movement mostly the strength of their convictions. Mustafa Khar was also there but he was of a different mettle—someone rather in Bhutto's own mould, fond of the good things of life; a man who enjoyed manipulating power and had an air of laughing up his sleeve. For political strength Bhutto had to rely almost entirely on his own standing as the champion of Pakistan's cause against India and of the cause of the poor against the rich.

However, at that stage, his ideas on economic issues were fairly vague and he saw little connection between a country's economic power and its standing in the world. Once, speaking to me, he scoffed at Ayub's Finance Minister: 'Shoaib thinks that the glory of a country comes out of smoking factory chimneys!' He expressed his view in a note to Ayub: '...the value and greatness of a country lies not so much in its per capita income, in the smoke and smog of its factories, or its balance of payments position as much as in the capacity and confidence of its leadership, in the minds of its men.' Bhutto admired the charisma of a Sukarno and a Nasser, the heroism of their freedom struggles, their stature on the world stage. He did not seem to notice that both leaders had outlived their triumphs, and now were feeding their people on slogans and mock heroics. In the long run what the people need is bread as well as circuses.

One evening in Tashkent, after a hard day's arguing with the Russians, Bhutto came into the room of our Moscow Ambassador, Iqbal Athar, to relax and chat. He said that nothing would be achieved in Pakistan unless there was a fundamental change in the system. But at the time I don't think he had formulated his ideas about what the desirable new system should be. He advocated socialism and the compulsory membership of Civil Servants in political parties. He may have thought in terms of establishing a one-party system as Ayub later accused him of wanting to do. This was implicit in what he said though he didn't say it in so many words. When I objected, he said 'But Civil Servants are already mixed up in politics and ever ready to be used by politicians. In my system the bureaucrat will be at least under party discipline, and accountable to it.'

I also demurred that the idea of welfare socialism was for rich countries such as Britain or Sweden. For poor countries like Pakistan, I submitted, the primary need at that stage was production not distribution. 'Besides we don't have a socialist party,' I said, 'the bureaucracy will end up being the Party and will have all the more scope for self-aggrandizement and the lining of pockets.' He said, 'Then there is no hope for Pakistan if it is to go on plodding along the same old rut.'

When he was called to power after the exit of Yahya Khan's military regime, one would have said that the time, the circumstance and the man had come together in a unique and rare combination to put things right in Pakistan; to put the train of democracy and development on the rails again. He came in with a whirlwind of reforms in many spheres and some of these have stood the test of time. The Civil Services were restructured; the general staff of the Armed Forces was re-organized for greater coherence and co-ordination among the fighting services, the foundations were laid for heavy industry and the indigenous manufacture of military equipment. Within the space of a year or so, he was able to pilot through and obtain the unanimous support of the National Assembly for a Constitution, a task over which two Constituent Assemblies had laboured for a quarter of a century without success.

Bhutto refashioned foreign policy to take into account the limitations faced by Pakistan (though it was out of character for him to be restrained by such considerations) and he managed to

bring Pakistan out of the isolation and obloquy into which the
Bangladesh adventure had plunged it. Within a couple of years
of the fall of Dhaka, Mujibur Rahman was in Lahore embracing
Bhutto before the heads of all the Islamic nations. And with
India he signed the much maligned Simla Agreement under
which not only were Pakistani POWs brought home, but India
was bound down to negotiate a settlement of the Kashmir dispute.

When he sent me as Permanent Representative to the United
Nations his advice to me was to maintain a low profile and to
avoid confrontational politics. His aim was to heal the wounds
and achieve a reconciliation with our estranged former fellow
citizens of Bangladesh. Indeed, within a couple of years Pakistan
was again at centre-stage at the United Nations and in the world.
It all seemed too good to be true.

And so it was. The ordeal by fire was to come again—a fire
lighted by India's underground nuclear test in 1974. Pakistan's
nuclear programme was at that time at an early stage, and such
nuclear installations as we had were all under IAEA safeguards.
But when India carried out an underground nuclear explosion,
not surprisingly, it was Pakistan's programme that became the
object of suspicion and concern. The Indian horse having fled,
the Western powers decided to lock the door of Pakistan's stable.
Bhutto became the focus of these efforts for he was seen as the
moving force behind Pakistan's nuclear policy. Henry Kissinger
came to Lahore in 1976 to urge him to come to terms on the
issue while a sympathetic Republican administration was in office,
for if the Democrats came to power, he warned, Pakistan would
find them far tougher to deal with.[4] Indeed when Jimmy Carter
became President, he made the proliferation issue his foreign
policy priority, and on top of his 'Do List' was the cancellation of
Pakistan's contract with France to build a plutonium reprocessing
plant. It was widely believed that the dispute over Pakistan's
nuclear programme was one of the causes, and not the least
important among them, of the political crisis that developed three
years later and led to Bhutto's overthrow and Ziaul Haq's military
coup.

But of course there were other internal causes that were no
less important. In the troubled political history of Pakistan,
Bhutto's was a unique position—he was a Sindhi Prime Minister,
elected by Punjabi voters; a feudal land-owner who had mobilized

the masses and led a political party that cut across Pakistan's complex provincial, ethnic, linguistic and class lines. Having started off with every advantage, Bhutto began along the way to dissipate his political capital—not only by what he did but by the way he did it. Nationalization of industry is a case in point. Its stated objectives were to promote industrial development with social justice. But these became mixed up with other subjective elements—intimidation, even vindictiveness. These gave the policy an arbitrary and unpredictable character. The predictable result was a massive flight of capital which was not reversed in Bhutto's time despite all the enticements the government offered subsequently.

On the political plane Bhutto made two errors of policy that were of a strategic nature and cut at the roots of his political strength. The first was the removal of the provincial governments in Balochistan and the North-West Frontier Province headed by the opposition National Awami Party (NAP). The second error was in the way he dealt with the question of the Qadiani[5] sect whose beliefs were the cause of doctrinal conflict with the orthodox *ulema* and indeed the average Muslim. The Qadiani question had periodically led to trouble in the Punjab, where the sect had originated and had most of its adherents. In 1950 an extensive outbreak in the Punjab had to be put down by the imposition of Martial Law. In 1974 a relatively minor scuffle in Rabwah, the headquarters of the sect, was threatening to spread, and a clamour arose from the ranks of the orthodox that the Qadianis should be declared to be non-Muslims. Bhutto, fearful of a repeat of the 1950 turmoil, declared that he would leave it to the National Assembly to take a decision on the matter. This was done in due course and in a free vote the assembly—where Bhutto's PPP had the majority—proclaimed that the Qadianis were a non-Muslim minority. In point of fact this did not place the average Qadiani under any material disability (other than that he could no longer aspire to the post of president or prime minister) and as a minority the community would enjoy the same rights and protections as were guaranteed by the Constitution to other citizens. Bhutto sounded rather pleased with himself at having resolved this knotty and long-standing issue with minimum damage. But he had given the religious parties a sign of weakness and whetted their political ambitions. They gave him no credit and quarter and were in the forefront of the movement against Bhutto after the 1977 elections. Later, in the heyday of the mullah under Ziaul Haq, an ordinance was promulgated under which harassment and persecution of the Qadianis on a medieval scale were systematized and given legal sanction.

In the first years of Bhutto's rule when these events took place, neither the Opposition parties nor the religious elements were much more than irritants in political terms. The threat to democracy and to his rule came, as before, from the army, though for the moment it was chastened by the defeat in Dhaka. His personality seemed to over-awe the generals, but the army was by no means fully under civilian control. To bring that about, he needed the support of, and he needed to strengthen, the other institutions of state—Parliament, the judiciary, political parties, a free Press and civil society as a whole. However, like many rulers that had gone before, Bhutto chafed under institutional restraints and maintained a state of emergency in order to get around them. And when he dismissed the Balochistan government, he was obliged to call in the army to pacify the rebellious province. In doing so he again lent respectability to the idea of a political role for the army, and revived the army's own sense of political mission.

For an elected Prime Minister, who had put in place a unanimously-adopted Constitution—whose whole political strength lay in popular support and constitutional institutions—for him to rely on the military, the intelligence agencies and a praetorian guard of security police, was paradoxical, egregious and suicidal. It was as if Bhutto from the height of seemingly absolute power could not see where lay the roots of his real power.

Bhutto had a controversial personality and almost always contention and dispute swirled around his head. He was demonized by his opponents during his lifetime for everything in which he was involved—the 1965 War, the secession of East Pakistan, the surrender at Dhaka, the Simla Agreement. To this day his role in these events remains the subject of debate. A 'flawed angel' is the expression used by the former British High Commissioner in Pakistan, Morrice James in his admiring but unsympathetic portrait of Bhutto.[6]

Bhutto was above all a man of action, and he made mistakes and he had his flaws. He was accused by opponents of being power-mad and ruthless in the pursuit of his ambition, a demagogue who roused the rabble and threatened the established order. His rule did indeed have a capricious and despotic stamp that came both from the crookedness of Pakistani politics and the complexity of his own personality. But a Borgia though he may be called, and self-consciously Machiavellian, arrogant and authoritarian as he undoubtedly was, there was something in him that transcended crude ambition, that went beyond a simple hunger for power. Behind Bhutto's demagoguery and love of power was a genuine zeal to transform society, modernize institutions, change the shape of things. His unquestioned contribution was that he aroused the political consciousness of the masses and gave them an awareness of their rights. Like most charismatic leaders, he was intoxicated by the adulation of crowds, and sometimes personal glorification and national greatness seemed to become mixed up in his idea of glory. He had a vision of Pakistan—perhaps a bit grandiose and expressed in grandiloquent terms. But many of those who opposed him had no programme, no vision, no constructive aims, nothing except meaningless slogans and jeremiads against Bhutto's doings.

But sometimes he too seemed to be a tactician without a strategy, not hesitating to give up fundamental positions in order to gain a temporary advantage or to avert an immediate crisis. Often he would manipulate people to no purpose, keeping them off balance, setting one off against another. He seemed to prefer exploiting the weaknesses of the men around him, rather than rallying their strength to his purpose. He was too worldly-wise, too cynical to be taken in by flattery and sycophancy, but still seemed to value subservience over sincerity if sincerity stood in the way of his purpose. He was not a good judge of men for he kept some very dubious characters in his entourage. Yet, Bhutto could show a keen perceptiveness of the qualities of a person, as is evident in the following pen portrait of Nepal's King Mahendra drawn in a note he submitted to Ayub:[7]

The monarch is the central authority in the country. The men around him are young, eager and enthusiastic, but they are all mediocre. Enthusiasm alone is not sufficient. The king therefore has to build the personality of some of the more intelligent men and also create a new leadership. The King is an outstanding gentleman, superstitious to the point of ridicule, and too much under the influence of astrologers. However he has many sterling qualities which more than make up for this deficiency. He is brave and magnanimous. Magnanimous because he has been very tolerant towards his opponents inside the country. At the banquet given for the King we invited two of the King's bitterest opponents, and I watched carefully his demeanor towards them. Never at any moment did he betray his inner feelings. He received them in exactly the same way that he received the other guests including his own retinue. In a democracy it is part of the drill to be normal and natural towards opponents, but not so in a monarchy particularly in a despotic oriental monarchy. I have made this observation as it gives an insight into the man's character. He is a man of few words, silent and shy, and as forceful as he is silent.

Perhaps at heart for all his outward cynicism and sophistication, for all his grandiose visions, Bhutto remained as he himself often said, a wadera, a rural grandee, eager to show off and to please, avid for authority as well as impressed with it. He manipulated men and institutions for his own ends, hounding enemies as he let down friends. In the process he demoralized friend and foe alike, and undermined the very institutions that were the source of his strength, and thus eroded the foundations of his own power.

Towards the end of 1976, Bhutto decided to call mid-term elections early in the following year. The decision was well received at home and abroad. It was seen as a sign that democracy was beginning to take root in Pakistan. The foreign Press drew the inevitable contrast with India, which was chafing under the state of emergency imposed by Mrs Indira Gandhi. Writing later, Henry Kissinger said that Bhutto's decision was meant to show up India. When Mrs Gandhi followed suit and was ousted in the elections, Atal Behari Vajpayee, Foreign Minister in the successor government, also apparently expressed the opinion that Mrs Gandhi had been goaded into calling elections by Bhutto's action.

Bhutto's decision indicated that he had consolidated his political strength. Its timing may have been influenced also by the seeming disarray among the many small opposition parties. But they had been cooking up things on the quiet, and as soon as Bhutto announced his decision, they sprang an unpleasant surprise on him by emerging on the scene as the Pakistan National Alliance. The PNA had only one policy point in common, and one shared aim—the ouster of Bhutto.

The election was a hard-fought affair, full of sound and fury and spectacle. Bhutto's campaigning covered the country from the shores of the Arabian Sea to the snow-bound highlands of the north. With a Mao cap on the head, and clad in the national costume (consisting of baggy *shalwar* trousers and over that a long, loose-fitting shirt) that he had popularized all over the country, he harangued mammoth crowds everywhere, danced and sang for them, told them of all that he had achieved for the people, for the country, for Islam, and the great things that he and they would do together in the future. He mocked the Opposition leaders and derided their slogans.

Among Opposition leaders the only one with the charisma and a popular persona approaching Bhutto's was the former Air Force Chief, Asghar Khan, who too travelled all over the country, denouncing Bhutto's autocratic rule and arbitrary ways and decrying everything Bhutto had done. Asghar Khan emerged as the main figure in the Opposition campaign against Bhutto, though Bhutto belittled him as a figure-head and a naïve front man for others. I was in Karachi on home leave and watched the 'Battle of Karachi' between the two of them in February. It was fought by means of monster processions of supporters led by each—the winning criteria being which one had the most people, was the noisiest, lasted the longest. The first one was Asghar Khan's made up mainly of Pathans who come to the city to find work and live in Karachi's shanty towns. Asghar Khan, flying in from the north, was greeted by a delirious crowd at the Karachi Airport, and walked at its head taking hours to reach a public square in the city where he made a speech. Bhutto also arrived by air, but instead of walking, drove in an open truck doing a mile an hour, and reached the working class suburb of Lyari fourteen hours later, at 3.00 in the morning. There he made an hour-long speech to the waiting throng. Obviously the one thing required for this kind of politics is tremendous physical stamina. Later I talked about it to Ghulam Mustafa Jatoi, who had stood at Bhutto's side throughout, and he mentioned another aspect of this sort of electioneering that had not occurred to me, 'We had to be very careful about taking liquids, as there were no sanitary arrangements in the truck!'

Bhutto's crowd was made up largely of Karachi's indigenous Makranis and of Sindhis trucked in from outlying villages. Thus both crowds had an ethnic complexion. Another common point between them was that both processions were made up of people who did not have the vote in Karachi. In the event, the PPP bagged only one seat from the Makrani suburb of Lyari, and the Opposition got all the rest; Asghar Khan's own party got none.

I also watched the voting in villages on the outskirts of Karachi, almost all with PPP's black, red and green flag fluttering on roof-tops. At most polling stations the crowds were large and orderly, but with no sign of the trucks and buses in which voters are normally hauled to vote by interested candidates. It was a sign of growing political awareness and involvement that people had turned up to vote under their own steam.

It was widely assumed that Bhutto's PPP would win and win handsomely. Iqbal Burney, an eminent journalist and a leading Opposition adviser, told me on the eve of polling that he did not expect the PNA actually to get a majority, but enough seats in the National Assembly to prevent Bhutto from doing anything he pleased. The general view was that the PPP might emerge with a majority of 'only' sixty per cent in the National Assembly. A sixty per cent win would normally be considered a smashing victory, but in the present case the word 'only' signified that Bhutto would not have the numbers required to amend the Constitution to a presidential system—a thing many people suspected him of wanting to do; nor would he be able to prolong the emergency under which he had been ruling the country. Bhutto's position was expected to be weaker after the election in another way. The old ideological PPP leadership having been sidelined or having left the party in dudgeon at Bhutto's waning anti-imperialist fervour, Bhutto had given party tickets to candidates capable of winning seats in their own right. Hence, it was thought he would be dealing with a party ideologically less coherent and less easily amenable to being run by his personal fiat.

Nobody had expected the landslide that occurred. In a lakeside rest-house in Karachi's hinterland, we watched with surprise and growing dismay as the results began to come in on TV and showed the Opposition being virtually wiped out. At the end of the count, the PNA had won only eight seats in all! I was told that Bhutto himself was startled at the excess of zeal shown by the party's campaign managers. The Opposition immediately cried foul. In a TV press conference the following day, Bhutto appeared tense and contentious in dealing with blunt questions from foreign pressmen. He denied rigging and pointed to the Karachi results and the close wins in the Punjab—'if the election was stage-managed, we would surely have allowed the PNA a more convincing figure of seats than eight!' He said, 'Look at the vast crowds that joined my Karachi procession, and yet the PPP got only one seat there.'

The Opposition cited cases of intimidation, and of irregularities, and pointed to the uncontested return of all senior PPP men, and of Bhutto himself, as evidence of rigging. In Bhutto's case, the rival candidate, a certain Maulana Jan Mohammed, had been 'kidnapped' as he was on his way to file his nomination papers, and was released only after the last date for doing so had expired and he could no longer run against Bhutto. Was this done at Bhutto's behest or through ill-advised zeal on the part of the local officials? At any rate Bhutto himself took no action to rectify the situation or disown the action. On the contrary, in the same way, though perhaps less flagrantly, all provincial governors and chief ministers belonging to the PPP were also elected unopposed. The fact is that none of them, least of all Bhutto, faced a serious challenge from their opponents and would have been re-elected without difficulty in the normal course. The phenomenon of unopposed election can perhaps only be understood in terms of the feudal ethos prevailing in the rural areas where it was thought a sign of political macho that nobody should dare to oppose a leader in his constituency. At any rate, the rigging was overall a relatively marginal affair, involving perhaps twenty-odd seats—not a number that would affect the PPP's control of the National Assembly. Even Ziaul Haq, before he started publishing White Papers against Bhutto, publicly minimized the impact of the rigging on the overall outcome of the election.

Asghar Khan who had declared beforehand that the PNA would not accept a PPP victory, denounced the whole election as a fraud and launched a movement to overthrow Bhutto. There followed months of *hartals* (a protest strike, which is in spirit, more than a simple strike, but a gesture of rejection and dissociation) hunger-strikes, sit-ins, demonstrations and processions. This is a legacy of Mahatma Gandhi to the subcontinent's politics that Pakistanis, who tend to disown any and everything Indian, have adopted wholeheartedly and without the Mahatma's squeamishness about violence.

I drove around the city the night after the trouble broke out. Around Empress Market in Karachi, an area within a half mile radius looked like a battlefield—rubble, rocks, broken bottles, and shards from the broken windows of looted shops and smashed liquor stores lay everywhere. Returning from Hyderabad one afternoon, at one of the so-called labour colonies on the city outskirts inhabited by Pathans, we saw Federal Security forces alighting from trucks and taking up positions all around it. It was an unsettling sight to see armed men in battle dress laying siege to a cluster of mud huts and straw shacks in the main city of their own country.

Police did their thing: laying about with staves and spraying tear-gas. The authorities banned this and banned that. The government's information people did their thing. The Press stepped gingerly on tricky ground. Thus on 16 March the daily *Dawn* carried a headline 'Situation Normal All Over Country' with a sub-heading 'Twelve Hurt in Lahore Tear-gassing'. A government press release in the same paper stated 'A few people gathered near the Regal Cinema at 16.00 hours presumably in response to a call by the Opposition parties...after some time they dispersed without violating Section 144 of the Criminal Procedure Code.' On the back page was a photograph with the caption, 'A view of the procession near Regal Cinema', showing a large, belligerent-looking crowd marching forward, carrying anti-Bhutto banners.

Bhutto spoke again over television. I heard the speech at a dinner given by Chief Minister Mustafa Jatoi. A number of PPP bigwigs were there—among them Bhutto's closest advisers at the time, Hafiz Pirzada and Jam Sadiq Ali, both looking tense and exhausted. Bhutto spoke for an hour and a half, sounding defensive at the start, but warming up as he went on. He was defiant and combative, contrasting his vision of the country's future with PNA's obscurantism and negative policies. But overall the speech was a call for dialogue and a signal of his willingness to compromise.

The one thing that I found surprising in the whole situation, a trend that ran counter to the conventional wisdom on the subject, was the appeal that the Right-wing, fundamentalist platform of the PNA seemed to have for many young people. The accepted thing was that young people tended to be Leftist and turned Right-ward as they grew older and stiff in the joints. I asked Tariq Siddiqui a distinguished Civil Servant and a somewhat Left-leaning thinker himself, about this phenomenon. His analysis put things in a different perspective in regard to Pakistan (and possibly the Muslim world as a whole). 'The usual Left-Right polarization does not hold here,' he said. By turning to Islam, the young in Pakistan are in fact turning left-wards in a social sense. The mullah whose influence tends to be underrated, speaks to them, albeit in crude and uneducated idiom, of Islamic egalitarianism, and against corruption in high places, the high-handedness of the powerful and sinfulness of the rich. The mullah lives with the people to whom he speaks, and lives in the same way, sharing their problems and concerns. The ideological leftist often belongs to the Western educated elite, is brought up in a foreign language and mode of thought, and is used to spending his evenings discussing the problems of the poor over a scotch and soda at the club. The gulf in Pakistan, said Tariq, is not between the Left and Right, but between Sind Club and Jacob Lines.[8]

In the West, the initial reaction to the sudden upheaval in Pakistan was of surprise and sympathy. Pakistan had been trying to turn a new democratic leaf and had done well on the international scene. Bhutto's previous baiting of the West was not quite forgotten, but he had earned admiration for the way he had pulled the country out of the slough of despond after the Bangladesh defeat. The post-election troubles received an apt headline in an American newspaper: 'Pakistani voters elect trouble!' As the crisis dragged on, sentiment varied between doubt at Bhutto's ability to surmount it, and concern for the future of Pakistan itself. Meanwhile a general election had been held in India, in which Mrs Gandhi was defeated and the aberration of Emergency rule ended. The dramatic turn-around in India's situation and the orderly change that took place there, had restored the old stereotypes of a democratic, secular, modern India versus a Pakistan beset by inner contradictions and unable to come to terms with itself.

Ambassadors were asked to report reactions in their countries of accreditation to the Pakistan situation. I wrote to the Prime Minister conveying the view from the UN: as to the elections, the general view was that rigging, intimidation and other malpractices did take place, but not as extensively as alleged, and that the PPP would have emerged with a majority anyway; and finally, that the extensiveness and persistence of the protests indicated that more deep-seated grievances were at issue than the conduct of the elections. Given the image of stability and progress projected by Pakistan in the previous five years, there was puzzlement that this should be so. Little was known about the personalities of the Opposition leaders, the grievances which animated them, or the policies and programmes which they were advocating. What little was known of these (the demand for the abolition of family planning, the establishment of a fundamentalist social order) did not evoke sympathy; but other demands, notably for the lifting of the Emergency and of Press restrictions, were seen as reasonable. In general it was thought that there would have to be renewed polling.

More than a month after it was launched, there was still no let up in the Opposition movement. Administrative measures and police action had remained without effect as had Bhutto's offers and invitation to a dialogue. The Opposition would accept nothing other than his resignation and fresh elections. Their stand left Bhutto with little choice between surrender and ignominy or the reassertion of his authority by brute force. Indeed the Opposition's strategy appeared to be to provoke a situation in which Bhutto would be obliged to call in the troops who, the Opposition expected, would in the end refuse to fire on their brethren. There was an unspoken ethnic assumption behind the strategy, Bhutto being a Sindhi and the military non-Sindhi. The refusal by a single police inspector or army subaltern to fire on demonstrators could start the fatal decline.

There was of course a third choice available to Bhutto: without entering into negotiations with the Opposition and acting on his own, he could have announced the dates for fresh elections to be held under the supervision of the higher judiciary and the armed forces. It was by no means an easy decision for him. It would amount to a tacit admission of the Opposition's charges and could demoralize his partymen. Jam Sadiq Ali to whom I mentioned the idea, raised a more down-to-earth objection: the winning candidates had spent small fortunes to get elected and most of them had won their seats fair and square; they would not take kindly to being told to go back and start all over again. On the other hand, as Jam Sadiq conceded himself, it wasn't possible to run a democratic system when (on account of the Opposition's boycott of the provincial elections) the provincial assemblies were made up entirely of PPP members. It was a choice between evils. Bhutto did not make a clear choice, but tried a combination of stick and carrot that weakened the impact of the one and soured the taste of the other.

In the last week of April he declared Martial Law in the cities of Karachi, Hyderabad and Lahore. It seemed like the last throw of the dice and it did not work. Trouble on the streets did not abate, but the troops having to shoot at their own kind and to face their taunts, began to falter and jib and made a quiet withdrawal that was officially described as tactical. A month later the Lahore High Court, by a unanimous decision of the full bench, held that the imposition of Martial Law was *ultra vires* of the Constitution. The decision further weakened Bhutto's position *vis-à-vis* the Opposition leaders.

In May a team from the National Defence College visited the United States and called on me at the United Nations. It was an occasion to get an idea of the military frame of mind. Most were colonels, commanders and group-captains, and spoke their minds freely enough. I found that their mood was not mutinous, but one of uneasiness at the role the armed forces were being called on to play in an essentially political crisis. They pointed to the fact that martial law had *not* put a stop to the demos and street trouble as proof that the crisis could only be resolved through a political settlement. The leader of the group, General Azmat Awan, without naming Bhutto, was critical of the actions he had taken in dismissing the Balochistan and the Frontier Province governments and amending the Constitution in order to increase his hold on the judiciary.

In the last days of April all embassies and missions abroad were alerted that the Prime Minister would address the nation on the twenty-ninth to make a very important statement. In New York all personnel serving in the UN Mission and the Consulate-General gathered in my office to listen to the speech on the radio. There was a buzz of speculation about what the Prime Minister would say. The general consensus was that he was going to take the plunge and announce new elections. There was an almost tangible sense of relief all round and the feeling that the country was going to come out of the woods. It was to be nothing of the sort. Instead Bhutto announced a ban on Sin—drinking of alcohol, gambling, horse-racing, night-clubs, pornography; a Council of Islamic Ideology was to be set up; and so on. The move had no effect whatsoever on the situation (and not much, for that matter, on the level of sinfulness). The Opposition dismissed it all as cosmetic and opportunistic, and declared that the movement's primary aim was to put an end to Bhutto's rule.

Bhutto prided himself on his political shrewdness and dexterity in dealing with opponents and difficult situations. But, now some of his decisions seemed to indicate something unsure about his touch. Many of his actions were defensive and reactive—or, as in the case of the Islamist measures, based on impulse or misjudgement. He seemed able neither to put down the Opposition onslaught—which for all its intensity was confined to the larger towns and cities—nor to muster the support of his own political legions among the urban working classes and the rural masses. On 17 March I went to see Sindh Chief Minister Mustafa Jatoi, and found him sitting in an upstairs lounge, in front of a coffee-table piled with files. A wireless transmitter-receiver was crackling on a side-table. Using the code name Tariq I, he was receiving reports of trouble on the streets. Crowds were defying the Section 144 order banning public gatherings; lampposts and other public property were being damaged; private cars were set on fire. I asked him why the government was daily promulgating Section 144 and thereby providing demonstrators the occasion to defy it. Couldn't the Opposition be allowed to hold its demos and the PPP hold its own counter-demos? He said instructions to deal with the trouble were coming directly from Islamabad and from Bhutto himself, and that it was very difficult to get any ideas and suggestions across to the top.

While the mobs were out on the streets and howling for his head, Bhutto, who had once compared the art of diplomacy to that of dancing, was also engaged in executing one of the most intricate diplomatic minuets of his career. The pressure from the American administration on the nuclear issue was relentless. In a meeting on 18 March, marked by a little forced jocularity to cover up the underlying tension, Ambassador Byroade demanded insistently that the receipt of technical equipment and blueprints for the plutonium reprocessing plant from France should be suspended forthwith. Bhutto tried to laugh it off: 'If our two countries can arrive at a settlement, we will let you take away the entire plant and install it on the US East Coast.'

There was a touch of gallows humour about the way he cast a line for a personal meeting with Carter, 'If the CIA does not pump more money into the Opposition coffers and if I am still around and alive, I would welcome a face to face encounter with Carter.' Around this time he had also phoned Ambassador Yaqub Khan in Washington and myself in New York to take discreet soundings about the possibility of a meeting with Carter.

There was not much doubt about where American sympathies lay in the Bhutto-PNA tussle. Washington had studiedly abstained from sending Bhutto a congratulatory message on his re-election. On the other hand, when elections were held soon afterwards in India, and Morarji Desai succeeded in ousting Mrs Gandhi, Carter's greetings pointedly expressed the hope that India's elections would serve as an example to others in the area. When Bhutto spoke to Byroade of US interference in Pakistani politics, Byroade's denial was distinctly pro forma.

On 28 April, a day before he announced the Islamist measures, Bhutto had summoned a joint session of Parliament and made a fiery speech describing the movement as a massive international conspiracy to punish him for the independent stands he had taken on various issues, and in particular for refusing to give up Pakistan's nuclear programme. He accused the United States of masterminding the conspiracy and providing help, advice, money and political support to the Opposition movement. In Washington Ambassador Yaqub Khan was summoned to the State Department and read a sharp representation by an Assistant Secretary of State, and small shipments of equipment of various sorts were ordered stopped in retaliation. In New York at a reception given by US Permanent Representative Andy Young, Assistant Secretary of State Atherton took me aside and spoke of the United States' 'distress' at the Prime Minister's accusations and said to me, 'Please believe me, it is not true that we have interfered in Pakistani politics in any way'. I told him that the

Prime Minister had not made these charges lightly, and that evidence in support of what he said had been presented to Ambassador Byroade.

In the nature of things the evidence of American involvement was circumstantial in nature. The Opposition dismissed Bhutto's charges as a diversionary move as well as an attempt to rally the armed forces to his side. This may well have been so, but neither the nature of the evidence nor Bhutto's motives in making the charges, necessarily make them less believable. There were a number of American actions that were indicative of the US attitude and involvement. The administration stopped a shipment of tear-gas to Pakistan on the ground that it would be interpreted as an endorsement of the Bhutto government's action against the Opposition. But didn't stopping it send an even stronger signal of support to the Opposition? The *Washington Post* took issue with the US decision, and in an editorial comment asked if there was electoral rigging, was it more heinous than what had happened in Cooke county in 1960? (whereby John F. Kennedy is said to have manipulated his victory over Nixon). There was the PNA's very effective *paiya-jaam* (wheel-jam) movement, recalling the CIA-sponsored and financed truckers' strike in Chile with which began the process of the overthrow of Allende. I personally had my first doubts about US intentions when *Newsweek* abruptly and without apparent cause, cancelled its cover story on Bhutto—only a week after Bob Christopher, editor of the international edition, had gone out of his way to say to me in the presence of a number of people at a party: 'We are doing a story on Mr Bhutto next week—not just a story but a cover story.'

Another indicator was an unexplained fall in the value of the dollar which Bhutto ascribed to CIA funding for the Opposition operations such as a co-op to assist the families of PNA activists who were arrested, disabled or killed. *Washington Post*'s Lewis Simon confirmed the fall of the dollar's rupee value, and also noted that after Bhutto's 28 April speech, Washington had hurriedly cancelled the proposed nomination of a nuclear expert as the new Ambassador to Pakistan. *The New York Times* went as far as admitting to some 'small scale dabbling' in the elections by the United States, but tried to minimize its significance by alleging that the Soviet Union and even the Arabs and China, had done the same sort of thing. Small scale dabbling was perhaps all that was needed at the time to set a light to the fuse in Pakistan.

The one thing about which there was no doubt was the obsessive character at the time of American fears as to the dangers of proliferation. In a seminar on the subject that I attended in Colorado in 1976, a Harvard professor spoke about how he had nightmares of a Libyan cargo ship sailing into New York carrying a nuclear weapon with which to blackmail or blow up the city! *The New York Times'* first editorial comment on the Pakistan political crisis made the point that it proved the danger of exporting plutonium reprocessing plants! Jimmy Carter's intense concern over Pakistan's plutonium reprocessing project, together with the political polarization in Pakistan, appeared in the eyes of many to provide the Americans with the motive, the excuse and the opportunity to intervene. Members of the French delegation at the UN hinted to us more than once that their plutonium reprocessing project in Pakistan had something to do with the turmoil in the country. The Education Minister of Iran, Hoshang Ansari, who came to Islamabad around that time, said that the US had admitted to interfering in the Pakistan crisis but 'to give Bhutto a jolt', not to overthrow him.

Bhutto thought he would rally public opinion and put the Carter administration on the spot by going public with charges of US involvement in the Opposition movement against him. When Secretary of State Cyrus Vance wrote a letter proposing that mutual grievances be discussed 'silently and dispassionately', Bhutto took this as showing America's guilty conscience and its fear of being 'exposed'.

Nevertheless, Bhutto did not want to break with the Americans. Minister of State Aziz Ahmad, and Cyrus Vance had a meeting in Paris on 1 June and reached agreement to let bygones be bygones. However almost simultaneously another American signal went out in the form of a report (leaked by the *Washington Post*) by a US Narcotics Agency representative, a certain O'Keefe who, in an *obiter dicta,* expressed the opinion that 'Mr Bhutto's days are numbered', and that the State Department as well as the National Security Council shared this opinion. Both hastened to deny it and affirmed that the narcotics official had no business to express personal opinions, but the message had already been received by those concerned.

On 1 May, two days after his Assembly speech on US interference, Bhutto called me in New York on the phone and gave me a pep-talk. He hoped I was not losing heart, and asserted that all would turn out well in the end. I was not to be apologetic to the Americans about what he had said in his speech. (But he sounded a little defensive, saying that he had to expose the American role, and to take the people into confidence. In a democracy the people are the government's best support, he affirmed.) The Americans had got to work, he told me, as soon as he called elections, and that already in February they had practically come out into the open and begun to pour money and men into the operation against him. He talked about his remonstrances to Byroade and the latter's half-hearted denials. His doubts had been first aroused (as were mine) when the *Newsweek* people suddenly cancelled their Bhutto cover story just a week before it was to appear and when preparations for it must have been completed. (The cover instead was on the problems of middle age, 'The Greying of America'.) Bhutto recalled that *Newsweek* had done exactly the same thing to Ayub in the latter's last phase.

Then he said that he had just been talking to Yaqub in Washington to see if a meeting with Carter could be arranged for him. 'All and sundry are being invited to meet Carter. If the Americans want to resolve the present crisis with Pakistan, then it must be discussed at the highest level'. He wanted Yaqub and me to put our heads together to try to bring about a meeting with Carter but to do so without making a formal move. This sounded as if he was preparing to compromise on the reprocessing plant, but he added 'Make it clear to them that Pakistan will never compromise on principles [the reprocessing project] and that after all the public fuss that had been raised, even to discuss the issue has become difficult, if not impossible.'

He went on, 'If the Americans think they can browbeat Pakistan by cutting off economic aid and military supplies, they should think again. We are not without options. We can turn to the Soviets and strengthen relations with them. We can do so, as many other non-aligned countries are doing, without jeopardizing our relations with China.' I asked him about the prospect of a settlement with the Opposition. He said that his statement about American interference had created an impression on the public mind and now the Opposition would have to compromise. 'I am in full control of the situation now,' he asserted. But already there had been rumours about the army's intentions. I asked him about this but he dismissed all that as the usual rumour-mongering and said, 'The armed forces are alright! There is no problem from that direction.' This was not how it looked from where I was. He seemed to be losing steam and direction. Opposition had the will and means and guidance to keep the movement going and knew exactly what it wanted—Bhutto's exit, and perhaps his head. In May, the retired Air Force Chief, Asghar Khan called for it publicly, and in a letter to the Chiefs of Staff and officers, called on the armed forces to overthrow Bhutto.

That was the last time I ever spoke to Bhutto, and the sound and tone of his voice are still in my mind. He was trying to be reassuring, but there was a note in it also of someone seeking reassurance.

Some years later a senior Foreign Office official told me that at the height of the agitation, the Soviet Ambassador had called at the Foreign Office to warn that the Americans were trying to create divisions within the army in order to prepare the way for bringing down Bhutto. The official was sent to Lahore where Bhutto had gone that day for various meetings, among them one with the Chief of Army Staff, Ziaul Haq. He spoke to Bhutto over the phone and said, 'Sir, I have been sent with a very important piece of information that I can convey only to you personally.' Bhutto was obviously not as complacent as he sounded on the phone to me, for he asked, 'Does it have something to do with the gentleman I am seeing this morning?' Why then did he not act decisively to nip the danger in the bud? Was it already too late? Or was Ziaul Haq, forewarned by friends, quicker on the draw?

In response to Bhutto's directive, I flew to Washington to discuss tactics with Ambassador Yaqub. He thought that if the American purpose was to engineer Bhutto's exit, then they were hardly likely to provide him with the public relations boost and political support of an invitation from the President. The situation was not such that they needed to make up with Bhutto. At any rate we were going to make a try, and it was agreed that the best and least obtrusive channel would be Andrew Young, the US Permanent Representative at the UN who was said to have Carter's ear. Accordingly, I spoke to the Ambassador and it was arranged that he and his wife would come for tea at the Embassy in Washington the following week. We went over the ground with him. While not directly refuting Bhutto's charges, Andrew Young pointed out that in view of recently toughened up legislative controls, the CIA would find it difficult to mount this kind of operation without the Congress getting to know about it. I said that the Prime Minister for his part, had put forward evidence in support of his charges but that the important thing was to defuse the crisis in the relations between the two countries and prevent the matter of American interference becoming an issue in any renewed polling. Pakistan was prepared to discuss its nuclear plans with the US, though the current situation had made such discussions difficult. We also made it clear that while Pakistan was ready to discuss a solution to the problem, there could be no question of compromising principles.

Andrew Young,[9] who had no doubt been briefed for the meeting, thought such a meeting could not take place until fresh elections had taken place in Pakistan, but that he would bear the idea in mind and discuss it with Assistant Secretary of State, Phillip Habib. The response was much as expected, and I don't suppose that it surprised Bhutto.

At all events, Bhutto did not intend to burn his bridges with the Americans though in his 28 April speech he had threatened to take Pakistan out of CENTO. Speaking to the American Chargé d'Affaires some weeks later, Bhutto explained why he had decided to speak out, despite the fact that some of his own partymen had advised him against it and counselled a low-key, non-confrontational approach towards the United States. But, he explained, it was his belief that a national policy became meaningless if the people were not taken into confidence. In the past Pakistan's relations with the United States had never had the sanction of popular support. President Ayub Khan had given various assurances on behalf of Pakistan to the United States but he had done so confidentially, in drawing-room conversations. Similarly, Yahya Khan had not taken the people into confidence on developments in relations with the United States. Bhutto said, that he on the other hand, had made the US-Pakistan relationship one that was supported and endorsed by the people of Pakistan.

Nevertheless, he pointed out, there were differences within the PPP on policy towards America, on membership of CENTO and other related issues. Bhutto said to the American official that he had lost the support of close associates like J.A. Rahim, Khurshid Hassan Mir and Mairaj Mohammad Khan, because they didn't approve of the softening of his original 'activist' posture against the US. His own view was that Pakistan's interests did not conflict with the interests of the United States and the West in general. In fact he was giving careful thought to 'activating' Pakistan's participation in CENTO, and had noted with interest American ideas for a link between Pakistan and NATO through CENTO.

But at the same time he was also taking soundings from the Soviets about their intentions with regard to Pakistan. Ambassador Azimov of the Soviet Union called on the Prime Minister some days after the 28 April speech and said that the 'historic' speech had evoked much interest in Moscow, though the Americans were telling the Soviets not to believe Bhutto's offers to leave CENTO. Bhutto was using the threat, the State Department asserted, only to put pressure on the US. The Ambassador said that it was in Pakistan's own interest to quit CENTO and if it did so, 'broad vistas' would open up for the development of Pakistan-Soviet relations. But Bhutto wasn't settling for diplomatic platitudes, and asked the Ambassador: 'What is meant by broad vistas? Will there be Soviet co-operation with Pakistan in defence or will the Indo-Soviet Friendship Treaty stand in the way? And why is membership of CENTO considered an impediment to closer Soviet relations with Pakistan, if it had not hindered the development of Soviet Union's relations with Iran and Turkey?'

Bhutto had discussed the subject in several meetings with Azimov during the previous year. Now he spelt out what he expected in return for Pakistan leaving CENTO. Firstly, Pakistan must have a definite and specific Soviet agreement for continued and uninterrupted supply of military hardware. He added that 'apart from vital security factors', Pakistan had to maintain a large and well-equipped army in order to satisfy the 'historic martial traditions' of the country which had been the breeding ground of armed forces even in British times. Secondly, he said, it must be understood that if Pakistan did decide to quit CENTO,

it would not be done immediately and in a precipitate manner;
cool and careful consideration would be needed and he would
have to talk to the Americans to study their views. He would not
want the action to look like a desperate step taken in anger. A
prelude, though not a long prelude, was needed.

The record thus belies the rumours that were given currency
at the time that Bhutto had agreed to give the Soviets a naval
base in Gwadar on the Arabian Sea in exchange for their political
support to his government! Ambassador Azimov could not of
course answer Bhutto's questions himself and responded with
broad generalities: Soviet policy was to create conditions that
would render US bases totally unnecessary in the region; US was
far away and the Soviet Union was close to Pakistan; geopolitical
factors and common history dictated that the Soviet Union and
Pakistan learn to live with each other. America, the Soviet
Ambassador declared, behaved towards developing countries like
a cowboy; if Pakistan quit CENTO, it would see the US itself
becoming more responsive to Pakistan's sensitivities.

There was no ambiguity however about Soviet support for
Bhutto himself. On 9 May, in his first meeting with the Prime
Minister after the PNA trouble broke out, Azimov assured him of
the Soviet Union's full sympathy. He wondered whether Bhutto
had done the right thing in deciding to hold a dialogue with the
defeated parties. The ambassador's analysis was that even if
Bhutto made every concession and held fresh elections, the PNA
would not accept the results if these went in favour of the PPP
again. His leaders in Moscow had asked him to find out what the
Prime Minister intended to do if the dialogue yielded no result.
Pakistan's Western friends, he said, were backing the clamour
for Bhutto's resignation, but the Soviets did not consider that
this would be in the interest of Pakistan, or of peace and security
in Asia.

Bhutto and Azimov met again after a month. The ambassador
had received Moscow's reaction to Bhutto's queries and
comments at the previous meeting. It was on the lines of what he
had already conveyed to the Prime Minister in his meeting with
him on 14 December 1976: quitting CENTO was in Pakistan's
own best interest and would also open a new chapter in relations
with the Soviet Union. Bhutto was disappointed with these
bromides and told the ambassador that he was conveying nothing

new. He said that it was wrong to underestimate the importance
of CENTO and the value of Pakistan's decision to leave it. He
again pressed the ambassador for a reply to the specific and
substantive proposal he had put to him. Echoing the parallel
Soviet argument about the effect of Pakistan leaving CENTO, he
said that if the Soviets were concerned about India's reaction
they should realize that by befriending Pakistan, they would get
more leverage in India.

Reverting to the domestic situation, the Ambassador said that
the Soviet government strongly condemned the US role in the
present crisis in Pakistan and saw it as part of an 'ugly imperialist
scheme'; the Soviet Union was fully aware of what was being
discussed in the State Department and the National Security
Council on the situation. The United States had postponed its
plans against Pakistan to the period between August and
November. Azimov warned that Pakistan should remain vigilant,
for the US and its allies will be resorting to 'other actions and
other means' to attain their ends. He urged Bhutto to be specially
careful about his personal security in the existing circumstances—
nothing was to be ruled out, not even an attempt at assassination.

I ran into George Bush on the street in New York one morning
around the middle of June. I had known him when he was US
Permanent Representative at the UN. Since then he had been
Head of Mission in China and CIA's Director. Now he was looking
after his business but also keeping an eye on the Republican
nomination for the following year's Presidential elections. He
said his political drawback was that he was not a publicly-known
figure and added, 'But then nor was Jimmy Carter when he
started.'

Bush was very affable, expressed concern about what was
happening in Pakistan and the rising tension between Pakistan
and the USA, and said that he would like to talk to me about
these matters. A couple of mornings later, at his invitation I
joined him for breakfast at his club in Manhattan. He said he
could guarantee that the CIA was not involved in the anti-Bhutto
movement. Preparations for any such venture take a long time
and would have had to begin while he was the CIA head and he
would have known about it. (And if he had, I didn't suppose he
would be telling me all about it over a nice cup of coffee!)
Moreover, at present such covert operations had become very

difficult since they required the approval of the appropriate Congressional committee. He could not say who, if it wasn't the CIA, could have carried out the sort of clandestine activities mentioned by Bhutto; he himself seemed sceptical about there being any foreign hand at all in the business.

I said that the Prime Minister had made very serious charges bearing fully in mind the importance of Pakistan's relations with the United States. Foreign Minister Aziz Ahmad and Cyrus Vance had met and agreed to let bygones be bygones and look to the future. But the fact was that the basic Pakistan-US difference remained unresolved. The question of plutonium reprocessing had acquired in the eyes of the Carter administration an importance that was out of all proportion to its real implications and that simply disregarded Pakistan's energy needs and security concerns. Pakistan was prepared to discuss ways of satisfying the US about Pakistan's nuclear programme and intentions, but the administration was not to be satisfied with anything short of the outright cancellation of the project. This, I told him, was out of the question. It was plain that the US was adopting double standards in this matter—it was resuming shipments of enriched uranium for Tarapur to India merely on Prime Minister Morarji Desai's word as to India's peaceful intentions, whereas it refused to be satisfied with the extremely stringent safeguards to be applied to the French reprocessing plant in Pakistan. At the very least the US could have insisted on an accounting of India's accumulated plutonium stockpiles and supported Pakistan's call for a South Asian Nuclear Weapons Free Zone. Bush skirted discussion on the reprocessing plant, saying he did not understand its technicalities. As for India, he said that a whole group of people in America held India in quite irrational regard, and in their eyes India could do no wrong. This view had been reinforced after the recent restoration of democracy in India. He spoke of Bhutto warmly, recalling their meetings in New York and Islamabad. He asked me to convey his regards to him and hoped that the trouble with the US would not be allowed to become too big an issue in the elections; if the US were attacked too strongly, he felt, the task of Pakistan's friends in Washington would become more difficult, specially at a time when India's supporters and propagandists were ensconced in influential positions in the Carter administration.

PPP-PNA Negotiations

As the end of April approached and the PNA's politico-theological campaign continued unabated, Bhutto decided to turn to Saudi Arabia's religious-cum-financial influence in order to bring the Opposition to a more amenable frame of mind. The Saudi Ambassador Shaikh Riyadh el Khatib was summoned to the Prime Minister's on the twentieth, and asked to seek the Saudi monarch's mediation between the government and the PNA. Minister of State for Foreign Affairs, Aziz Ahmad, said to him: 'Events are moving very fast, and time is of the essence.' The ambassador was urged to fly to Riyadh to brief the King personally and meanwhile the Prime Minister would also cable a personal message to the King requesting him to urge the PNA leaders to enter into a 'constructive dialogue' with the government.

Bhutto apparently felt some qualms about involving a foreign power in the country's domestic politics, for in his message to King Khalid he found it necessary to rationalize the request. Given the negative interference of 'a certain power' in Pakistan's internal affairs, he wrote, he felt that it was 'morally right' for him to seek the Saudi monarch's positive and constructive intervention to help resolve the crisis. Saudi Arabia was, of course, on the closest possible terms with this 'certain power', and Saudi Arabia's own attitude to Bhutto and his policies was by no means unambiguous. Presumably, Saudi Arabia was not unsympathetic to the Opposition's demand for establishing a Saudi type Islamist regime in Pakistan. It was known that some of the Islamist parties within the Opposition alliance had been receiving financial support from the kingdom. Bhutto was of course well aware of the position and also knew that not long before, two Opposition emissaries had been received by Prince Saud bin Faisal: Hakim Said, and A. K. Brohi ('an able lawyer and jurist but with an ego bigger than himself'). In an oblique remonstrance, he said to the ambassador that 'such persons could not give the Saudi leaders an objective analysis of the situation.' If Bhutto nevertheless chose the Saudis to act as mediators, it was precisely because they had connections with the Opposition and the clout to make it see reason.

In the event, Ambassador el Khatib proved to be not only diligent and skilful in carrying out his difficult assignment, but was objective and impartial in assessing the nature of the difficulties in the way of agreement. He started his mediation a week later on his return from Riyadh with instructions from the then Crown Prince Fahd, and Foreign Minister Saud bin Faisal (King Khalid was in London receiving medical treatment) to act as a special envoy to the Opposition leaders, to convey to them Saudi Arabia's concern at the continuing crisis in Pakistan, and to urge them to reach a settlement with Bhutto. The ambassador received the latter's permission to meet the PNA leaders who were under detention in the Police Training Academy at Sihala. Records of Bhutto's discussions with the Saudi envoy were maintained in the Foreign Office, and throw an interesting light on the ups and downs of the ill-fated negotiatons, and the frame of mind in which Bhutto approached them. He began by giving the ambassador an analysis of the situation, and added some titbits—sardonic and sometimes fairly near the mark—of the personalities and motives of some of the actors on the scene:

Mufti Mahmud who headed the PNA, was chief of the Jamiat-e-Ulema-ul-Islam—a party that he said had bitterly opposed the creation of Pakistan, but he was personally inclined to break the deadlock and open a dialogue.

On the other hand, the retired Air Marshal Asghar Khan, he said, was opposed to a negotiated settlement as such, and his was a hard-line stance in the present crisis. An effective speaker, he attracted large crowds, but he harboured illusions about his popularity among the masses and in the armed forces, that were not borne out by the facts. He was allowing himself to be used as the 'front man' for the PNA, whose other leaders fully expected him to fall by the wayside in due course on account of his own political blunders and impulsive speeches.

The PNA was spearheaded by two parties that were otherwise poles apart in their policies and general outlook, namely the religous Jamaat-e-Islami, and secular National Awami Party (NAP). The latter party was led by Khan Abdul Ghaffar Khan who once had declared, 'We are first of all Pakhtoons, then Muslims, then Pakistanis.' NDP, the National Democratic Party, was the NAP's *alter ego*, set up when the latter was banned. Nasim Wali Khan, the principal NDP leader, seemed to have no political programme beyond getting her husband, Wali Khan, out of jail where he was kept pending a trial for sedition.

The Jamaat-e-Islami, he said, was another party that had opposed the creation of Pakistan, and was the moving force behind the PNA's Islamist platform; yet, said Bhutto, when he announced the ban on alcohol, gambling, etc., Maulana Maududi's reaction was that enforcing Shariat was not the real issue for the movement!

Of the lesser components of the PNA, Bhutto said that the Muslim League had two factions, one headed by Malik Qasim and the other by the Pir of Pagaro. Neither amounted to much in terms of organization and popular following. The Pir he said, was basically a gentleman and thus open to reason, but was susceptible to the influence of unscrupulous relatives, notably his brothers-in-law, Hassan Mahmud, and uncle Ali Ahmed Rashdi. 'You and I are the only true leaders, the rest are paper figures,' Bhutto recalled the Pir as telling him in a recent meeting. They had both been sorry at having fallen out though the families had known each other for generations. Later, when Pir Pagaro began to make himself disagreeable in a number of ways—demanding Bhutto's resignation as a *sine qua non*, calling him a mere *de facto* Prime Minister, and so forth, Bhutto revised his amiable assessment of the Pir's personal qualities and antecedents. 'The man has literally gone mad,' he said to Ambassador el Khatib, and told him about the Pir's father, a 'tyrant, fanatic and terrorist', who was hanged by the British and betrayed to them by his own cousin, Ali Mohammad Rashdi, the same Rashdi who was among the present Pir's closest advisers and confidants.

Nawabzada Nasrullah, headed yet another party that had opposed the creation of Pakistan, and whose total membership at present was made up of some three or four individuals. The Nawabzada was a man, Bhutto said, who possessed a unique gift— he could be obstinate and reasonable at the same time, obstinate in public and reasonable behind the scenes. His strength lay in his long experience in politics, his shortcoming in that it had been acquired almost entirely in the Opposition.

Azad Kashmir Muslim Conference's Abdul Qayyum Khan had at one time spoken of him—Bhutto—as 'the only leader who could stabilize and strengthen Pakistan', but he was now, Bhutto said, against everything—the PPP, the government, parliamentary democracy.

Bhutto did not try to conceal from the Saudi envoy the seriousness of the situation created by the crisis. The economy had been badly hit, the lives and property of people had become unsafe, and the country as a whole was suffering. In another reference to the situation a month later he sounded even more despondent. The country had gone through a nightmarish experience, the economy was ruined, deep hatred had been created between different regions; the Opposition, he said, had fanned religious and regional animosities and was exploiting them for its ends.

Bhutto also tried to draw out the ambassador on the question of foreign interference in the crisis. He recounted his conversation with Kissinger the previous year when the latter had warned, 'You might have to pay a very heavy price for obtaining a reprocessing plant.' But the Saudi ambassador did not rise to the bait. When one day Bhutto put the question to him pointedly, el Khatib opined that the major foreign power involved in the crisis was the Soviet Union. By this time Bhutto too had been disappointed with the Soviet reaction to his overtures. He agreed that the real danger to Pakistan came from the Soviet Union who was 'breathing down our necks' through Afghanistan, and that therefore he did not want to take a negative attitude towards the United States. But he added that for Pakistan the nuclear reprocessing plant was a necessity and he would not give up the project.

El Khatib's mediation took the form of proximity talks between the sides with the ambassador shuttling between the Prime Minister and the Opposition leaders detained in Sihala near Islamabad. At that point the Opposition were rejecting any sort of dialogue with Bhutto and simply wanted him to step down at once and let the judiciary and army hold elections all over again. Not so long ago the Opposition had boycotted the Balochistan provincial elections on the ground that the army's presence there would make free elections impossible! Now, through the Saudi envoy, Bhutto sent an offer to let the PNA win another additional forty seats (so that PPP would not have the majority needed to amend the Constitution). A form of rigging by consent! Also he would release Wali Khan, Bizenjo and others who had been undergoing a slow-motion treason trial for the last several years, and allow the formation of PNA governments in the NWFP and Balochistan.

Reporting to the Prime Minister on his first meeting with the PNA leaders, the envoy said that they had read with care the Prime Minister's message and listened with 'rapt attention' to what he himself had to say, occasionally consulting among themselves. Mufti Mahmud was their chief spokesman. They told the ambassador that they would prepare counter-proposals to Bhutto's offer, in consultation with legal and constitutional experts. They had asked whether King Khalid would guarantee any agreement reached between them and the Prime Minister. The ambassador replied that there was to be a written agreement which itself constituted a guarantee and a guarantee was also implicit in the King's mediation. The ambassador made it clear that the Saudi King wished to help the parties reach a compromise but that a demand for the Prime Minister's resignation could not be part of a compromise.

The PNA counter-proposal was handed to the Saudi envoy about two weeks later. It consisted of a list of thirty-two demands ranging from the formation of a caretaker government to details of the arrangements for holding the elections. It was accompanied by the disarming explanation that it was only a framework for discussion and that many of its points were really for 'public consumption'. In reality, Mufti Mahmud declared, the PNA had only one basic demand, and that was for fresh elections to the National Assembly to be held under the supervision of the army and the judiciary. They were not asking for Bhutto's resignation, but were not prepared to talk to him until this demand was accepted.

Bhutto was ready to discuss this demand and any others in the course of negotiations, but refused to concede anything before hand. However he accepted the principle of fresh polling in the shape of the formula put forward by Yahya Bakhtiyar, which was that new elections would be held first for the provincial assemblies, and depending on their results, be followed by fresh National Assembly polls. The ambassador urged upon the PNA leaders the need for compromise and accommodation. He said that to everything he suggested their answer was, 'For us, King Khalid's word is a command!' but for all that they were not willing to heed his counsels of moderation, and he found, from meeting to meeting, that their positions were hardening. He also complained that the PNA were leaking the substance of their discussions with him to the Press. Moreover, Mufti Mahmud who had promised to persuade and convince the other PNA leaders to be flexible, had failed to do so; indeed it was the ambassador's view that he had chosen not to do so.

A week later el Khatib came to the Prime Minister's house at around midnight and told him that he had done some more talking with Mufti Mahmud and had come with a message from the Maulana that he would like to meet the Prime Minister in strict secrecy. Mufti Mahmud had also said that if they could hammer out an agreement between the two of them, he felt sure he could persuade the other leaders to go along; if one or the other of them didn't, they would be free to go their own ways. El Khatib said that the Maulana had spoken with great authority, thus indicating his desire to reach an agreement.

According to the ambassador's information, Mufti Mahmud, Nawabzada Nasrullah Khan, and the Jamaat-e-Islami, were willing to accept the Bakhtiyar formula whereas Asghar Khan and Shah Ahmad Noorani were against any dialogue at all with Bhutto. At Bhutto's meeting with Mufti Mahmud two days later, the Maulana confirmed that if agreement was reached between them he would overrule any dissenting minority; no one would be allowed to wield a veto. Bhutto for his part said that he had come with his final offer: the PNA should drop its preconditions and enter into a dialogue in which he would be willing to accept the dissolution of the National Assembly, subject to agreement being reached on the timing of the new elections, setting up of an independent election machinery, and other connected matters. (Earlier he had said to the Saudi envoy that a cooling-off period of about a year would be needed before fresh elections could be held.) As for the demand that he resign, Bhutto offered to put the matter to the country in a referendum. He explained to the PNA leaders that he couldn't just walk out of the scene; he had to take into account the interests of his supporters, his partymen and public opinion in general. The PNA's support came mainly from shopkeepers in urban areas, whereas the PPP had wider support with deep roots in the rural areas as well as among the urban masses.

After some more footwork, by the end of the month the Saudi envoy had succeeded in getting all nine PNA parties to agree to hold a dialogue with Bhutto. But when he brought to him a draft of a letter they wanted him to write putting everything down in black and white, Bhutto smelled a rat. He suspected they were trying to trap him into accepting unconditionally to dissolve the Assembly, whereas he had agreed to do so only if there was agreement on the various prerequisites that he had outlined. If agreement was not reached on these connected issues, the PNA would turn around and accuse him of going back on a written pledge; also the draft made polemical references, with an eye to propaganda, to the conditions in which the *détenus* were kept. El Khatib feared that Bhutto was now making pre-conditions of his own that would give the hard-liners an excuse to sabotage the negotiations. He urged the Prime Minister to accept the PNA's draft or add a memorandum setting out his own understanding of the agreement. After a great deal of discussion in which Abdul Hafiz Pirzada also took part, the whole idea of exchanging letters was dropped.

More palavers followed between the Saudi emissary and the PNA and between Bhutto himself and Mufti Mahmud. By mid-June Bhutto had conceded the PNA's main demands; a date, 16 October 1977, was set for the new elections; the Emergency would not be lifted but it would be 'frozen' with the same practical effect. There were still some sticking points left including the PNA's demand to share power in the interim; on this matter, despite el Khatib's pleadings that it would 'do no harm' to take two or three PNA nominees into the government, Bhutto remained adamant. 'It would be the end of my party!' he exclaimed.

There were other hiccups. The Pir Pagaro issued a colourful statement ('This is the story of Samson and Delilah...drop scene in the drama...') at which Bhutto's advisors took umbrage. The Pir also said that the Opposition did not recognize Bhutto as the legitimate Prime Minister. Ambassador el Khatib tried to smooth ruffled feathers and told Bhutto that he himself had found the Pir to be a rather complicated man to deal with. He said that the Pir should not be taken seriously and asserted that he was not trusted even by his PNA colleagues. The ambassador recounted that on one occasion they had spoken to him in Arabic so that the Pir would not understand.

The Saudi envoy soldiered on in the face of these difficulties and by the beginning of July seemed to have everything tied up.

However the difficulty and risk of this type of negotiation—where negotiations take place not only between the parties but within the inner councils of the various negotiating parties—is that any one person or group can dig his heels in and bring things to a halt or bring everything toppling down. The Opposition had a historic opportunity at that juncture, acting as a vocal and vigilant custodian, to play a role in curbing Bhutto's authoritarian and arbitrary ways and to strengthen democratic institutions. But the Opposition leaders were in a vengeful mood and out to get Bhutto's head and to undo everything he had done, good or bad. To oust Bhutto was the lowest common denominator among the PNA's political and ideological conglomerate—either because they hated his policies, or hated him personally and because some of them nursed their own ambitions. So, although Mufti Mahmud had said that no one would be allowed a veto, in practice when the PNA's agreement fell short of unanimity, Ziaul Haq who was in the wings, waiting and watching—and weaving his web, was handed the chance he needed.

Two things strike one about the process of negotiations before it finally—and almost inevitably—came to grief. Firstly, that despite the note of desperate urgency struck by Aziz Ahmad at the start, it took more than six weeks before agreement was reached on a matter on which essentially Bhutto had already decided to cede, that is, the holding of fresh elections. He had also agreed that the elections would be held under the supervision of the judiciary and the armed forces. He had gone further and offered that the PPP would not run candidates in forty of the National Assembly seats to put at rest the Opposition's fear that he wanted an absolute majority in order to amend the Constitution. One could blame the Opposition's inflexibility and their internal dissensions for the slow pace of the progress, but some of the delay—risky for Bhutto's own position—was also caused by the PPP's quibbling over words and gestures, by its mental reservations, undercurrents of doubt and suspicion, by side issues of prestige and 'face'. All this seemed out of character with Bhutto's normally decisive style and was completely divorced from the demands of the increasingly critical situation.

The other singularity of the process was Bhutto's frequent references to the role and wishes of the armed forces. Thus when the ambassador reported to him on his first meeting with the Opposition leaders, Bhutto said that he would have to consult the armed forces on certain matters such as the situation in Balochistan. Then, he said that at some point he would have to call on the Service Chiefs to 'express their opinion' before the PNA and government leaders. Again in rejecting the demand that he step down and hand over the administration to a caretaker government, he affirmed that he was the legally and constitutionally elected head of government and that the Chiefs of Staff of the Armed Forces had declared that they considered him as such. When the Pir of Pagaro taunted him with being only a *de facto* Prime Minister, his reaction was similar—if he were treated as such it would compromise his position as the head of the Armed Forces. Whenever he received a briefing from the Saudi Ambassador on the status of his mediation, Bhutto said that he would inform the Service Chiefs of the day's developments.

When agreement was in sight, the ambassador suggested simultaneous action by the PNA to call off its actions in the streets and by the government to lift Martial Law. Bhutto said that he was a politician and realized only too well the implication of prolonged military control, but then added that he would have to consult the Heads of Armed Forces in the matter because they had borne great responsibility in bringing the situation back to normal.

It was as if he was constantly looking over his shoulder at the military while negotiating with the PNA through the Saudi envoy. Bhutto had an ambivalent attitude towards the armed forces. He had developed close personal links with many senior officers, and shared their views on India, Kashmir, and the nuclear issue. On East Pakistan his first reaction to the military action ordered by Yahya Khan had been to declare, 'Pakistan has been saved!'

Yet at heart he remained suspicious of the military's intentions and of the ambitions of military strongmen. He was at the UN General Assembly the year that the army carried out a *coup* in Chile, and he personally added a very strong condemnation of General Pinochet to the draft of his speech to the General Assembly. 'The horrid events that occured in Chile last week when a selfish myopic junta overthrew a child of revolution, can only strengthen the forces of emancipation in that country and add further passion and fire to the resolve of the Chilean people...' (But he also added, 'But, we in the Third World should not be swayed by conspiracy theories and forget that the fault lies within ourselves. We are betrayed by what is false within'.) I asked him why Pakistan should express such strong views on the controversial affairs of a far-away place. He told me, 'My words are not addressed to the Chilean generals, but to ours.'[10] His anxiety in this regard led him to make the fateful choice of Ziaul Haq as Chief of Army Staff.

The Soviet Ambassador had asked Bhutto a pertinent question, indeed the key question: what did the Prime Minister plan to do if the dialogue with the Opposition did not succeed? The chances of success were less than even, for there were many among his opponents, if indeed not most of them, who wanted not fair elections, but Bhutto's head. By entering into negotiations, he put into their hands the power to set the agenda, to agree or not to agree, even to negotiate or not to negotiate. There was in fact no rational answer to the Soviet question, for in the absence of a settlement it would come to a trial of force. And in that case...

Ziaul Haq had in fact been urging the Prime Minister to reach a settlement with the Opposition, and had warned that failing a political settlement, recourse to the 'military option' might become unavoidable. According to Ziaul Haq, Bhutto took this to mean that the armed forces would intervene to restore order on the government's behalf, for he said to Ziaul Haq (or so the latter claimed), 'Alright but don't do anything until I tell you to.' Recounting this to a friend, Ziaul Haq said that he could hardly keep from laughing out aloud. I find it hard to believe that a person of Bhutto's shrewd temper hadn't thought things through to their logical conclusion and would have taken such a naïve view of the Army Chief's words.

On 5 July, the army was back on the scene. At first I half-believed that the army meant what was implied by the title of Operation Fairplay chosen for the *coup*. It is said that all that changed when Ziaul Haq called on the detained ex-Prime Minister at his place of detention in Murree, and Bhutto warned him of the consequences that he would have to face for his action, under Article 6 of the Constitution (which prescribes the death penalty for a person guilty of trying to subvert the Constitution). Perhaps the fatal turning came when Bhutto set out on a tour of the country and was greeted by huge crowds wherever he went. The crowd in Lahore was said to be a million strong, and the sight must have given the authors of the *coup* something to think about. It was possibly the single event that sealed Bhutto's fate. These developments were significant for Bhutto's own fate. But, in retrospect, it seems clear that the generals had come back to stay. Among the very first of Ziaul Haq's official acts was to proclaim that henceforth thieves would have their hands cut off, and other wrongdoers would receive the prescribed Islamic punishments. None of this happened then or has been done since, but this was not the action of a person who claimed to have assumed power for the sole purpose of ensuring the holding of fair elections. As one former general said to me, 'If the purpose was to hold elections and hand power back, then why should the Bhutto government have been dismissed in the first place?' George Bush, whom I met at a dinner soon after the *coup*, shook his head sceptically when I spoke about Operation Fairplay.

In the first few weeks Bhutto was shown consideration, even respect. Ziaul Haq praised Bhutto's efforts to reach a compromise with the Opposition, and minimized the extent of the alleged election rigging. But after a minimal period of courtesies and amenities, the gloves came off. A young man, a mutual friend of the Bhutto children and mine, told us that he was at Bhutto's house in Karachi a short time before Bhutto was arrested, and he heard him say, 'They are going to come for me. I know it, and this time they won't let me out alive.'

Soon he was being assailed on all sides by writ petitions, enquiries, and complaints, about his alleged acts of omission and commission during his rule: abuse and misuse of power, the arbitrary dismissal of Civil Servants, transfer of funds abroad, illegal detentions, arrests, torture. Old J.A. Rahim, a PPP founding father, gave a harrowing account on TV of what was done to him by FIA goons when he fell foul of Bhutto. The sinister Masud Mahmood, Bhutto's Security Chief, was in army custody, incommunicado for an indefinite period, and would in due course, begin to sing and help send Bhutto to the gallows.

On one occasion Ziaul Haq told a group of senior Pakistani officials that he could have solved the 'Bhutto question' in the first hours of the *coup*—that is, had him shot out of hand—but that he had preferred to go the judicial way. Bhutto's murder

trial was a long-drawn-out affair and, except for skipping the
initial Sessions Court stage, meticulously followed the procedures
laid down for criminal trials—from High Court to Supreme Court
and through the final Judicial Review. Foreign observers were
impressed with the formal solemnity of the proceedings, the skill
and erudition of the prosecution and defence lawyers, the
references in arcane Latin phrases, the citing of judicial
precedents from the Privy Council of the House of Lords, the
Supreme Courts of India, Australia, Canada and elsewhere. It
was a judicial spectacle of the highest standard transposed from
Britain, with the judges wearing black robes and wigs, lawyers
addressing them as 'M' Lord', and each other as 'My Learned
Friend'. But throughout the months of tortuous proceedings,
one thing was never in much doubt—the outcome of the trial.
Right at the beginning of Bhutto's prosecution, Justice Samdani
of the Lahore High Court released Bhutto on bail. The late
G. Mueenuddin who was our house guest in New York at the
time, jumped out of his chair when I told him the news: 'They
must put him back in straight away! He is a most dangerous man
and must not be allowed out and about on the loose.' He need
not have worried. Bhutto was immediately put back in and Justice
Samdani himself removed from the bench to avoid further lapses
of this kind.

The Lahore High Court found Bhutto guilty and sentenced
him to death. The Court's findings were based on motive and
circumstances. The cartridge empties did not match the bullets
taken from the victim's body. The murder weapon was never
found. Justice Mushtaq, whose removal from the bench Bhutto
had requested on grounds of personal bias, gave ample
demonstration of it by his treatment of Bhutto during the trial
and the *obiter dicta* in his judgement on Bhutto's unfitness to be
the Prime Minister of an Islamic state. Talking to me Justice
Aslam Riaz Hussain, then acting-Governor of the Punjab, was
critical of the conduct of the trial and held that Justice Mushtaq
should have followed the traditions of judicial propriety by
stepping aside from the bench as soon as the accused made a
charge of bias against him. Curiously, this conversation took place
at a dinner at Ziaul Haq's place in the presence of his Military
Secretary, General Saghir, who listened to it without demur or
comment.

The appeal in the Supreme Court was heard in a more judicious atmosphere. The Lahore Court's strictures on Bhutto's lack of Islamic virtues were expunged as irrelevant to the question at issue. Bhutto was allowed a personal appearance in the Court, in a departure from the usual practice. Yet here too the outcome was not different. French lawyer Robert Badinter talked to me at a lunch in Paris after a visit to Islamabad to watch the proceedings. He had no criticism of the proceedings of the Supreme Court, but said: 'I have returned with the clearest impression that Bhutto's fate has already been decided.' He had met and talked to Justice Anwarul Haq and could not help but note the Judge's intense personal animus and prejudice against Bhutto.

That Ziaul Haq wanted Bhutto dead, of that he himself left no one in any doubt. No appeals, no feelings of gratitude, or compassion would have the slightest effect on him. But he was flustered at the flood of mercy appeals arriving from all over the world. After the death sentence pronounced by the Lahore Court, the German Permanent Representative to the UN, Baron von Wechmar asked to see me urgently and brought a personal message from his president appealing for Bhutto's life, and offering to accept him as an exile in the Federal Republic if Ziaul Haq would let him go. New York's ex-Mayor John Lindsay wished to go to Pakistan to join Bhutto's defence team.[11] Later, when I was ambassador to France, President Giscard d'Estaing spoke to me on the subject on every occasion that we met and wanted to send an emissary, former Prime Minister Edgar Faure, to go to Islamabad and personally plead for Bhutto's life. French Foreign Minister de Guiringaud said to Agha Shahi during one of the latter's visits to Paris to discuss the nuclear question, that in case of Bhutto's execution, the reaction in France could be emotional and would cause repercussions on relations.

It was all to no effect. Ziaul Haq said to a Reuters correspondent, 'If we are to give in to such pleas, we had better quit....' Not a bad idea as such, many would have said! He sent official delegations abroad to discourage foreign intercession on Bhutto's behalf. The Martial Law administration's nervousness and uneasy conscience was evident from the fact that even after Bhutto was hanged, Agha Shahi was sent to an Islamic Conference meeting held in Morocco to lobby against any condolence or sympathy being expressed to the family.

Many people hold that Bhutto was led to his downfall and death by a destiny even more inexorable than the one decreed by Ziaul Haq, a fate written not in his stars, but in the lineaments of his character, like the pre-ordained unfolding of a Greek tragedy. Talking to me on one occasion, his sister Munawwar Begum, recalled that NAP leader Wali Khan had said to Bhutto when he was at the height of his power, that if he went on as he was doing, 'You won't return to Larkana on your two feet.'

'A threat?' I asked her.

'No, a warning!' she answered.

Bhutto is said to have declared on one occasion, 'I would rather go down in a pool of blood than die a sordid death in crumpled sheets!' He created tension and conflict around himself and seemed to relish and thrive on it. 'I am a man of crisis!' I recall him saying in New York when Dhaka's fall was imminent and the Indian Army was closing in on our men from all round. He said on another occasion, 'Sometimes you have to *create* a crisis; bring things to a boil, in order to open the way to the resolution of a conflict.'

Now he faced the ultimate crisis of his life. On 18 December, at the conclusion of his appeal trial, Bhutto was allowed his day in court and made his last appearance in the world of living men. When he entered the court room, the entire audience spontaneously rose to its feet as if he was still the Prime Minister. According to the *Guardian*, at the beginning he was 'pale and trembling' and not fully in command of his faculties. At one point he broke down, tears running down his face, and a stillness came over the court room. He spoke for four days altogether, regaining his composure and self-confidence. 'I have smashed the prosecution case to smithereens,' he declared at the end of it. But he had dealt relatively briefly, in an almost cursory way, with the charges of murder and conspiracy on which he was standing there under a sentence of death. The telephone, he said, was the main witness against him, 'The telephone has been my prosecutor and adversary. The whole alleged conspiracy was carried out by me on the telephone, with no witnesses, no record.' Why, the *wadera* in him asked, if he had wanted to do away with some insignificant Raza Kasuri, would he need the police to do the job?

His statement was a bravura performance characteristic of Bhutto at the top of his speaking form—eloquent and impassioned. It was in turn lofty, moving, ironical, emotional and shrewd—addressed as much to the judges sitting on the bench with the thread of his life in their hands, as to the 'people' who had remained strangely passive throughout the long trial, and to the world beyond, that had shown intense concern with his fate. He defended himself as a man, as a politician, as a statesman, as a Pakistani who had fought for Independence 'shoulder to shoulder' with Nehru and Jinnah; as a true Muslim who had served Islam, by holding the Islamic summit in Lahore and settling the Qadiani issue. 'My life matters little to me, but the Lahore High Court's unjust attack on my devotion to Islam is a calumny worse than death,' declared Bhutto, falling in with the current official ethos. He even commended the Supreme Court for their decision in the Nusrat Bhutto case, saying that it was positive 'in a way and under the circumstances'; only, the Court should have set a time limit for the holding of elections and should not have given Ziaul Haq the power to amend the Constitution.

The Court had stretched procedures to allow Bhutto to make a personal appearance. Ziaul Haq had grumbled at this, but in the face of the international interest in the case, and widespread criticism of the flimsy evidence on which it was based, no doubt the court was anxious to be seen as bending over backwards to give Bhutto a fair hearing. Moreover, unlike the Lahore judge, Chief Justice Anwarul Haq was personally courteous towards Bhutto—an ominous sign in the circumstances.

Bhutto was hanged in the dead of night on 4 April. In a Dublin hotel, I had been fiddling with the bedside radio from time to time throughout the night. At 5 o'clock the BBC said there were strong indications that the former Prime Minister's death sentence may have been carried out—its correspondent who along with others from all over the world had been keeping vigil outside the Rawalpindi jail, saw a military vehicle emerge from the gates in the early hours and head for the airport. From there shortly afterwards a military transport plane took off and headed south. In a later bulletin the BBC said that Radio Pakistan had confirmed the death and burial in his home village of the former Prime Minister. Begum Nusrat Bhutto and Benazir were denied permission to go to the funeral, at which only a couple of elderly relatives and his first wife were present.

The desperate deed was done and the country launched into the unknown. It was hard to take it in. I moved about in a daze, going from the bedroom radio to the TV in the sitting-room, watching and listening to the same thing over and over, throughout the day. The BBC spoke of the flaws in his character: 'overbearing arrogance, and an all-consuming contempt for opponents'. Bhutto's voice was heard, high-pitched, a little fluty: 'I am not arrogant, I would never like to be arrogant. But when stupid things are said, naïve things, certain absolutely absurd things....' The TV screen showed him haranguing vast crowds, tearing up a sheaf of papers and walking out of the Security Council, going up the steps of the Lahore High Court, jaunty in a blue leisure suit, with the familiar look of cynical amusement on his face. In those last moments, what thoughts had gone through his mind as he stood alone, hands and feet bound, the black hood of death over his head, the noose fastened around the neck? It was hard to accept the reality of what had happened. One was thankful only that he went like a man, with dignity and standing straight, and that his enemies failed to break him and bring him to his knees. His treatment in jail, specially after the Supreme Court confirmed the death sentence, had been shabby and vindictive in the extreme.

The regime had got rid of Bhutto but only by investing him with a martyr's halo. It showed a morbid sensitivity on this score. When the BBC correspondent reported that Bhutto was calm as he walked to the gallows and said, 'Help me my God, for I am innocent!' three retired—and no doubt officially inspired—judges of the Lahore High Court issued a press statement saying that he had not said any such thing. How would they know? In fact to this day no one is certain in what manner Bhutto met his death, and rumours persist that he was manhandled, or tortured or even killed before being hanged.

The regime continued to show signs of nervousness about the situation and about world reactions. Agha Shahi was sent to the Islamic Conference meeting held in Fez in June to stop it from passing a condolence resolution because even condolences could be construed as an implicit criticism of the execution and a diplomatic setback.

Ziaul Haq had asserted that Bhutto's execution would cause no upheaval in the country. The regime freely used the whip and knout to scotch protests and divert peoples' attention. PPP leaders capable of stirring up trouble were taken into custody. The police laid about with their staves as they always do. On the day of the hanging, a man was found who was running some sort of a house of assignation in Rawalpindi and the regime put on a spectacle worthy of the Middle Ages. The man was publicly flogged, his face was blackened, and he was paraded through the city on a donkey's back. Stocks of liquor were discovered and destroyed in public ceremonies. A great to-do was made about cleaning up vice and iniquity for ever from the pure soil of Pakistan. Nevertheless demonstrations took place in various towns and cities and despite all precautions and prohibitions, 60,000 people turned up at Bhutto's grave site for the *chehlum*, the ritual fortieth and last day of mourning.[12]

In Paris too, with its small population of Pakistani immigrants, the embassy received threatening letters and witnessed some demonstrations. President Giscard d'Estaing, in a public statement expressed his 'deep emotion' at Bhutto's execution, and released to the Press the text of a letter Bhutto had written to him a year earlier from the death cell in Pindi jail. A strange letter from such a place—it was defiant and polemical but also very human and emotional; there was no pathos in it, no appeal to compassion. On the contrary Bhutto had written, 'You will understand that writing from behind the heavily fortified bars of this death cell, my pride and vanity inhibit me from expressing to you my gratitude for your thoughtful concern...' It was in part political analysis, in part personal credo with a characteristic polemical touch: 'I never did subscribe to the belief in the decline of the West. This [idea] was Spengler's tactical device for the West to attain her strategic aim of world mastery.' Referring to the West's struggle against Communism, by means of its superior technology and technique, he wrote scathingly:

> the 'chewing gum' *coups d'etat* of military dictators...usurp constitutional authority to meet the 'menace' of communism, but in truth are the harbingers of communism. By defending them the West sows the seeds of its own destruction....The chaos of democracy represents, in its tumult, greater inherent stability than the mortal silence of our dictatorships....

With his own life hanging in the balance, he thought of death but not with despair or despondency. He did not believe there would be a third World War and annihilation, but even if such a war did break out...

There is too much beauty in the world for it to be annihilated in a victory of the dying over the dead. Something of it will survive to bloom into fullness once more...If I am done to death, my blood will fertilize and strengthen the resolve of the young men and young women of this country. The most shining of my idylls, I have lived with the people of my country...

NOTES

[1] He sent me a set of these on leaving Rawalpindi after being dropped from Ayub's Cabinet in 1966. The citations in this chapter of his views on various subjects are mainly from these papers.

[2] Bhutto admired Sukarno who in turn treated him with fatherly affection. When Sukarno was overthrown and Foreign Minister Subandrio was sentenced to death, Bhutto wrote an open letter to Indonesia's military regime to plead for a reprieve for a man who was a personal friend and who had stood by Pakistan in the 1965 War. It was almost as if a premonition came to him, across the turbulent years that lay ahead, that some day he too would be facing extremity and would be in need of friends to speak up for him. When his hour came many did indeed stand by him—the German Chancellor, Giscard d'Estaing of France, Syrian President Hafiz al Assad, the Kuwaiti ruler, Jaber al Ahmad al Sabah.

[3] RCD (Regional Co-operation for Development), an association for economic development among Pakistan, Iran and Turkey, is now known by the acronym ECO (Economic Co-operation Organization) and has expanded to include some Central Asian states. The IPECC (Indonesia-Pakistan Economic Co-operation Council) no longer exists.

[4] The story current in Pakistan was that Kissinger had threatened that a 'horrible example' would be made of Pakistan—or of Bhutto personally—if the nuclear programme was not given up. When I asked Henry Kissinger about this some years later, he denied having used the expression 'horrible example', and said that in any case he was not talking about Bhutto personally.

[5] The Qadiani sect was founded in the Punjab in the nineteenth century by Mirza Ahmad, a religious reformer who claimed to be, or was considered by his followers to be a messenger of God—a belief which runs counter to the cardinal Islamic doctrine that the prophet Muhammad (PBUH) was the last of the prophets sent by God, and none other would follow him until the advent of the Mehdi or Messiah.

[6] Morrice James, *Pakistan Chronicle*, Oxford University Press, Karachi, 1993.

[7] Papers with author.

[8] Sind Club founded by the British in 1879 and closed to 'natives' during the Raj, is today the equally exclusive haunt of Karachi's plutocracy. Jacob Lines, during the Raj, was a sprawling complex of barracks for the 'other ranks' of the Indian Army. Today it is an unsalubrious semi-slum in the heart of Karachi.

[9] Andrew Young fell victim not long afterwards to a secret meeting with the PLO representative at the UN, Labib Zehdi Tarzi, at the residence of the Kuwaiti permanent representative. When news of the meeting leaked, it provoked such a furore in Israel and pro-Israeli circles in the United States, that Carter had to disown Young and let him resign. Tarzi told me later that the incident had been a public relations bonanza for him and he was flooded with invitations from all over America afterwards for speaking engagements.

[10] UN General Assembly, A/PV 2122, 20 September 1973. In fact the Chileans did not take the thing too much to heart. The Chilean Chargé d'Affaires called on me sometime afterwards to say that Prime Minister Bhutto had misconstrued Pinochet's action, and he proposed the establishment of direct diplomatic relations between our countries.

[11] He could not do so on account, ironically, of a law passed under Bhutto requiring foreign lawyers first to be registered for practice in Pakistani courts—a lengthy procedure.

[12] This is not an exclusively Islamic custom and its origins apparently go back to Pharaonic Egypt. The process of mummifying the body of the dead Pharaoh—drying it out over slow heat, injecting resins from the cedars of Lebanon into the veins and arteries took forty days, at the end of which the Pharaoh was considered to have finally passed on to the netherworld.

CHAPTER 14

A SIMPLE MAN

Early in 1978, a cable came from the Foreign Ministry asking me
to report to Islamabad as soon as I could for a meeting with the
Chief Martial Law Administrator. I supposed that he wanted
personally to size up an ambassador holding a key diplomatic
post, who was known as a 'Bhutto man'. I had worked closely
with Bhutto at the United Nations and in the Foreign Ministry,
but I was not a Bhutto man in any political sense and did not go
along with all of his political ideas. On the other hand, I did not
share any of Ziaul Haq's political ideas at all and I assumed that
after hearing my views, he would have me transferred to a less
sensitive post or decree a more summary fate.

When I was ushered into the living-room of the Army Chief's
house in Rawalpindi—the relatively modest house where he
continued to stay even after taking over as President—Ziaul Haq
was standing in the middle of the room. He came forward to
shake hands, saying, 'I have heard a lot about you and thought
we ought to get acquainted .' A man of medium height, he still
wore his handlebar mustachios but did not cut the dashing
cavalryman's figure that newspaper pictures had led one to
expect. In a uniform not too well cut, with the plain khaki
trousers ending a little above the ankles, he had indeed a rather
homely appearance. The striking feature of his person was the
eyes, a cold grey of opaque tint.

I was taken aback a bit when the General explained the specific
purpose of his summons to me. So many petitions and appeals
were being received on Bhutto's behalf from various foreign
countries, he said, that there was a need perhaps for a special
effort to clarify matters to the world. So, a start was to be made
with the Muslim countries and four delegations were being sent
out to 'explain' to them the Bhutto case. Three of these were to

be led respectively by A.K. Brohi, a constitutional lawyer, Sharifuddin Pirzada, the Attorney-General, and retired ambassador Agha Hilaly. What did I think of the idea, Zia asked, and would I be willing to lead the fourth delegation? And he added, 'I would also appreciate your views on the whole Bhutto situation.' It was evident that this was to be a test of where I stood, for I was by no means in the same league as the three other persons—all declared and vocal opponents of Bhutto; nor was there any lack of other such eminences willing and eager to go on such a mission. I decided to give the General my opinion without beating about the bush. The appeals and mercy petitions, I said to him, were being made on humanitarian grounds and were understandable in view of Mr Bhutto's international standing and his extensive personal contacts and friendships in many countries. But they were inspired mainly by the feeling that he was on trial for his politics. The General's own statement on BBC television two days before—in which he had spoken as if Bhutto had already been found guilty of the murder for which he was on trial—could not have failed to convey the same impression. An official campaign to discourage mercy petitions would reinforce the suspicion that the authorities did not want any obstacle in the way of carrying out a predetermined decision. To my surprise the General did not take issue with any of these points, and only corrected me about his TV interview, saying it was to the ITV, not to the BBC. We were later joined by Agha Hilaly and by Foreign Secretary Shahnawaz. After some discussion the idea of sending out missions was dropped; instead the Foreign Secretary was to instruct our envoys in various capitals to explain to all concerned the working of Pakistan's judicial system, its independence from the executive, and other such abstract and lofty notions.

At the Islamic Foreign Ministers' meeting held in Dakar some months later, Agha Shahi used this line in his lobbying against any possible moves by the Conference on Bhutto's behalf. With great earnestness he expounded Pakistan's Anglo-Saxon legal tradition, explained that it would be contempt of court to entertain mercy petition in a case that was *sub judice*, and affirmed that the Martial Law regime greatly respected the judiciary's independence and stood in awe of the law.[1] Most of them listened in silence and must have thought that all this high-powered official lobbying in regard to a *sub judice* case was surely no less a contempt of court. However PLO's Abu Muzeir put matters plainly: 'Mr Shahi, we know only too well what all that means, we know what is the reality of laws and courts and procedures under Third World regimes. Bhutto's trial is political and nothing else, and you know this as well as I.' He went on to remind Shahi of the zeal with which, at the previous year's session of the Islamic Foreign Ministers' Conference, the Pakistan delegation headed by him had lobbied on behalf of the Bhutto government for a resolution against foreign interference in Pakistan's internal affairs.

The Palestinians had a bone of their own to pick with Zia. Farook Kadoumy, the PLO's Foreign Relations adviser, reminded Shahi of Ziaul Haq's role in King Hussein's operation against the PLO in the so-called 'Black September' action in Jordan in 1970. 'That man hit the PLO; *he* made the plans for King Hussein's massacre of Palestinians,' Kadoumy said to Shahi, and added, 'Bhutto is being punished by the Americans for trying to make a nuclear bomb and for his support of the Palestine cause.' However Kadoumy did not bring up all this in his speech at the plenary session of the conference in which he declared, 'At this session, let us not be forgetful of one man, a leader of a friendly country, the Chairman of the Summit of this conference, Zulfikar Ali Bhutto. We appeal for his life and for his dignity.' The other delegations maintained an embarrassed silence on the subject, though in private Foreign Minister Sabah al Ahmad of Kuwait and some others remonstrated vigorously against the death sentence on Bhutto.[2]

The question will always remain why Bhutto picked Ziaul Haq over the heads of more senior and competent officers, to be the Chief of the Army. Ziaul Haq was unknown in Pakistan outside army circles, and within the army itself opinions about him were mixed. Bhutto had been advised by a number of persons against his intended choice. Retired General Fazal Muqeem who had been Bhutto's Defence Secretary, said to me that he had warned him, 'Zia is a deep one', and not the right man to lead the army. The former Chief of Staff, General Gul Hassan, whom Bhutto had sent away as ambassador to Austria and whose opinion he asked during a stop-over in Vienna, told me that he advised him: 'Whatever else you do, don't touch *that* man with a barge pole!

. (He joked: 'Bhutto must have thought that any one whom Gul Hassan dislikes can't be all bad!') In fact nobody had recommended or suggested Ziaul Haq for the job; the choice was Bhutto's alone.

One is tempted to speak of the workings of a perverse destiny leading Bhutto to make wrong decisions at critical junctures, or a Greek tragedy playing itself out to its predestined end. But I got a matter-of-fact answer from Bhutto's sister, the late Manna Islam, when the subject came up in conversation on one occasion. She said that Bhutto was looking for a COAS who would not get up to any funny business and thought Zia was the man because he did not have a following in the army and would be loyal out of gratitude at being given such a big leg up. She also told me a story that was revealing of the very different personalities of the two men and of their inter-relationship; possibly, it casts a light also on the particular spite and vengefulness that marked Ziaul Haq's treatment of Bhutto once he had him at his mercy. Around the time when the question of choosing a new Chief of Staff was being considered, Bhutto was on a political tour in Multan where Ziaul Haq was the area GOC. He came over to the Prime Minister's camp unannounced, and asked the Military Secretary if he could get to see the Prime Minister. Bhutto who had a very busy schedule, did not want to receive him, but Zia would not give up and just kept sitting in the Military Secretary's room to take his chance. Then after a long wait, and at the embarrassed Military Secretary's pleading, Bhutto finally relented and had him shown in. Zia said to Bhutto that all he had come to do was personally to present the Prime Minister with a copy of the Holy Koran and to swear fealty to him upon it. The whole thing was rather transparent and not very becoming. Bhutto was too astute and cynical a man not to see through it, but what he may have seen as abject submissiveness was surely the reflection of a great and ruthless ambition. Moreover the fact that Ziaul Haq had no personal following in the army was not very material; the army follows orders, not individuals, as Bhutto ought to have remembered from Ayub's case.

When after Bhutto's overthrow, Zia visited him in the President's House in Murree, his deluxe, initial detention place, Bhutto no doubt recalled and perhaps reminded Zia that he had picked him as Army Chief over the heads of many others. Bhutto was still taking a high tone with the General and the General was still being deferential. But his answer, as I heard from a friend of Zia's, was blunt: 'Sir, I owe my rise to my prayers—not to you or to any mortal man.' The truth is that Bhutto was not a very good judge of men. In the end he was betrayed by some of those who were closest to him. This was ironical, for Bhutto's was not a trusting nature. He did not put his faith in many people, nor did he demand that they give him their trust. For him it was enough that they feared him. He manipulated and controlled people by keeping them on tenterhooks.

In the beginning people did not know what to make of Zia and of the *coup* he had carried out in such a seemingly tentative manner. There was indeed some talk at the time that the whole thing had been stage-managed by Bhutto himself, and that he would be back in power as soon as the army had subdued the political turmoil. Zia himself took a soft line in talking about Bhutto, paying tribute to his ability and to what he had done for the country and minimizing the impact of the alleged election rigging. He declared that Bhutto had gone as far as he could to accommodate the Opposition. But this amiable phase did not last, and no doubt was meant only to justify the name Zia had chosen for the *coup:* Operation Fairplay. From the start, the hand of Martial Law weighed more heavily on the PPP and soon the regime was openly going for the PPP and for Bhutto personally. White Papers, virulent and voluminous, began to appear about the alleged rigging of elections. A press release which we received for distribution by the embassy, spoke of Bhutto as 'frothing with rage'; pronounced that 'his thirst for publicity was as unquenchable as his megalomania was infinite'; and exulted that 'not all the Chairman's men could save his chair, for you cannot fool all the people all the time'. I sent it back to the Ministry, with the comment that such language was not appropriate in diplomatic communications. As an example of the reaction abroad to the anti-Bhutto campaign, I also sent to the Information Ministry a cutting from the Paris daily *Le Monde* which said,

A White Paper condemning the attacks on the liberty of the Press by Mr Bhutto was issued on Sunday by the Government of Pakistan. On the other hand, sixteen persons, including journalists and typesetters have been arrested in Karachi between 22 and 26 August while they were demonstrating against government restrictions on Press freedom. Seventy-six persons are now in jail for the same reason, and some of them are reported to have been maltreated.

In my first meeting with him, Ziaul Haq had asked me what I thought of the 'whole Bhutto situation'. We got to the subject after dinner at his place the next evening. I had not warmed to the man at our meeting the previous morning though he received me with great courtesy and did not take amiss my plain-speaking about Bhutto. At the dinner I was impressed by his capacity to keep the peace and listen to opinions that, on the face of it, were quite the opposite of what he himself was saying and advocating, and ran counter to the policies he claimed to be trying to enforce. The conversation ranged far and wide and was notable for its 'liberal' orientation. The attractive wife of a senior General— wearing make-up and dressed in a sari and sleeveless blouse— talked about the economic roots of corruption and the need to foster 'progressive thinking in the country rather than emphasizing ritualistic Islam'. These were indeed simple notions which elsewhere and at other times would be considered self-evident, but they seemed daring and radical at the table of the Chief Martial Law Administrator who was proposing to enforce Nizam-i-Islam at the point of a gun. But Zia himself joined in the general deprecation of the mullah's retrograde and negative role in society. The truth is that though he was in his personal life devout and observed all the religious rites and prayers, Zia was by no means a zealot. I observed one instance of his relaxed attitude on these matters. During an all-day session of an Envoys' Conference that Zia was attending, rugs had been laid out for midday prayers under an awning on a lawn, off the foreign ministry's meeting hall. At the lunch break, he rose and went down to join the gathering—Foreign Ministry staff—for prayers. Not one person from among the conference participants, ambassadors, federal secretaries, senior officials, followed him. Many kept walking back and forth and chatting on the terrace alongside the prayer tent. I thought this would rate us a homily on one's Islamic duties from the General who claimed that Martial Law was there in order to turn everybody into a good Muslim. But he never said a word or showed that he had even noticed the truancy. Islam was his political platform and in the absence of any other sanction or justification, he had made 'Islamization' the *raison d' être* for continuing his rule.

After dinner was over, he asked Brohi and me to stay back for a review of foreign relations. After a general chit-chat on relations with various countries, it was Brohi who asked me what the world in general and the United States in particular thought of the present situation in Pakistan. In the United States the reaction had been mixed. The Carter administration had put the nuclear issue, and specifically Pakistan's attempts to match India's nuclear capability, on top of its foreign policy agenda. The fall of Bhutto, who was the moving force behind Pakistan's nuclear policy, cannot but have come as welcome news to the administration— whether or not they actually connived at, or engineered his fall. In public they maintained a discreet, one should say, expectant silence. At a lunch given by Jimmy Carter at New York for the Heads of the Asian delegations to the UN General Assembly's 1978 session, as he went around greeting guests, he stopped to say to Agha Shahi, 'General Zia is doing a good job in a difficult situation. Please convey my good wishes to him.' This was America's 'Human Rights President'—commending the 'good job' of a regime that was flogging journalists and carrying out public hangings! But the Carter administration's nuclear hopes in the Zia regime were soon to be disappointed.

Another rather amusing indication of US officialdom's ambivalence with regard to Bhutto, came a couple of years later at a lunch at the American embassy in Beirut. Ambassador Robert Dillon who had been in Turkey before being transferred to Beirut, talked about the Menderes case, the way charges had been cooked up in order to hang the deposed Prime Minister, and he was hanged because the authors of the *coup* were alarmed by his continuing popularity and afraid that if he made a come-back, *their* necks would be in the noose. A woman from the State Department sitting on my left said to me, 'Really, it is *so* much like the case of...', then suddenly realizing who she was talking to, fumbled, 'like er,...the case of Mary, Queen of Scots!'

On the other hand, public and Press reaction in the US and abroad generally to Zia's *coup* had been adverse, specially as it was carried out apparently to forestall an imminent agreement between the government and the Opposition. But criticism and questions were temporarily set aside because following his pledge to hold fresh elections, news continued to come of preparations going ahead for holding elections and the re-establishment of democratic institutions. Thus *The New York Times'* editorial on the *coup* expressed doubt rather than outright disapproval. The paper's editor, Richard Ullman, explained to our press attaché that they were making a 'temporary exception' in view of Ziaul Haq's pledge to hold elections. Nevertheless, a good deal of scepticism persisted on the basis of the general experience of military *coups*. The question was whether, whatever he might say, Ziaul Haq would stand by his pledge or find in the evolution of events reason or pretext to revise his position.

In reply to Brohi's question, I said to Ziaul Haq that in the most sympathetic view in the West the army was riding a tiger (whereupon he smiled a wry smile) and the general belief was that the regime was saying what all such regimes say, but it would not hold elections or give up power. I also spoke about the change of mood that had occurred in the Pakistani community in New York and elsewhere. Whereas, before the *coup*, I used to face heckling from audiences about the doings of the Bhutto government, now the questions and criticisms only concerned the intentions of the military regime. However I did not tell him that at a *qawali* in New York, organized under Yusuf Haroon's sponsorship a couple of months after the *coup*, Sabir Qawwal brought the house down with a Bhutto one-liner:

Yes! I drink wine, I do confess, but
I do not drink the blood of the poor!

The General nodded at all this and refrained from taking issue. When I finished he said, 'I am not surprised at these Western reactions. It is true that military regimes do not ordinarily give up power. But this time we shall surprise them. We *shall* hold elections as pledged, please be sure of that!' But in answer to a question from me he said that a 'national government' could not be set up for another three or four months and until 'this Bhutto affair is settled one way or another'. He also said that the PPP was holding together as a party so far, but was not as strong in the Punjab as was generally assumed. Then, as he had done in public statements, he volunteered his personal opinion that 'the only way Bhutto can be destroyed is by political means'. Then why the trial, why the Lahore judgement, why all the frantic efforts whose logical aim could only be the physical elimination of Bhutto? Was there a difference of opinion in the top brass, with Zia taking the moderate line? Or, was his remark a part of his deviousness? Some people hold that Zia had not originally intended to hang Bhutto but had been brought to the decision by the force of circumstances. Of these the decisive factor was Bhutto's continuing political hold and the popularity, that had been spectacularly demonstrated by the vast crowds that turned out to greet him at Lahore when he went there after being released from detention. I myself think the Lahore visit was probably the decisive event for the fate of Zulfikar Bhutto. It was now his neck or theirs. During a visit to Paris in September 1978, General Fazle Haq made no bones about the matter. 'If Bhutto lives, jail or no jail, he will be out one day and hang the generals who threw him out...,' the General said to me during a dinner given for him by the Military Attaché. He went on to say that if he had his own way, he would have imposed *real* Martial Law: 'To begin with, I would have had some six to seven chaps shot out of hand—Bhutto himself, his cousin Mumtaz, Hafiz Pirzada, Mustafa Khar... '

But Zia was no bull in a china shop. He felt the ground as he went. He was selective in choosing his targets. 'What then do *you* think we ought to do, Akhund sahib?' Zia asked me during that after-dinner chat in Islamabad. I said that the course of action he had announced seemed to me precisely the right one: fresh general elections on the dates proposed, and the army to go back to the barracks and to its duties under the Constitution. I said that the idea that the army should clean up politics before handing power back to the politicians may be a tempting one, but it was more likely that the army would itself get corrupted, and certainly it would get involved in partisan politics, by staying on. The General nodded politely as if agreeing with it all. I did not delude myself that this was the case, but at that stage I did believe that the compulsion of events, the awakened political awareness of the people and international pressures would help to keep the General to his promise.

'This Bhutto problem', as Ziaul Haq called it, came up formally twice again in meetings with him. In January 1979 at an Envoys' Conference in Islamabad, Ziaul Haq addressed an audience which besides the envoys, also included a number of other high civil and military officials. His statement was devoted entirely to 'the one problem that has kept the country in a turmoil for eighteen months, the problem of Mr Bhutto'. He gave an account of the events preceding the military *coup*, his warning to Bhutto two weeks earlier to find a political solution otherwise the army would have to move, and he explained why on 5 July he finally decided to move. 'Nawabzada Nasrullah told me that the agreement reached between Bhutto and Mufti Mahmud was not acceptable to the PNA as a whole....' Ziaul Haq went on to say that he could have done away with 'the Bhutto problem' on that very first day of the military take-over, 'but no, I decided to act through the Courts, to let the law take its course...' As if the significance of this statement was not clear enough, the General went on to make a slip of the tongue (a 'Freudian slip!' as someone sitting next to me whispered), 'When we engineered the case, er...I mean when we *instituted* the case against Mr Bhutto...' And then he continued, 'Any way, it is a case arising out of a private complaint, the Government has nothing to do with it. We are only giving all necessary help in its investigation and prosecution.' The case had been conducted scrupulously in the Supreme Court where, he said with a touch of exasperation, against all precedent, Bhutto was allowed to speak personally and 'such funny things have happened as were never heard of before'. Now, he warned, the country must be prepared for the repercussions of the judgment, 'whatever they might be'. But he appeared to know what the verdict was going to be, for he added that any trouble that occurred would be confined largely to the interior of Sindh.

At night he entertained the visiting ambassadors and others to dinner, and I found myself seated at Ziaul Haq's table. Almost the first thing he said was that the timing of this particular conference had been set in the expectation that 'the Bhutto affair would be over by then', and the envoys would be able to see for themselves that everything was going on as usual. Everyone suspected that the Supreme Court *would* confirm Bhutto's death sentence and that Ziaul Haq knew all about what the Court was going to decide. Yet for a moment a hush fell upon the conversation as Zia's cold-blooded and cynical remark, uttered with a jolly little laugh, lifted the veils of accountability, judicial procedures and equal justice with which the regime had publicly covered the deed it was going to do.

After dinner he detained some of the ambassadors including myself, and called us in one by one for a tête-à-tête. When my turn came, he said he had seen my telegrams about the French President's appeal on Bhutto's behalf and assumed that all these appeals arose from the fact that in Europe the death penalty had been abolished. I repeated what I had been reporting by cable: that the French President had shown great personal concern at Mr Bhutto's fate, had spoken to me about the matter on every occasion that we met, and that he had wanted to send former Prime Minister of France, and elder statesman, Edgar Faure,[3] to Islamabad to personally plead for the former Prime Minister's life to be spared. I recalled Giscard's warning that Bhutto's execution would have international repercussions for Pakistan. At the Quai d' Orsay I was told that the concern expressed by France over Bhutto's fate reflected the unanimous opinion of the nine members of the European Community. Others too had spoken to me in the same vein, such as André Fontaine, editor of the influential daily *Le Monde.*

I told Zia that in Dublin they had urged clemency for Bhutto and talked about the harvest of bitterness the country was still reaping on account of the political killings that had taken place on Ireland's independence. The Turkish ambassador had recalled the Menderes case. Zia listened without arguing or indicating in any way what he intended to do with Bhutto and only said a few words on the supremacy of the law and that the law was equal for all, high or low. I said, 'General, I speak, as you know, as a friend of Bhutto's. You will no doubt discount my words for that reason.' He reassured me, 'No, no, you have every right to say what you wish.' I urged him, 'Justice is supreme but mercy is a divine quality. You have Bhutto's life in your hands. I pray that you will temper the Court's decision with the prerogative of mercy that is also in your hands.'

'It will be done,' he said, 'it will be done.' What would be done? I had not the slightest illusion that the General would show mercy towards the man whom he seemed to fear above all men and things and had come to hate with a personal, vindictive and unremitting hatred.

Earlier, at the dinner Interior Minister Mahmud Haroon said to me that there existed a strong leftist element among the younger army officers who might have been sympathetic to

Bhutto, but they had been alienated when, on emerging from detention in Murree, Bhutto attacked and threatened the army as such. But the mere fact that there was such a tendency within the armed forces increased in the eyes of the regime the risks of letting Bhutto live. Mahmud thought that Bhutto was certainly going to be executed, though the Cabinet was divided on the subject. Brohi, Mir Ahmad Ali Talpur, and the Jamaat Ministers were all for hanging. When I asked the Mir about this subject later he vehemently denied that this was so in his case, '...even though,' he had added, 'we had our own blood debts to settle with Zulfikar Ali.'

Every time I visited Islamabad and drove to the President's House past the blank walls of the jail, I felt, as it were, the immediacy of the presence of that proud man, once so powerful, sitting now in his death cell, still proud and unbending, but alone with his thoughts and without recourse. The only recourse lay, whence it would never come, in the heart and mind of one man, who had closed them to every appeal. I felt acutely my own powerlessness to do anything effective for Bhutto in his extremity. I knew it wasn't much use, but I talked to any one who I thought might have some influence on Ziaul Haq. A number of such persons visited Paris where I was Ambassador at the time. I have already mentioned the hard-fisted response of General Fazle Haq. Another visitor to Paris was Air Chief Marshal Shameem, a Zia crony, who agreed that Bhutto would not be able to do much from jail or exile, but he expressed the regime's visceral fears in pointing out that the PPP remained a political force and would be returned as the largest single party if elections were held. The Aga Khan suggested the possibility of using Martial Law powers to suspend Bhutto's trial and send him out of the country, on pain of the case being resumed if he returned. Several countries had offered to accept Bhutto in exile and keep him from playing politics. I put this to Agha Shahi when he was passing through Paris, but he demurred that the government had no authority to suspend a trial. I thought that in a country in which the Constitution itself could be suspended, such a consideration was not very relevant.

Mustafa Gokal, Ziaul Haq's Shipping Minister, came often to Paris and was said to be close to him. When I asked him what was to become of Bhutto, he was silent for a while as if searching for

the right words, then blurted out, 'We are trapped! Many people
will be sorry if he is hanged, specially the poor masses. We don't
know what is the right thing to do.' Then he gave what sounded
like a rationale for getting rid of Bhutto nevertheless, 'Look,
today Bhutto is locked up in jail under heavy guard and the most
stringent security precautions. And yet people are afraid of him;
his party men still cling to him, perhaps only out of fear but just
the same.' I said that the influence of Bhutto alive could perhaps
be contained and eroded, but of Bhutto martyred, never! His
killing would leave a scar on the soul of the nation, his ghost
would stalk the politics of Pakistan for a generation. Even if
Bhutto was guilty of murder, let not the army take his blood
upon its hands!

Perhaps, in spite of himself, Gokal saw the force of my
argument, for he said to me, 'You must talk yourself to Zia on
those lines.' I said that I had little personal influence with the
General who moreover thought of me as a 'Bhutto man' and
would put me off with some courteous platitudes. Someone who
was close to him and was not a friend of Bhutto's, perhaps even
an opponent, could perhaps argue more convincingly with the
General. On his next trip to Paris, Mustafa Gokal told me that he
had talked long and hard with the General on the lines of our
discussion in Paris, but found him immovable. Zia had argued
that things would never settle down as long as Bhutto lived, and
he believed that once he was out of the way it would be possible
to break up the PPP and play off against each other the many
small parties and groups that were likely to emerge thereafter.
Ghulam Ishaq Khan, Secretary General of the Martial Law
regime, echoed the same idea in talking to me about the election
prospects. 'Afterwards,' he said (Bhutto was still alive), 'the PPP
may be willing to come to terms with other political parties and
the Military.' This was the scenario on the basis of which Yahya's
collaborators had prepared for the elections in 1971. It would be
again the assumption on which after Zia's death the
Establishment proceeded with the 1988 elections.

The next occasion when the 'Bhutto problem' came up was
another Envoys' Conference held in July 1979. Bhutto was already
dead. Ziaul Haq dismissed the matter in one sentence of his
opening statement. 'Bhutto was hanged to uphold the supremacy
of the law, and that chapter is now closed.' And alas for you,

General! Alas for the country! History is not a series of closed chapters. It is an endless interweaving of a multitude of threads which make the fabric of a nation; in the case of Pakistan, its brief and blood-stained history is made up of a web of clashing ambitions, factional rivalries, regional loyalties—a tangle from which was knotted the noose for Bhutto's neck. Ziaul Haq had added more strands to the tangled skein—religious intolerance and sectarian animosities and a pseudo-ideological dogmatism, and in the end, himself fell victim to the forces of discord and contention that he had let loose.

The General had resolved the 'Bhutto problem' to his satisfaction but another knotty one remained, and that was his pledge to hold elections. One could see early on that his heart was not in it at all. In his statement to the envoys he renewed the pledge, but added wistfully, that although the world did not look with favour upon military governments, a number of countries were in fact under military rule and doing quite well. He reverted to the theme on another occasion when, criticizing the diplomatic missions for not effectively projecting the country's image abroad, he conceded that they faced a difficult job. 'It is not considered a good thing for a country to be under military rule, though I for one, am certainly not ashamed of it—but that is how the world looks at things.'

Nor were his advisers great believers in democracy and democratic procedures. Ghulam Ishaq Khan visited Paris in January 1979 and I asked him whether the promised elections would really be held. 'Yes, I suppose one might as well have elections', he said with a weary air, as one might speak of a childish whim that has to be indulged. Many Establishment figures saw democracy not as a system of government, but as a matter of who was to exercise power: incompetent, opportunistic, corrupt politicians, or those who have the experience and skills to run the administration and can rise above petty political considerations. Behind it was the unspoken question of who would enjoy the perks and profits of exercising power. Over the decades, regardless of the nature of the prevailing regime, in effective terms Pakistan has been ruled and regulated by the higher bureaucracy. In the beginning the Civil Servants were the only ones who had the requisite experience and skills. Then, as government took on an increasing variety of functions, from allotting evacuee property, residential plots and agricultural land, to fixing the prices of rice and cotton, issuing import licences and industrial sanctions, Civil Servants got their fingers in every pie. In the process the bureaucracy has acquired a reputation for corruption, self-aggrandizement and opportunism, and is held responsible for the instability of the country's politics and its failure to make a social and economic breakthrough. In fairness the blame ought to be more evenly shared. But, while as individuals some of the top Civil Servants can stand with the best in the world, as a class, the bureaucracy trained in the colonial purpose of maintaining the *status quo,* has remained imbued with that spirit, with this difference that the British concept of the neutral Civil Servant, has fallen by the wayside and instead, through political pressures as well as self-interest, Civil Servants willingly act as the tools of the government of the day, ready to do its bidding right or wrong. Such people have kept the country going in the face of all odds, but kept it going round and round in small circles. The key failure of Pakistan's bureaucracy lies not so much in a lack of professional integrity or financial probity— South Korea's case shows that spectacular progress can be made notwithstanding—but in its lack of dynamism and motivation, and commitment to the future. But in this respect the failings of the bureaucracy, its self-absorption and attitude of *carpe diem* perhaps reflect a deficiency on a broader, national scale.

Zia's remarks about military rule indicated how his mind was working, but meanwhile moves were already afoot at damage limitation—in case a way could not be found to avoid elections altogether. A month after Bhutto was hanged, I received a letter from the Foreign Secretary seeking information about the relationship between the President and Prime Minister and the role of the armed forces under the French Constitution. Similar queries had gone out to other missions. France's political set-up and ethos are in some ways quite like Pakistan's—at least on a superficial level. There exists a highly centralized system of government with a powerful and elitist bureaucracy running the administration; a very politicized and bitterly divided society, but at odds more over political and class affiliations than issues; a people possessed of great pride in the nation's military prowess and history, and inclined to be cynical about the competence and integrity of the leadership. De Gaulle's Constitution had introduced a sort of diarchy—a sharing of power between the President and the Prime Minister. The French President has very large powers in most matters, and in an emergency can personally assume all state powers. But he may do this only in consultation with the Prime Minister and the Council of State; he cannot dismiss Parliament and certainly may not amend the Constitution. All this made for a strong government under de Gaulle but has caused problems and sometimes stalemate in subsequent administrations, specially when the two government leaders belong to different parties. The special emergency powers were invoked only once and that was when de Gaulle used them to put down an attempted revolt by a group of generals opposed to his plans for Algerian independence.

The concept of diarchy does not exist in Anglo-Saxon systems, though the British relied on it in doling out small doses of self-government to their colonial possessions. But diarchy is something very dear to the heart of the Pakistan Establishment and is proposed as a way of introducing checks and balances in the system. Zia spoke of it as more in keeping with Islamic law. This is of course a fallacious idea. It is not more Islamic to have a powerful indirectly-elected President than a powerful directly-elected Prime Minister. The idea of checks and balances among the different arms of government—the legislative, executive and judiciary—is a salutary and essential principle of democratic government. But introducing checks and balances *within* the executive branch is a very different thing, and a recipe for discord and paralysis. The eighth amendment of the Constitution introduced by Ziaul Haq was not designed with constitutional checks and balances in view, but to allow him to retain—as the governor-general did under colonial rule—ultimate decision-making power in all matters.

As for the role of the armed forces, in France as elsewhere (including Turkey, whose case is often but inaccurately cited in Pakistan) their constitutional role is to defend the territory and independence of the country, and to come to the aid of civil power at its request. That and nothing else. In Pakistan, Zia had conferred upon the armed forces (and therefore, himself) the task also of defending the ideology of the country, something that they could only do—since ideology is a purely political concept—by putting in jail, flogging or hanging those who did not fall in line with the rulers' concept of ideology.

In October Ziaul Haq took the plunge, postponed elections indefinitely, banned all political parties, and announced that Martial Law would now be applied as it is meant to be, its orders no longer subject to review or appeal in civil courts. I was leaving Pakistan service very shortly to go to Beirut as the UN Secretary General's Special Representative in Lebanon. A phone call came from Islamabad one evening and it was Ziaul Haq. He said, 'You must have seen my announcement about elections...We have postponed them, this time without setting a new date. We have just had the Local Bodies elections, so we thought, let's see how that works....' (The non-party Local Bodies elections had not gone as the regime had wished; despite all kinds of handicaps, PPP backers had won a majority of the seats). Zia was on the defensive, 'People who live abroad have a different view of things....Western newspapers will set up a howl...our real problems are economic...' I wondered: Why is he calling me of all people to say these things? I am not a political figure, or one whose views matter. He knows these well enough from my conversations with him on the subject and what I have been saying to various people close to him. Why now, when I am about to leave Pakistan's service, does he bother to explain and justify his actions to me? I supposed that it was to see whether I was going to resign, call a press conference in Paris, and make a public relations scandal for the regime as some Pakistani diplomats had done for Bhutto during his last days in power.

I told him I was sorry that he had cancelled elections and felt that the turn he had decided to take was not the right one for the country. I believed that fresh elections were the only way out of the dead end and I believed this not because I was living abroad, but on an objective view of the country's situation. He said, 'Well, anyway....', and wished me well in my new job and said that I should look him up whenever I was in Islamabad.

Before leaving for Beirut the next day I wrote him a letter in which I said, *inter alia*:[4]

Politics by its nature is a fractious activity. Is it possible for the armed forces if they stay in the field of politics on an indefinite basis, to remain immune from the debate, division and discord that are natural to political activity and which democratic institutions are designed to contain and reconcile? Martial Law may, for a while, make things go more efficiently but dictatorship, by bottling up dissent, denying the citizen a voice in his own fate, builds up tensions which inevitably lead to upheavals.

It is said that our people are not fit for democracy and that they will only respond to the stick...on the contrary they have shown the capacity, however rarely the opportunity was offered to them, to elect their representatives intelligently, to sift slogans from realities, right from wrong, fair from unfair.

True, there exist among our people corruption, inefficiency, lethargy, sectarianism, provincialism and many other evils, but the same vices can be found in people of other countries, including our neighbour India...moreover, the wearing of a uniform is no protection against these evils.

To a great degree they arise from the fact that our institutions— the legislatures, the civil services, the judiciary, the Press—have never been allowed to function as they are meant to and over the years, through misuse, neglect and cynicism, have become servile and ineffective. You have said that all our institutions have been destroyed or eroded and that only the armed forces remain to provide stability...I beg you to reflect whether placing on them the burden of being the political arbiters of the country, indeed in the prevailing circumstances, political partisans, would not put under strain the very qualities that have made the armed forces an effective and dependable national institution.

After a few weeks, I received in Beirut a personal note from the General acknowledging the letter, with a polite word of appreciation for its sincerity and candour. This was Zia's way. He had enough self-assurance to listen, without getting upset—and without paying any heed—to criticism or adverse opinion. He did not make it a matter of *lèse majesté* or take umbrage at dissent or contradiction. However his tolerance stopped at anyone who could be a real threat to his position or stood in the way of his aims or interests.

At an Envoys' Conference in July 1979, one session was devoted to the subject of Pakistan's image abroad and similar matters. Ziaul Haq came to the session and sat through it. The Information Minister was a little man with a pointy beard, pot-belly and teeth stained with beetle juice. He told the envoys how they should be going about their job. Ambassadors Mehdi Masud and Anwar Saeed—the latter rather aggressively—pointed out that the difficulty about projecting the country's image abroad was that every five years or so embassies were asked to repudiate everything that had been done by the previous government, the same government whose deeds they had been extolling until then.[5] I said that Pakistani diplomats knew quite well what to say about the country and how to say it, but it was no part of their duties, functions or competence, to enter into issues that were the subject of political debate and controversy within the country, and they should not be required to do so.

In his speech at the UN General Assembly's 1977 session, the head of the Pakistan delegation asserted that the Press in Pakistan was in fact more free under martial law than it had been under Bhutto's rule. A Karachi journalist explained to me the sense in which this was true: there was no 'overt censorship' as such, he said, but Press control was exercised in a subtle and selective manner. Some newspapers of limited circulation were allowed to write whatever they pleased, preaching mainly to the converted. For example, the English language daily *The Muslim*, published from Islamabad and read mostly by the bureaucracy and the diplomatic corps, wrote pretty much what it liked, questioning and criticizing Zia's policies and actions. This enabled many diplomats to report back on the comparative freedom enjoyed by the Press under Martial Law. Newspapers and journals with a wider circulation were more closely watched, but again without being given any express instructions or orders, only a 'friendly telephone call' offering suggestions and guidance if they were getting too far out of line. Only those that were considered congenitally intractable were censored or banned altogether. This was the case with the PPP newspapers.

In reality, control was not always exercised in such subtle ways. In May 1978 four journalists were flogged in Lahore when they went on a hunger strike to protest the closure of the PPP paper *Musawat*. Under-Secretary General Buffum called me in his capacity as the UN official responsible for human rights questions, to seek a 'clarification' of the report. Then one morning some officials of Amnesty International called at the mission to give me a copy of their current report on Pakistan which spoke of flogging as an 'inhumane and degrading' punishment, and also expressed regret that the last part of Bhutto's trial in the Lahore High Court was held in camera. Not without a touch of irony, the report also recalled the complaint made by the Pakistan government in the preceding year—when Bhutto was still Prime Minister—of Amnesty International's alleged bias against the government.

I saw Ziaul Haq nodding at the hometruths he was hearing from the envoys, things with which he couldn't possibly have agreed. In his own summing up, he thanked the envoys for speaking frankly, 'even bluntly', and said: 'We give too much importance to what the world thinks of us and not enough attention to the views of our own people, nor to putting things right. Embassies cannot achieve what the government at home has failed to do.'

Everyone was much impressed—indeed left open-mouthed— by these impeccable sentiments, but then the General himself put things in perspective: 'One cannot change the BBC's mind, but there are unpatriotic Pakistani publications like PPP's London paper, *Millat,* that are printing lies and the envoys must do all they can to discourage them.' Earlier a minister had hinted at how overseas trouble-makers making trouble from the safety of exile abroad, could be discouraged: '... many of these people have relatives here'.

When I met Ziaul Haq again it was during his visit to the UN several years later. He greeted me in a friendly way, and in the course of a brief conversation at the dinner given by Permanent Representative, Sardar Shah Nawaz, said: 'Well, soon we will also have democracy!' In his speech after dinner, he even made a little joke about it: 'I shall have more free time in the future than I have had in recent years, to the great satisfaction of our parliamentarians who have been anxious, as you know, to make sure that I get more time to myself!'

The other good thing that had come Zia's way, thanks to the Afghan War, was renewed American patronage and the resumption of American military and economic aid to the point where Pakistan was the fourth largest recipient in the world. Pakistan was treated now as a country at the front line of the free world, and Zia himself as a champion of freedom, and in Brezhinski's epitaph, the 'architect of the Soviet Union's greatest defeat'.[6] This was a complete turn around from the situation in which Zia had found himself after Bhutto's execution. The PPP, contrary to expectations, had not come apart even though its active workers were flogged in public and Benazir was constantly

in and out of jail or under house arrest. In the world at large
Pakistan's stock was low and Zia himself was shunned. No one
was inviting him to visit and no one of any consequence was
coming to pay visits in Islamabad. I had been asked about
arranging a stopover for him in Paris on the way back from the
non-aligned summit in Havana in September 1979, but I advised
against it. President Giscard d'Estaing had been deeply moved by
Bhutto's death and was vexed that Zia had not responded to his
appeals and had not allowed his emissary, Edgar Faure, to go to
Pakistan.

The Americans were disappointed with Ziaul Haq's
equivocation on the nuclear issue. They had wasted no time, as
soon as Bhutto was toppled, in setting in motion action to bring
Pakistan in line on this issue. The French President sent a special
envoy to Islamabad to suggest a modification of the design of the
reprocessing plant so that it could not produce plutonium. Hard
on the heels of this French proposal, US Ambassador Hummel
came to the Foreign Office and read out a series of demands: no
statement should be made regarding the French envoy's visit;
Pakistan should not go ahead to build the reprocessing plant on
its own (the French having delivered the plans and drawings). If
you do that, the ambassador said, Pakistan will lose the
reprocessing plant as well as the benefits of giving it up. The
Americans recognized that the Zia regime had a serious public
relations problem in this matter, and were therefore not
demanding any overt assurances from Pakistan. The ambassador
wanted Zia's tacit unspoken agreement to an arrangement
whereby France would, acting unilaterally, quietly drop the
project. He also wanted assurance that Pakistan would not go
ahead to build the plant on its own. In this regard too the United
States did not seek an overt and explicit assurance as it had the
means, the ambassador indicated, of determining what Pakistan
was up to.

After trouble broke out in Afghanistan, reports came from
Washington that 'rethinking' was going on within the Carter
administration about Pakistan. In June 1978, Secretary of State
Cyrus Vance came back with answers from President Carter
himself to a set of specific questions that Agha Shahi had put to
Vance. These answers were that: (1) yes, the US did share
Pakistan's concern over Afghanistan, and was sending a high-

level official to Iran and Saudi Arabia to discuss the situation. He
could go on also to Pakistan if we agreed; (2) the territorial
integrity and independence of Pakistan—as of all countries—
were important to the US which gave due importance to its
obligations in this regard under the UN charter and its bilateral
commitments to Pakistan under CENTO; (3) the differences with
Pakistan had arisen over its projected reprocessing plant; if this
question was satisfactorily resolved, the administration would be
able to resume and perhaps enhance economic aid and would
also consider the matter of military sales. This response made it
plain that for the United States, the Afghan situation was only
another lever for pressurizing Pakistan to give up the reprocessing
project—and that even if we did so, no great rewards should be
expected.[7]

In the following year in the face of the worsening situation in
Afghanistan, Pakistan was told that the United States had moved
away from a unidimensional approach to world problems—
meaning, do not expect any cold war favours. George McGhee,
former US ambassador at Ankara and Bonn, told me that the
Carter administration had foreknowledge, through reliable
intelligence reports, of a major Soviet move into Afghanistan,
but did nothing about it. At that stage there was little public
concern in the US over Afghanistan; even Reagan, running for
President and under pressure from the agricultural lobby, had
opposed a retaliatory grain embargo against the Soviet Union.

The Non-Aligned Conference held its summit in Havana in
September 1979. Some time before that, at the foreign minister-
level meeting in Colombo, Pakistan's application to join the
movement had at long last been approved, and the summit
conference provided an interlude in the diplomatic doldrums of
the martial law regime. Havana has a beautiful site, stretching
along the Caribbean sea front. In the bad old days, Havana was a
flesh-pot, a glittering sin city and a playground for the rich and
wicked, run by the Mafia. Castro's revolution had cleaned all that
up and had gone to the other extreme. Now Havana was a dull,
stodgy sort of place. But it was still not puritanical enough for
everyone's taste. One evening the Cubans organized a 'Cultural
Evening'. The affair consisted mainly of uplifting songs about
the achievements of the revolution and comedy routines making
fun of Imperialists, Yankees, the Chinese, and other such droll

characters. But there was a brief and earthy interlude when a bevy of buxom, scantily-clad dancers erupted on the stage, shaking and shimmying. After a moment's stunned pause, the entire Iranian delegation rose together like a flock of startled birds, and gathering up their black robes, fluttered out of the hall.

The ordinary Cubans one talked to, that is, the proverbial taxi-driver and shopkeeper, complained about how things had gone from bad to worse. Generally speaking, the population looked dispirited and a shoddiness, peculiar to 'People's Democracies', hung over everything. Shops exhibited mostly empty shelves. A commodity specially in short supply was news of the outside world as no foreign newspapers were allowed to come in. If one didn't have a transistor radio, one could only read 'revolutionary news' published by the local Press—such as the doings and sayings of Castro, and items like: Comrade Mengistu hails Cuba's Selfless Help to Ethiopia!; Eucalyptus Plantation up in Fraternal Burma! Yemen President opens Youth Centre!

For Ziaul Haq the conference was his first venture on the international stage after he made himself President and hanged Bhutto. Nobody knew how he would be received. It turned out to be Zia's 'coming out party'. He had been agreeably surprised already, he told the delegation of which I was a member, at the warm welcome Castro gave him at the airport, and quite impressed by the man himself. 'Castro isn't as terrible as he is made out to be,' he said. They had talked, among other things, about sugar-cane. Castro said to Ziaul Haq, 'We will show you how to grow better sugar-cane, and you teach us how to make the atom bomb!'[8]

When Ziaul Haq entered the conference hall for the opening session, every Press photographer made a beeline for him, swarming around him, hopping and scrambling and snapping away as if he was a pop star. Ziaul Haq was a celebrity as the man who had hanged Bhutto and was making the Islamic bomb. He was also greeted in a cordial fashion by the heads of state and foreign ministers on nearby seats, and got a warm embrace and a buss on the cheeks by Yasser Arafat whose colleagues had spoken so bitterly about him at the Islamic Foreign Ministers' conference not many months ago. Shahi told me later that back home Zia's fellow generals were very elated by his reception at Havana, and were less inclined than ever to hold elections and give it all away.

Pakistan joined the non-aligned movement as a full member at Havana. The Indian Foreign Minister offered self-congratulatory congratulations: 'The flag of non-alignment flies now over the whole subcontinent!' as if it wasn't India that had moved heaven and earth for years to prevent this from happening. The session was notable for the rifts between various groups and tendencies in the movement. The OPEC and the oil-consuming countries exchanged words. Castro complained that most of the new-found Third World oil wealth was being deposited and invested in industrialized countries while the non-oil producing countries were left to fend for themselves. All the sugar produced by Cuba, he said, couldn't pay for its fuel needs at current prices. President Kaunda of Zambia was reproachful: 'We broke relations with Israel for principles and not for oil, but we see OPEC's billions being channelled into buying hotels and properties in the West and from there into Zionist hands to be used by Israel against the Arabs themselves.'

The major schism was over relations with the Soviet Union. The Cubans were trying to move the non-aligned conference from non-alignment to 'a close and special relationship' with the Soviet Union on the ground that the Soviet Union gave 'selfless support' to non-aligned causes. But Tito was there to foil the attempt. The only surviving founder of the movement, he recalled the memory of all those founding fathers 'who are no longer with us and who had made the non-aligned movement what it was'. He reminded members that the movement had never been a rubber stamp for anyone and must resist attempts to 'insinuate alien interests' into it. He castigated imperialism, colonialism and neo-colonialism but also 'hegemonism'—a code word for Soviet domination.

The Foreign Minister of Senegal was less circumspect and took on Cuba head on. Castro, he said, was ramming through his own pro-Soviet views and decisions on the conference, 'without us, in spite of us, and against us', with the 'mechanical applause and parrot-like speeches' of its claque of supporters. He brought a storm on his head from those who took the remark personally. Kaunda of Zambia admonished 'this young man who insults his elders' and who dared say that they take instructions from others. 'Look at my white head!' he cried indignantly. The Foreign Minister of Benin called his Senegalese colleague the 'devil's advocate', and said that God would punish him; and then remembering that his country had just adopted Marxism-Leninism as its ideology, added a caveat, '...that is, if God exists'.

The Cubans were not the least bit fazed by all the fuss and carried on regardless. Castro thundered, 'When Cuba speaks, let the miserable rats [anyone who held a different opinion] remain silent.' The way they handled things was simplicity itself. There was the bitterly fought question over the Cambodian seat, and the question was who should sit in it: the representative of the Soviet-supported Vietnam puppet, or that of the unspeakable and bloodthirsty Pol Pot regime favoured by the majority? The Cuban Chairman of the Political Committee proposed as a 'compromise' (but only because the Soviet-sponsored Cambodian was going to lose) that the seat be kept vacant, and invited the views of the Committee on the subject. Fifteen out of sixteen members having opposed the Chairman's proposal, he ruled that the consensus was in favour of *his* proposal on the basis of consultations he had held outside the Committee room. Then he banged the gavel and adjourned the meeting before any of the dumbfounded members could open their mouths. The ASEAN and other Asian members made a commotion in the corridors, sputtering and fuming, and held a meeting under the chairmanship of President Jayawardene of Sri Lanka, to consider how to cope with the Cuban parliamentary style, and could find no answer to the problem.

Castro dominated the conference by his sheer presence. An impressive figure, big and broad shouldered, his bushy beard gave him the appearance of a biblical prophet or an extra in a Western movie. His voice was stentorian and his manner domineering. But he had charm and could leaven his dogmatism with irony, as in an interview that I read at the time in *The New York Times*:

> President Castro, what explains your enormous energy and dynamism?
> Appearances!
> Is it true you are fifty years old?
> That is an imperialist fabrication. I am only twice twenty-five!

His stamina was as prodigious as was his determination to get his own way in the conference by hook or by crook. He was in the Chair throughout, always puffing at a huge cigar, and never missed a cue even in meetings that went on all night. His speeches were unabashedly partisan, full of extravagant praise for the Soviet Union and for Vietnam, and attacks on China as an ally of Yankee imperialism, of the Shah in Iran and of Pinochet in Chile. However on the matter of Afghanistan he was strangely circumspect; the only reference he made to it was to welcome it as a new member of the socialist fraternity. He did not say anything in praise of the Afghan revolution, or to justify and laud the Soviet Union's intervention. He refrained from making any direct or indirect criticism of Pakistan. I thought that this was not accidental, and together with Cuba's generally friendly attitude to Pakistan at the conference, it may have been intended to signal the Soviet Union's desire not to burn its bridges with Pakistan over Afghanistan.

Afghanistan

Ziaul Haq had taken a leap into the dark over the Bhutto case, but Afghanistan proved to be his parachute. The Afghan events were discussed at the July 1979 Envoys' Conference in Islamabad. There was a good deal of talk about Russia's 'grand design', its thrust to the warm waters, and the threat to the oil supplies of the free world. My views were not on all fours with this time-honoured line of thought. I was of the view that much had changed since Peter the Great worried about Russia's ice-bound coastline, and there were shorter ways to the oil lifelines of the Gulf than through Afghanistan. The trouble in Afghanistan had its roots in the familiar Third World syndrome of poverty, social injustice, and arbitrary government, complicated in Afghanistan's case by tribal, ethnic, linguistic, and other tensions. It had been brewing for a long time independently of the Soviet Union's aims and designs. The regime's Marxist label too had to be viewed against this background, and it was too early to treat Afghanistan as having gone irretrievably into the Soviet camp.

Soviet support for the *coup* came from mixed motives. They no doubt feared that the direction in which Daud was taking Afghanistan, including a definitive reconciliation with Pakistan, would erode Soviet influence in Afghanistan and open up the prospect of an anti-Soviet bloc stretching from Pakistan through

Afghanistan into Iran and perhaps beyond. Daud's Foreign
Minister Wahid Abdullah, talking to me in New York, blamed
Pakistan for not having moved fast enough in giving effect to the
preliminary agreement reached between Bhutto and Daud. He
said that during his visit to Kabul the year before, Bhutto had
promised to release Wali Khan, Bizenjo and other political
prisoners, but had delayed matters until after the election. It was
a great mistake on Bhutto's part to have arrested these leaders,
Wahid Abdullah said, and was the beginning of his problems. He
affirmed that the Balochis and Pathans did not want to secede
but only to enjoy in practice the autonomy given to them by the
Constitution in principle. The Afghan Foreign Minister assured
me that Daud was not out to break up Pakistan; if he had wanted
to, Pakistan's crisis was a good opportunity for Afghanistan to
make a try.

For Pakistan the danger came from Moscow, and to my mind,
we had therefore to try to come to terms with the Soviet Union.
Those who saw in the Afghan crisis above all an opportunity to
get back into America's good books, need not have feared that a
settlement with the Soviets would preclude an approach to
Washington. It could on the contrary add a chip to Pakistan's
bargaining position. I discounted the danger of direct military
intervention by the Soviet Union in Afghanistan, because, I
argued, no vital Soviet interests were at stake in that country; it
would be bad for them in the non-aligned world and would be
the end of their idea of an Asian collective security arrangement;
it would put more steam into the Sino-American *rapprochement*;
and all that to gain what? Only a foothold in a country where
they were already fairly well-entrenched and which presented no
great intrinsic strategic interest. My conclusions as to Soviet
intentions proved to be wrong, as shortly afterwards Soviet tanks
trundled into Kabul. But my analysis was not too far off the
mark, and in due course the Soviets realized that they had made
a fatal mistake in invading Afghanistan. Perhaps I should have
sent a transcript of my remarks to Moscow!

Soon after the Envoys' meeting of 1979, I left the Foreign
Service to join the UN and was no longer concerned with Afghan
policy. In Beirut where I was posted by the United Nations, they
had their own worries and there wasn't much news of Afghan
developments in the local media. But I did follow things from a

distance and through occasional meetings with people involved
in the issue. In Pakistan, Zia's critics accused him of having stirred
up the Afghan trouble because he profited from it, and of
tailoring the Afghan policy to serve his own ends. In point of
fact, at the outbreak of the Afghan trouble, Ziaul Haq had reacted
to it in a restrained manner. Pakistan gave recognition to Taraki's
coup, and Zia held a meeting with him in Havana at which
apparently there was some meeting of minds. He did not grasp
at the $400 million carrot held out by Jimmy Carter, and he kept
his head in the face of Soviet threats. Objectively speaking, his
response to the Afghan crisis at the start was, by and large, the
right one. Over all, he showed grit and a cool head. If
Afghanistan's domestic upheaval turned into a major cold war
conflict, it was not because of anything Pakistan or Zia personally
did, but because the Soviets themselves completely misjudged
the situation. Eventually, the Afghan crisis did bring dividends to
Zia, far beyond anything he could have hoped for, but at that
early stage when Pakistan stood alone in the face of the Soviet
threat and a rising flood of refugees from Afghanistan, nobody
could have foreseen that Soviet cold war policy was going to
meet its nemesis in Afghanistan and that Pakistan's Chief Martial
Law Administrator would emerge as a champion of the free
world!

It is difficult to find a rational explanation of why the Soviets,
disregarding the lessons of history, blundered into Afghanistan.
Moscow apparently had not consulted its Warsaw Pact allies about
the move, and some of them learned about the Soviet invasion
from the newspapers. Most of them disapproved because they
felt that the Soviet Union was stepping beyond the spheres of
influence agreed upon at Yalta and creating a bad precedent.
Nor apparently was there consensus within the Soviet Union itself
about the move. Vassily Safronchuk, Under-Secretary General at
the UN, who had been the Soviet Union's deputy satrap in Kabul
at the time, put it down to the advice of the local Soviet
representatives in Afghanistan, who out of 'stupidity and hubris',
had misled Moscow and led it up the garden path. An early
signal of the minefield it had walked into, was Hafizullah Amin's
coup. According to Safronchuk, who knew him well, Amin was a
man driven by ambition and thirst for power. But the Soviets also
saw him as a Tito-like personality who would follow a policy of

playing off China and the USSR against each other, as soon as he had consolidated his power. Such a turn would endanger the whole Soviet position in Afghanistan, and they were determined not to allow Hafizullah Amin to stay in power.

Safronchuk said that Hafizullah's relations with the Soviets were tense from the beginning, and told me of an incident that showed how matters stood. There was bad blood between President Taraki and Amin who was Prime Minister. The Soviet Ambassador proposed a meeting between the two of them in his presence at Taraki's house in order to patch things up. Amin refused, saying he feared for his life at the President's house. The ambassador was indignant, 'Are you suggesting that the Afghan Prime Minister is to be killed in the presence of the Soviet Ambassador and that the ambassador is to be an accomplice in the act?' In the end Amin was badgered into agreeing to go to the meeting. A little after the appointed hour, as the ambassador and Taraki waited for him to arrive, Hafizullah Amin's motorcade was heard entering the palace grounds. (It seemed that Amin went everywhere in a motorcade with armed guards preceding and following his car.) Suddenly shots rang out and there was an exchange of fire for several minutes. Soon some guards came running in and said that firing had broken out as soon as Amin's motorcade entered the gate. No one could tell where the shots came from or who started the shooting. Amin's car had turned round as fast as it could and had gone back.

Next morning, all East European diplomatic envoys were summoned to the Foreign Ministry and were informed of what had happened by Foreign Secretary Shah Wali who went on to accuse the Soviet Union of having set a trap for Amin. Safronchuk who had gone to the meeting on behalf of his ambassador, said he walked out of the meeting in protest. In due course, Hafizullah died in the same palace in a hail of bullets. Safronchuk acknowledged that Hafizullah was killed in a shoot-out there, but he would neither confirm nor deny that, as rumoured, Soviet officers were present when it happened. However the circumstances of the earlier incident recounted by Safronchuk do point the finger at Soviet involvement.

I met Hafizullah Amin when he came to the UN as head of the Afghan delegation to the General Assembly in 1978. In his speech he called for a solution of the political problem with Pakistan on the basis of 'the will of the Pashtoon and Baloch people.' Agha Shahi and I went to see him and to find out what exactly he meant. He said to us, 'The Afghan revolution was a real revolution and not a *coup d'etat* like Daud's.' His references to Pakistan, he explained, reflected the agreed policy of the revolution and were meant to be friendly. Afghanistan wanted a peaceful and permanent settlement with Pakistan, he told us, and added, 'Daud was not sincere in his approach to Pakistan.' He said, 'We don't intend to start any trouble with Pakistan nor to go beyond what I said in the General Assembly unless Pakistan's actions and words push us into doing so.' Amin was suave and amicable in manner, but one could sense the toughness underneath the veneer and a note of threat in the soft-spoken words. It was plain that this man could be bad news for Pakistan; on the other hand, if he was looking for a deal with China, then he must have been willing to include Pakistan in it. Thus his enigmatic words left open various possibilities.

In the early eighties there were indications that the Soviets might consider a pull-out from Afghanistan given certain conditions. At an international seminar in Aspen, Colorado, a senior Polish official suggested that the Soviets might be ready to withdraw their forces within the framework of a general agreement to neutralize Afghanistan and provide guarantees against Chinese intervention in Afghanistan and US intervention in Iran. I discussed the subject with him afterwards, and asked if Poland could play a role in bringing about a settlement. He said, 'The Russians are very touchy about receiving advice from anyone on their Afghan venture', but that President Gierek had discussed the subject with Ziaul Haq when they met in Belgrade on the occasion of Tito's funeral. After they had got rid of Hafizullah and the danger of his doing a China finesse had been removed, the Russians themselves apparently put out hints that if Pakistan would recognize Babrak Karmal, there could be a deal involving Afghan recognition of the Durand Line. In 1984, at a dinner at the UN in New York, Ziaul Haq told me about his talk with Andropov at the Kremlin and the latter's keenness to settle the Afghan issue. 'He wants Pakistan to help in the matter,' Ziaul Haq said.

When I reported my conversation with the Polish official, Academician Szcepansky, to Foreign Secretary Shahnawaz, he confirmed that Gierek had talked to Ziaul Haq but that when Agha Shahi was sent to Warsaw to follow up, the Polish President was unable to meet him. This was not surprising, the Poles being immersed very much at the time in their own problems at home and with the Soviets. The matter could have been pursued through other channels. What I found surprising in the Foreign Secretary's letter was a sort of 'immobilism' and a reliance on diplomatic gimmickry such as resolutions of the Islamic Standing Committee. 'We do not exclude limited Soviet strikes against Pakistan,' he wrote but went on, 'our best option is to continue with the OIC Standing Committee's initiative and ensure world-wide support as a deterrent.' Rather a thin reed to lean on, I thought, sitting in Beirut where Arab League and Islamic and other committees and their initiatives bloomed and died like desert flowers. As a senior Pakistani ambassador put it to me at the time, we were 'drifting on Afghanistan', and nobody knew quite what to do other than to go on asking one international forum and another to call for the withdrawal of Soviet troops.

I do not know whether any serious attempt was made by Islamabad to explore the possibilities of compromise and the Soviet peace feelers received from various quarters. A settlement then might have spared Afghanistan much of the travail it suffered in the years that followed and that did not end with the Soviet withdrawal in 1989. It would also have spared Pakistan the many woes and evils including drugs and gunrunning that afflicted the country as it became increasingly enmeshed in the war.

Of course, it is a moot point whether an acceptable compromise was in fact available—a compromise that would be acceptable not only to Pakistan, but also to the Afghan refugees and armed factions present in increasing numbers in Pakistan, and to the major powers, namely, China and the United States, who had become involved in the issue. On the whole there may have been an even chance of finding a settlement. The mujahideen might have resisted a settlement which allowed a role to the PDP, but they did not jib in 1988 when Ziaul Haq put forward his proposal for an interim government composed of equal thirds of the mujahideen, the PDP and 'intellectuals'—viz., King Zahir Shah's men. Moreover, they could hardly have rejected a settlement that was backed by Pakistan and would lead to the withdrawal of foreign troops from their country. As for China, after a visit to Beijing, Ziaul Haq told the Foreign Office that the Chinese leaders had said to him that Pakistan should go ahead and normalize relations with Russia as they didn't expect them to attack Pakistan physically; nor did they expect India to do so and they didn't mind at all if we normalized relations with India.

In parenthesis it is worth noting that at the time India was being relatively circumspect with regard to Afghanistan. In Delhi there was the right-wing Hindu government of the BJP, and contrary to conventional wisdom, in general it displayed a more accommodating attitude towards Pakistan than the secular Congress. There was no reference to 'Pashtoonistan' in the joint communiqué issued at the end of Foreign Minister Vajpayee's visit to Kabul after the *coup*. He had spoken there in terms that seemed indirectly to accept the Durand Line as Pakistan's western border. The Indian Foreign Secretary told his Pakistani counterpart, Sardar Shahnawaz, that India would not react adversely to any steps Pakistan considered necessary to ensure her security *vis-á-vis* Afghanistan. However such rationality was unaccustomed in India-Pakistan relations, and one could not accept the Indian gestures at face value. The situation in Afghanistan was volatile, and Pakistan itself faced an uncertain prospect. India could not be expected to foreclose its options, if an opportunity occurred to profit from it.

The crucial position was that of the United States, and this had undergone a complete change with Carter's exit and Reagan's election. The nuclear issue was put on the shelf—momentarily—for Afghanistan was the Vietnam of the Soviets, and Reagan was not going to allow them to be let off the hook. With American economic and military aid beginning to flow, the Martial Law regime was acquiring a vested interest in the Afghan War, and in time developed rather grand concepts of the shape of things after a successful conclusion of the war—the Oxus River as the strategic frontier of Pakistan, and a vast area of 'strategic consensus' extending from Pakistan through Afghanistan and Iran to Turkey. Such pipe dreams seemed to have clouded the view of policy-makers who gave no thought to exploring the possibilities offered by the new situation of finding a solution to the Kashmir dispute, or settling the Durand Line problem and the difference with the United States over the nuclear question. In line with the religious turn given to everything in Zia's time, the Afghan struggle too became a religious war, a Jihad, with its own theological rules and tactics and strategy and purposes, that could scarcely be discussed in ordinary terms. Zia built up the military capability of like-minded Afghan groups and factions, so that after the war was won, Afghanistan would be not only Pakistan's strategic hinterland, but the Martial Law regime's political hinterland. Americans were content to play the game by Zia's rules and went along with the special momentum and direction that he was giving to the war. In these circumstances, the idea of a compromise was far from any one's mind. Speaking to me in 1984 about the UN mediator's efforts, Secretary General Pérez de Cuéllar told me of his impression that neither the United States nor the Ziaul Haq regime seemed to have an interest, each for its own reasons, in seeking an Afghan settlement at that stage.

The Soviet administration fell into weak and unsure hands, and as one sick and dying leader succeeded another, this showed up, as often happens, in a hardening of the Soviet position. In July 1984, Pérez de Cuéllar told me that during a visit to Moscow, he had discussed Afghanistan with President Chernenko who read out what he had to say on the subject from a piece of paper that had been written for him (to make sure, given his state of health, that he got it right). Banging both fists on the table, Chernenko said to the Secretary General that there was no question of Soviet troops leaving Afghanistan and letting China and the US have the run of the place. Pakistan would *have* to talk directly to the Karmal regime, the Soviet leader asserted, if there were to be serious negotiations.

The Soviets lost the Afghan War and doubtless, that was one of the factors in the calamitous loss of self-confidence that overtook the Soviet system. But the Afghans did not win it. Pakistan gained no lasting benefit out of its support to the Afghan struggle. The US and the rest of the West washed their hands off the affair and went away. This was one war that everybody lost.

The Peace Accords, painstakingly worked out by the UN over years of negotiations in Geneva, left many loose ends.[9] On the eve of signing the Accords, Prime Minister Junejo told me that they had omitted to make a provision in the agreement for the

Soviets to stop supplying arms to Kabul. This was then taken care of in an exchange of letters between the US and the Soviet Union by which the latter accepted the idea of 'symmetry' whereby either both sides would have to stop supplying arms to their respective allies, or both may continue to do so. But how was this to be squared with the provision that Pakistan would prevent arms supplies from reaching the Mujahideen?

Junejo asked me if at the UN people believed that Gorbachev really meant what he was saying about quitting Afghanistan. There was a hard-line Western view that he was only trying to divide the free world and get its guard down. My view was that objective conditions and Gorbachov's reform platform made it necessary for the Soviet Union to disengage from Afghanistan, but that he would extract a price, more from the United States perhaps than from Pakistan. As for Pakistan, my assessment was that once the Afghan issue was settled, we may find ourselves facing more problems from our American ally than from the Soviets as the nuclear issue would then quickly move back to the top of the agenda and Pakistan having no lobby in Washington, other than the Afghan lobby, would have to fend for itself.

Ziaul Haq was opposing the signing of the Geneva Accords for reasons of his own, but Junejo, who had decided to sign, finessed him by calling a Round Table of all political parties and getting their approval to go ahead. Benazir went too, after making sure that Ziaul Haq wouldn't be at the table. In her statement she called (echoing Ziaul Haq on this one point) for establishing an interim government in Kabul and also asked that a settlement of the Durand Line question should be negotiated as part of the Geneva settlement. Both proposals were, on the face of it, essential components of a general Afghan settlement, but unfortunately, were not included in the Geneva Accords.

For Benazir there was a domestic aspect to Junejo's Round Table. She saw it as useful at that stage to strengthen Junejo's hands *vis-à-vis* Ziaul Haq, and to try to widen the gulf between them. She said to Junejo, 'We want *you* to be the voice of Pakistan in the negotiations on Afghanistan.'

The tussle between Zia and Junejo (*muka-dhaki* in the words of the Indian Ambassador) had intensified and become common knowledge. Zia had picked the relatively unknown Muhammad Khan Junejo to be Prime Minister, expecting him to be docile and do what he was told (rather the same reasons for which he himself had been picked as Army Chief by Bhutto). Moreover, it seems that there was an unwritten understanding when Zia restored parliamentary government, that the subjects of Foreign Affairs, Defence and Intelligence would remain Zia's exclusive domain. Now Junejo was gradually getting a grip on things and tried to assert to the full his powers under the Constitution. However the situation remained inherently contradictory since Zia continued to hold the post of Chief of Army Staff—a situation that was clearly contrary to the Constitutional provision forbidding any person from holding two offices of profit at the same time.[10] A sympathetic American correspondent suggested that by retaining the job of Army Chief, Zia was forestalling a *coup* by another ambitious general, and thus really protecting democracy!

I called on Junejo in Karachi shortly after his appointment as Prime Minister. A tall, lanky, soft-spoken and sad-eyed man, one could picture him as a Don Quixote tilting at the roof-top wind-catchers of lower Sindh. He was not articulate and had a somewhat diffident air, but he made up for this by an innate dignity. He would soon show that he did not lack self-confidence. He became animated in talking to me about the advent of democracy and other recent developments. Martial Law was as good as gone, he said; the 1973 Constitution and fundamental rights stood restored; the civilian government was fully in control, there was no division of power. I congratulated him for the way he was handling a most delicate situation and added, 'The train is being pulled by two engines, let us hope both will pull in the same direction.'

'Yes indeed that was true for a while,' he said, 'but now we have uncoupled the second engine.'

But then, what about the Eighth Amendment? 'Oh, that has no practical effect', Junejo claimed; with the lifting of the State of Emergency—which, he reminded me, had remained in force since the 1965 War and throughout Bhutto's Prime Ministership—people could go to Court to obtain relief and get redress. It all sounded a little blithe and too good to be true, but Junejo apparently wasn't just whistling in the dark; that is how he intended to, and in effect did try, to play the game with Ziaul Haq.

However Zia who 'gave' Pakistan democracy had done so on the principle that 'He who giveth can also take it away', and that was the underlying purpose of the Eighth Amendment.[11] In its decision on Mustafa Khar's petition against his detention under a Martial Law order, the Lahore High Court held that the Eighth Amendment indemnified and validated all ordinances and laws promulgated under Martial Law, but not all the acts of omission or commission performed thereunder, if any of these were done without proper authority and jurisdiction, showed malice or violated constitutional provisions. Self-evident, one would think, but in the prevailing circumstances it was considered a 'historic judgement'. The sad fact is that Pakistan's constitutional history is strewn with such historic judgements, each contradicting the previous one, a process of which the Lahore judgement itself gave a mournful summary.

At a seminar in Lahore a participant raised the following question: 'We rightly blame the generals for usurping power, but what should be said about the role of our Establishment and in particular the judiciary, which has always found some legalistic basis for the actions of the usurpers?' The Judges answered for themselves. The Lahore decision cited the Supreme Court's judgment in the Asma Gillani case against Yahya Khan's Martial Law in which Justice Yaqub Ali had expressed the judiciary's dilemma:

> ...my own view is that a person who destroys the national legal order in an illegitimate manner cannot be regarded as a valid source of law-making. Maybe that on account of his hold on the coercive apparatus of State and the people, the courts are silenced temporarily, but let it be laid down firmly that the order which the usurper imposes will remain illegal and courts will not recognize its rules and act upon them *de jure*. As soon as the first opportunity arises, when the coercive apparatus falls from the hands of the usurper, he should be tried for high treason and suitably punished.

But then meanwhile?

It would not be long before the courts were once again face to face with the dilemma. This time the Supreme Court did not reverse the judgment given against Yahya Khan, but in order to dismiss Nusrat Bhutto's petition against Zia's Martial Law, had

recourse to a so-called Doctrine of Necessity. Discussing the
decision with me, an eminent judge of one of our High Courts
who was visiting New York at the time, took a pragmatic line.
Once an authority was *effectively* established, he said, no court in
the world could hold such an authority to be illegal, however it
may have been established. So what is the point, I asked, of
having a Constitution that lays down how legitimate authority
should be established and exercised? His justification was that at
least the courts remain in existence and can provide some
redress. The point of the learned Judge's reasoning was that
respect for form is not without importance. But if institutions no
longer protect freedoms and legality, what good is form and
procedure except as a charade and to provide justification for
their infringement. The Supreme Court had not only provided
legitimacy to Zia's *coup* but had given him the authority to amend
the Constitution at will.

The man who appeared in the case on behalf of the regime
was Pakistan's famous constitutional lawyer, A.K. Brohi. He
should have been pleased with the decision, but was not, and
explained to me the reason why when he came to New York a
few days after the Court's judgment. He had set out his views on
the matter more fully and cogently in a letter to Ziaul Haq, a
copy of which he gave me. The reason for his unhappiness was
that the Court had treated Zia's *coup* as a 'constitutional
deviation' justifiable under the 'Doctrine of Necessity', whereas
the view he had urged on the Court was that the declaration of
Martial Law had created a new legal order in which the Chief
Martial Law Administrator was the fountainhead of all legality.
This was the famous Kelsen Doctrine cited by Justice Munir to
legitimize Governor-General Ghulam Muhammad's *coup*, which
was the first of Pakistan's many 'new legal orders', and this was
the same Brohi who had argued the opposite thesis in the case
against Yahya Khan, the fallen fountainhead of one of these!

As to the Doctrine of Necessity, Brohi said that the principle
of necessity was one that renders lawful what would otherwise be
unlawful. It was not unknown to English law in which there is a
defence of necessity, albeit of uncertain scope in criminal and
constitutional law. Its application in the case of Martial Law was
but an extended application of the same concept(!). But the
necessity must be proportionate to the evil to be averted, and

acceptance of the principle did not normally imply total abdication or acquiescence in the suppression of the legal order since it was essentially a transient phenomenon.

This sounded like a criticism of Ziaul Haq's action in suspending the Constitution and taking over the government. But really what bothered him, Brohi pointed out in his letter, was that the 1973 Constitution would still remain the law of the land, and the Superior Courts would retain the power of judicial review. This decision, he said solicitously, might make the CMLA's powers to issue orders and regulations 'somewhat vulnerable' to the opinion of the Courts on whether or not they were commensurate with the objectives of the 'necessity' that had impelled him to act.

He need not have worried. Among the first things that Ziaul Haq did was to put the judges in their place by having them take a new oath—an oath that implicitly was a repudiation of the one they had taken to uphold the Constitution. Justice Anwarul Haq who had given the CMLA the right to amend the Constitution, indulged in a bit of heroics by refusing to take the oath. Ziaul Haq did not take it amiss and put him up as Pakistan's candidate in the elections for the International Court of Justice. Before the election I saw the man standing by himself in a corner of the Delegates' Lounge of the United Nations, where he had come personally to lobby his candidacy. In the election too his isolation was conspicuous: he received one vote, that of Pakistan.

But Brohi did have a point to make. Accusing the lordships of indulging in mock heroics, he held that their stand faced the country with something worse than executive tyranny. By taking it upon itself to decide what action of the Martial Law regime was or was not justified by the original 'necessity', the Court had opened the way to judicial despotism, against which there was no recourse or remedy. Brohi explained to me that in case there was discontent with a decision of a ruler, whether a democratically elected prime minister or a dictator, the people can come out on the streets and agitate against it; if the movement was strong enough, the government might give way. But a decision of the supreme judicial authority of the country is final, no appeal lies against it and no amount of public discontent can affect it. Subsequently the principle of judicial despotism was institutionalized by Ziaul Haq when he granted virtually absolute powers to the Federal Shariat Court (restricted only by the right of appeal to the Supreme Court) to strike down any law that it considered to be inconsistent with Islam—even one that might have been adopted by the unanimous vote of the National Assembly. It is argued that these powers and functions are no different from the United States' Supreme Court's power of review and interpretation. But this is a fallacious analogy. When the US Supreme Court rules that a law or government decision is incompatible with the Constitution, there is nothing to prevent the Congress from amending the Constitution itself. The Shariat Court (together with the Supreme Court in appeal) on the other hand has been given the responsibility of interpreting the word of God. Their decision is therefore final and absolute by definition, and not subject to amendment by any human agency. A handful of men, and behind them the one man who appoints them, are thus invested with the quasi-divine power to make and unmake laws in their own lights and interests over the heads, and in disregard of the will of the elected representatives of the people.

In 1986, with the Constitution restored, even though it was mutilated by Zia's amendment, Zia was sailing in unfamiliar waters and soon his navigation began to falter. He was furious at criticism coming from within his own creation, the semi-appointed Majlis-i-Shoora: 'I won't have my own cat growling at me!' Junejo was nibbling away at what Zia considered as his prerogatives and trying to build a power base by 'revitalizing' the Muslim League with a progressive liberal-sounding programme, bravely devised by technocrat Sartaj Aziz. But it was rather a desperate mission to build a viable political party on the foundations of the Pagaro group, a splinter of a mutant of an offspring of the original All India Muslim League of Jinnah, which itself, but for him and some of the higher leadership, was led by a patchwork of special interest groups, feudal landlords, pseudo-socialists and Empire loyalists. Meanwhile, over the years the Muslim League had become a political foster mother willing to lend its persona to every military regime. The magic of the brand name!

The first reef Zia struck was the Ojhri[12] disaster in which a munitions dump, situated between the twin cities of Rawalpindi and Islamabad, blew up killing and maiming thousands of persons in both cities. Ziaul Haq's reaction was almost nonchalant; on television he appeared at a loss for the right words to say, the appropriate demeanor to adopt, and seemed strangely disconnected with reality. (Americans, on the other hand, were impressed, in the words of the Consul-General in Karachi, with the 'awesome' stability of Pakistan noting that there had been no protest demos, no demands for heads to roll, no outcry against the Afghan policy.)

Then Zia really ran aground by dismissing Junejo, for now, unless he was to carry out a *coup* against his own system and himself, he was obliged to order fresh elections. But actually the turning point in Zia's fortunes had come even earlier when, with a view to securing his own position, before restoring the limited democracy he was preparing to concede, he held a referendum. The one loaded question the voters were required to answer was whether they were in favour of Islam, and hence of Ziaul Haq's programme to Islamize the country. The question had to be answered with a 'Yes' or a 'No', and answered as a whole. The corollary was that a 'Yes' answer would mean that Ziaul Haq stood elected, *ipso facto*, President for another five years.

Zia declared, 'You have the freedom to say "No" *in* the referendum and to say "No" *to* the referendum.' In smaller print on the same page of the newspaper carrying this declaration was a single column headline stating that five persons were held for opposing the referendum!

Ziaul Haq engaged in the unfamiliar activity of electioneering, going to all four provinces, donning the local costume, and finding something to say in the local language. I watched on TV his visit to Sindh—looking not very convincing in embroidered Sindhi cap and an *ajrak*,[13] and opening his speech with some carefully rehearsed words in Sindhi about how truly great the province of Sindh was, how deep its devotion to Islam, and how very much everyone loved Sindh.

In Karachi, Zia revealed his four-point programme on TV for solving the country's problems: (1) the path of Allah; (2) the precepts of the Holy Koran; (3) Islam's greater glory; and (4) Pakistan's stability. Nothing was said about such little details as the eighty per cent illiteracy, the galloping population growth, the spreading drug addiction. 'People ask,' he said, 'what are your qualifications for the job of President?' And piously he responded: 'My answer, in the words of the song we have just heard, is that I am the mendicant of Muhammad!' (gada-i-Mustafa). The official claque that is always present at these occasions raised 'full-throated' cries of 'Mard-i-Momin, Mard-i-Haq, Ziaul Haq! Ziaul Haq! [Oh righteous man, oh man of truth! Oh, Ziaul Haq!]' One had the impression that unconsciously, Zia was trying to emulate Bhutto's populist style, in the same way that Bhutto had in some ways, tried to adopt some of the military panache of his predecessor, Ayub Khan.

It was assumed generally that Zia had the referendum all sewed up with his ten million vote bank of armed forces personnel and government employees, all of whom had received formal orders to vote, the local councillors, the mullahs, the numerous monitors (nazimeen) he had appointed to check if everyone was saying their prayers. To make doubly sure, Zia decided at the last moment that voters would not need to produce their ID cards in order to vote. But when the day dawned and the referendum got underway, like a ship launching gone awry, it immediately bogged down in the mud swamps of public cynicism and indifference.

I happened to be in Karachi on home leave, and with some friends and family went round polling stations in various parts of the city to see how things were going. Everywhere it was the same desultory picture. Under marquees erected outside polling stations, one for men and another one for women, yawning officials sat on plain tables handing out little chits to voters. Except that there were no voters to speak of. The officials beckoned, like merchants in an oriental bazaar, to every passer-by to please come in and vote. Our chauffeur Ayub— member of the Jamaat-i-Islami, a Nazim-i-Salatin (monitor of prayers)—wore a fine beard, and was an altogether model example of the New Islamic Man of Zia's professed ideals, but even he did not think much of the referendum or that it would do anything for the greater glory of Islam.

BBC's evening bulletin remarked upon the very thin turn-out of voters and reports of extensive fraud and malpractice. Trouble was reported from Lahore and some other cities, where the police had made baton-charges against protesting crowds. But Pakistan Television carried shots of massive crowds at polling stations and estimated that Zia would get ninety-eight per cent—the time-honoured percentage in such exercises—of the vote for his policies and person. Zia himself appeared on TV in due course and, in order of priority, thanked his five comrade generals, the army as a whole ('My only constituency') and the Civil Services for the sweeping mandate he pretended to have received in the referendum.

Ziaul Haq was putting a brave face on the outcome of the referendum. Perhaps he wasn't really surprised by it. For him it had provided what he wanted—a legal basis, however contrived—for continuing as President. But in the long view it weakened his position by exposing to 'his only constituency', the officers and the rank and file of the armed forces, how slight was the popular base of their chief.

On the surface all was well, American aid and weapons were flowing in as never before, and the economy was picking up according to World Bank figures. But the credibility of the government and what it said and did was almost non-existent. A. K. Brohi said to me (though not about the Ziaul Haq regime of which he was a fervent admirer), 'In Pakistan never believe anything until it is officially denied.' The country's institutions were being eroded by this loss of public faith and Ziaul Haq's ill-conceived measures to give them a so-called 'Islamic' orientation.

When I was in Beirut, Faiz Ahmad Faiz who was editing a PLO literary revue from there, used to drop in from time to time for a chat. In March 1982, back from a visit to Pakistan and a meeting with Ziaul Haq, he made an analysis of the situation that was almost prophetic. He said that Islamization had only meant the weakening and destruction of existing institutions insofar as they interfered with Zia's liberty of action. Zia had dropped all pretence of restoring democracy and was, in effect, telling politicians, 'Come and get it if you can'. Politicians were in disarray and did not know what to do. But the nature of politics was changing in Pakistan; the old political leadership was lost in the wilderness and had little following among the people whose basic concerns were economic and social. In Lahore 20,000 village school teachers had staged a protest demonstration at their plight—the fact that these simple folk, ill-shod and wearing patched clothes, were able to get together in such a large number and organize a protest in the face of all the bans and rigours of martial law, was a portent in Faiz's eyes.

Faiz said that rebelliousness was taking roots in the peoples' minds and the country's social norms. Bhutto had exposed the inequities and fundamental disorders in Pakistan's society. He had awakened ordinary people to their rights and changed their attitudes. But he had not done much to change things: the institutions and structures remained the same. Army rule over the years and specially the current spell under Zia, without changing anything, had removed or weakened the buffers—the elected legislative bodies, trade unions and the free Press—that stood between the established order and social revolt or anarchy. Ziaul Haq was now out to destroy all political parties; if he succeeded, eventually there would remain nothing between the rule of the gun and mob rule.

Faiz also told me how he was held up by Immigration at the airport because he was on their Exit Control List. It took twenty-four hours to sort things out. Meanwhile he stayed with the Chief Minister, Mir Rasul Baksh Talpur. They spent the evening over a bottle of whiskey, notwithstanding the Islamic regime of which the Chief Minister was a pillar. It was a heartening illustration of the paradox and eccentricity that redeems and mitigates things in Pakistan, even under an ideological Martial Law regime!

When I took leave to return to New York after the first meeting with him, Zia said to me, 'If you have any problems or want to talk about anything, please call me directly. I am really a simple man!' It was a condescending remark but he meant it literally. I took him at his word, and when the *babus* at the Ministry of Culture tried to throw a spanner in the works of a UNESCO project to save the 5,000 year-old Mohenjo-Daro ruins, I called him on the telephone about it. He was as good as his word and authorized me on the spot to go ahead and sign the accord with UNESCO.

But Zia was far from being a simple man though he had unassuming manners. Like Bhutto, he evoked the most conflicting reactions among those who knew him. Many saw him as perfidious, opportunistic, two-faced, crafty, and sadistic. Others lauded his piety, humility and courtesy. He had no outward arrogance—unless one saw a sort of reverse arrogance in his somewhat self-conscious humility. Thus he made it a point to see off visitors, high or low, to their cars—but there seemed something a little demonstrative and excessive about the gesture.

Ziaul Haq undoubtedly had personal charm and made a favourable impression on many of those he met. Secretary-General Pérez de Cuéllar after his first meeting with Ziaul Haq on a trip to Pakistan, said to me in a tone of pleasant surprise, as if he had expected to meet an ogre, 'But your General is really a very agreeable person.' When I accompanied a mission to Pakistan, led by the Chairman of the UN anti-Apartheid Committee, Nigeria's Ambassador Joseph Garba, Zia bowled him over by personally arranging some portions of his trip and letting him use the President's helicopter to facilitate his visit. He asked people about the welfare of their families, showed concern for the problems of individuals and was considerate in small ways.

'One may smile and smile and yet be a villain!' said Hamlet of his dissimulating uncle, the usurper king. But one thinks rather of Iago in considering Ziaul Haq's gratuitous and limitless animus against the man to whom he had every reason to be grateful. There was something incomprehensible in the implacable vindictiveness with which he pursued Bhutto and Bhutto's family. However, unlike Iago's mischief, Zia's malice against Bhutto was not entirely unmotivated nor was it wholly personal. Bhutto had an overweening air and sometimes deliberately humiliated and put down people. Quite possibly Bhutto may have done so, knowingly or otherwise, to Zia whose obsequious and ingratiating ways made him an obvious target. But it went beyond personal considerations; Bhutto had threatened the established order and the power of the Establishment with the moves and reforms he had made since assuming power. His 'socialism' had frightened businessmen and scared capital away from the country. In his last budget he introduced an agricultural income tax, the nightmare of Pakistan's feudal class, of which he was himself a prominent member. Even before that, as Minister for Industries, he had infuriated the Establishment panjandrums, when he tried to open a door to the Soviet Union—feared by them as the source of dangerous ideas and social revolution. Their fury was all the greater because it had to be suppressed, or expressed in whispers among the like-minded. For Bhutto inspired fear and hatred in equal measure. When Bhutto was overthrown, Sahibzada Yaqub who has an apt Urdu couplet for every occasion, phoned me from his embassy in Washington and expressed these pent-up emotions in the following verse:

Idd-i-nazara hai shamsher ka uryan hona
(A feast for the eye is the unsheathing of the sword!)

Zia did much harm to the country in destroying and damaging institutions and undermining respect for the law. But in truth, all Pakistan's rulers with few exceptions, had abused power, twisted rules and regulations, and flouted the Constitution in order to retain power and to be free to do whatever they wished. Zia was more systematic in this respect and taking cover behind the slogan of 'Islamization' he trampled over procedures and damaged institutions, in some cases perhaps beyond repair. Moreover, he lasted longer than any other ruler, and had more time to corrupt and distort the system. The harm Zia did on this score was not always wilful. It came from the man's innate limitations, from the background from which he had risen, from the conformism, the philistine and anti-intellectual spirit, the dogmatism and doctrinal obscurantism, that has gradually been gaining the upper hand in Pakistan in the name of a so-called 'Pakistan Ideology'. Leaders without political convictions or attachment to principles of any kind, committed only to grabbing and enjoying political power and the perks it brought, had succeeded each other and reduced politics to a game played without rules. Bhutto too gave in to this spirit when he feared that his hold on power was threatened, as on the Qadiani issue and, in his last days in power, the futile decrees to ban drinking and gambling.

About Bhutto one could say that he had a modernistic vision even if it was a bit grandiose and without a very specific direction. He sought power not merely in order to enjoy it but to get the country moving. No such aim and purpose illuminated the obscurity of Ziaul Haq's eleven years. In the name of economy, many large scale and vital projects launched by Bhutto—among others, the Indus Highway, an underground railway in Karachi, and an integrated truck manufacturing plant—were immediately cancelled. But they were not revived in all the years of Ziaul Haq, when the country was awash in money from foreign aid, the Afghan War, overseas remittances, and not to mention the drug traffic, smuggling and other underground sources. Not a road or a power station, no major industrial plants, no centres of higher learning were built in those years. Vast quantities of arms and ammunition were coming in for the Afghan War. Pakistan's own forces were upgraded with sophisticated weapons. Yet there was no attempt to obtain technology, to upgrade and improve the defence industry established in earlier years. The worst indictment—next to the systematic destruction of institutions and public morality—of the Zia years is that for the country they were years that went down the drain. Little was achieved or attempted, the country as a whole fell behind in social and economic terms though, thanks to the Afghan War, drugs and other such sidelines, people were living better. But they were living off jam today.

Zia displayed an undoubted gift for political manipulation, that, according to some, put Bhutto's political savvy in the shade. Having used one politician or another, time after time, to gain some end of his own, Zia then outfoxed the lot of them. But then perhaps the task was not too difficult since many politicians were only too willing to be used for his purposes, if there was something to be had for themselves at the end of it.

Still the question remains, where did this obscure man, with little standing in the army itself, find the inner strength and self-assurance that enabled him to overthrow and hang a duly elected prime minister, abrogate the Constitution, bring the judiciary to heel, keep the politicians at bay, and turn his whims and fancies into state policy? Was it the inertia of the system, civil and military, that caused orders to be carried out—apathetically and not without a murmur—but carried out nonetheless? Was there a weakness in the system or in the national character that allowed it to happen?

But Zia who had thought that he would ensure his own neck by hanging Bhutto, was led by this wanton, craven and tragic act from one false move to another. Zia's original instinct—if that is what it was, and not a feint—had been right when he affirmed that if Bhutto was to be eliminated from the political scene, it could only be done by political means. Much of the evil that Zia did or that was done during his long reign, flowed from that fateful decision. He smiled and smiled, but the ghost was always there egging him on—in his hounding of the Bhutto women, the mysterious murder of Shahnawaz Bhutto, the army's rampage in Sindh in 1983, even the Sindhi caps he affected, his attempts to imitate Bhutto's populist style, the continuation of the worst of the Bhutto economic policies such as nationalized industries.

When Zia's plane crashed, the Paris daily, *Liberation* carried the news of his death under a banner head line, 'Dictator Falls Out of the Sky'. It called to mind in ironic counterpoint, Zia's own words at a Friday prayer gathering two days after he had toppled Zulfikar Bhutto, 'We have brought Mr Bhutto down from the skies to the earth...'

NOTES

[1] Listening to Shahi's legal exposition, I recalled a story I had read in an Indian newspaper about the trial of a certain Mr Guha, accused of poisoning his wife. The man pleaded innocent, and alleged that she had committed suicide. The evidence was inconclusive, and perhaps as a gimmick for the Press, the defence lawyer decided to summon the spirit of Mrs Guha personally to clarify matters. But the lady proved as scrupulous about legal niceties as our delegation.

'Did you commit suicide Mrs Guha, or did your husband poison you?' she was asked on the planchette board.

'I cannot tell,' she replied.

'Why not?'

'Because the case is *sub judice*!'

[2] Author's notes.

[3] Edgar Faure, President of the Council of State, had moved a number of times to be allowed to go to Pakistan. One Sunday morning he came to the embassy residence without an appointment, and asked me to press his request with Islamabad, which I did. But I told him what the answer would be: the case was *sub judice*... He phoned me from Dublin a couple of days later to ask if a reply had come to his request. I conveyed to him Islamabad's response—which was as anticipated. After Bhutto's execution, I ran into Faure coming out of a Chinese Embassy reception. He didn't say anything, but stood in the street staring at me across the moving crowd, and shook his head in regret and reproof. A couple of years later I saw him again in Beirut, and he told me that after failing to get Pakistan's permission to go to Islamabad, he had flown to Saudi Arabia to ask the royal family to intervene on Bhutto's behalf. He was told that the Saudis had already tried their best, but that Ziaul Haq was adamant.

[4] October 1979.

[5] Author's notes.

[6] *International Herald Tribune*, Paris, August 1988.

[7] When Carter eventually offered $400 million in aid, Zia dismissed it as peanuts, taking a dig at Carter's peanut farming business. At a conference I attended in 1980, Henry Kissinger scoffed: 'Carter has called the Afghan crisis as the "greatest threat to world peace since World War II", and he wants Pakistan to face it with $400 million.'

[8] Author's notes.

[9] The UN mediator on Afghanistan, Diego Cordovez, feeling bullish one day about the prospect of agreement, said to me that he was giving a dinner that

CHAPTER 15

BEIRUT

On a Sunday morning in the spring of 1975, a car driving past a church in a suburb of Beirut fired shots in the direction of a gathering at its entrance, killing four men, some of whom were members of the Falangist party's militia.[1] The car sped away but it was generally assumed that the assailants were Palestinians. In the afternoon of the same day, a bus load of Palestinian workers returning home through the same suburb was ambushed and all its passengers were killed. The events of that fateful 13 April marked the opening of the Lebanese civil war, though tension had been building up in various cities and towns of Lebanon for quite some time before. The Lebanese themselves avoided calling it a 'civil war' and preferred simply to say 'the events'. It was in fact an over-simplification to call it a civil war or to view it as a religious conflict between Christians and Muslims. This was only one aspect of a situation of great complexity in which communal and religious affiliations were often overshadowed by factional and personal rivalries within the different communities; where at the back of the contenders stood their two powerful neighbours— Israel and Syria—and behind them, their cold war supporters, the United States and the Soviet Union. Nor was it always the case that Muslim Syria supported the Muslims and Israel supported the Christians. Hafiz al Assad's Ba'ath government was secular and socialist and not Islamic. The ruling Alawites are an esoteric sect whom orthodox Muslims would probably not consider to be Muslims in the proper sense. On the political level, Muslims were ambivalent about Syria—as the Druse journalist Merwan Hamadé put it, 'In Lebanon Syria has self-serving friends and sincere enemies.'

When the Syrians appeared on the scene in 1977, it was at the desperate appeal of the Christian factions who were on the verge evening for the Pakistan delegation at which the main course would be their own sceptical words about a settlement. But, he said, Western countries were not pleased, and he was told by the representative of one, 'Who is Pakistan to go and get an Afghan settlement on its own!'

[10] A petition against Zia on this matter was filed in the Sindh High Court, but the Court declined to consider it on the ground that it had no jurisdiction as the respondent was resident in Islamabad.

[11] Under it the President may dismiss the Parliament and call for fresh elections, and act on his own discretion on a number of specified subjects including the appointments of Service Chiefs and higher Judges. In addition, he has discretionary powers in respect of 'any other matter'. In short, he can do anything he pleases. This so-called 'sweet will' clause was qualified in later negotiations by making it subject to review by the Supreme Court. The Eighth Amendment, by splitting executive authority, has caused the transfer to the courts of many matters that are essentially political in nature.

[12] A huge munitions dump situated at Ojhri between Islamabad and Rawalpindi blew up in April 1988 causing many casualties and much damage in both cities. The cause and circumstances of the event have not been revealed to this day.

[13] A cotton print shawl worn over the shoulders, that has become something of a political totem in Sindh.

of being routed by a joint force of Sunnis, the Druse socialists and the Palestinians. But the Syrians had come only to save the Christians from defeat, not to help the Maronites resume their minority rule over the Muslims. The disappointed Falangist faction of the Maronite Christians then turned to yet another foreign power—Israel this time. The Israeli invasion of 1982 occurred with their connivance. But Israel too sided with them only to the extent that it suited its purposes, and the Maronites soon found that the Israelis were backing their Druse enemy in the Shouf, and the Sunnis against the Christians in the Iqlim area. The Maronites came full circle through help from Syria to dependence on Israel and then the United States and in the end back to the detested but unavoidable Syria again.

Lebanon's communalism was rooted in intangibles—attitudes, prejudices, memories—in short, the intoxicating power of history that Paul Valéry talks about. There was a strong element of tribalism about it. Sometimes the Lebanese saw the rights and wrongs of the civil war in the simple way football fans judge the merits of their respective teams. But in the years of fighting the situation had become entangled in other interests and concerns, the battle for turf among war lords and their diverse foreign patrons.

Each religious group and sect was also riven by internecine rivalries more bitter still than their quarrel with the other sects. There were three Maronite factions each with the blood of the others on its hands; the Shiahs were in undeclared rivalry with the Sunnis, but were also split within themselves into the moderate Amal party and the Hezbollah fundamentalists backed by Iran; the Druse fought Shiah as well as Sunni when they were not in temporary alliance with one side or the other. Only in extreme situations did any community close ranks—in 1978, the Christians and in 1982, the Muslims. By 1979 the war was not between Christians and Muslims, but a variety of armed factions and mafias pursuing their own ends or fighting proxy battles on behalf of foreign paymasters. Fire-fights were not always across the 'green line' that divided the Christian zone in the east from Muslim West Beirut ('Muslim' was misnomer for West Beirut because in fact it had a mixed population including a scattering of Jews). Often the violence was gratuitous, with no clear or attainable aim. As the war went on and the war-lords acquired weapons and wealth and power, the line between militia and Mafia became increasingly confused. The war was fought in the name of ideology and religion, but its wheels were kept turning also by smuggling and drug trafficking, gunrunning and looting. At dinner at the new home of the Tarazies'—a prominent Beirut family—the host told me that their old and quite grand seaside apartment in Ramlet el Beida was 'bought' by K___ , one of the lesser war-lords of Beirut; that is, he sent over some gunmen who gave him a cheque and showed the family out.

When I arrived in Beirut in October 1979 as the UN Secretary General's Special Representative, the civil war had already been going on for five years. When I left it was in its tenth year. Every year one said that it could not go on much longer and had to stop. There was a good deal of talk—and a good deal of cynicism—about reconstructing war damage and developing the economy. My own main responsibility was to assist the Lebanese government in this effort. But the war, which nobody was winning, and in the end nobody did win, would go on for more than fifteen years before petering out. A great number of people were killed or wounded, much of the country was destroyed, and nobody gained anything out of it—neither any of the Lebanese factions, nor Israel and Syria nor the great power players off-stage. More than most wars, it illustrated the folly and mischief that prevail in the affairs of men. But my purpose here is not to tell the story of Lebanon— it is too complex to be told in one brief chapter, and much already has been written about it. What I am setting down are some personal impressions of the way things were and some vignettes of life during the years my family and I spent there. I had first seen Beirut in 1949 during an overnight stop on my way to Paris as a Foreign Service probationer. It was a small, sleepy town overlooking the Mediterranean that lapped at the foot of the St Georges hotel where I spent the night. Now in 1979 the legendary hotel was a burnt out hulk, but the seaside pool was still functioning and lined with bikini-clad girls—a symbol of how far Beirut had fallen and of the never-say-die resilience of the Lebanese.

As a Pakistani there were certain parallels and contrasts that I could not fail to notice in the history and situation of the two countries. Each had come into being in the breakup of an empire. Lebanon, carved out of the Syrian velayat of the Ottoman

23. Prime Minister Bhutto at author's reception for him, New York, 1973.

24. Director General M'Bow of UNESCO and author. Signing an agreement to safeguard Mohenjo-Daro, 1979.

25. CMLA! Cartoon by Lala Akhund.

"Before the court awards punishment, may I point out that the defendant is a promising left-hand spin bowler."

26. Bhutto's trial—a wry comment by *Punch*, 20-26 July 1977.

27. Giscard d'Estaing and author at a pheasant shoot at Marly near Paris, 1978.

28. Quaid-i-Azam's centenary, 1976. Quaid's daughter Dina Wadia speaking to Secretary-General Waldheim and author at the UN mission's reception.

29. A Palestine Refugee Camp in South Lebanon after Israeli air attack, 1981.

30. Secretary-General Pérez de Cuéllar accompanied by Under Secretary-General Urquhart and the author, receives briefing from UN force officer during visit to Beirut, 1981.

31. Author and UN military observers visit city centre Beirut, 1983.

32. Author's son, Birjis, in their Beirut apartment after it was hit by an anti-tank shell, 1983.

33. Scene of explosion in American Embassy, Beirut 1983.

34. The ruins of the embassy building.

Empire, was established as a distinct entity (in the shape first, of a semi-independent French mandate) after World War I by the fiat of the conquering powers. Pakistan came into existence when the British Raj was wound up after World War II. Each country was created to provide a homeland for a cultural and religious minority. Pakistan was born in bloodshed and civil strife though it was created by an agreement among all the concerned parties; Lebanon's Christian character was ensured by a power-sharing accord among its various communities. Lebanon faced Syrian resentment as Pakistan continues to face Indian hostility, due in both cases not to any offense or misdeed on their part, but to the simple fact of their existence. Syria has never opened an Embassy in Beirut in token of her refusal to treat Lebanon as a foreign country.

In other ways the roles were reversed: unlike Pakistan, in Lebanon it was the Muslims who called for a secular, non-religious regime (which would allow their majority to weigh) and the Christians who clung to a religious dispensation that assured their predominance. It was the Christians who wanted job quotas and reservations in Lebanon, whereas the Muslims favoured a system based on merit and free competition. Unlike Pakistan, Lebanon did not have separate electorates, but the various communities were allotted seats in the Parliament in accordance with an agreed formula: Maronites, twenty; Greek Orthodox, eleven; Sunnis, twenty; Druse, six; and so on. Overall, in a House of ninety-nine, Christians had fifty-four and Muslims forty-five seats. This six to five ratio between the two major communities was observed also in the composition of the Cabinet and in major jobs and other important institutions. (When in 1983 the negligence of officials caused the death of sixty people in a blizzard, a newspaper wryly noted that the government had maintained the proper communal balance in taking disciplinary action: two Maronites were dismissed for two Sunnis, and two Shias for one Greek Orthodox.)

In 1943 when the French mandate was brought to an end and Lebanon became fully independent, a 'national pact' was concluded between Muslims and Christians, formalizing the practice of allocating the top political offices on a sectarian basis and also laying down two guiding principles of state policy. The first was that the Christians would not seek Western protection for their position; and the second, its corollary, that the Muslims would not seek to make Lebanon part of a larger Arab nation. However, in time a number of factors began to unravel these arrangements. The first was demography. Multiplying faster than the Christians, Muslims (in particular the under-privileged Shia community) began to chafe at being junior partners for ever and started claiming a share in power commensurate with their larger numbers—in effect a change in the six to five ratio to parity—and also asked for some of the more important government posts reserved for Christians. A small matter, one would think, over which to fight a fifteen-year war! Discussing the subject with me once, Najib Dahdah, editor of the daily *Le Reveil*, the Falangist party's ideologue, said that the numbers game did not give a decisive advantage to any of the communities since whoever may have the majority, the minority would be numerically only a point or two behind; nor, he said would a secular non-communal system necessarily give the Muslims an advantage since in competitive examinations the Maronites usually did better. Nevertheless, in principle the idea of reform was accepted by the Christians. But they always put off sitting down with the Muslims to settle the matter. The Shiah-owned *Daily Star* illustrated the Christian attitude to the Muslim demand for reforms, by quoting the youthful St Augustine's prayer: 'Give me chastity and continency—but not just yet!'

Arab nationalism was another source of discord in Lebanon. The irony was that the concept of 'Arabism' had been initiated and propagated by Lebanese Christian intellectuals in the early years of the century. But then it had been a platform for uniting all Arabs, Muslim and Christian, in the common struggle against the rule of the Ottomans. Now the Christians felt apprehensive at the anti-Western and anti-capitalist shape and direction Arab nationalism was taking after the creation of Israel and under Nasser's leadership.

Michel Khoury, Governor of the Bank of Lebanon and son of Lebanon' first president after independence, wondered: 'What will remain of Lebanon's special and unique character, of its opening to the West in culture, language, and many other things, under a Nasserist dispensation?'[2] Khoury was a Maronite but not an adherent of the militant Falangist party, nor a man of a partisan temperament. To a man of his background—cultivated, westernized, a little bit dilettante—the prospect of Lebanon turning into a heavy-breathing, ideological, Arab Nationalist state was unsettling and unwelcome.

For Pierre Jemayel, head of the Maronite political party and movement, the Falange, Lebanon was a bird with two wings: cut off one or the other, and it would fall to the ground. He said to me once:

> Lebanon is neither for the Christians alone, nor for the Muslims alone. Neither should try to dominate the other. A Christian does not feel entirely at home in Muslim-dominated Arab countries. In the Christian countries in the West, a Muslim does not feel that he belongs, but here in Lebanon, both feel that this is their land and home. Lebanon is a civilization on its own.

A man of contradictions, Pierre Jemayel fought the French for Lebanon's independence as early as 1936 and did time in a colonial prison. But after independence, he became a staunch supporter of the French connection to the point of denying or belittling Lebanon's Arab roots. He led a party that was wedded to perpetuating Maronite domination over the country. He spoke fervently of Lebanon's democracy, but headed a more or less totalitarian one party regime in Christian East Beirut. He embodied in all this the contradictions inherent in the position of the Christians in Lebanon.

Anis Yassine, a Sunni banker, said about Pierre Jemayel that he was not an anti-Muslim fanatic, but a pro-Maronite fanatic. The complexity of Lebanon's crisis lay in nuances like that. His wife, Mai Yassine, added that the trouble with the Maronites was that they were pushy and lacking in 'class'. 'We the Sunnis,' she said, 'we are at ease with ourselves, wherever and whatever we might be; we are not concerned with putting on airs and being other than what we are.' This referred to the Maronite pretension of being 'Western'. A Maronite girl once said to me a little shamefacedly, 'We pretend to be Western to avoid being Arab.' The Maronite credo was a mixture of myth and illusion, fear and narrow-minded insularity, ethnic pride and sense of cultural superiority—a cross-breed racism based on the assimilation by the elite of a foreign language and foreign culture. The Maronite connection with France goes back to the Crusades when many of them sided with their European co-religionists against Muslim fellow-Arabs. Now again, faced with the tide of Islamic 'Arabism', they began to identify themselves with France and the West. It was perhaps illustrative of this frame of mind that during the Christmas of 1982, a French language newspaper started a collection to offer gift parcels—not to the tens of thousands of disabled and homeless fellow citizens, but to well-paid men of the Western multinational force! The truth, despite all their anxious disowning of their 'Arabity', however, is that almost everything worthwhile the Lebanese Christians have done, they have done in Arabic.

Still, left to themselves the Lebanese might have reached a new national accord as many of them, specially among the Christians, professed to believe. But the ideological climate of the time did not favour a spirit of compromise, and there were too many external pulls and tugs for the Lebanese to be left alone.

The principal external factor, was the Palestine question. From the moment Israel was created and the displaced Palestinians began to flee to other Arab countries, Lebanon's fragile communal equilibrium was under threat. The first wave of refugees, made up of Christians for the great part, and not being too numerous, was relatively easily absorbed. In fact they brought money and business skills and launched Lebanon's initial economic boom. Then came other, larger waves—after the 1967 War, then King Hussein's clean-up of the Palestinians in 1970, and various other episodes in the Palestinian travail. By the mid-seventies the PLO had become a state within a state in Lebanon. It maintained a large and well-armed military force in the south and was running the show in many parts of Beirut.

The PLO used the South as its base for launching attacks on northern Israel. These were of doubtful military or political value and led to Israeli retaliation. In 1978 this took the form of a full-scale military incursion and the occupation of south Lebanon, which has continued to this day. When the Security Council adopted a resolution asking Israeli forces to withdraw, Israel went through the motions but set up a 'security zone' nominally under a renegade Lebanese major, Sa'ad Haddad, where Israeli forces came and went as they pleased.[3] To the Muslims Haddad was a quisling but he was seen with mixed feelings by the Christians for whom the source of all trouble was the Palestinian presence.[4]

A UN peace-keeping force, the UN Interim Force in Lebanon (UNIFIL) was sent to the area with a three-fold mandate: to oversee and confirm the withdrawal of Israeli troops; prevent guerrilla attacks on Israel from the area; and help the Lebanese government re-assert its authority in the South. Soon after arriving in Beirut I paid a visit to the UNIFIL area of operations. The helicopter that took me there first headed some distance out to sea, and then flew south on a course parallel with the coastline until the UNIFIL area of operations was reached when it veered back inland, and landed at the force headquarters at Naqoura. The purpose of this detour was to avoid providing a target to any armed mavericks along the way.

The UN force consisted of battalions from a number of countries—France, Ghana, Ireland, Nepal, Nigeria, Norway— each in charge of a different area and all under the overall command, at the time, of General Alexander Erskine of Ghana.[5] I hopped by chopper from one battalion area to another. The situation of the Nigerian battalion at Taibé was not typical, but showed the intricate and singular nature of the UN's peace-keeping task in the area. The battalion's main observation post was at a high point on a spur extending from the village and from there all the country around could easily be seen and controlled. A hundred metres or so downhill, was installed a unit of the Israeli-controlled Haddad militia with an APC (Armoured Personnel Carrier) and some light guns. This post, in turn, overlooked another Nigerian post situated a couple of hundred metres further down the hill.

I was told that the situation had come about when the Haddad APC had simply driven up one morning and taken up position. The UN protested, but did not think it appropriate to oust the militiamen by force or threat of force. Across a gorge was the Beaufort crusaders' castle held by the PLO. The imposing ruins of the castle commanded the countryside from its precipitous site on top of a sheer crag, and were a visible symbol of the Palestinians' defiance, resolve and dominating position in this part of the country. In Taibé town itself, one or two buildings including the mansion of National Assembly Speaker, Kamel el Assad, were in the possession of the Haddad people. Shells were lobbed from time to time by one or the other side, making a noise but not causing much damage. My Nigerian escort remarked, 'Fortunately the range finding is not very good around here!' UN's blue helmets and Haddad's men in camouflage fatigues, intermingled on the streets without taking too much notice of each other. Lebanese authorities were not much in evidence in the south as a whole, for the region had effectively passed under the control of the PLO on the one hand and Israel on the other.

The Israeli-controlled militia had made a number of other encroachments in the UNIFIL area of operations and had been allowed to get away with it. On the other side, the PLO had increased the number of its armed men in the area and the UN force was only partially successful in interdicting guerrilla attacks on Israel. A more serious dereliction was that the deployment of the UN troops had left an eight kilometre gap in a key sector between the villages of Blat and Taibé. Through this gap armed men of both the PLO and the Haddad militia, were able to move more or less freely. Lebanon's Army Chief, General Victor Khoury told me that the Israelis used the gap for their forays in the South, and would never allow UNIFIL to close it. The new Force Commander, General Callaghan of Ireland, explained that the 'gap' could not be closed without occupying Merjayoun which was the headquarters of the puppet Major Haddad and that the move would be strongly resisted by Israel. All this was quite true but still there was no satisfactory explanation of why this conspicuous and inexplicable lacuna in the deployment of the UN force had been allowed in the first place. And to leave things as they were meant that UNIFIL was in effect, serving as a shield for Israel's strategy in the area.

It is not that there was active and deliberate UN connivance with Israel. However some of the decision-makers shared the general Western tolerance of Israeli policies and showed a lively awareness of the fact that behind Israel stood the might of the United States. At any rate they were reluctant to put their hand in a hornet's nest. A UN official stationed in Jerusalem spoke to me of the 'strategic importance' to the Israelis of the Blat-Taibé gap—almost as if there was a tacit agreement to allow them to use this channel for maintaining pressure on the PLO.

As for helping the government to strengthen its presence in the South, an attempt to post a unit of the Lebanese Army alongside a UNIFIL contingent came to grief when it was fired on by the Haddad militia and withdrew. The PLO too was more than happy to see the Lebanese Army stay out of the South. For the PLO, the army was a hostile force that stood aside when Israeli commandos carried out operations against the PLO on Lebanese territory and had itself taken repressive action against the PLO. Victor Khoury told me that the Lebanese Army had come to an unwritten arrangement with the Israelis under which the latter would leave in peace Lebanese villages where there were no Palestinians, and in return, he said, 'We used to tell them where they could find the Palestinians they were looking for.'

Clearly, the UN force had failed to accomplish any of the principal functions it had been set up to perform. The immediate and evident cause of its failure was Israel's defiance of the Security Council's demand that it pull its troops out of Lebanese territory—a defiance that seemed to have the tacit backing of the United States. But this was not the only reason—the PLO's armed presence and activity in the area, Lebanon's internal dissensions, and the UN's own institutional weaknesses were also responsible for the deficiencies in the performance of UNIFIL. At the end of 1980 the Security Council adopted a resolution asking the Secretary General to do something about this state of affairs. Waldheim asked me to enter into discussions with all concerned (except—in view of my nationality—the Israelis)[6] in order to mobilize support for UNIFIL and to enable it to complete its mandate. The circle to be squared was to induce Israel to evacuate south Lebanon by ensuring its security from PLO attacks and in exchange, offer the PLO something for desisting from such attacks. That done, the Lebanese Army could return to the area and gradually resume its normal responsibilities for security and defence.

Foreign Minister Fuad Boutros suggested a reasonable compromise: let the European Community offer to 'recognize' the PLO in return for the PLO agreeing not to launch any more attacks on Israel from south Lebanon; or prevail upon Israel to stop 'pre-emptive' strikes and to attack only when attacked. Then Israel could begin to withdraw its troops from south Lebanon and the Lebanese Army gradually assume its normal responsibilities of ensuring security in the area and defending the country's borders. As an alternative to formal recognition, I had earlier suggested to Ambassador Rudi von Wechmar of West Germany who was UN General Assembly's President for the year, that he pay a visit to Lebanon in that capacity and meet Arafat. It would not amount to EEC recognition, but would constitute a signal of some sort. But Western countries were not prepared to recognize PLO or make even a gesture in that direction. The crux of the problem was that Israel was not prepared to give up its foothold on Lebanese soil. It used the security issue as a pretext for pursuing larger aims and was already planning the invasion of Lebanon by means of which it expected to put an end to the Palestinian problem once and for all.

Arafat was the other main player at that stage and I called on him late one evening. For security reasons, one was never given a fixed time for a meeting with Arafat, nor told where it would be held. So one night, while we had some guests to dinner, the UN military liaison officer suddenly turned up with a message that the Chairman could receive me in half an hour. I left my mystified guests and proceeded through darkened streets to the sinister ruins of the Chamoun Stadium where the PLO had its set-up. From a small house there, we picked up Arafat's Security Chief, Abu Humeid, who led us to Arafat's hide-out for the night—which was never the same place two nights running.

Arafat, as always, was bouncy, cheerful and grinning from ear to ear. He took the line that the PLO presence and actions in Lebanon were 'legal' (under the so-called Cairo Agreement brought about by Nasser in 1969 shortly before he died) and it was not the UN's business to try to cancel or modify these agreements. However he had given his *parole d'honneur* [word of honour]' to the Secretary General not to mount military operations against Israel from South Lebanon, and he would stick by it. But he could not keep it if Israel continued its pre-emptive attacks; moreover he made it clear that PLO was *not* giving up its military option overall.

The PLO, he complained, was blamed for everything that happened in the South no matter who caused the trouble; in fact, he said that the PLO had the thankless task of trying to restrain groups such as the National Movement and the Arab Liberation Army from getting up to mischief. (This was true, and in fact it was the PLO that guaranteed the security of the US Embassy in Beirut. When the embassy was blown up in 1983, it was partly because this protection was no longer available to it, the PLO having been ousted from Beirut.) Pointing out that the Israelis had apologized to Syria when three Syrian soldiers were killed inadvertently in Israeli crossfire, Arafat said that Israel had done so only because Syria had a powerful ally in the USSR, with whom the US did not want any trouble. 'Is the US waiting for the PLO too to enter into a "Friendship Treaty" with the Soviet Union? Will the US pay heed to the PLO only if Arafat became another Mengitsu?'[7] he asked.

General Abu Walid the PLO's military chief who was present at the meeting, made a specific suggestion: the UNIFIL should close the eight kilometre 'gap' in the UN lines, or at least set up an observation post in the sector through which infiltration and attacks were taking place. Abu Walid said, 'The PLO is accused of using the gap to infiltrate into Israel, whereas Israel claims to use it only in order to retaliate. Yet the PLO itself is asking for a UNIFIL presence there in order to put a stop to all military activity through the gap.'

In my report I proposed the following measures to the Secretary-General:

(1) UNIFIL should begin by making a determined effort to remove the four encroachments made by Israel in its area of operations, and at the same time it should get the PLO to reduce its strength therein to the original 200 armed men. UNIFIL's number two man, Norway's General Odergaard, agreed with me that it was possible for UNIFIL to assert its presence and authority more vigorously than had been the case, for example, by preventing the free run of its area of operations to any of the sides;

(2) the Lebanese flag should be shown in the South by inducting more Lebanese troops into the area, initially on nation-building tasks;

(3) measures be taken to improve relations between UNIFIL and the local population, by involving UNIFIL engineer units in reconstruction work and other such activities.[8]

The UN headquarters thanked me for these 'eminently reasonable' proposals, agreed that UNIFIL must indeed make a start towards consolidating its area of control and preventing infiltration through its lines, and then qualified the whole thing by saying that 'a fine distinction had to be drawn between firmness on the one hand, and descending into the fray, on the other.' Of course UNIFIL had neither the means nor the political backing to enter the fray, nor was any such action called for. What was lacking in the UN action and attitude was precisely the proper degree of firmness. The least it could do, if it could not compel the Israelis to withdraw, was not to allow them to nibble away at the UNIFIL area of operations. In the end UNIFIL acted largely as a symbol and provided a presence that was nevertheless useful to all. The consensus behind its presence was a negative consensus, for everyone felt they would be worse off without it.

On the whole the year 1979-80 was a relatively quiet period. The Arab League Conciliation Committee had set up an Arab Dissuasion Force (that became a purely Syrian force in time) to keep order; and the oil countries pledged $4 billion for Lebanon's reconstruction. PLO commandos took guerrilla actions and invited Israeli retaliation. On 27 August, Israeli aircraft hit a residential block on Fakhani Street where one of the buildings housed an office used by Arafat. He was not there, but the incident showed that Israel had a good intelligence network in Lebanon. The bomb went through the middle of the high-rise building and into the basement, killing hundreds of residents. I watched the rescue work—the building was being taken down piece by piece in case there were survivors in the rubble. Ten days earlier I was caught in an Israeli air raid and recorded the event in my diary:

17 July: Meeting at 11 a.m. with Abu Jaffar, PLO political counsellor. First must pick up Security Chief Abu Humeid who will take me to meeting place. All hell breaks loose as car enters the Chamoun Stadium area. Overhead is sound of aircraft flying low and criss-crossing the sky. Demented rattle of ack-ack guns that dot the sky with white smoke puffs—decorative and ineffectual against supersonic Phantom fighters. Past the stadium walls, thin plumes of white smoke rise from the ground straight up into the air like gigantic and noxious weeds—markers for the raiding aircraft. There are several explosions, sharp as whiplashes, the sound of rockets hitting the ground. Abu Humeid leaps into my car and we speed off to the office of the Political Bureau. Abu Humeid is shouting instructions from the moving car. A big one falls somewhere close by, causing the car to bounce and makes the driver jump in his seat. Streets are narrow and crowded with people running helter-skelter for cover and others with

Kalashnikovs in hand, staring at the sky for something to shoot at, and finding nothing, let off bursts from the rifles anyway.

At entrance of street too ñarrow for the car, we get out and run, sidling along walls to a ramshackle building and up a flight of creaky wooden stairs. We stop, out of breath, at the third floor, and I am shown into a dusty room to wait for Abu Jaffar. No one appears for a long while. I sit in the empty room, body tensing to the sounds of battle going on beyond its flimsy walls. Then a door creaks open and a woman puts in her head to ask, 'How would you like your coffee, with sugar or without?'

In the beginning of 1981, the US emissary Phillip Habib arranged a cease-fire in the south between Israel and the PLO resistance. But the lull did not reflect reconciliation and was not a prelude to negotiations. It was a period when all the numerous players were watching and calculating, manœuvring and preparing the ground to pursue their conflicting aims. There was plenty to keep people occupied as well as preoccupied. Chic new boutiques and restaurants opened in Beirut; in a lightning and bloody raid the Falangists eliminated the militia of ex-President Camille Chamoun, the nominal head of the Maronite National Front, and blew up the home of his son, Dany; models flew over from Paris for a fashion show; an art gallery exhibited Dali drawings; French Ambassador Delamare was shot dead in front of his residence and within sight of a Syrian checkpoint.[9] The presidential election was due in 1982 and not only the Lebanese political parties, but Israel, Syria as well as the US were critically interested in its outcome. Tension increased as the time for the elections came closer.

Another latent source of tension was the cease-fire itself for it had given political advantage, in terms of prestige, implicit recognition, and relief from military pressure to the PLO, militarily the weaker side. In general, even while the PLO was improving its diplomatic position on the world scene, on the ground in Lebanon the Palestinians felt increasingly vulnerable, facing pressures from Syria and a resuscitated Lebanese Army, under attack from Israel and threat of attack from the Falangists, receiving less support than in the past from their Lebanese allies. The PLO too was building up its fighting strength as best as it could, receiving shiploads of weapons at clandestine ports as well as by air on small improvised airstrips.

Abu Iyad, Arafat's close adviser, told me that they had received from Dany Chamoun details of a planned four-stage Israeli invasion of Lebanon that would circumvent the UNIFIL area of operations and occupy Beirut Airport, the suburbs of Khaldé, and Ouzai at the southern entrance of the city. But the aim of the operation would not be territorial gains, but to kill the maximum number of Palestinians and take important prisoners. He added an interesting motive for the Israeli operation: to drive the bulk of the Palestinians into Syria or Syrian-held territory and put them under Syrian control. Abu Iyad thought that Begin may want to launch the plan before the coming elections in Israel if he thought that they might go against the Likud. Abu Iyad considered that Israel would not embark on a venture of this sort without the approval and support of the US. He was not sure that these would be forthcoming, but was very sceptical that Reagan's election would improve matters for the Arabs.

When I met Arafat again a month later, he expressed great concern over a statement made by Vice-President George Bush accusing the PLO of helping the leftist guerrillas in El Salvador. This statement, he was sure, was intended to give Israel the green light for the 'major and decisive' action it was planning to take in the coming months against the Palestinians in Lebanon.

Israel had no need of any such oblique hints from the US administration for as is now known, the US Secretary of State Alexander Haig was aware of, and had encouraged Sharon's plans for the invasion of Lebanon. At a dinner party at the home of Foreign Minister Boutros a year later, the wife of a senior European official repeated to me something said to her by a US Embassy counsellor when Israel invaded Lebanon: 'It is all unfolding according to plan. You will find it unbelievable if one day you learnt the truth...'

Another straw in the wind was the fate of a peace effort mounted by the UN in consultation with the US in order to consolidate the cease-fire. Under-Secretary General Brian Urquhart came to Beirut in the midst of these rumours and alarums of impending war. We went to see President Sarkis who said that he had been receiving reports on the subject from various sources, including Lebanese embassies. They were couched in identical terms, indicating a common origin. The United States, he said, had shown an inexhaustible tolerance for

Israeli actions and Israel felt free to do whatever it pleased. 'I no longer have the nerves, Mr Urquhart, I no longer have the nerves!' the distraught President of Lebanon cried out.

We also met Arafat who looked preoccupied and lacked his usual bounce. 'Yes,' he said, 'we do face problems—the post-Fez atmosphere in the Arab world,[10] the Iran-Iraq War, the West Sahara dispute and the ever-present threat of an all-out Israeli attack.' Arafat complained that Israel was offering the Palestinians not self-government but self-administration—and in saying this he seemed to signal a softening of his attitude to Camp David. He reiterated his pledge not to mount military operations on Israeli territory from the South but emphasized that it did not mean that the PLO was giving up its military option.

At that point however, the PLO's 'military option' if it was exercised, would serve only as a pretext for the all out attack Israel was preparing to launch. A couple of weeks earlier I had discussed the situation with PLO's political adviser, Abu Jaffar. He showed a down-to-earth sense of realities and did not waste time on rhetoric or polemics. He anticipated that an Israeli attack, when it came, would be a very massive affair; small operations brought Israel limited benefits, he said, and only got it a bad name. He thought that Israel might first do an airborne operation in the Beka'a to knock out the Syrians and then the PLO would be on the spot. Abu Jaffar added, 'But we are on the spot whatever happens. Our Chairman says, "PLO is ready for anything, but...."'

In the beginning of 1982, the Lebanese government gave the Secretary General a memorandum setting out a series of proposals that would, step by step, bring about complete Israeli withdrawal from Lebanon and restore Lebanese sovereignty over the whole country. The Secretary General's response while fully supporting these objectives, was to put forward a two-phase programme that, in the initial stage, was concerned almost wholly with consolidating UNIFIL's existing area of operations; in other words, with firming up the *status quo*. As for the other problem, that is, ending Israeli occupation of South Lebanon, which was the subject of UNIFIL's real mandate and its *raison d'être*, this was to be taken up in the second phase, in the form of seeking the agreement of Israel and its client, Major Haddad, for the 'orderly entry and deployment of UNIFIL forces' in the area.

General Callaghan, the UN's man in Jerusalem, Claude Aimé
and I, were asked to put our heads together over this plan and
give the Secretary General our considered reactions. The reality
was that the UN's mandate was being flouted and there was little
prospect of its being carried out. After four years of fruitless
efforts by the UN, the threat of a new war was looming over
Lebanon, the internal situation was completely polarized, and
the authority and legitimacy of the Lebanese government had, in
practical terms, been eroded almost to the vanishing point.
UNIFIL, in the circumstances, had become an alibi—a screen
behind which Israel had established a puppet regime in South
Lebanon, while PLO and other groups continued to mount
guerrilla operations that did nothing to further the Palestine
cause, but provoked massive and disproportionate Israeli
retaliation. The solution lay in a two-fold effort (1) Israel's
withdrawal from Lebanon and the restoration, via UNIFIL, of
Lebanese sovereignty over the South; and (2) consolidating and
extending the recently concluded PLO-Israel cease-fire, so that
South Lebanon would cease to be a base for PLO's ineffectual
guerrilla war against Israel. In my view, it was time for the
Secretary General to confront the Security Council with the facts,
and ask it to face up to its responsibilities instead of going on
with the make-believe of a step-by-step attempt to implement the
Council's resolution.

Nobody quarrelled with this approach, but since it meant taking
on the United States, it was no doubt put aside as unrealistic,
and we continued to pursue the pseudo-pragmatic two-phase
programme. On the basis of first things first, this came down to a
plan for the separation and limitation of weapons of long-range
capability—artillery, Katyusha multi-rocket launchers, etc.—that
were in the hands of both sides in the area. I was informed that
the State Department had been consulted about this proposal
and, presumably, approved it. Arafat, for his part, said he was
willing to consider it, but made the point that Israel could always
move back its guns in short order, and that moreover, it remained
free to hit the PLO targets from the air and sea. But even this
diffident UN effort was to come to nothing, for abruptly, without
explanation or any further word, a cable came from New York
one morning, stating that the proposal was shelved and the UN
mediation effort was not to be pursued for the present. It was a

sign that the hounds of war that had been straining at the leash, would soon be let loose. The Security Council's search for peace in Lebanon was soon overtaken by events.

On 5 June, on a visit to London, driving back from a dinner with friends, we noticed a commotion outside the Dorchester Hotel—police cars, people rushing about, spot lights, TV cameras. I thought they were shooting a film. At home, flicking on the tube for the late news, I learned that the Israeli ambassador had been shot at and seriously wounded while attending a dinner at the hotel.[11] Three days later Israeli troops swept into Lebanon and by 10 June they were at the outskirts of Beirut. UNIFIL troops looked on like spectators as the Israeli tanks and APCs drove past; only the Nepalese battalion made an attempt to resist. General Callaghan sent an indignant message to the Israeli commander, General Rafi Eytan, protesting at his troops pushing through the UNIFIL area of operations and 'the indiscriminate and totally unnecessary bombardment from the sea, land and air of Tyre and Sidon.' He received a curt and enormously arrogant reply: 'The Israeli Army is not here with your permission, and will carry its task to completion whether you like it or not.' The Israeli general's supreme self-confidence was not unjustified. Secretary of State Haig, reporting on the war and speaking of losses on the Israeli side, said 'We lost one plane, two helicopters...'

In the first days of the war, Israel downed seventy-nine Syrian planes thanks largely to the Hawk Eye 'Battle Management Aircraft', AWAC's junior brother, used by the Israeli Air Force. According to an account published in a New York newspaper, this aircraft could from the safety of Israel's own air space, observe a Syrian plane from the moment it took off to the point when it came within range; and calculating its speed, altitude, and direction, and being able to distinguish enemy craft from friendly ones, it could bring down the former at the touch of a button.

After three days at the gates of Beirut, the Israelis made a lightning move into the suburb of Ba'abda and took up positions in front of the Presidential palace and astride the road to Damascus. The move cut off the PLO leadership's only land exit. Newspapers reported that the Israelis intended to go in and get the trapped leaders one way or another.

For the Palestinian people, robbed of their land, homes, identity, opposed by the might of some of the most powerful countries in the world, betrayed by fellow Arabs, weakened by internal dissension, and now caught in a web of their own weaving, things now seemed to be moving towards a terrible and tragic denouement.

From London I went on to New York, where the Secretary General asked me to start organizing emergency relief for war victims. There was no real shortage of anything in the country, but in West Beirut there was a crisis on account of the embargo the Israelis had clamped on the besieged city. To add to the privations caused by the embargo on foodstuffs and medicines, the city's water supply and electricity were also cut off from time to time. The Security Council held meetings and called for a cease-fire, but generally proceeded in a rather desultory fashion. On 19 June, France presented a draft resolution on the condition of civilians in West Beirut, but the Council's meeting was delayed for five hours while the State Department pondered over the text. Then the Council had to wait another forty-five minutes because, it being Sabbath, the Israeli delegation had religious scruples about being driven to the UN by car, and chose to come on foot! The Secretariat too was permeated with a concealed pro-Israeli bias, and though UN officials shook their heads and professed frustration at Israel's actions, the bias appeared in small and subtle ways. Thus, when a draft for the Secretary General's statement to the Security Council said that relief would be provided to Beirut 'as soon as freedom of movement is allowed', a secretariat official wanted that changed to read, 'when freedom of movement becomes possible'.[12]

To show the UN flag and organize relief work on the spot, I returned to Beirut via Larnaca in Cyprus in a boat which was taking over the first shipment of relief grains. A tiny little tub it was, badly in need of a coat of paint. It had no passenger accommodation but the captain and crew were most hospitable and vacated their own quarters for me and my group which included the Swedish Ambassador to the UN, Anders Thunborg, who was to make an assessment of relief needs and war damage on behalf of the Secretary General. However we stayed on deck and on a little portable radio listened to Jimmy Connors make a great comeback by beating McEnroe at Wimbledon. In the morning the Beirut headland came in sight but the city itself was hidden in a haze from the previous day's bombardment. After being interrogated over the wireless by an Israeli patrol boat about the ship's cargo, and the names and nationalities of passengers, the Captain brought the ship alongside at Jounieh, a former marina for pleasure boats, and now the Falangist seaport. UN officials and a man from the Foreign Ministry received us with the news that all hotels were fully booked (a tourist boom in the middle of the war?) but that President Sarkis had very kindly offered to put up Thunborg and me at the Palace until accommodation was found.

Before going to the Presidency we decided to make a morale-raising tour of the UN offices that had been toughing it out. From the FAO office, which was opposite the President's house, we could see smoke rising from the grounds and were informed that it had been hit that morning by an artillery shell, injuring the Foreign Minister's chauffeur. The ambassador and I began to have second thoughts about the President's gracious invitation to stay that we had accepted with such alacrity. The matter was clinched during the audience with the President, when another shell exploded in the grounds. In the reception hall many windows were broken from previous hits, and carpets were rolled up and stacked on tables. The President's own office room had been badly damaged by a direct hit, so he received us in a little side room belonging to a junior secretary.

The President told us of the negotiation that was underway to end the Israeli attacks by an arrangement under which PLO fighters would withdraw from Lebanon, and in return the security of the Palestine civilians and leaders who remained behind, would be guaranteed. The US, he said, had given firm assurances regarding the post-withdrawal arrangements and guarantees. The President said that one had only to look at the prevailing situation to see the futility of the Palestinians' military option.

That was very true, but the war also showed the limited utility of the military option for Israel and the transient character of its most decisive victories. For, already at that point the war had ceased to be mobile and become a war of attrition. The Israelis did attempt from time to time to break through into the city, but essentially they stayed in place and tried to break the Palestinian resistance by means of artillery and air bombardments. These were merciless and undiscriminating. I saw one that evening as we dined in the mountain village of Beit Mery at the home of Ghassan Tueni, Chairman of the *Al Nahar* group of newspapers, and at the time Lebanon's permanent representative to the United Nations. We also heard an argument between two young Christians. Ghassan's son Gabriel, Greek Orthodox but whose mother was Druse, spoke of the reality of Lebanese nationalism, the need for a strong government, a common educational policy and democracy. His Maronite friend, Joseph Moawad held that all that was illusion and wishfulness. The reality was that Muslims and Christians had different historic memories, different ways of looking at the world, and different national myths. He himself, he said, could only identify with the Maronite community and culturally with the West. When he thought of history, he affirmed, he thought of the Kings of France!

From the terrace one could see Beirut, and listen to the sounds of the Israeli bombardment. The eastern Christian half of the city was brightly lit up while the western half, the target of Israeli action and embargo, was in total darkness, relieved only by the flash of exploding bombs. It was a metaphor, the city neatly sliced in two by Israel's electricity cut off, as was Lebanon in the mind of the young Maronite with his memories of the kings of France!

From the balcony of my hotel room (one having been arranged in the meantime in the hill top town of Brummana), with the whole of Beirut laid out like a map before one's eyes, there was a ringside view of Beirut's agony. I made notes in my diary of some of the worst attacks:

7 July: Rockets streak across the cityscape from east to west and the answering fire from west to east, making red gashes in the night sky. Where they land, tongues of flame leap up from the ground. Katyusha rockets, the so-called Stalin organs, play their dreadful drumbeat chords. Israelis are using flares to assist the range-finders. They hang in the air for a while and then come down slowly, casting an eerie yellow light on the target area.

In the hotel's basement disco, music is pounding away but does not drown out the rumble and thunder of death coming across the moonlit sky. Young people walk in and out, laughing gaily or sit chatting by the swimming pool. Not one of them turns to look at the torment of their capital city. The fire is concentrated on the

Palestinian areas in the south of the city—Bourj Brajneh, Sabra, Shatila. They have been receiving a merciless pounding since the war began three weeks ago. One wonders if anyone is left there, and how they manage to survive.

11 July: The sound of shelling wakens me at 4 a.m. The attack goes on throughout the day and all evening and stops only at 9 p.m. The city has disappeared behind a grey pall of smoke and dust. Firing from land and sea is so concentrated that the sound of explosions can no longer be distinguished, but is like a continuous roll of thunder, reverberating from one end of the city to the other. A newspaper reports that 8,000 shells fell on the city in yesterday's bombardment—1,800 during one infernal hour; two per second! All this on a densely inhabited city area no more than a square mile or two in extent.

Meanwhile negotiations for an agreement are going on and an Israeli official says, 'Attacks between cease-fires are a necessary adjunct to political negotiations.'

12 July: I drive down with Thunborg to West Beirut to see the damage. Men at the Israeli checkpoint in the port, looking like high school kids, are very polite and friendly in manner. Across the line, we are suddenly a world away—tank traps and huge earth-works block the passage at many streets. The Wadi Jamil whores at the outskirts of the port have closed shop and taken their business elsewhere. The St Georges swimming pool is empty and abandoned. Most shops are shuttered and very few people are out on the streets. A variety of armed men in sundry uniforms or costumes stand about in the streets or go careening madly in jeeps. Debris from yesterday's attack litters Mazra Boulevard and the sea-front apartment houses of Ramlet el Baida. Cars, trucks, lie in piles of twisted and burnt out metal. In some places fires are still smouldering. A dead cow and two horses lie by the roadside, their legs raised stiffly in the air. The stench of putrefaction seeps in through the closed windows of the car. In the midst of this desolation an old man sits besides a carefully constructed pyramid of American cigarette packs, as he has always done, waiting for customers.

21 July: Another heavy day-long attack on West Beirut. When it stops in the evening the twilight is like a welt over the haze shrouding the city. But above it the sky is limpid—the crescent moon of Ramazan hangs over the murk below. 'A Wagnerian set,' says the Greek Ambassador as we watch from the balcony of his hotel room. I think of Iqbal's verse, *O dagger of the crescent moon, you are the symbol of the nation of Islam.*

6 Aug.: A quiet day. No bombs have fallen on Beirut all day long. In the afternoon as I sit reading on the balcony, a single plane flies

in over Beirut, makes a leisurely circle over the western part, drops a bomb and then flies away. A small cloud of dust rises from where the bomb has impacted. BBC's evening bulletin announces that a building was hit in the Saraya quarter where the Prime Minister's office is situated, and that 250 civilians were killed. A Bangladeshi UN official, a former Pakistan Air Force pilot, explains to me that it was an implosion bomb; set to explode a few meters directly above the target, it causes an intensely hot fireball that sucks up all the surrounding air and thereby creates a vacuum. The walls of the target building implode like an eggshell under the pressure of the outside atmosphere and the building collapses on itself; anyone inside the building or around it is asphyxiated.

I visited the place some days later and indeed the rubble was piled up in a quite small radius around the hit. Later it was said that the target was Yasser Arafat who was in the building, but miraculously had left a short while before the attack.

12 Aug.: Yesterday when my office phoned the Israeli HQ in B'hamdoun to ask for clearance to go into West Beirut through one of their checkpoints, the Israeli official said, 'Okay, but you must check with us before setting out. Tomorrow could be a bad day.' Indeed it was, probably the worst in this war of relentless and implacable destruction. I have some difficulty getting back to my hotel in the east because the Israelis have closed all exits. A soldier on guard duty tells us, 'Nobody is getting in or getting out now.' Fortunately, my Iraqi colleague, Mustafa Jaff, recognizes the man's Iraqi accent, chats him up a bit about Baghdad, discovers that the families had known each other, and so the gates of Inferno are briefly re-opened.

Without a moment's respite or breathing space, tanks, aircraft, artillery and naval guns rain down destruction on the devastated city. In the evening, after eleven non-stop hours, the attack suddenly stops. Lebanon Radio announces that Reagan, outraged, has phoned Begin with a peremptory demand, 'I want this stopped, and stopped right now!' It confirms the Arab belief that if the US wanted to, it could bring Israel to heel in no time. In Israel itself there is indignation at the senseless carnage and the Knesset holds a stormy session in which everyone blames Sharon for it.

Israeli embargo on West Beirut was very rigorous in the initial weeks. Whenever we crossed over to the West, Israeli guards thoroughly searched the car for any food or drink we might be carrying in and confiscated any sandwich or bottle of Coke they found. This continued despite a firm word to the Secretary

General from the White House that Israel was being pressed to lift the embargo. However when Spain moved a resolution in the Security Council calling on Israel to lift the embargo, the US delegation abstained in the voting on the ground that the resolution was 'one-sided'. When at last it was lifted, it was done with the whimsical logic of a Kafka story. Petrol and fuel of any kind was not allowed in—for obvious reasons—but then without fuel, wheat that was allowed to go in could not be baked into bread. Rice could be taken in, but not sugar nor skimmed milk. Blankets, yes; tents, no. The logic, one supposed, was to assuage Western public opinion without really easing the pressure on the besieged city.

Together with a UN team I visited the battle-hit area in the South to observe the war damage. We took dusty back-roads in order to avoid the Israeli-Palestinian front line. On the way we saw that a nomad shanty town that had nothing of any military importance, had been razed to the ground. Later I learnt that the site belonged to a Beirut tycoon who had been trying for years to clear out the squatters. The war gave him the opportunity to do so and to let the blame fall on the war. In Sidon the municipal building was gutted and the picturesque eighteenth century souks along the sea-front destroyed. In the Ain Helwi refugee camp old men and women stood apathetically or rummaged in the rubble. One saw few young men; most had gone off with the fighters and many had been carted off to detention camps. A bus load of Israeli tourists turned up and the people got off to take photographs of the ruins.

The Israelis had changed all the road signs into Hebrew for the convenience of the military, but as a result, the Lebanese were unable to find their way around in their own country. There was talk of pillage and looting by the Israelis—we saw a truck load of uprooted lampposts being trundled off to Israel.

I called on Bishop Haddad, Greek Orthodox prelate of the region. When the Israelis were approaching Sidon he went to the entrance of the city and—in the fashion of the Middle Ages—interceded with the Israeli commander for a few hours respite to permit the civilian population to get out of harm's way. So it was that there was comparatively little loss of life in Sidon and 7,000 men, women and children sat out on the beaches for two days without food, drink, or shelter, but alive.

The Battle of Beirut should go down in history as no less
heroic than the Battle of Britain. It was possibly an even greater
example of fortitude and courage for here the enemy was not
across the sea, but at the door, indeed inside the house, walking
the streets, sipping coffee in cafés, eating in restaurants,
controlling traffic, and arresting people. The disproportion
between attackers and defenders was overwhelming. Israeli forces
were equipped with the most modern technology and all kinds
of cost-effective weapons and were free to use them at will—
cluster bombs and phosphorus bombs, supersonic aircraft, heavy
tanks. Yet no one showed fear, no one complained, and not
many thought of escaping. People went about their business as
well as they were able to, continued producing newspapers and
magazines, reading out the news on TV and radio, driving
ambulances and fire-engines, burning garbage, selling vegetables,
even throwing parties! No one got robbed, raped or molested.
Sometimes young men would stop a car and siphon off the petrol.
It happened on one occasion to a UN car. They apologized to
the chauffeur, 'I hope you will understand. We need the fuel to
fire our Katyushas!'

It was an unequal fight and for the Palestinians it could only
end in one way. Negotiations for an end to the war, conducted
for Israel by the US Deputy Secretary of State Phillip Habib, and
for the PLO by Lebanese Prime Minister Shafiq Wazzan, were
making slow and tortuous headway. The essence of the proposed
settlement was that the Palestinian leaders and fighters would
leave Lebanon and a multi-national force (MNF) with contingents
from western countries would come to maintain order and assure
the security of Palestinian civilians. The crucial question, but
meaningless in the light of what happened subsequently, was at
what point the MNF would enter the scene and take over. Israelis
wanted the Palestinian fighters to leave first, but the PLO feared
treachery once its fighters had put down their arms and emerged
from their well-protected hide-outs. Israel suspected double-
dealing by the PLO: once their security was assured by the
presence of the MNF they would find all sorts of excuses for not
leaving.

Arafat argued and bargained to the last. It was all to no avail
in the end, but it said something about the state of PLO's morale
that in their extremity they were still putting forward terms and

conditions. Arafat declared that the PLO was not negotiating from a position of weakness. The Israelis, he pointed out, had nowhere been able to cross Palestinian lines in Beirut and only advanced where traitors had opened the gates for them. At a meeting with him, one of his assistants spoke to me of putting up a desperate fight. Arafat pulled him up, 'There is no desperation. We shall not fight to the death. We shall fight to victory!' But Wazzan firmly put down Arafat's bravado about making Beirut the Stalingrad of the Middle East. The task was to save Beirut from further destruction, the Lebanese Prime Minister declared.

The agreement on Palestinian withdrawal from Beirut was finalized by the middle of August. The MNF would stay in Beirut for a month to keep order and ensure security, meanwhile helping Lebanon's own forces to assume these tasks. Israel made a new condition at the last minute—the return of the bodies of nine Israeli soldiers missing in action in the 1978 War. Social Affairs Minister Abdur Rahman Labban was bitter, 'For the sake of those nine cadavers, a hundred more Lebanese are going to be killed.'

At dinner one night with friends in an apartment near the green line, we heard heavy and sustained firing—rifles, machine guns, and rocket propelled grenades, all suddenly going off together and non-stop. It was close enough to cause the silver, crystal, and candlesticks on the beautifully laid out table to rattle. It seemed like a scene from a surrealistic Buñuel film. Every one jumped in his seat when there was a particularly big bang, but nobody was really frightened. It was not the sound of battle but of celebration, a *feu de joie*. The Palestinians were leaving the following day. And who was celebrating their departure? Not their sworn Falangist enemies, but the Palestinians themselves. It was partly an exercise in morale-building but there was also a genuine sense of triumph at having stood up for so long to one of the mightiest war machines in the world. A Maronite girl at the dinner said to me, 'We can't abide the Palestinians, but one has to admire their grit. Not a single one among them came out with a white flag in all these weeks of non-stop Israeli punishment.'

Next morning the celebration was still on. The fighters were leaving with heads held high and carrying their side-arms in token of honourable withdrawal. Radio Lebanon described West

Beirut's emotional farewell to its unwanted guests: from crowded balconies, flowers, rice and sugar (in a place still under an embargo!) were sprinkled on the fighters as they marched through city streets to the waiting ships; the traditional *yoo-yoos* of the women mingled with salvos from machine guns and Kalashnikovs fired into the air.

Arafat left a week later, amidst unprecedented security precautions provided by the US marines who were among the first of the MNF contingents to land after the exit of the PLO fighters. He was seen off by the Prime Minister and by a Christian Cabinet minister representing the President. A year or so later Arafat would start talking about returning. Talking to me about this, Wazzan was angry, 'I saw him off last year with all honours, drove with him to the port, and everyone else was there too: Mufti Khalid, prominent politicians, government officials. And now the same Arafat wants to come back to Beirut. Why doesn't he try to return to Jerusalem?'

A year after the war's end Shafiq el Hout, the PLO representative in Beirut, gave me a hard-headed analysis of the Palestinian plight. He said that the grit shown by the PLO fighters should not eclipse the bitter reality which was that the Israeli invasion had been an 'earthquake' for the Palestinian struggle, not only in Lebanon but elsewhere, and that it had imposed limits on the important military aspect of the Palestinian struggle. The Palestine leadership and intelligentsia, he said, must search for new strategies to face the situation. Speaking to me at a dinner party, the Palestinian wife of a Lebanese Cabinet minister put matters more plainly, 'We can't go on like this, families divided, suffering oppression with no end in sight!' She was sure that Arafat would prevail (in the armed insurrection by the hard-liners within the PLO) and reach a settlement with Israel. She was surprisingly prescient about the nature of the settlement: if Labour won in Israel, Shimon Peres would give back the Gaza Strip, Jericho and some other parts of the occupied territories, but Jerusalem, never!

Under the agreement painstakingly negotiated by Phillip Habib and Wazzan, the MNF were to stay in Beirut for a month in order to maintain order and ensure security, meanwhile assisting the Lebanese government to reassert its control and take things in hand. But the multinational force withdrew abruptly and before schedule at the initiative of the United States. During its stay, mines were cleared, defensive earthworks demolished, tank traps removed, and the way into the city reopened. Was this an effort to restore normalcy and freedom of movement, or did it have a more sinister significance? There were many who believed that all this, followed by the MNF's premature departure at a time when the Israelis were still at the gates, was part and parcel of a plot to eliminate the PLO from Lebanon once and for all.

After the massacre at Sabra-Shatila, Prime Minister Wazzan was very bitter. He told me that the premature withdrawal of the multinational force was a mistake and a betrayal. In the course of his negotiations with Phillip Habib, he had always raised the question, 'Who will guarantee the arrangement? Who will see to it that its various provisions are carried out faithfully?' Phillip Habib, Wazzan said, would solemnly thump his own chest by way of an answer. But, said Wazzan, he was not content with gestures and verbal assurances and got a written commitment from the Americans that the Israelis would *not* enter West Beirut after the PLO's withdrawal. But Lebanon was deceived, Wazzan said, and so was the United States.

Were the Americans deceived? Had they been naïve? I got a different perspective on the matter from a senior European representative who attended meetings of the European Community envoys. He came back from one of these to tell me in strict confidence that the Americans had decided to withdraw their marines from Lebanon. The Italians indicated that they would follow suit. The French opposed the move and proposed indeed that the role of the MNF should be extended beyond the agreed date. But they could not stand alone in the face of the US' determination to leave. I asked my informant why the Americans wanted to pull out before time. He said, 'One can only guess at the reason why the Americans are in a hurry to leave—I am afraid it may not be a very worthy reason!'

On the one hand, Reagan proposed a peace plan the substance of which was that Israel was not to keep the conquered territories of 1967 nor build any more Jewish settlements therein; on the other hand, there would be no Palestinian state but full autonomy for the West Bank in a federation with Jordan. So it looked as if Israel had won the battle but was going to lose the war! However nothing came of the Reagan plan; the Begin government set about at once to undermine and sabotage it, getting full help from not only the pro-Israeli lobby in the United States, but also from the intransigence of the Palestinian hard-liners.

President's election

The next move on the Lebanese chequer-board was the election of a new president. The date set by the Constitution for the election was approaching, and its outcome was a matter of vital importance not only to the Lebanese themselves, but also to neighbouring countries and other powers. The election undoubtedly had been a factor in the timing and magnitude of the Israeli attack, for a major objective of Israel's strategy in Lebanon was to install a compliant government in Beirut. Israel's connection with the Falangists was by now well-established, and Israel's choice for the job of president was Bashir Jemayel, chief of the Falange militia. However not all Israelis were sure of Bashir's loyalty. On the eve of the election, Israel's President Chaim Hertzog said in a BBC interview that gratitude was not a Middle Eastern virtue, and that once he was elected, Bashir was quite capable of turning around and coming to terms with Syria. In fact the Falangists had disappointed the Israelis during the war by staying out of the fray. They did not allow the IDF to off-load supplies at their private port of Jounieh. Apparently Bashir had not been forthcoming about signing a formal peace treaty with Israel. He had refused to permit El Al flights to Beirut, or to give the Israelis a helipad in East Beirut. Begin had made his irritation known by keeping the Falangist chief waiting for a couple of hours in his ante-chamber when he came to see him in the Israeli border town of Nahariya, after the invasion.

For the Lebanese the election was more than a struggle between factions and communities; it involved the question of Lebanon's survival as a legal entity. National Assembly Speaker Kamel el Assad, who would preside over the elections, and who was staying at the same hotel as I, explained the matter to me one morning over a cup of coffee in the lounge. People in West Beirut, he said, were opposed to elections being held while the country remained under Israeli occupation.[13] Their real reason was that they feared that no candidate other than Bashir Jemayel would come forward in the existing circumstances and that Bashir would be elected unopposed. Kamel el Assad did not disagree with that view but felt that such considerations were secondary to the importance of upholding the legal framework of the state which was about the only thing that was still left of Lebanon's statehood. The president's office was a symbol of Lebanon's unity, the only shred of 'legality' that covered the *de facto* rule of warlords and militias. If elections were not held in due form and on the due date, he said, there would be no Lebanon left to worry about and the country's *de facto* partition would become partition *de jure*.

The election was held on the exact due date laid down in the Constitution. When I arrived at the improvised National Assembly hall, the Press, both local and international, was there in force, and a scattering of ambassadors and other dignitaries was present in the visitors' gallery. But the House itself was empty and the seats of the MPs were all unoccupied. Some were confabulating in caucus rooms but many had not arrived. The critical question was not whether Bashir would get the requisite majority, but whether the sixty-two members required to make the quorum would show up and permit the election to be held. Around ten o'clock, members started drifting into the hall, in ones and twos, but by noon only twenty-odd seats were filled while another twenty or so members were milling around in the lobbies. At noon the Jemayel family was present in full, but there was still no quorum and it seemed that the election might have to be postponed. If so, the chances were that Camille Chamoun, calmly installed in his seat, would be the compromise candidate. At one o'clock there were still only fifty-eight members present and Bashir's chance seemed to be slipping away. The tension in the house was palpable and in the visitors' gallery people were taking bets. Then at 1.45 p.m. just before the house would break for lunch, there was a sudden hubbub and a great flurry among pressmen and photographers. The four missing members were seen marching—or being marched—down the aisle by their escort of Falangist militia-men. The rest went fairly quickly and Bashir was declared elected at the second ballot. Firing of weapons of all descriptions broke out outside the building and was picked up by neighbouring areas and soon was going on all over East Beirut. Later it was learnt that the four truant members were caught by a Falangist jeep within a few kilometres of the Syrian-held area where they were fleeing to avoid having to vote.

I had paid a visit to former President Suleiman Frangié in his mountain retreat at Ehden in the north sometime before this, but at a time when Bashir's election was a foregone conclusion. Frangié's eldest son, Tony, daughter-in-law, little grand-daughter, and even their pet dog, had all been done to death with the utmost brutality one night by a Falangist commando despatched by Bashir. The old war-lord had sworn vengeance upon the clan of the Jemayels and their children and their children's children, until 'the very name Jemayel shall no longer be heard'; the bodies of his own children lay in caskets in the family morgue, to be properly buried only when the vengeance was accomplished. He predicted that Bashir Jemayel would not live to be president: 'He shall be killed by one of his own.' He said to me, 'It is ever so— he who has lived by the sword shall be cut down by the sword.'

On 15 September, only three weeks after the election and before he could be sworn in, Bashir was killed in a huge blast that blew up the Falangist headquarters in East Beirut. In those three weeks Bashir had moved like a whirlwind on Lebanon's political scene, proposing changes, preaching unity, and trying to allay Muslim fears. He had begun to talk about the need to reconcile the interests of Lebanon's different communities and eased away from too open an association with the Israelis. In the Muslim communities, voices were being raised in Bashir's favour.

On the way to Bashir's funeral with a delegation of UN officials, I ran into a convoy of Israeli tanks trundling back into the port area which they had vacated upon the arrival of the MNF. In Bikfaya, the Jemayel's ancestral village, Amine, red eyed and grief-stricken, received condolences while his father the old Shaikh Pierre, ramrod straight and bearing himself with great fortitude and dignity, was sitting in the midst of old friends and ancient enemies. Maronite, Greek Orthodox, Sunni, Shiah— everyone was there: Saeb Salam, Rashid el Solh, Takieddin el Solh, all Sunnis, and former prime ministers; and Camille Chamoun in a bright green suit that made him look like a large and wise old leprechaun. All were there except Suleiman Frangié, who expressed regret—that Bashir had not died at his hands! The Saudi Chargé d'Affaires when he was ushered in, stood in the doorway and declaimed in a very loud voice, the condolences of King Fahd and Saudi condemnation of the killing, recalling how Saudi Arabia had suffered a similar bereavement in the assassination of King Faisal. Clearly, the Saudis wanted everyone to know on which side they stood. The Israelis were there too, in the shape of air force Phantoms that criss-crossed the sky over Bikfaya in a tribute to the dead and to tell everybody that Israel was there, so beware!

On the previous afternoon Sharon had flown in by helicopter to Bikfaya to offer personal condolences—and as the Kahan Commission report on the Sabra-Shatila massacre revealed later—to urge the Falangists to join the 'fighting' now that Israeli troops were to move into West Beirut. This was something the Israelis had not been able to achieve in three months of heavy fighting and intense pressure against Beirut's defenders, but since MNF's clean-up during its brief stay in Beirut, the roads were open and they were waiting only for a pretext to move in. A bulletin issued by the Israeli Army after Bashir's assassination stated, 'It would be immoral for Israel not to assist in keeping the peace...the present Israeli troop movements ensure that calm will prevail and anarchy will be forestalled...'

They moved into Beirut in the early hours of the morning following Bashir Jemayel's funeral. I woke to the rattle and clink of tanks trundling up the street below our apartment and went out on the terrace to watch. The tanks were followed by a column of infantrymen, bulky with weapons, advancing single-file like a line of grey ants. They stuck to the sides of walls for cover and moved on the double wherever there were gaps in cover. There was no resistance, but the Israelis were firing off their guns just in case. Many of the loudest bangs were shells exploding in the air that were meant to discourage any opposition and generally to make an impression.

Later in the day, Mrs Sirin Shahid, a Palestinian social worker who lived on a lower floor, came up with some others including house guest Jean Genêt the well-known novelist and playwright, and PLO sympathizer. We watched from the terrace while Israeli soldiers lined up some two to three hundred men on a sea-front esplanade behind an old Turkish mosque. Sirin's teenage niece was pale with fear and asked me, 'What are they going to do to these people? Are they also coming up here to check everybody's papers?'

Another Israeli bulletin issued later in the day said, 'IDF [Israeli Defence Force] is in control of all key points in Beirut. Refugee camps harbouring terrorist concentrations remain encircled and closed...contrary to the agreement large numbers of terrorists remain in Beirut with arms of various kinds.' A US spokesman was quoted as saying that the Israeli intervention may help to prevent a blood bath in Beirut in the wake of Bashir Jemayel's assassination. By two o' clock in the afternoon the Israelis were in position everywhere and quiet descended upon the city. But at nightfall the sound of gunfire and the explosion of shells was heard again. From the terrace I saw flares lighting up the sky to the south, in the direction of the Palestinian refugee camps. I was impressed that the Palestinians still had fight left in them and the ammunition to carry on.

On Friday, Sirin Shahid came to see me along with a young Norwegian girl who was engaged in doing social work with the Palestinians in the Akka Hospital near the Shatila camp. The girl was in a very distraught state as she told me of the atrocities that had been perpetrated at the hospital—patients killed in their beds, doctors taken out and shot out of hand. She also told a not very coherent tale of something dreadful going on in Shatila—a massacre in which hundreds of people, perhaps more, had been butchered. I was inclined to be sceptical; such things do not happen, why should the Israelis, whose Lebanese adventure had already given them a bad name in the world, want to massacre unarmed Palestinians? Then some officials of the US embassy came to see me with scraps of information they had received about a gruesome massacre that had been perpetrated at the refugee camps of Sabra and Shatila. I had no independent source of information and the Israelis had restricted movement in the city, and in particular, to and from the refugee camps. I drove over to the ICRC office to ask the director what, if anything, they knew about these reports. He too had heard them and said that Red Cross representatives had gone to the spot to investigate. A phone call from them came while I was still at the ICRC office. The director said that he was sorry ICRC rules did not permit him to divulge information to third parties but the look on his face said it all plainly enough. Later the director of UNRRWA,[14] the UN agency looking after Palestinian refugees, phoned me to confirm the news, which was also reported on the BBC evening bulletin. The sounds and sights of the previous night were not those of the Palestinian fighting a last ditch-battle, but of hundreds of men, women, children being done to death in the still of the night under the eerie light cast by Israeli flares; they were unarmed civilians whose main fault was that they existed. The Norwegian chargé d'affaires who was in the vicinity, told me that he saw a bulldozer trundling down a road, and he sensed that there was something strange about it. It took him several moments to take in the fact that there were human bodies piled in its scupper. They were being taken out to be dumped in a mass grave.

I was informed that many bodies were still lying where they had been killed two days before. The conditions inside the destroyed camp were unspeakable, and there was danger of pestilence and disease spreading from it to the rest of the city. In government circles, split between factions and communities, after the first reactions of disbelief and shock, a schizophrenic paralysis had set in. Along with a UN delegation consisting of representatives of WHO, UNICEF, and UNDRO,[15] I went to see Prime Minister Wazzan about the situation and to offer UN's services. He sent me on to Brigadier Koraytem, the Army Deputy Chief of Staff and with his assistance a task force was formed that, with the help of a number of Lebanese NGOs, notably Rafiq Hariri's construction firm, Oger-Liban, and the Lebanese Army, arranged to bury all the bodies and restore sanitary conditions in the area.

In my diary I entered a note on a visit to the camps:

Two-storied house with façade blown away—in sitting-room on first floor, arm chairs and a sofa arranged around a TV set, picture of Virgin Mary on the wall. Some of the Palestinians are Christians. On a kitchen table in another house, the remains of an unfinished meal. In a narrow cul-de-sac, the walls and door of a cinder-block shack are spattered with blood. On the walls of another house, a slogan in Arabic: 'Tony was here, for God, Fatherland and Family.' A grey haired woman sitting under a tree, weeping silently. Her husband, looking in a pile of rubble, straightens up as we approach. He tells us the trouble started early on Thursday. They noticed Israeli tanks taking up positions at high points overlooking the camp. The inhabitants feared that they were preparing to attack the camp under the impression that armed fighters were still present there. A delegation was sent carrying white flags, to explain to the Israelis that only civilians remained in the camp and they meant to give no trouble. When none of these emissaries returned, panic began to spread in the camp. In the afternoon a phosphorus shell landed near the old man's house. He took his family and fled to the house of a brother who lives in town. So he wasn't there when the killers came, but he had heard from others that they wore militia uniforms and were accompanied by Israelis.

The old man tells us the story of his life. Originally from Ramallah in Palestine, he was chased out of there when the Israelis came in 1948. He went to Gaza for refuge hoping to return to his home town when the trouble was over. But this proved impossible. So he found his way to south Lebanon. Then he came to Beirut looking for work and settled in Shatila. Settled isn't quite the word because he had to keep leaving it on account of outbreaks of one kind or another, and coming back in search of livelihood. He now looks at the mound of debris which was part of his home and beyond, to the back half of the wretched cinder block hut which is still intact—walls painted a bright green, framed photographs on the walls, some sticks of furniture. He fears that this too may be knocked down when the bulldozers come to clear the rubble. He wants to patch up the damaged front portion, rebuild the front wall, plant a new tree uprooted by a bulldozer.

There is an innate dignity and courage about the man as he talks quietly about putting together his family's life again—he is not railing against Jews or the Lebanese or fate, as, for the third or fourth time, he contemplates the ruins of his life around him. Persecuted for no reason that he can understand, but only because he and his family and their likes exist.

The massacre has now been forgotten or filed away with so many others that mark the history of the Arab-Israeli conflict. But at the time there was an international outcry at the massacre, not least in Israel itself where a hundred thousand people took out a candle-light procession in the streets of Jerusalem and obliged the Begin government to appoint a commission to examine what had happened and how and why. The commission's basic finding was that the massacre was committed by Falangist extremists (which is true) and that the Israelis who had sent them in and were in full military control of the place, were guilty of nothing more than negligence, blunders, carelessness and acts of omission—a conclusion that was hard to believe. In the words of an Israeli writer, somewhere along the line, with Israeli troops and tanks surrounding the camps, with Israeli flares lighting up the place, with sounds of gunfire being heard miles away, the number of killed being reported to Israeli officials, there must have been some acts of commission.[16] In fact an Israeli soldier's ID card was found in the camp; at the Gaza hospital, two German-speaking men, presumably Israelis, had interrogated Norwegian volunteer nurses; Israeli tanks had fired at the camps. The Kahan Commission dismissed all these facts as tendentious or unbelievable or irrelevant, and concluded that 'absolutely no direct responsibility devolves upon Israel or upon those who acted on its behalf'.[17] However by the appointment of a commission, and by its findings against Sharon and some other top brass, Israel was able to dissociate itself from the event and maintain its reputation in the West as a country that can do no wrong.

Indeed the President of Israel chose to take the high moral ground and called on President Amine Jemayel to discover and punish the killers of Palestinian refugees and warned that if he failed to do so, all the help in the world would not save his presidency, and the fires from the graves of Shatila would rise up and burn down the cedars of Lebanon. In the camps in the South, devastated by Israeli firepower, the IDF mounted briefly, an 'operation charm': men of the Tsahal (Israeli Army) helped old women, played with children, and tried to be nice to all and sundry. In the Ansar prison camp they showed a film on the Shatila massacre to make the point that things could be much worse and how much better off the refugees were under IDF's benign control.

Israel's war was called Peace for Galilee—but the real purpose of the war was not to protect the Galilee, but to secure the West Bank. The limited objective was attained in the first few days when Israeli troops reached the Awali River and Israeli aviation and artillery destroyed the PLO strongholds and refugee camps in the area. But the war's defensive title concealed larger ambitions: to destroy the PLO as an entity, to set up a pro-Israeli government in Lebanon and get it to sign a peace treaty and then to sit back quietly to absorb and digest the West Bank. To attain these aims, Sharon wanted to make a go for the lot— Beirut, Tripoli, the Beka'a and, in the words of French ambassador Paul Marc Henry, settle everything with firepower.

However in the French Army's view, the ambassador added, the Israelis were already at the end of the tether financially, economically, politically and even militarily. They did not have the stamina to push out the Syrians, or dislodge them from the mountain crests, nor could they take Tripoli. In Beirut itself, the Israeli Army had been halted at the gates. To attempt to storm the city street by street and fight from building to building would have imposed a cost in lives that Israel could not afford to pay. Already with nearly 500 dead, the invasion of Lebanon had been for Israel its most bloody venture upto then. So now beyond striking at the Palestinian quarters in a sort of blind rage and malevolence, there seemed to be no clear aim to Israel's war.

But now with Israeli troops sitting in West Beirut, the Palestinian fighters gone, and the other anti-Israeli groups disarmed, Israel felt that the road was clear. Lebanon was asked to sign a full-fledged peace treaty and much more besides—continued Israeli military presence on Lebanese soil, joint patrols with the Lebanese Army, diplomatic relations, open borders, full economic relations and free trade. Even Bashir had prevaricated over demands of this kind; Amine Jemayel, who had been elected President after his brother's assassination, was caught between his Falangist party's need of Israel's support and his own need to win acceptance among the Muslims and come to terms with Syria. On the eve of Secretary of State Shultz' visit to Beirut in April 1983, Amine declared that he would do nothing that might jeopardize Lebanon's relations with the Arab world. Antoine Fattal, who conducted the negotiations with the Israelis, told me that during a lengthy negotiating session Israel's General Tamir, a blunt tough-talking soldier, thumped the table in frustration and cried out, 'Let us forget all this quibbling about the number of patrols, the calibre of guns and all that. Let Lebanon make peace with Israel and we will throw out every foreigner from your soil and guarantee the security of your borders.' Fattal said he had to explain to the Israeli soldier that Lebanon was an Arab country after all, it lived in an Arab environment and could not cut itself off from the Arab world.

The Lebanese dilemma *vis-à-vis* Israel was summed up for me by a Christian friend: 'Egypt and Israel have entered into a marriage without love. Why won't the Arabs allow Lebanon to make love with Israel without a marriage?' Shultz had come to arrange the match and he did a tireless shuttle that finally led to Lebanon signing a Peace Treaty with Israel. However the event changed nothing much for any of the parties: the internal conflict went on in Lebanon; the Israeli military occupation continued in the South; the Syrians stayed on in the Beka'a.

Syria's position was crucial to a settlement in Lebanon and to overall peace. Syria loomed large in Lebanon and not as a friendly presence at that time. In a meeting with an Islamic delegation from Lebanon, a year before the Israeli invasion, Hafiz al Assad had replied bluntly to their request for the withdrawal of Syrian troops from parts of Lebanon: Syrian troops entered Lebanon without the authorization of any third party, he said, and had no need of any one's approval in order to stay there. Their presence in Lebanon was not only an Arab duty, but also a national duty.[18] Syria had the capacity to help or hinder a settlement in Lebanon. In fact its presence in Lebanon gave Syria a similar capacity with regard to a general Middle East settlement. It was surprising therefore that in most current moves and thinking about peace in the Middle East, Syria continued to be left out of the reckoning. A Lebanese newspaper wrote: 'One cannot make war without Egypt, and one cannot make peace without Syria.'

In March 1984, ten months after it was signed and hailed by Israel and the West as a historic turning point, the treaty was abrogated. Now it was the turn of the other side to talk of the 'historic turning point' marked by the treaty's abrogation. In general, Muslims felt pleased and vindicated. The Christians took the matter philosophically. Antoine Fattal wrote an erudite article in a Beirut review to explain that the agreement that he had negotiated, was *not* being abrogated since it had never really existed in the first place. Shultz who had put a lot of personal effort into the treaty, apparently took it very badly but in public only said something about 'waiting and watching'. Israelis felt spited and showed it by bombing the Druse mountain towns of Aley and B'hamdoun the next morning. Syria, which had won this round, reacted in a very low key manner. For Syria the treaty had represented another step in the Camp David process, and by undoing it she had scotched the chance of the process being carried forward, leaving her in the lurch.

Syria took a hard-headed view of the realities. Farook Shara'a, the new foreign minister, affirmed that whatever the Israelis say soon becomes American policy with a coating of sugar to entice the Arabs to swallow it. He added that any attempt to flatter the Americans would only increase their contempt for the Arab mind and their humiliating treatment of the ingratiating Arab rulers.

But Lebanon's time of troubles was not over by any means. Israel gradually pulled its troops from Beirut and elsewhere back to square one,[19] with nothing to show for its military adventure and the many dead, but new and more implacable enemies in the shape of the Iran-backed Hezbollahis in south Lebanon and a strengthened Hamas in the West Bank. But the Palestinians too fell out among themselves and the PLO with the Syrians in Tripoli. Yasser Arafat came back to Tripoli and another compulsory but less ceremonial exit had to be organized for him. I was privileged to play a role in the event by arranging to provide the UN flags under which the ships carried the Chairman to his new destination!

The Secretary General asked me to go to Tripoli to find out what was going on there. The trouble was among the Palestinians this time. Arafat and his loyalists were being expelled by a dissident faction backed by Syria. A Member of Parliament from Tripoli, Abdel Majid Riffai, summed it up for me: at bottom it was, he said, the usual story of Arab politics—a brew of ideological intransigence combined with political opportunism; Trotskyites turning into Islamic fundamentalists, the PLO arming the militias of Shaikh Shaban, the Sunni firebrand who was getting inspiration as well as money from Iran; Iran allied with Syria but backing the PLO in the latter's proxy fight with Syria which in turn, was arming and egging on the rebel Abu Moussa against Arafat...

The multinational force had returned after the Sabra-Shatila massacre, and stayed for nearly eighteen months this time. Its presence did not materially change the situation, even though the USS *New Jersey* participated in some of the hostilities by shelling Druse or Shia positions on the Lebanese government's behalf (billing the latter at $700 a shot). Then the MNF left again after suicide bombers blew up the barracks housing the American and French contingents. The American embassy was blown up twice, first in the sea-front premises in West Beirut, and the second time in its new refuge in Christian East Beirut where it had moved for greater safety. Each time it was done in exactly the same manner—by someone driving a truck full of dynamite upto the premises and blowing it up, and himself with it. On the second occasion, the bomber was able to carry out his mission despite all the rigorous precautions that were in force, because an iron grill that was to go on the entrance gate was not yet in place. President Reagan explained things in his homely way saying that anyone who had ever had their kitchen done over, knew that things never get done on time...

Some weeks before the election of his brother Bashir as President, Amine Jemayel took me out to lunch in a mountain restaurant overlooking the sea. He was driving his own car and I noticed a sub-machine gun in a holder alongside the gear shift. It was like something out of the movie *Godfather*. I asked him about his own prospects for or interest in the job. 'Not while my brother is in the field,' he affirmed, 'but if he were to be blocked, it would be another matter.' However he listed his own superior qualifications for the presidency: wider acceptability among Lebanon's various communities; close ties with the Saudis and other Arabs; plans for economic reconstruction and social reform. But he was against making the constitutional changes demanded by the Muslims. Not now, he said to me, perhaps in time and gradually, once the country had been put back on the rails, and '...any way, *we* are the winning side!' he declared to clinch the argument, forgetting that at the beginning he had said that the Israelis were there for their own ends and not to hand the place over to the Christians.

When Amine was elected President after his brother's assassination, he started off on the right foot, but in the end floundered between the two attitudes reflected in his lunch time remarks to me—appreciation that a new settlement among Lebanon's communities was needed, and the hubris of 'We have won!' The most important challenge before him on becoming President with the unanimous support of all sides was to consolidate that consensus. But he was in a hurry to reassert governmental authority and sent in the army to 'clean up' the city's Shiah-majority southern suburbs. The army which had recruited a lot of Muslims under Amine's instructions, broke up when Shiah units refused to fire on their kinsmen and fellow-Shiahs in the suburbs. All the Muslim members of the Cabinet, including the Prime Minister, resigned. Amine lost it all in one throw of the dice, and suddenly Nabih Berri, head of the Shiah Amal, found himself the master of West Beirut. This was a development that caused disquiet among the Druse and the Sunnis, but for the moment they maintained a common front.

I called on Nabih Berri a couple of days after all this had happened and found him in a moderate and conciliatory mood. He said he did not want Amal to rule West Beirut as a conquering militia, nor to break with the legal authority, and certainly he did not want to split the country. He said he would not allow the defecting Shiah units of the army to join the Amal militia or even to fraternize. His aim was to reopen the passages to East Beirut and restore normal conditions in the city. He compensated owners of bars and other such establishments that had been wrecked by zealots in the first flush.

Perhaps more than in most wars, in Lebanon's war, those who paid the price were the nameless, faceless, 'ordinary' people on both sides, for the war was 'fought' by militiamen who fired their mortars, grenades and rockets from behind protected bunkers and suffered relatively few casualties themselves. Their shells fell on residential localities, shopping centres, or parking lots, killing people going about their daily chores. In 1983 a Beirut newspaper estimated that there had been 179 cease-fires in the eight years since the war began. On the occasion of one such cease-fire, opposing militiamen fell into each others arms, hugged and kissed, noble-mindedly forgiving each other and forgetting the hundreds of innocent fellow citizens they had killed, maimed, orphaned, widowed, and made homeless since the previous cease-fire!

In visits to camps of persons displaced from one side to the other, I saw the mirror image contrasts of the sufferings on both sides. In the Christian suburb of Ain Remmaneh, in a building whose roof was hit by a rocket, families—two to three to a room—huddled on the lower floors, sleeping on mattresses laid side by side on the floor. This looked like comfort compared to the airless basement of a dispensary across the green line with puddles of water on the floor, which was home to a group of very old persons. These were people with no relatives or friends to go to, and without the means to find something better. 'This is the end of the road for this lot,' said our guide, an unshaven, chubby young militiaman from the Falangist party. Then across the street again, at a trot after our militiaman, we went into the cavernous interior of a hanger or warehouse. At the far end a door opened into a dark and narrow passageway. The man used his flash light to lead us down several flights of stairs which terminated in a room without windows. It was hard to imagine what purpose this dungeon-like space, airless and lightless, normally served. Now it offered refuge to a displaced group of aged people, clad in pyjamas or shapeless dresses, huddling around the glow of a kerosene heater which provided a sinister gleam of light and the illusion of heat. The place was right on the green line and we heard the sound of shells exploding and the rattle of gunfire as these people mumbled their stories. Here in the bowels of this shell-battered building they lived in constant fear that 'they' (Muslim militiamen) might still come and slit their throats. Coming up from this netherworld, worthy of a Piranese prison drawing, into the sunlight, everyone was sent back scurrying into the hangar when a rocket fired from the Muslim side across the green line hit a wall outside with a shattering crash. The explosion was followed by sustained fire from this side as a riposte. During the brief lull that followed, we raced up the street—bent over double in order to reduce the snipers' target space—to get back into our cars, feeling afraid as well as foolish.

Then we went across to the Red Cross office in Jounieh where things were really upscale—coffee and cookies passed around by leggy blondes in tailored suits and chic women driving up in their Volvos, looking distraught and demurely selfless. The final stop was the basement garage of a shopping and amusement complex where a large number of Christian refugees from the Shouf were sheltered. The Falangists had invited TV cameras and newspapermen for the occasion, but a black-frocked, black-browed priest had a mind to be polemical, 'So! Are we too at last to be vouchsafed something from the United Nations, or is this just another photo opportunity?'

On the other side it was the same story, Druse families displaced by bombardments, cowered in flooded basements. In a vast, bare, dark space a few pinpoints of light were single candles around which families sat silently. But in the midst of the ruin and desolation, the laughter of children would ring out sometimes like an intimation from another world.

The military fiasco in the Shiah suburbs led, among other things, to a change of army chiefs. Ibrahim Tannous who was carrying out the president's orders during the ill-fated operation in the suburbs, was relieved of his command, but by way of compensation received the Grand Cordon of the Order of the Cedar. Walid Jumblatt remarked that Lebanon was the only country where officers were decorated for shelling their own countrymen! Michel Aoun the new chief had the reputation of being sympathetic to the extreme wing of the Falangist militia— a reputation he would confirm some years later when he tried to mount a rebellion against Lebanon's agreement with Syria. When I paid him a courtesy call, he spoke with great confidence and assurance. 'This is peace,' he said to me, 'this is the end of Lebanon's war. It had to end one day and that day is the fourth of July.' Sadly, he was off by a number of years.

The fourth of July was the day on which a 'Security Plan'— one of many before and since—was to go into force; the army was to take up positions everywhere and take over from the various militias; Christian officers would resume their posts in West Beirut; and Muslim officers in East Beirut. Aoun explained that the reality was that the balance of power was now roughly equal among the various contenders and none of the parties could expect to gain anything by more fighting. (That, however, had been true for a long time. Walid Jumblatt, in answer to my question, said puckishly, 'We go on fighting because we still have all this ammunition left'.)

A new so-called Government of National Unity took office after a 'reconciliation conference' in Geneva among the war-lords who were now themselves holding various Cabinet posts. At my suggestion UN's new Secretary General Pérez de Cuéllar paid a visit to Beirut in June 1984. The Secretary General's visit was in the nature of a morale booster for these efforts, but the situation was uneasy and things were still very tense. At the Presidency, Amine Jemayel, fresh from his various setbacks, strode in exuding vigour and self-confidence. It seemed a little forced, a sort of compensatory mannerism, as when a short man draws himself up to walk tall. Pérez de Cuéllar, a plain spoken man eschewing niceties, said pointedly that it would be 'short sighted' to assume that one could isolate the Lebanese problem from the general Arab-Israeli conflict. The Lebanese view, and in particular that of the Christians, was quite the opposite of this, and Amine rejoined that the Lebanese problem was *sui generis* which must be solved on an *ad hoc* basis and not be lumped in the same basket with the larger issue. The Secretary General conceded the point, but said that what worried him the most, was that among the major powers at that time there was so little concern over the Middle East and an almost complete lack of movement on any of the problems, whether it be the overall Arab Israeli conflict or the situation of Lebanon. Meanwhile, he said, *faits accomplis* were being consolidated on the ground, creating difficulties in the way of an eventual settlement. The passage of time, in his view, did not favour the Arabs. He himself stood ready to help in whatever way he could, but the scope for this, as everyone knew, was very limited under the UN Charter.

Amine concluded these discussions of high policy by passing to the Secretary General a chit recommending the extension of the contract of a middle-level UN employee! Slightly taken aback, the Secretary General passed it to me with a shrug, as if to say, 'Now what is all this about!' I had no difficulty of course, in recognizing one of our own most deeply-rooted social customs!

The new Prime Minister, Rashid Karamé was present at the meeting with the President, but protocol and considerations of communal balance made it essential that the Secretary General should pay a separate call on him in his office on the other side. So, allowing the Prime Minister a little time to get there himself, we took a UNIFIL chopper to West Beirut—the Wild West Beirut, where everyone carried a gun and nobody was in full control. The chopper landed at the Bains Militaires—the army's once smart and exclusive beach club. As soon as the Secretary General emerged from the craft, he was surrounded by a jostling, pushing, scrambling mob of soldiers in scruffy uniforms—men of the famous 6th Brigade, now almost wholly made up of Shiah Muslims. The atmosphere of pandemonium was not very reassuring as to the efficiency of the unit, nor was the bearing of the individual soldiers very professional. But they were the only remnant of the regular army in West Beirut, and when the rare occasion arose, served to symbolize the existence of the Lebanese state.

At the Prime Minister's, all having already been said at the President's meeting, the discussion took a somewhat philosophical turn—national versus international responsibility for Lebanon's crisis; the concept of 'Arabism' and the question of Lebanon's Arab identity; the shortcomings of the international system and of the UN charter. '*Une Charte piegeé* [a booby-trapped Charter]' Pérez de Cuéllar called it, which had left him without the power to enforce UN decisions and made all major decisions subject to the veto, including any move to take away or attenuate the veto power. Karamé spoke of Israel more in sorrow than anger—Israel should learn to coexist with the Arabs instead of trying to dominate them. In South Lebanon the population was being subjected to daily oppression and humiliations in the areas under Israel's military occupation.

Next was a meeting with Nabih Berri who was minister for the South, a departure from protocol since the Secretary General normally calls only on presidents or prime ministers. But Berri was the effective ruler of West Beirut via the 6th Brigade and his own Amal militia, and insisted on the Secretary General paying him a call at his office.[20] The pandemonium here was worse, for in addition to the regular soldiers, there were Amal militiamen, reporters and Press photographers, falling over each other, crowding around the lift, bounding up the stairs, fingers cocked on triggers or poised on camera shutters. Nabih Berri in a natty shantung silk suit was sitting in his chair and trying to be above it all. He made the point that the people of the South in the past had never themselves attacked Israel, yet now Israelis had made enemies of them by treating them exactly as the Nazis treated the Jews. All this was going to create a worse security problem for Israel than the Palestinians ever did—every single day one or more attacks were being made on the IDF and these were likely to intensify if the Israeli occupation continued. The Amal supported the Palestine cause but had never approved of guerrilla attacks across the border. Let Israel evacuate the region, Berri said, and he would send his militia to the South to make sure that there were no attacks on Israeli territory from there. Under what principle of international law could Israel demand security arrangements for its territory on the soil of a neighbouring country, he asked. If such a thing was accepted, then, Berri said, Cuba may well ask to station its troops in Miami! Israel wants to turn South Lebanon into the North Bank, he affirmed, saying that the question of security was only a pretext.

The Secretary General's visit was my last notable official activity in Lebanon before leaving to take up a new appointment in New York. The last interesting thing that happened to me personally was that an anti-tank shell was fired at our apartment one fine morning from the East side. It was a 140 mm tank-fired missile going 1,100 ft. per second, or 2,500 miles an hour, when it hit. Luckily it exploded outside on impact with the wall, and on entry only damaged what was in its way; luckily also, I had just moved out of its path to answer the telephone. And miraculously the thing entered through a narrow blank space on the wall just missing a valuable eighteenth century tapestry cartoon from the school of Goya (belonging not to me, alas, but to the landlady) leaving it unscathed. Who dunnit? UN experts told me that these missiles, guided by computer, are very accurate. Later some friends from the East came to enquire and warned me that there was a group of Christian 'ultras' there who disapproved of a Muslim being in my position in Lebanon, and wanted to make this clear. This was quite contrary to my experience during my five years in the country when all doors were open to me and I never felt that anyone had reservations on any score. The trouble that morning had actually started from our side, when a couple of shells were sent eastwards from somewhere behind our apartment building, and we were all tensed for some retaliatory fire. I think the hit was just one of those things—statistically almost inevitable.

We had other brushes with unpleasantness in these years—an armed hold-up one night in the Beka'a; bullets ricocheting off the terrace roof from duels in the street below. One not very agreeable moment was when shells began to drop outside a glass-fronted supermarket where I was doing some last-minute shopping with two of my boys. It had been a bad day overall. The shop was almost empty, and the assistants seemed tense, waiting only for us to finish in order to shut up shop. Shelling started as I went to the check-out counter to pay. Two RPGs exploded just outside, making everything rattle on the shelves. The girl at the counter stiffened, and on the third explosion dropped everything and went to huddle in a corner. The few shoppers, a couple of old ladies and the assistants, all moved to the back of the shop, but in this aseptic place with open shelves and floor-to-ceiling glass windows, there wasn't any real cover. I did not fancy the idea of being found dead in a pile of burst tuna fish cans. When a lull ensued, we quickly paid and drove off, somehow manœuvring a way through cars screeching around corners and scurrying off in every direction like scared cockroaches.

One morning a heavy shell fell on nearby Hamra Street and our apartment seemed to shake with the impact. My wife asked me later if I had been afraid. It was difficult to define what one felt then in the heat of the moment. Undoubtedly fear, but also anger—which can be a sublimation of fear—at the brutality of the mindless gunmen who fire their guns, and at the chieftains who set them their murderous task. But sometimes one felt more real fear when all was suddenly quiet, with joggers running along the sea front and birds twittering in the bushes. It seemed all too peaceful—like an illusion, a piece of deception conjured up by a sorcerer, or a refinement of the unavowed anxiety with which one constantly lived.

In July 1982 I paid a visit to the town of Chtaura in the Beka'a and was taken to a hospital run by Christian nuns who attended with exemplary devotion and selflessness to their patients, most of whom were Muslims. A sister took us through some of the wards. A mother and child both had lost limbs. She held the child in her arms, giving him the warmth and comfort of her own torn and pain-wracked body. A man lay inert with hideous burns from a phosphorus bomb—phosphorus once lit, cannot be put out by water or anything else, and the fire only goes out when it has burnt itself out. An old woman in her seventies, with silvery hair, was propped up against the pillows. She had fine, delicate features, and when we approached her bed, she tried to sit up. The smile that lit up her face cast its radiance on the whole room. The sister lifted up the sheet covering her legs and we saw that one of them had been amputated right up to the top of the thigh. The beauty and gentleness of her smile were like a reproach, but also an absolution of all that is ugly and vindictive and filled with hate in this world.

NOTES

[1] The Falangist party was the most important political-cum-military grouping of the Maronite Christian community, and was founded by Shaikh Pierre Jemayel after a visit to Germany in the 1930s. Its name, organization and ideology were to some extent, influenced by the Nazi party.

[2] Conversation with author.

[3] Moshe Sharett's diaries cite a remark made by Dayan in 1955, that the only thing that was necessary to secure north Israel was to find a Lebanese major who would create a Christian regime in the South allied to Israel.

[4] The Major continued to receive his pay from the army headquarters for years, though he refused to receive its orders, and fired on an army contingent sent for duty to the South.

[5] 'Command' being understood in a formalistic, administrative sense; for operational purposes UN troops take orders only from their own officers who receive instructions from their governments.

[6] During their invasion of Lebanon, the Israelis raised a small fuss with the Secretary General about keeping a Muslim in Beirut, but generally this question was never raised in Lebanon. Once a French businessman asked me if it was awkward as a Muslim to be in charge of things in a situation of conflict between Muslims and Christians. It wasn't, and I thought the question would not even have been asked if I had been a Christian.

[7] Marxist leader of the *coup* that overthrew emperor Haile Selassie and established a pro-Soviet regime in Ethiopia.

[8] In response to a similar suggestion on a subsequent occasion, General Callaghan wrote to me: 'You will appreciate that under no circumstances will I order men under my command to change their uniforms for civilian attire...' I recalled this bit of military punctilio when a year later these men in their uniforms stood gazing while the Israeli Army swept through their area of operations.

[9] He had ignored threats and warnings and refused to be accompanied by bodyguards. 'What good will it do?' he said. 'Instead of one person being killed, there will be two or three!'

[10] Where King Fahd had proposed a controversial peace settlement based on Arab recognition of Israel in exchange for the return of lost Arab territory.

[11] The ambassador, hit in the head, hovered at death's door for months, but when he recovered he was very critical of the invasion.

[12] A UN Secretariat paper of 1981 spoke of safeguarding 'the interests and concerns of all those involved in South Lebanon...', seeming to give legitimacy to Israel's presence in the area, whereas the mandate of UNIFIL was to see to the withdrawal of its forces from Lebanon. In April 1984, another Secretariat plan proposed the disengagement of Syrian and Israeli forces in the Beka'a, and deployment of UNIFIL in the buffer zone between them—a buffer between two foreign armies that were on Lebanese soil and had no business to be there. The Lebanese saw it as an amputation of Lebanon supervised and guaranteed by the UN. Amine Jemayel said to Urquhart who presented the proposal, 'I am glad this is the third of April and not the first!'

[13] Among these was Bashir's brother Amine, who said to me that a president should not appear to have been imposed on Lebanon by Israel.

[14] United Nations Relief, Rehabilitation and Works Agency.

[15] World Health Organization; UN Children's Fund; UN Disaster Relief Organization.

[16] Ammon Kapouliak in *Le Monde Diplomatique*, June 1983.

[17] The Commission of Inquiry into the Events at the Refugee Camps in Beirut. Final Report; 1983.

[18] Author's conversation with a member of the delegation.

[19] The paradox of the situation was illustrated when the Lebanese government protested the 'premature' Israeli withdrawal from the Shouf where Druse and Falangist militias were at each others' throats!

[20] Some East Beirut newspapers held me personally responsible for bringing about this meeting, which was not true. This was the only time during my five years in Lebanon that the question of my religious affiliation was brought up.

EPILOGUE

After five years in Beirut I returned to New York to head the UN's Centre Against Apartheid. The job was concerned with mobilizing diplomatic and political pressures against the South African regime to compel it to put an end to its iniquitous system. After Beirut, it seemed like another thankless job. When I took up my post at the UN headquarters, my friend Sardar Shahnawaz who was then our permanent representative, tried to console me with the thought, 'At least from the fire you are back into the frying pan!' South Africa's racist policy aroused passion, fury, outrage and indignation, not only among the South African protagonists themselves, but all over the world. The future promised nothing except more bloodshed and perhaps a racial holocaust. Nobody could have imagined at the time that in just five years, not only would apartheid collapse under the weight of its absurdity, but that the dominant white minority would peacefully give up power to a black majority in a multi-racial democratic regime. There cannot be many instances in history where a problem of such deep-seated irrationality and involving irreconcilable interests, was resolved on the basis of plain common sense.

Then I returned briefly to the Foreign Office as an adviser in the Cabinet formed by Benazir Bhutto after the Peoples' Party won the elections of 1988. This was Pakistan's third attempt at democracy, and like the previous two, it had taken place against a background of political turmoil and in a constitutional semi-vacuum. But the omens seemed favourable this time: the post-Zia transition had taken place as laid down in the law; the army had refrained from taking over. Benazir, who had experienced great personal tragedy and endured years of persecution, anguish and pain, stood before the world as an image of youthful idealism, courage and fortitude. Western media spoke of her as the 'Woman of the Year'. One French newspaper went further and proclaimed Pakistan as the 'Country of the Year' for the exemplary and unprecedented manner in which it had made the transition from dictatorship to democracy. But all that is a separate story, and an epilogue is not the place for telling it.

An epilogue, the concluding word, should neatly tie the loose ends, set out appropriate conclusions, and draw the moral of the story. I am not sure that there is a straightforward moral to the story or that any cut and dried conclusions can be drawn from the vicissitudes, wars and alarums, the manœuvres, moves and counter-moves that mark Pakistan's political evolution and diplomatic history. 'Memoirs are a mental indulgence,' a friend remarked on being told the subject matter of the book I was writing, 'a form of escapism!' There is no doubt some truth in that view. Looking back at what was, one is led inevitably to wonder about what might have been, how things could have turned out if certain decisions had been different, or the decision-makers had been other than who they were.

An often-debated question in Pakistan has been over the decision of Prime Minister Liaquat Ali Khan in 1950 to go to Washington, discarding an earlier invitation to visit the Soviet Union. Many believe that matters would have gone better for Pakistan if he had not put all his bets on Washington, but maintained good relations with both Washington and Moscow. Personally I am not at all sure what the right answer is. There are other, larger questions that invite speculation. What if Nehru had not aborted the confederation proposed by the British Cabinet mission? Or the Congress party had not rejected Shaheed Suhrawardy's proposal—a proposal that the Quaid for his part had accepted—to set up a separate Bengal-Assam state? Or, going back further, if the Congress had agreed to share power with the Muslim League after the 1937 provincial elections? Supposing the Quaid had agreed, as in the case of the Frontier province, that the future of disputed princely states should be decided by referendum? The most consequential question of all, is perhaps, what if Independence and Partition had taken place under the aegis of a Viceroy who acted as a referee, instead of playing centre-forward for one of the sides? The questions are almost rhetorical in nature, and in pondering the answers one can only note, sadly, that the history of the independence struggle in India and of the British connection, was at many key points a story of opportunities lost and wrong turnings.

One ought to use the lessons of the past to meet the challenges of the future. That, after all, is the purpose of history. The trouble with writing about the future is that the future almost always has more surprises up its sleeve than analysis or imagination can conjure up. The past is not always a good guide. Extrapolation can lead one into absurdity and anachronism. In a thought-provoking talk on the subject in 1975, Lord Allan Bullock, Master of St Catherine's College, Oxford, took the audience back to the beginning of the century and then forward through it in twenty-five-year segments, in order to demonstrate the pitfalls of political forecasting. Thus in 1900, no one foresaw a World War or knew what such a war could be. The great war took the world unawares, and swept away the Hapsburgs, the Ottomans and the Tsars and their powerful empires that had seemed destined to rule the world for the foreseeable future. Again in 1925, when Germany lay prostrate and in the grip of uncontrollable inflation, who could have foretold that she would rise in a few years to proclaim a thousand-year Reich, and then fall to the uttermost depths of defeat and devastation, but only to rise once more as a leader of a united Europe? In the same period the British Empire that seemed to be at the zenith of its glory and self-confidence, would begin to decline and disintegrate. In 1950, with the triumph of Mao in China, communism looked like an all-powerful monolith stretching across the globe and threatening to take the whole world in its ideological embrace. But by 1975, China and the Soviet Union were at daggers-drawn and Communist China, the erstwhile enemy number one of the 'free world', had become an unavowed American ally. Even more astonishing and momentous transformations were to occur, as we know, in the years remaining before the end of the century.

One often thinks of the future in terms of Utopia, though in literature sometimes this can be of the negative kind—for instance, the *Brave New World* of Aldous Huxley or Orwell's *Nineteen Eighty-four*. I myself saw the future in a not very cheerful light in a monograph on the international order that I wrote in 1983:[1]

It could happen that the existing order may break down altogether in the face of the widening rich-poor gulf, uncontrolled population growth, scarcity of resources and living space, racial conflict and social revolt. In that case, urban guerrillas, terrorism, political as well as criminal, drug and gun Mafias and covert operations by intelligence agencies, death squads and vigilante justice, streamlined by technological developments, may disrupt and dominate international relations and generate a Mafia-like underground of organized violence and lawlessness on the international scene.

But generally speaking, Utopia is a very desirable place where all is as it should be. Now, as we stand at the threshold of a new century, one should be looking to the future in an upbeat mood. Indeed the twentieth century, one of history's bloodiest, most tumultuous and revolutionary periods, seems to be closing with a 'happy ending' as the curtain falls on apartheid, the Arab-Israeli conflict, the Irish question, and many other intractable and long-standing quarrels, and above all on the cold war that dominated and distorted world politics for the last half of the century.

But there is a question mark over things as the twenty-first century approaches. In some ways, with the end of the cold war, international politics has lost its focus and moving force. Many new and complex problems have arisen, and no one now claims that with the collapse of communism the evolution of history has attained its final goal. The initial euphoria has given way to a political and moral vacuum in which it is not easy to understand what it is that moves and motivates human beings—ideology, religious faith, patriotism, primeval instinct? How is one to understand the mindless cruelty of the Bosnian War, the existence of sects devoted to evil for evil's sake, the atavistic rise of extremist groups that extol and propagate violence, intolerance, racism?

Some see the modern malaise as a symptom of the loss of religious faith and the erosion of traditional values. I don't know how such things are measured. On the face of it, people do not appear to be less religious or more wicked than usual; on the contrary, religion is now openly practiced in places like Russia where previously it was banned or discouraged. Elsewhere, specially in parts of the Islamic world, religion has assumed a political role, and fundamentalist groups seek political power in order to impose their agenda.

A word in parenthesis may be appropriate about 'Islamic fundamentalism' which is spoken of by some in the West as an even greater menace to its values and way of life than communism ever was, *casus belli* of the ultimate cold war—a 'Clash of Civilizations'. Western media and polemicists have over-simplified what is in fact a complex phenomenon. Islamic fundamentalism is part nostalgia, part xenophobia. It has a revivalist aspect—the search for a pristine age when justice and godliness prevailed and when the banner of Islam flew over the world. It is an attempt also to preserve and reaffirm Islamic identity in the face of the high tide of 'Westernization' sweeping the world.

Fundamentalism has a populist side when it raises a voice against despotic rulers, corrupt officials and the selfish rich. It is a protest at the unfairness and social inequality, the profligacy in the midst of poverty that prevail in many Islamic countries. But the cardinal Islamist demand is not merely that laws should conform to the spirit of Islam—a matter on which there is no dispute—or even that Islamic injunctions should be enforced on the individual by the state, but that the *ulema*—religious scholars—and not the elected representatives should have the final say in all public affairs—an idea incompatible with democracy and inconsistent with the absence in Islam of priesthood or a pope.

Islamic fundamentalism is anti-Western for specific reasons that are not ideological or doctrinal, but political—the injustice perpetrated against Palestine and the indifference to the plight of Kashmir. Its ideological target is not the West, but the Westernized ruling elite, and all those who reject theocratic rule. Some of the governments faced with the challenge of economic and social modernization have, in some cases, gone in for a quick fix in the shape of a superficial and imitative Westernization. This was the choice of the Shah, and it fatally widened the rift between him and the people.

In passing one might note the curious fact that whereas Islamist parties have made gains in a Westernized country like Algeria and even in secular Turkey, in Pakistan where Islam figures so prominently in every sphere of activity—politics, diplomacy, banking, education, sports—the Islamist parties have never during the half century of Pakistan's existence, altogether obtained more than three per cent of the popular vote in any election held at any level. One has to assume that notwithstanding the Islamist rhetoric employed by political parties on all sides, the Pakistani voter draws a distinction between religion and politics. (No doubt it says something also for the political skill of the closet secularists who have run Pakistan's public affairs through these years.)

The cold war simplified things and presented the pursuit of national interest and power politics in the form of a morality play. The future prospect is not of another fight between good and evil. The problem will rather be that of managing an increasingly complex, over-populated, socially and politically fragmented world. Change has become a constant of modern life, but it occurs in quantum leaps, shifting life and life styles into different orbits, creating disconnections between peoples, generations and classes. As new discoveries and progress in electronics, telecommunications, biological engineering and other such technologies change the way people live, operate and think, they also create new problems and in some cases, raise difficult questions on the moral and ethical planes.

In some respects, the world system is beginning to show signs of stress: in some cities and countries, if not yet in the world as a whole, there are already more people than can be supported properly; too much travel and too easy contact has not created better understanding, but is breeding more friction, xenophobia and racism. This can be observed specially where immigration of workers has caused concentrations of alien populations, as in the suburbs of many Western cities. I recall the remark of a Jamaican colleague at the UN to a Western diplomat during an argument on the new economic order, 'If the rich countries will not allow a fair economic deal to Third World countries, Third World people may come and get it in your countries.'

Another unsettling factor, brought about by the ease and speed of modern telecommunications, is the constant interplay between domestic and international politics. No country's business is wholly its own today. The value of the US dollar is not a matter fully in the hands of the United States. Nor is the Pakistani carpet-exporter free to have his carpets made as he pleases. Traditional diplomacy establishes rules for the conduct of states among each other. Today organizations such as Greenpeace and Amnesty International are setting norms for the behaviour of states towards the world as a whole, its environment, and even towards their own citizens.

The issues of war and peace, of economic growth and social justice, poverty and population explosion, are structurally interconnected. Many of the most critical contemporary problems—drugs, terrorism, computer crimes, ozone depletion—can only be dealt with on a global basis and through international co-operation. In a world that is more and more intricately interdependent, the nature and role of the state in the world order cannot remain unchanged. Even the largest and most powerful state cannot cope with such issues on its own. At the same time, in many cases the nation state is also under pressure from within, for when there is no longer an enemy at the door, the concept of nation and the appeal of nationalism is weakened by the narrower but more powerful pulls of ethnicity, language, and culture.

In such a complex world, what will be the meaning of 'sovereignty', what will be the substance of independence? Even today the possession of military power is not a decisive or even a relevant factor in the influence and authority exercised by a state. The United States is the sole superpower at present, not on account of the nuclear warheads in its possession—Russia has as many—but because of its world-wide economic, cultural and social reach. Is it likely then that war will gradually cease to be an instrument of policy, that the concept of sovereignty, already meaningless in some ways, will disappear? It is perhaps too much to expect such developments in the foreseeable future, but the trend is likely to be in that direction.

Many people would like the United Nations to develop into a world government in order to manage the world's complexity. Some feel that it is not possible for the United Nations to be effective in a world of sovereign states. One must remember however that in a world where the international rule of law is still weak, 'sovereignty' is a concept designed to protect the weak states against interference from stronger states. The concept of world government has been a staple of political Utopias but it only begs the question. Who will run such a government, and for whose benefit? In practice a world government may give us the worst of both worlds—the unresponsiveness and bureaucratic remoteness of the modern state apparatus, as well as war in the shape of police actions against dissenting or non-conforming nations and peoples. Indeed the most difficult problem in the future may be not that of preventing war between countries, but of making countries co-operate for the common good, and overcoming the indifference of life's winners to the plight of the losers.

In conclusion, I turn again to the situation within Pakistan and India, and the relationship between them that has been the central theme of this book. In a world caught in change and movement, and moving away from old quarrels and military confrontations, in a dynamic Asia that is now in the front rank of economic and social progress, South Asia seems to be moving in an anti-clockwise direction. India and Pakistan, despite all their advantages of size, population and resources, remain laggards in the economic and social race. While the world is trying to turn away from nuclear weapons—weapons that, like the battleship, may be on the way to obsolescence—India and Pakistan are on the verge of starting a nuclear arms race. While each tries to keep up with the other in military terms, both are falling behind the rest of the world in almost every other field. Are the two countries doomed to become the world's most heavily armed states but remain among its poorest and least developed societies?

The basic problem remains what it always was, Hindu-Muslim antagonism. Despite centuries of living side by side, Hindus and Muslims neither found common ground—except the few who became Anglicized —nor came to terms with each other's separatness. They remain locked in an ambivalent relationship that defies solution or definition. Partition did not resolve the problem, but has turned it into a contention between sovereign states. Communalism remains a motivating force in the politics of both countries. In nominally secular India it can be presented as the democratic principle of majority rule; in Pakistan, on the ground that the country was created in the name of Islam, there is an unspoken postulate that while all citizens are equal, Muslims are more equal than the rest.

Part of the problem between them, perhaps much of it, lies in the psyche of the two communities, their self-image and the way each looks upon the other, indeed perhaps in their very nearness to each other. In his *Civilization and its Discontents*, Freud remarks

upon the peculiar fact that people whose territories are adjacent
and who are otherwise closely related, are always at feud with
and ridiculing each other—for example the Spanish and the
Portuguese, the North and South Germans, the English and the
Scots, and so on. He saw in this tendency a harmless means of
satisfying aggressive tendencies, and strengthening cohesion
within a group. But in the subcontinent the juxtaposition has
not been innocuous, for it is weighed down by too many rancours
and resentments of the past.

India's history is peculiar and without parallel in that for
centuries on end, the native Indian, the Hindu, was not master
in his motherland. It surely colours the way Indians look upon
themselves and at the world around them. 'Do not forget that
every Indian carries on his shoulders the burden of a thousand
years of history,' an Indian diplomat once said to a Pakistani
colleague. It was this burden that stood in the way of a settlement
that might have kept the subcontinent united; it is a factor in the
resentment that continues to smoulder in India at Pakistan's
creation. India has the ambition and the potential to become a
world power. But India's emphasis on military power, even at the
expense of social and economic priorities—her aircraft carriers,
ICBMs, nuclear bombs, weapons without any obvious targets—is
it not also an over-compensation for a history of subjugation?

The historic and racial memories of the subcontinent's
Muslims in contrast, are memories of conquest and rule, and
though the majority of Muslims are converts whose cultural and
ethnic roots lie in India, they tend to seek their identity in the
connection with the lands of Islam. From the pragmatic roots of
the Quaid's two-nation theory there has grown a dogma based
on intolerance and self-delusion. But the doctrinal vehemence
with which Pakistan denies any bond or connection with India
has a defensive character and is plainly contradicted by day to
day reality.

The path to a rational relationship between Pakistan and India
is thus encumbered by conflicting emotions and aspirations. In
the best of circumstances, one cannot expect to see a logical,
linear progression to peace. At Tashkent, Kosygin had said to
Ayub Khan that the world had learnt to live with more difficult
problems than Kashmir, and cited the division of Germany as an
example. The Berlin Wall was demolished only in 1989, but the

ice was broken by Willy Brandt's Ostpolitik (policy towards East Germany) twenty years earlier when he became Chancellor, and decided to make a break with the policy of ignoring the existence of East Germany. In 1976, when he was heading a World Bank Commission on the North-South dialogue, he came to discuss his mandate with the Group of 77 of which I was chairman. He explained that the German situation at the time was like a drama in which there was little movement of any kind, and the actors went on repeating the same lines. Brandt said that he could change neither the play nor the actors, so he thought that in order to get things moving, he would try to modify the script, or perhaps just the decor. That was the thinking, he explained, behind his Ostpolitik. The policy faced much scepticism and opposition at home and abroad, but gradually it changed the terms in which the question was discussed. The denouement took a long time to develop, and many different forces operated to bring down the Berlin Wall, but undeniably Willy Brandt's opening to the East set things in motion.

Would the Brandt approach be useful in breaking the fifty-year-old India-Pakistan deadlock? India has always held that the way to a Kashmir settlement lies through the normalization of relations in all fields. Pakistan considers that this is putting the cart before the horse, and that normalization in the circumstances would only legitimize the *status quo* in the territory. However the argument is now being settled in favour of normalization by the compulsion of events and outside pressures—regulations of the World Trade Organization, satellite TV, Internet, and so on. The fact is that the establishment of normal relations in the fields of trade, culture, and communications will do neither the one thing nor the other. War broke out in 1965 although normal relations existed in all these fields until then. Nor has their absence since then generated pressures for a Kashmir settlement.

One way, the ultimate way, of changing the scenario is war. In history territorial disputes have usually been settled by the arbitration of arms. But India and Pakistan have been to war three times already without matters being settled definitively in favour of one side or the other. Even the 1971 War, despite the Pakistani capitulation in Dhaka, was not conclusive in the larger context. There is no reason to suppose that if there were another conflict, either side would be able to prevail in a decisive manner; the only certainty is that both countries and peoples would suffer an irretrievable set-back to all their plans and aims and hopes.

A factor against a fourth India-Pakistan war, paradoxically, lies in the fact that both antagonists have acquired nuclear capability. A nuclear war in South Asia will not be a long-distance affair fought across oceans and on the territory of third countries. It will be fought mainly on the plains of the Punjab and against major cities in both countries. Whoever 'wins' it, a nuclear war will leave total devastation on both sides and its after-effects will continue to be felt long after it is over. One supposes that neither in India nor in Pakistan is the civil or military leadership so irresponsible or emotional as to risk such a catastrophic outcome. A nuclear balance between India and Pakistan may in practice, therefore, make them as careful about provoking a conventional conflict as the recognized nuclear powers have shown themselves to be. A nuclear stand-off might even lead both countries to recognize that military equations are not the ones that really count in the modern world—least of all in developing countries whose military credibility depends, in varying degrees, on foreign supplies, and who have many other pressing claims on their resources.

But even if its incidental consequence is to diminish the risk of war, the idea that peace should be maintained between two developing countries by means of a mini-balance of terror, is surely repugnant and incongruous. It condemns essentially peaceful people, who are deprived of so much in their lives, to live henceforth in the shadow of the nuclear bomb, with the knowledge that annihilation is only minutes away. Yet the remarkable fact is that the two countries have never once sat across the table seriously to discuss the nuclear issue and all its implications. The introduction of nuclear weapons to the subcontinent, if it does come about, will have happened in a policy vacuum. There are no self-evident strategic or military reasons to justify it, and it is not likely to alter the India-Pakistan equation in any significant way.

On the face of it, the outlook is not encouraging; the best hope seems to be for a grudging coexistence based on a nuclear stand-off, and a peace that is no more than the absence of war. In a situation of 'no war, no peace', diplomacy becomes—to inverse Clausewitz—the pursuit of war by other means. The India-Pakistan relationship, which is at bottom the Hindu-Muslim question, lies beyond the reach of conventional diplomacy. The two peoples, bound inextricably in a love-hate relationship, can be led as easily to war as to peace. The choice for peace may seem the more difficult one in disputes of a highly emotional, indeed non-rational nature. But it has been made elsewhere—in Algeria, the Baltic States, South Africa—by clear-eyed leaders who took the hard decisions to obey the dictates of good sense, and the people followed. Personally I am not pessimistic that good sense may come to prevail in the relationship between India and Pakistan, and through a settlement between the two states bring about an understanding between the Hindus and Muslims of the subcontinent that has been long sought for, and which was the purpose of the creation of Pakistan.

NOTES

[1] 'On Revitalizing the International Order', Aspen Institute, New York, 1983.

APPENDICES

APPENDIX A

Extracts from Quaid-i-Azam's speech on being elected President of the Constituent Assembly of Pakistan; 11 August 1947:

...I know there are people who do not quite agree with the division of India and the Partition of Punjab and Bengal. Much has been said against it, but now that it has been accepted, it is the duty of everyone of us to loyally abide by it and honourably act according to the agreement which is now final and binding on all. But you must remember, as I have said, that this mighty revolution that has taken place is unprecedented. One can quite understand the feeling that exists between the two communities wherever one community is in majority and the other is in minority. But the question is, whether it was possible or practicable to act otherwise than what has been done. A division had to take place. On both sides, in Hindustan and Pakistan, there are sections of people who may not agree with it, who may not like it, but in my judgement there was no other solution and I am sure future history will record its verdict in favour of it. And what is more, it will be proved by actual experience as we go on, that was the only solution of India's constitutional problem. Any idea of a United India could never have worked and in my judgement it would have led us to terrific disaster. Maybe that view is correct; maybe it is not; that remains to be seen. All the same, in this division it was impossible to avoid the question of minorities being in one Dominion or the other. Now that was unavoidable. There is no other solution. Now what shall we do? Now, if we want to make this great State of Pakistan happy and prosperous, we should wholly and solely concentrate on the well-being of the people, and especially of the masses and the poor. If you will work in co-operation, forgetting the past, burying the hatchet, you are bound to succeed. If you change your past and work together in a spirit that every one of you, no matter to what community he belongs, no matter what relation he had with you in the past, no matter what is his colour, caste or creed, is first, second and last a citizen of this State with equal rights, privileges and obligations, there will be no end to the progress you will make.

I cannot emphasize it too much. We should begin to work in that spirit and in course of time all these angularities of the majority and minority communities the Hindu community and the Muslim community—because even as regards Muslims you have Pathans, Punjabis, Shias, Sunnis and so on, and among the Hindus you have Brahmins, Vashnavas, Khatris, also Bengalees, Madrasis, and so on—will vanish. Indeed if you ask me this has been the biggest hindrance in the way of India to attain freedom and independence and but for this we would have been free peoples long ago. No power can hold another nation, and specially a nation of 400 million souls, in subjection; nobody could have conquered you, and even if it had happened, nobody could have continued its hold on you for any length of time but for this. Therefore, we must learn a lesson from this. You are free; you are free to go to your temples, you are free to go to your mosques or to any other place of worship in this State of Pakistan. You may belong to any religion or caste or creed—that has nothing to do with the business of the State. As you know, history shows that in England, conditions some time ago, were much worse that those prevailing in India today. The Roman Catholics and the Protestants persecuted each other. Even now there are some States in existence where there are discriminations made and bars imposed against a particular class. Thank God, we are not starting in those days. We are starting in the days when there is no discrimination, no distinction between one community and another; no discrimination between one caste or creed and another. We are starting with this fundamental principle that we are all citizens and equal citizens of one State. The people of England in course of time had to face the realities of the situation and had to discharge the responsibilities and burdens placed upon them by the government of their country and they went through that fire step by step. Today, we might say with justice that Roman Catholics and Protestants do not exist, what exists now is that every man is a citizen, an equal citizen of Great Britain, and they are all members of the Nation.

Now, I think we should keep that in front of us as our ideal, and you will find that in course of time, Hindus would cease to be Hindus and Muslims would cease to be Muslims, not in the religious sense, because that is the personal faith of each individual, but in the political sense as citizens of the State.

APPENDIX B

Excerpts from statements by the author on the international economic order:

(These statements were made in the seventies and some of the pessimistic forecasts made then, have fortunately, not come to pass. Moreover, the idea of a dirigiste New Economic Order has given way to the development philosophies of the IMF and the World Bank and the 'magic of the market place'. Nevertheless the persistence of mass poverty among vast populations in the Third World and the recurrent economic malaise in the industrialized countries, show that the basic maladjustment in the world economy has not been removed.)

(I) From the presidential address to the UN Economic and Social Council, Geneva, 2 July 1975:

The attainment of independence by many countries formerly ruled by colonial powers has transformed the character and concerns of the United Nations. Not only have the former colonial territories and peoples obtained a voice on the world stage, but they have awakened to their rights and potentialities. They have become aware that the means to redress their plight are available. At the same time the unchecked growth of population in the developing countries and the growth of consumer demand in developed countries have created pressures on living space, on resources and environment that give a sense of crisis to the situation. We know all too well the statistics of poverty in the midst of prosperity, of waste and prodigality on the one hand, and penury and deprivation on the other.

The situation is indeed serious, for rich countries as well as poor, and worse lies ahead if we cannot agree on measures to redress it. But it is not such as to cause disillusionment or provoke despair...as we look back over the span of thirty years since the United Nations, Charter was written, how can we fail to note the evolution that has taken place in the concept of international responsibility, a concept which the Charter embodies in the pledge to promote social progress and better standards of living in larger freedom. The Marshall Plan was in its time a remarkable innovation in international economic relations, but it was limited in scope and confined to a single region of the world. The institution of foreign aid embraces a much larger part of the globe, but its underlying purposes have been only partially economic and social in nature. It is a long step from there to the

idea of an economic order, expressly designed to ensure greater
equity and greater rationality in the economic and social relations
among nations.

The call for re-shaping economic relations among nations is not
necessarily a demand for redistributing existing wealth, it serves little
purpose to discuss how that wealth was accumulated in the past. Nor
is the New Economic Order a move for the bureaucratic regulation
and control of economic activity on a world-wide scale. It is a call for
change at a time when the need for change is all too evident. It
introduces on the international plane, ideas that are taken for granted
in national policies, but which have been lacking in the relationships
and structures of the existing international order...the idea of equity,
of justice, fair shares; and the idea that the future growth of the
world economy should be consciously directed towards eradicating
the poverty, disease and ignorance that afflict vast numbers among
the world's population.

(2) At a Round Table organized by Business International, Puerto
Rico, 9 January 1977:

The misery that exists in the midst of wealth is deeply troubling for
the moral conscience, but we cannot hope to understand the problem
if we approach it from one side and the other on a purely moralistic
plane. I do not minimize the importance of the moral impulse, for
without it all human intercourse would be a matter of calculation
and expediency. However, the poverty we are speaking of, that affects
not hundreds of thousands, not millions, but hundreds of millions of
people, should arouse not just compassion, not merely horror, but
the deepest foreboding for the well-being and future of all the people
of this planet. Poverty of such depth and magnitude represents an
enormous waste of the earth's human and material resources, and
provokes a terrifying alienation of the spirit and mind.

The man who finds his bed on a city pavement, what share does
he have in the things of this world? What can he hope to get out of
it, what does he give to it, what is his role in life? In hopeless
frustration he turns to violence for release. The cities of the poor are
cities of anger and hatred, a hatred without an object, a violence
without a purpose.

(3) At a seminar on the North-South dialogue organized by the
Centre for Research on the New International Economic Order,
Oxford, August 1978:

> The nature of the economic crisis is global and all-embracing, and it
> should be tackled on that basis. What hope can one entertain that
> mutual give and take and a rational approach will be applied to the
> present world-wide malaise? The history of nations, including those
> that are today the most highly developed and politically stable,
> indicates that struggle and confrontation, conflict and violence, rather
> than reasoned debate and civic action were the instruments for
> bringing about changes in social and economic structures, of re-
> distributing wealth and power among contending groups and classes
> within a country. Is the world doomed to repeat this experience on
> the international scale? If so what would that mean for the peace,
> stability and well-being of the planet since the protagonists in the
> contention are sovereign and independent states, and peoples
> differing from each other in race, culture, faith and ideology, political
> institutions and historical background? Is the world's future to be a
> future of conflict and violence, of a revival of gunboat and paratroop
> diplomacy, of boycotts and embargoes, of terrorism and the urban
> guerrilla?

(4) At a conference of the Christian Democratic Union, Bonn,
1 March 1978:

> Economic and social development is a complex process; it is not
> possible to single out one or two levers with which it may be set in
> motion and sustained. The injection of capital or the application of
> technology will not by themselves provide the impetus for
> transforming economies and make them capable of self-sustaining
> growth. Excessive growth of population, social disparities, lack of
> education and diversion of resources to military expenditures—and
> in this regard one must address also the major industrialized
> countries—stand in the way of economic growth and social progress.
> The important thing is to adopt an integrated and global approach
> which would enable the poor countries to develop their full potential
> and the rich ones to rationalize their growth and consumption...the
> greatest paradox of the present situation is that in the Western
> industrialized countries, men are unemployed and productive
> capacities are under-utilized when they could be put to work to meet
> the vast and pressing demands which remain unsatisfied in the
> developing countries for lack of purchasing power.

(5) At a symposium jointly organized by the Council of Europe and the OECD, Paris, December 1978:

The major developed countries dismiss as an exercise in rhetoric the Third World's demand for a New Economic Order. The dialogue is at a standstill however, not on the rhetorical plane but on concrete issues and specific points such as stabilizing commodity prices, Third World debt, deteriorating terms of trade, restrictions on manufactured imports, transfer of resources and official development aid; monetary reform. On all these issues, the demands of the developing countries are either rejected out of hand or made the subject of protracted and seemingly endless debate. In passing, one should note that almost every proposal in the past few years has emanated from the side of the developing countries, and that in turning down these ideas, proposals and demands, the developed countries rarely, if ever, offer any alternatives.

The reason for the present stagnation of the North-South dialogue lies in the absence of political will; there are no insurmountable technical differences and certainly no irreconcilable conflicts of interest that stand in the way.

...the economy of the world is today poised on a fault in the system; a discrepancy between economic realities and economic institutions, between the objective needs of the situation and the policies of governments. The crises which confront all countries and various parts of the economic system may be in the nature of warning tremors. An earthquake has its own way of rearranging the order of things and producing a new balance between the forces of the earth. Fortunately in the affairs of men we need not leave things to the blind working of uncontrollable forces.

APPENDIX C

Conference on Nuclear Energy and World Order, New York, 13 May 1979.

(Participants included Dr Ekland, Director General of the International Atomic Energy Commission, Governor Jimmy Carter, democratic candidate for president; Commander Jacques Cousteau, French explorer.)

Summary of statement by author:

Prometheus was punished forever because he stole fire from the gods, but no one has tried to put out the gift he brought to mankind. Nuclear energy despite its dangers, is here to stay. The promise of wind and solar energy and other new sources of power lies in the future, and there is no reasonable alternative at present, to an increased use of nuclear energy, specially in the developing countries. Developing countries such as Pakistan, possessing neither coal nor oil, with a per capita consumption of less that 200 kW per year (compared to the US consumption of 12000 kW per capita annually) have to turn to atomic energy for their economic development and to meet even the bare requirements of their people.

There is no dispute about the necessity of effective regulation of nuclear development. The relevant questions are what is to be controlled and regulated, how and by whom and to what ultimate end and purpose? Attempts to prevent the spread of nuclear weapons which began with the Baruch Plan when there was only one nuclear weapon power, today comprise a number of measures at the international level. Among these are the Nuclear Non-Proliferation Treaty, the safeguards of the International Atomic Energy Agency, regional arrangements to establish Nuclear Weapon Free Zones, and bilateral commitments and safeguards.

Recent developments, notably the Indian nuclear explosion of 1974 and fear of nuclear terrorism, have intensified concern and induced a new unilateral approach to the question by some powers. This is embodied in punitive measures such as the Symington Amendment (which would use United States economic aid as a means of pressure) or Canada's stoppage of nuclear fuel to Pakistan. Canada abrogated its existing agreement to supply technical assistance to the Karachi Nuclear Power Plant not because Pakistan had violated any provisions of the agreement—on the contrary, Pakistan had scrupulously fulfilled its obligations under the agreement and agreed to a further strengthening of its safeguard provisions. The action was taken in an attempt to prevent Pakistan from establishing a reprocessing plant.

It is important to remember that adherence to the Non-Proliferation Treaty, to Nuclear Weapons Free Zones and IAEA safeguards involves the voluntary acceptance by sovereign states of restraints on their freedom of action and abridgment of their sovereignty. Non-nuclear states will lose faith in non-proliferation, if the measures proposed jeopardize their security, hinder their economic development or relegate them to an inferior position in the political, economic and technological fields. Furthermore, it will be difficult to sustain and justify any regime of non-proliferation which leads to a permanent division of the world into nuclear and non-nuclear states—a freezing of the existing power structure.

The Non-Proliferation Treaty which was the first comprehensive attempt to attain this objective, was considered a compact between nuclear-weapon powers and non-nuclear weapon states in which the latter accepted restraints on their sovereignty in return for measures toward nuclear disarmament by nuclear-weapon states. The nuclear weapon powers have not taken such measures so far. The stockpiles of nuclear weapons have not decreased since the treaty was signed. The Non-Proliferation Treaty also failed to prevent the emergence of a sixth nuclear power. It has failed to provide effective protection to non-nuclear weapon states against nuclear threat or attack. And finally, it has done little to help non-nuclear weapon states to develop the peaceful uses of nuclear energy.

A viable non-proliferation system is yet to be evolved. Such a system must:

(1) recognize the energy needs of the world, particularly of the developing countries and their desire to attain self-sufficiency and independence (to the extent possible) in this field;

(2) recognize the inevitability of technological advancement;

(3) seek to prevent not the transfer but the misuse of technology, equipment, fuel, etc.;

(4) not discriminate as between suppliers and consumers, or among consumers. For instance, European countries carry out a form of self-inspection, whereas in the case of Third World countries, IAEA safeguards, and even the more stringent French and German safeguards, are considered insufficient; and

(5) be universal and based on voluntary acceptance.

A conference of suppliers and consumers could consider all aspects of the problem and devise a viable international system. It goes without saying that all governments are interested in preventing nuclear theft and accident. An international approach is also essential to devise methods of waste disposal.

We must assume that all countries have a stake in a safe and peaceful world, not that any country with the technical ability will inevitably go nuclear. Consent is the basis of international law, and a rational non-proliferation system can be built on self-restraint, mutual co-operation and due consideration for the legitimate security interests of all countries and the economic well-being of all peoples.

INDEX